THE SHADOW GOVERNMENT

About the Authors

Daniel Guttman received his B.A. from the University of Rochester, where he graduated *summa cum laude* and Phi Beta Kappa. He attended law school at Yale, where he was an instructor in political science. He is currently a practicing attorney in Washington, D.C.

Barry Willner received his B.A. from Lafayette College, where he graduated *cum laude* and Phi Beta Kappa. He attended the Georgetown University Law Center, where he was an editor of the *Georgetown Law Journal*. He is at present a practicing attorney in New York City.

THE
SHADOW GOVERNMENT

THE GOVERNMENT'S MULTI–BILLION–DOLLAR GIVEAWAY OF ITS DECISION–MAKING POWERS TO PRIVATE MANAGEMENT CONSULTANTS, "EXPERTS," AND THINK TANKS

by Daniel Guttman and Barry Willner

WITH AN INTRODUCTION BY RALPH NADER

PANTHEON BOOKS
A Division of Random House
New York

Copyright © 1976 by Center for Study of Responsive Law

All rights reserved under International and Pan-American Copyright Conventions. Published in the United States by Pantheon Books, a division of Random House, Inc., New York, and simultaneously in Canada by Random House of Canada Limited, Toronto.

Library of Congress Cataloging in Publication Data

Guttman, Daniel, 1947–
    The Shadow Government.

    Includes bibliographical references and index.
    1. Government consultants—United States. 2. Business consultants—United States. I. Willner, Barry, 1947–   joint author. II. Title.
JK468.C7G87   353.09'3   75-10365
ISBN 0-394-49244-7

Manufactured in the United States of America

First Edition

To our fathers

ACKNOWLEDGMENTS

The authors are indebted to many for their advice and support. Len Rodberg was of singular importance to us in conceptualizing the themes in this book. Peter Schuck's editorial comments on the successive drafts of various chapters were invaluable. We wish to express special gratitude to Susan Gyarmati for her painstaking efforts in bringing this book to completion. Among others whom the authors would like to thank for either scholarly advice or moral support are Nancy Bekavac, Dave Calfee, Mary Calfee, Lucille Guttman, Ruth Jarmul, Kathy King, Art Klebanoff, Louis Mayo, Shellie Moskowitz, Pierce O'Donnell, Mark Raskin, Leo Ribuffo, Andy Rooney, Sharland Trotter, Billy Want, Bethany Weidner, Ellen Weissman, and Thelma Willner.

CONTENTS

INTRODUCTION

Not long after the passage of the National Motor Vehicle and Traffic Safety Act in 1966, the new agency created to administer the law duly noted its insufficient expertise and knowledge for carrying out its duties. However, instead of building these assets in-house, the National Highway Traffic Safety Administration (NHTSA) followed the custom of other Federal agencies and purchased studies that related to its mission on contract from outsiders. Soon, the agency began receiving these reports, paid for by the taxpayer at inflated prices, from a number of research and consulting firms.

I noticed several characteristics about these reports. First, they relied largely and uncritically upon auto industry sources, rarely criticizing the industry even though its performance was so insensitive to automobile safety that Congress had resoundingly invested NHTSA with the critical function of pushing the industry to higher levels of performance. Second, they did not equip the agency to carry out its mission more capably but, in fact, were so empty that the agency staff scarcely read them. They were, however, made to look weighty and impressive to justify their sizable cost. Third, the firms that prepared these reports were also open for business from the automotive industries. Fourth, they relieved the agency both from the burden of making controversial decisions—consequently affecting the scope and timing of safety standards—and from the need to establish its own review and research capabilities. Finally, it became increasingly clear that these alleged outside experts knew little about what they were paid to do and, more importantly, did not care to find out.

Throughout the Federal executive departments and agencies many similar studies have "rested heavily on government library shelves," as one former official put it. Nonetheless, the process and product have been of great significance. Whether shelved or used, these reports affect the expenditure of billions of dollars' worth of Federal contracts each year. Their importance stems not so much from what they say as from the status of the firms and individuals who have finely honed the techniques of the "think tank" game. Although hidden by considerable camouflage, this game is an instrumental one, designed to ratify, certify, or initiate what the Federal bureaucracies and their corporate beneficiaries—a well-fused duo—are doing or would like to do. It is a ritual involving millions of dollars each year that in turn directs annual expenditures of billions of dollars. But it is more than that.

To appreciate the significance of *The Shadow Government*, one must understand the extent and function of delegation of governmental responsibilities to private special interests by the Executive Branch in a society where government power so consistently derives from the generic power of corporations. Social Security and veterans' benefits aside, the predominant activity of government is letting contracts, grants, and subsidies to corporations for the purpose of performing governmental missions. Although the regulatory functions of government provoke the most publicized outcries, the contracting activities, in sheer dollars and personnel, are vastly greater—more than 100 times greater in revenue terms alone. The growth of Federal Government expenditures in the last twenty years (from $70 billion to $365 billion) has not resulted from an increase in the number of employees, which has remained relatively stable. Instead, it has resulted from a growth of government by contract and grant—a staggering $110 billion in 1973. The subcontracting of work—concerned with policy formation, organizational models, and even the recruitment of Federal executives—to private corporations whose stock in trade is alleged to be expertise accounts for the bulk of these huge expenditures. The mainstays of this private government-by-delegation are such firms as Booz, Allen, McKinsey & Co., Arthur D. Little, Stanford Research Institute, Institute for Defense Analyses, and several large accounting and management service firms such as Peat, Marwick, Mitchell & Co.

Not large by *Fortune* 500 standards, except such giants as Westinghouse which have consulting subsidiaries, these organizations are the brokers of "prestigious knowledge" whose self-styled independence from the rest of the corporate world is supposed to render to the Government detached and objective advice and plans. Notwithstanding conflicts of interest arising from their regular and sometimes simultaneous service to both governmental and business clients and also the absence of any meaningful external evaluation of their performance, these consulting firms are now a pervasive force in Government-business relations. It is not difficult to understand why. These firms form part of a career triangle with Government and business which features a continual shuttle of personnel from one to the other. Fortified by personal friendships and contacts, the consulting industry services the needs of public and private institutions in specific and by now routine ways. Federal department officials achieve significant insulation from criticism of their behavior if they can cite a "think tank" study. The imprimatur of consulting firms, sympathetic to and associated with the largest business interests in the land, conveys, to an inquiring Congressional committee for example, that a department's action has the backing of an industrial or commercial establishment. Obviously, developing or recommending the types of Government programs which enrich corporate interests, in turn, ingratiates the consulting firms with the business part of the triangle.

A combination of the abdication of its responsibilities by the Executive Branch and the assertiveness of the firms themselves insinuates them solidly into the governmental process. The myth that outside expertise is superior to and more efficient than the public bureaucracy ignited this combination, almost uncontrollably. Why, the tune went, establish a full-time operation to do what a specialized consulting firm could do in an ad hoc manner? The response that doing it within the agency could be shown to be cheaper never became a countervailing force on its own. Nor did other significant arguments gain any ground; for example, that the work could be done more accountably in Government or that the Government should have strong capabilities for reviewing work under contract. On the contrary, the consulting industry has operated outside the normal accountabilities of Government, beyond the reach of Freedom of Information rules and with conflicts of interest as a way of life. This situation has also served to deeply undermine comparative governmental performance by inducing the delegation of public duties and the departure of qualified employees unable to resist the higher remunerations outside Government. The Department of Health, Education and Welfare has estimated the cost of grant and contract personnel to be seven times greater than the cost of full-time Government employees.

The basic importance of the consulting industry officials, as *The Shadow Government* shows, lies in their almost exclusive influence to suggest, shape, and even implement much governmental policy in both its narrowest and its broadest sense. Hardly an area of governmental responsibility has escaped their involvement—an involvement that has even reached the point of assigning consulting industry executives to undertake daily, operational functions at critical levels of the public bureaucracy. Messrs. Guttman and Willner describe in unrelenting, rich detail the consulting industry's encompassing role in health, housing, defense, education, highway and mass transit, government reorganization, poverty and urban renewal, criminal justice, civilian technology research and development, executive recruitment, cost control and efficiency efforts, and private control over public spending. Through a variety of case studies, they show how incompetence and proven failures of expertise entrenched ever more deeply the firms' claim on future business. A burgeoning frontier—the advising and often running of departments of foreign governments—is not treated here because this phenomenon deserves a volume by itself.

The drive to merge Government and business power to the advantage of the latter has been unceasing in recent decades. This fusion has been accompanied by socializing corporate risk, using the public treasury. Business advisory committees, captive agencies, personnel exchange, campaign contributions, and other interlocking arrangements have dissolved the arms-length relationship which Government should maintain to facilitate equitable access and due process for all citizens. The level of *de facto* delegation of public government to private interests may be sufficiently cloaked in contractual and other formal approvals by the various executive departments in order to escape constitutional prohibitions. However, such delegation should not escape a decisive policy evaluation from the viewpoint of democratic principles—including representative as well as effective and efficient government.

Unfortunately, Congress has not strongly insisted that the Executive Branch develop a reasonable expertise of its own to fulfill its authorized missions. It has shown virtually no interest in ordering the creation of an executive process that would ensure quality evaluations of the work of contractors. Consequently, the abdication of responsibility has proceeded at a rapid pace through contracting and then subcontracting the assemblage of knowledge and ideas incident to functions that are clearly governmental. It is a useful index of the extent to which the contract-consulting bureaucracy has become a part of the nation's power structure that the current Congressional distaste for bureaucracy has not extended to the "shadow government." Yet, without a dismantling of this "shadow government" and a return to an accountable governmental structure, the surrender of governmental powers to corporate enterprises will become institutionalized—a quiet *coup d'état* encouraged by transient public officials hailing from or on their way to corporate positions.

The material in this book shows the need for remedial action which prevents the Government from abdicating in favor of special interest groups. The Congress is the most appropriate branch of Government to begin reasserting governmental supremacy over this massive delegation of power to private interests by the Executive Branch. Recently Congress began comprehensive studies of the regulatory agencies, reflecting a perceived inadequacy of legislative oversight in general. The contract-consulting bureaucracy should not be neglected any longer. However, it would be insufficient simply to expose the vast waste pyramided upon waste and the colossal incompetence and self-serving quality of so many of these consultantships. Nor is it enough to demonstrate the ways in which the taxpayers' contributions and expectations have been dashed by the grand schemes of economic reconstruction hatched to benefit the few at the expense of the many. What must emerge from such a Congressional review is nothing less than the establishment of an operational public philosophy of government.

Ralph Nader

Washington, D.C.
November, 1975

THE SHADOW GOVERNMENT

I.

OFF THE ORGANIZATION CHART

In the past two decades the Federal budget has increased from $70 to nearly $370 billion. Popular wisdom to the contrary, the number of full-time Federal civil servants has remained relatively constant. How does the Government manage? [1]

A large part of the answer lies in the growth of an invisible bureaucracy of private corporations whose services are contracted for by the official bureaucracy. In 1946 the largest single portion of the Federal administrative budget —30 percent—was spent on the civil service payroll. By 1966, 34 percent of the administrative budget was spent on contractors and only 22 percent on full-time Government employees. Today it takes almost 80,000 full-time employees to administer the close to $60 billion annually spent on contractors and the more than $50 billion given in grants to state and local governments and nonprofit organizations such as universities.[2]

The grant and contract budget pays not only for costly weapons systems and high-technology equipment but for an incredible array of hardware and services—food and fuel, paper and paint, construction and repair work, guard services, and trash collection. A smaller but significant amount purchases managerial or planning "expertise." In most cases the Government buys such expertise from private corporations that stock experts as if they were assembly-line commodities. Private expertise not only helps plan and manage the over $100 billion spent on grants and contracts, but virtually every other kind of Federal spending as well. Moreover, by writing and administering Federal rules and regulations, the experts exercise the kind of profound and continuing influence that has no ready monetary measure.

The corporations that market the expertise are largely unknown to the public, but perusal of the Washington, D.C. Yellow Pages suggests that they are the largest industry in the nation's capital. A recent edition lists about 120 "economic and social science researchers," 90 "economists," 150 "education researchers," 400 "management consultants," 60 "operations researchers," 60 "transportation consultants," and 15 "urban affairs consultants." Some are tiny operations, living on one or two contracts and with histories no longer than the Government programs that gave them life. Others are divisions of well-known industrial corporations, such as Westinghouse Electric Corporation or General Electric, the Washington offices of advisers to the corporate world, such as McKinsey & Co. or Price, Waterhouse, and "think tanks" that have been publicly associated with defense spending, such as the Institute for Defense Analyses and the Stanford Research Institute.

Lawyers have always been present in disproportionate number at the center of American government, but over fifty years ago Walter Lippmann had already perceived that men knowledgeable about the workings of industrial civilization, "known by all kinds of names . . . as statisticians, accountants, auditors, industrial counselors, engineers of many species, scientific managers, personnel administrators, research men, scientists, and sometimes simply 'private secretaries,' " [3] would be joining the lawyers.

Today they comprise the thousands who work on contract to the Government or oscillate between Government and contract employment. These people are clearly in the affluent portion of American society and reflect and sustain its biases. Blacks and women are underrepresented in positions of importance, and "credentials" are the mark of a man's worth. Many will have attended Oxford University or the Harvard Business School or any of a dozen other elite institutions. Still, there is a great variety in the income, education, and influence of the expert work force. At the lower levels salaries may be comparable to those paid by the civil service, but in the upper echelons of the more successful organizations salaries may range well over $100,000, far exceeding the approximately $40,000 maximum that most civil servants can attain.

If the Yellow Pages documents the existence of the consulting industry, it is unfortunately about the best information available. The bureaucracy of contractor experts is by and large invisible not only to the public but to a good many Washington insiders as well. The official organization charts provide no boxes for contractors. And of course, there is no suggestion of the role outsiders often play in the design of the Government organizations represented by the charts.

The Department of Defense is the largest single source of contract dollars. A Presidential panel, itself staffed by contractors, reported in 1970 on the Department's penchant for hiring contractors to make studies. "Accurate information on the nature and extent of contract studies within the Department," concluded the Fitzhugh panel, is "difficult and often impossible to obtain. Large numbers of contract studies are performed for various elements of the Department of Defense by both profit-making and not-for-profit research organizations. . . . It is not possible to go to one place in the Department, or even a few places in each of the services, and get a tabulation of recent or ongoing studies, including subject, purpose, significant findings, cost, or an assessment of the quality of work. There is," the panel concluded, "no effective control of contract studies within the Department." [4]

Information is no more readily available about the practices of the nonmilitary or, in governmentese, "civilian" agencies and departments. A Congressional study of the largest civilian department, the Department of Health, Education, and Welfare, found that while the Department annually reported the number of "man years" and the sums spent on "direct hire" employees, "for the most part agencies of the Department do not keep records of non-Federal employees supported by their grants and contracts." A "very rough" estimate supplied by HEW put the cost of grant and contract personnel at seven times the cost of full-timers.[5]

When records on "contracting for experts" are kept, the bookkeeping terms are often vague and subject to inconsistent application. Several agencies, for example, have rules that govern "management consulting" contracts. Officials who administer these rules are hard pressed to define "management consulting." The term, one official lamented, "is a mile high and a mile wide—we're working up a clarification." [6]

Other terms used by the Government to keep book on its contracts with experts include "research and development (R & D)," "training and technical assistance (T & TA)," "operations research (OR)," "planning," "evaluation," "systems analysis," "management studies," "professional services," and, of course, "consultant services."

The most sophisticated figures are those which account for R & D. These figures are collected by the National Science Foundation, and grand totals appear each year in the Presidential budget.

R & D is a contract sport. In 1973 over 50 percent of the $30 billion spent by America on R & D was provided by the Federal Government. Four and a half billion Federal dollars were spent on Federal installations. Eight billion were contracted to profit-making industry, and the rest was granted or contracted to private universities and nonprofit research organizations. The R & D figures reveal clear patterns of funding. Most Federal monies—an estimated $14 billion in 1975—are spent by agencies having to do with the military—the Defense Department, NASA, and the Energy Research and Development Administration. This money goes primarily to industry. Another large chunk, a little over $1.5 billion, is spent on medical research carried out primarily by universities and other nonprofit bodies. Further breakdowns show that a limited number of industries, corporations, and universities command a lion's share of the dollars in each category.[7]

R & D figures must be approached with caution. Most Federal money (about $11 billion in 1971) is spent not on "research" but on the "development" of costly hardware— spaceships and weaponry. R & D spending is as likely to reflect a political judgment as a technical one. When the Russians launched Sputnik, science became a salable item resulting in the escalation of R & D spending. Almost all of NASA's budget is classed as R & D, but scientists agree that NASA could have produced more "basic knowledge" if its prime mission had not been the politically attractive task of building man-carrying moonships.

The term "technical assistance" came into favor with the rise of America's foreign aid program and is currently a catchall for contract money aiding domestic and foreign agencies alike. In its first five years of existence the Office of Economic Opportunity spent $110 million on technical assistance contracts. Most of the spending, a General Accounting Office study found, was for work that was not very technical and probably not very helpful.[8]

If the free enterprise system is helped by Federal research subsidies, the Government also subsidizes the planning profession. Dozens of Federal programs require states and localities to prepare plans in order to qualify for Federal grants-in-aid. Often contractors are hired to do the work. A 1968 Federal study found that about $250 million was available each year for planning.[9]

Yet another category of contract expenditure was added when disillusion with Great Society spending programs increased. Politicians and experts, whose data-collecting appetite has no limit, agreed that the Government should study the effectiveness of its spending. From 1968 through 1970 the Office of Economic Opportunity awarded 237 "evaluation contracts," at a cost of about $30 million.[10] At the Department of Health, Education, and Welfare, the money available for evaluation increased from virtually nothing in the mid-Sixties to close to $50 million by 1974.

And then there are simply studies. The Government's clearinghouse for unclassified studies has logged in 360,000 titles since 1964, though it is not clear how many are the work of private organizations. One study found that in the years 1969–73 the Army spent over $126 million for contract studies. (About $30 million went for studies involving the use of the computer, $3 million went for "management studies," and the rest were classed as "operations research.")[11]

All of America's experts do not work for the Federal Government, and many who do are full-time employees. But the figures suggest that the conjunction of contractors and expertise is quite significant. Figures and accounting categories tell little about this conjunction. At the simplest, $1 million worth of expert assistance may have profound influence, or it may have none. To look beyond the figures and categories is not only to study the practical meaning of expertise in America but to learn much about the forces of profit, technique, and politics that shape the awesome growth of the Federal Government.

CONTRACTORS IN THE GOVERNMENT BUSINESS

Government contracting is a business, even though contractors may bill themselves as professionals and may claim to be working in "the public interest."

Like other private corporations, contractors aspire at least to survival, at best to growth. Like other private corporations, they must advertise their wares and cultivate new markets, even though these markets may be public agencies. They employ marketing techniques no less varied than elsewhere in private industry. Conferences are held, contacts are kept up, and employees are encouraged to join appropriate social clubs or professional organizations. When times are good, the brochures are printed in abundance.

In March 1971, the director of a major program for the United States Department of Housing and Urban Development received a confidential packet of information from the Westinghouse Electric Corporation. Inside was a document entitled "Business Strategy for 1970." [12]

Westinghouse, the document explained, was combing the Government in search of business for its new "Public Management Services" division. The division would engage in "selling services . . . literally the time of people" to public agencies. Intensive review had led to the conclusion that three "functional markets" were ripe sources of income: criminal justice administration, transportation, and public administration. Westinghouse acknowledged its lack of experience, but felt this to be a minor problem. The division would "use Federal contracts as a basis for developing understanding of state and local needs and to gain credentials and visibility."

Westinghouse's brochure featured a list of its potential competitors in the public management field. With some additions and exceptions, the list is as good a guide as any to the types of profit-making corporations in the Government contract business.

THE WESTINGHOUSE LIST [13]
Accounting Firms

Ernst & Ernst
Price, Waterhouse
Peat, Marwick, Mitchell & Co.

Management Consulting Firms

Booz, Allen, and Hamilton
Abt Associates
Organization for Social and Technological
Innovation (OSTI)

Software Firms

Computer Sciences Corporation
Computer Applications, Inc.

Planning Research Corporation
Systems Development Corporation

Computer Firms

IBM
UNIVAC

Industrial Firms

TRW
Sperry Rand
Lockheed

The Industrial Corporation

Why was Westinghouse, one of the world's largest corporations, hoping to make money as a public manager? Westinghouse is well known to the American public as a producer of consumer goods such as air conditioners and light bulbs. In recent years, however, the consumer divisions of Westinghouse have been corporate trouble spots. The corporation has done better marketing to large organizations than selling to individuals. Westinghouse, for example, is a leading producer of the expensive power-generating equipment purchased by utilities. It also receives substantial Government monies for its hardware. The Navy has paid for Westinghouse-made torpedoes, the Department of Housing and Urban Development has footed the bill for Westinghouse-produced houses, and the Department of Transportation for vehicles. Westinghouse's position as a major supplier of nuclear power plants was facilitated by its role as a manager of one of the United States' Atomic Energy Commission's laboratories.

Westinghouse, the marketing document explained, was entering the "public management" business in hopes that such experience would increase the profitability of the other Westinghouse divisions.

Westinghouse's efforts met with quick success. The public management division received a multimillion-dollar contract to redefine the jobs of over 700,000 postal employees, the largest "job evaluation" contract ever awarded by the Government. A subsequent Congressional investigation discovered that Westinghouse's marketing technique was far more advanced than its public management expertise. The inquiry found that Westinghouse's management experts were idle employees pulled together from throughout the corporation—refrigerator designers and engineers, for example. None had ever performed "job evaluations" before.[14]

The "Big Eight"

The accounting profession is dominated by the "Big Eight" firms, the largest profit-making organizations of professionals in the world. Arthur Andersen, the first Big Eight firm to issue an annual report (for limited distribution), reported over $315 million in earnings for the year ending March 31, 1974. Its 807 active partners averaged $91,400 in earnings, and the top twenty averaged well over $200,000 each. Peat, Marwick, Mitchell & Co. (PMM), another Big Eight firm, claims over 10,000 employees in nearly 300 offices throughout the world. "No other profession," financial journalist John Lyons has written, "is as deeply into the guts of the American system, and no other profession is concentrated into so few units." [15]

While the profession originated as a service to private managers, the growth of the accounting business has been sustained by investor demand for accurate information on business finances. Federal law requires "independent auditors" to certify annual financial reports for all corporations that sell stock to the public. By themselves, the Big Eight firms prepare and certify such reports for over 75 percent of the corporations on the New York and American Stock Exchanges.

Although their primary source of income is audit work, the Big Eight have developed "management services" divisions that do everything from locating prospective merger partners to setting up computer systems to studying possible investments. These divisions are among the largest management consulting organizations in the world. Up to 20 percent of the income of the accounting firm, reports *Business Week*, comes from this growing part of the practice.[16]

Little known is the amount of work that private accounting firms do as management advisers to the Government. "No private corporation," asserts Peat, Marwick, Mitchell & Co., "has experienced the degree of change in terms of growth, complexity of operations, or goals, objectives, and priorities that the Federal Government has during the past two decades, and in all likelihood will continue to experience in the future." In PMM's opinion, its expertise is essential to the Government in this period.[17]

To the extent that these firms work for the Government, their internal operations, the relationship between their consulting and accounting work, the development of their business strategy, and the manner in which corporate and private clientele are linked through internal structure become matters of public interest. Accounting firms, for example, are likely to have private clients that are benefitted or regulated by the public agencies the firm might contract with. Booz, Allen, and Hamilton's management consultants have reorganized the compliance division of the Food and Drug Administration at the same time that they have worked for drug industry corporations and advised a drug industry trade association, while the chemical-biological research division of Booz provided technical analyses for the drug industry.

Privately owned partnership accounting firms are not obliged to publish annual reports. There is no requirement that their financial state, much less the details of their advisory work, be placed on public record. The Freedom of Information Act, the law by which citizens are granted access to information from public agencies, does not apply to private organizations—even if they do much of the Government's work.[18]

Accounting firms have traditionally been quite secretive

about their business and have not altered their policy for public work. Accountants aver that they practice the low-profile techniques expected by corporate clientele.

The basic rule in pursuing Government business is a simple one. "We look," explains a top executive in the Lybrand & Cooper consulting practice, "to where the social action legislation is—that's essentially our priority-setting mechanism." [19]

With dozens of offices throughout America, the large accounting firms are ideally structured to market to a growing Federal Government. This is as true when the program involves industry as it is when Federal monies are given out to states and localities. The big firm may be contracted to help Washington organize a new program, then get paid over again as it helps localities spend Federal money.

Ernst & Ernst's success in monopolizing criminal justice planning in Indiana illustrates the point. When the United States Law Enforcement Assistance Administration was created, millions of dollars were made available to state and local law enforcement agencies. In order to qualify for monies, the local agencies had to submit plans—which the Federal Government would pay for. Ernst & Ernst won contracts to prepare Indiana's application for a planning grant, to prepare the 1969 plan, to prepare the 1970 annual report, to prepare the 1970 plan, to prepare the 1971 planning grant application, to prepare the 1971 comprehensive plan, and to prepare the 1972 comprehensive plan. When the Ernst & Ernst plans were implemented, Ernst & Ernst was in for more business. Thus a $7,200 planning grant was parlayed into a $20,000 action grant.

Finally, when the Indiana planning agency was called to testify before the Congress, Ernst & Ernst served as its consultant. "It sounds to me," marveled Congressman Dante Fascell, "as if an outsider prepares the whole plan for state operations starting at the local level, subgrantee, region, and the state, and he gets paid for that. Then the same consultant gets paid to see that it is implemented, and at this point one begins to wonder what the state agency is doing." [20]

Management Consultants

Management consulting firms, such as Booz, Allen, and Hamilton, trace their heritage to turn-of-the-century efficiency experts who studied the worker in the factory, timing and measuring his every action, testing his intelligence and motivation, with the aim of fitting him most efficiently into the new corporate machines. "Scientific management," writes the author of many popular works on management, "has proven to be the most effective idea of this century." The management expert, argues Peter Drucker, has not only produced a more efficient worker but has produced a politically and socially stable America. Without the gains of increased productivity, America would be a society divided between the haves and have-nots.[21]

Following their attention to the worker, the management experts acquired an interest in the practices of the men who managed corporations and in the processes of corporate growth. The Association of Consulting Management Engineers (ACME), a trade association to which Booz belongs, claims that its members have co-authored with corporate management "every accepted technique" of business management. Management consultants have made "distinct contributions to such central problems of managing a business as the design of the business, corporate strategy, human organizations, manager development, management relations, innovation, and keeping the enterprise relevant to the economic and social environment in which it functions." This environment increasingly means government.[22]

Who is the management consultant? No special credentials are required. A typical Booz, Allen résumé will note that the consultant has a bachelor's degree, and possibly a higher degree or two. Business degrees are common, but so are degrees in the natural or social sciences.

What does the management expert know? ACME breaks

down the "common body of knowledge" of management consultants into four categories—"general, managerial, a knowledge of the principles and practices underlying consulting, and technical or specialized knowledge." The general knowledge requirement sounds imposing, for the consultant should have "knowledge of, or background in, the humanities, history, political science, sociology, social sciences, business law, economics (both macro and micro), physical sciences, and engineering." Is the average consultant to be a Leonardo da Vinci, or simply a liberal arts graduate? [23]

What does the consultant do? Any expert résumé makes it compellingly clear that its subject has had a long and close association with such important matters as "budgeting," "long-range planning," "grants and contracts management," which may have required him to do "studies," to "assist in planning," or to "design a management system." By virtue of all of this, he may advertise himself as a man "experienced" in such arts as "organizational planning," the "management of research and development," or, perhaps, "the design of social experiments."

What does the management consultant do?

Whatever it is that consultants do, organizations have acquired an enormous appetite for their services. The American management consulting business, says ACME, is a $2 billion-a-year industry, employing between 40,000 and 60,000 professionals. The average consultant is himself likely to work in an organization, although, as with the lawyer, the closed partnership is the norm. There are about 3,000 consulting firms. While the vast majority employ only a handful of consultants, between 160 and 200 firms employ sixty or more professionals, and between 200 and 300 employ between five and sixty.[24]

Booz is one of the largest management consulting firms. To its management consulting, Booz has added a string of firms that specialize in areas such as transportation consulting, chemical research, computer consulting, acquisition and divestiture advice, and market and social science research. Today, Booz is a $60 million-a-year conglomerate of "professional services."

Booz claims that it has served "400 of the 500 largest U.S. industrial concerns, 25 of the 50 largest utilities, 25 of the 50 largest transportation firms, and 15 of the 50 largest insurance firms." This business has been complemented by income from Government agencies that suggests a dramatic penetration of management technique into public administration. In the years 1971–73 between 9 and 13 percent of the firm's income came from the Defense Department and NASA, and between 24 and 28 percent from other public agencies.[25]

While the accounting firms and many old-line management consulting firms remain closed partnerships, Booz has become a publicly held corporation, and though it now publishes an annual report, it discloses a minimum of detail. "To protect our clients' interests," they say, "we do not publicize our clients' names, the kinds of work we do for them, nor the results of that work." Booz employees are told that client work may be referred to if the client has chosen to make it public, in which case "the intent should be to reflect credit on the client's own capabilities and good management, augmented and not displaced by the firm." [26]

Whereas Booz initially advised clients on the management of men, Arthur D. Little, a Boston chemist and businessman, advised corporations on the use of technology. In Little's case, as in that of Booz, service to industry long preceded the development of substantial Government practice. The firm of Arthur D. Little, founded in 1886, virtually patented the idea of "contract research." In the original sense of the term, Little and associates would sell their talents to private corporations with the understanding that any product resulting from the arrangement would be the property of the buying organization.[27]

Arthur D. Little's practice adheres to the old ritual. "Because most of our work with private clients is confidential," says the firm, "we cannot discuss in detail what constitutes the majority of our work." This policy applies to

Government work as well. A series of interviews arranged for us with Little professional staff had to be canceled when the Chairman of the Board, General James Gavin, told his employees that they were not free to discuss their work with outsiders.[28]

ADL grew rapidly after World War II. During the war, Little employees were involved in important military research and began a long-time association with the Navy's underseas warfare programs. After the war, ADL became one of the first private firms to offer "operations research," a managerial by-product of wartime science, to private corporations. In the Forties, ADL's involvement with the economic development of Puerto Rico established the firm as an economic development consultant for both domestic and foreign aid programs.[29]

Since 1945, ADL's staff has increased from 170 to over 1,600 and, like Booz, it has become a publicly held corporation. Its 1973 income was $57.5 million. According to the 1969 annual report, 875 of the 1,000 clients served by Little were private organizations, but 30 percent of the firm's revenue came from public agencies.[30]

By the Sixties, the Government contract market was sufficiently large to be the prime source of income for new consulting ventures such as the Organization for Social and Technological Innovation (OSTI) and Abt Associates.

In the early Sixties, OSTI founder Donald Schon was a Little employee working on Government contracts in his field of specialty, the study of innovation in private industry. When a Government program was created to subsidize innovation in "research-poor" industries, Schon left Little for the Commerce Department, then left Government to form OSTI. Through OSTI, Schon hoped to apply the lessons he had learned in studying industrial innovation to the "urban" and "poverty" problems of the Sixties. (These efforts to apply industrial technique are discussed in the final portion of our study.)

Abt Associates was created by a political science Ph.D. who had been employed by the Raytheon Corporation, a major defense electronics contractor. Abt displayed entrepreneurial genius as he staffed his organization with bright young Cambridge graduate students and began to market to civilian agencies techniques that had been sold to defense managers. By 1971, the company was billing $4.5 million, and by 1974 its income was $16.5 million.[31]

Although the computer revolution has been a boon to all management advisers, Westinghouse's final group of competitors are most closely associated with the use of computers.

Planning Research Corporation was founded by a charter employee of the RAND Corporation. Where Booz and Little diversified from management and scientific bases, Robert Krueger was determined to build a "professional services" conglomerate from his initial computer services corporation. A $2 million business in 1960, PRC grew as Krueger acquired close to two dozen subsidiaries that specialized in areas such as air transport consulting, engineering, marketing, and the behavioral sciences. By 1973, PRC was doing almost $100 million worth of business.

Like Booz and Little, PRC has experienced severe growth problems. The firm overextended itself when it tried to operate a computerized travel reservation service, and Krueger was forced out of top management. Before he left PRC, Krueger put together the National Council of Professional Services Firms. The profit-making contract expert industry had reached maturity. It now had its own lobby. According to the Council, the industry, which encompasses architects and engineers, computer software, management consulting, and systems analysis organizations, does $11 billion worth of business each year—one half of which is with the Federal Government.[32]

The Nonprofits

The National Council argues that more and more of the business of government should be contracted out. It also claims that profit-making corporations are continually discriminated against by policies that assume that nonprofit corporations are better suited to work for the Government. (The Federal budget for grants-in-aid, for example, must be allocated to nonprofit organizations.)[33]

The National Council is correct in one respect. Nonprofit research and consulting corporations are not on the Westinghouse list, but they do much of the same work, and they are often found competing with profit-making corporations.[34]

What is a nonprofit? The clearest current definition is a traditional legal one. Nonprofits are not empowered to sell stock or to make profits and cannot, therefore, distribute profits to shareholders. To this basic difference have been added other legal distinctions. Tax law and government contract law, for example, treat profit and nonprofit organizations differently.

But the legal distinction is often far sharper than the practical one. Nonprofits are no less private than profit-making corporations. While boards of directors govern profit-making corporations, self-perpetuating boards of trustees govern nonprofits. If profit-making firms seek profits, nonprofits are no less interested in survival and growth. They are not allowed to finance growth with "profits," but they do so with "fees"—generally computed as a percentage of the cost of a given contract.

So powerful is the association of the term "profit" with private interest that simply by disavowing the term, nonprofits can project an image of "objectivity" and "public interestedness." Thus, a major Air Force contractor advertises periodically that "Mitre is a leading nonprofit systems engineering company working wholly in the public interest." Not surprisingly, those nonprofit Government contractors survive to the extent that they simultaneously promote corporate (profit-making) growth.[35]

There are two ways in which most nonprofits have entered Government service. Many were established by Government to service those agencies that subsidized the creation of the private atomic energy and space industry, and the growth of the private defense industry.

The Atomic Energy Commission, recently bifurcated into the Nuclear Regulatory Commission and the Energy Research and Development Administration (ERDA), has contracted out the management of the nation's atomic energy laboratories since its creation in 1946. These non-profit organizations are managed by a variety of private corporations, universities, and other nonprofit organizations. A study done by an Air Force nonprofit summed up the importance of these contracts as a bridgehead over which profit-making corporations crossed into the atomic energy industry:

> Some think that Westinghouse and GE attained their present dominant positions as the leading manufacturers and suppliers of nuclear power plants because of technological "know-how" obtained from their earlier experience as AEC prime contractors. And of course this is true. But some significance must be attached to the evidence that certain professionals at Bettis and Knolls Laboratories—who were Westinghouse and GE employees, respectively, and at the same time, quasi-employees of the AEC—occupied strategic positions which provided them with unique access to responsible officials within both the AEC and their own companies. They were able to act as agents for bringing policy positions of their industrial employers and the AEC into closer accord.[36]

The best-known nonprofits were created to serve the military. These include organizations that research new weapons technology—such as the Navy's Ordnance Research Laboratory, managed by Penn State University; organizations that manage industrial contractors—such as the Air Force's Aerospace Corporation; and organizations that perform studies of military management, technology, and policy—such as the RAND Corporation.

Nonprofits created by Government agencies have been dubbed "Federal Contract Research Centers," or "FCRCs." The term was coined by the National Science Foundation as part of its efforts to create accounting categories for Research and Development spending. In

1975, the FCRCs were estimated to have Federal contract incomes of over $1.7 billion. (Most of the money went to FCRCs sponsored by DOD, NASA, and the AEC (today ERDA). Additional sums went to the basic research organizations sponsored by the NSF itself and to the close to twenty "educational laboratories" created by the United States Office of Education to stimulate an "education industry." [37]

Often spoken of as an "invisible branch" of Government, the FCRCs are the only group of consulting contractors to appear with regularity in the public record. Sponsoring agencies account for FCRC expenditures as they treat civil service expenditures, providing Congress with annual totals. As one observer noted, "although the responsibilities and character of each of the FCRCs are different, what they seem to have in common is that they are not-for-profit institutions listed by name in the Federal budget as line items."

The FCRCs have been just visible enough to absorb perennial Congressional criticism of contracted expertise. As a 1971 Defense Department report acknowledged, "the tone and themes of Congressional comments ten years ago—too much growth, too great a cost to Government, too little control, and poor quality products—have been repeated in almost every succeeding year. Clearly, as viewed by the Congress, attempts by the DOD and the FCRCs to respond to Congressional concern have not been completely successful." [38]

When their budgets are threatened, the FCRCs respond like any profit-making business: they diversify or reorganize. When the Congress began to impose on the defense FCRCs financial ceilings similar to those imposed on civil service personnel, the organizations sought business from civilian agencies. "When the balloon goes down on one end," quipped a RAND vice president, "it goes up on another." RAND has successfully entered the civilian market. The Systems Development Corporation, an Air Force FCRC created by RAND to train airmen in the use of computers, has responded to raids on its employees by profit-making firms by turning itself into a profit-making corporation. SDC thus appeared on the Westinghouse list as a profit-making competitor.[39]

While the FCRCs were established to serve the R & D complexes and have diversified to serve other agencies and private industry, a second group of nonprofits was created to serve industry and attached itself to the R & D complexes.

A National Science Foundation survey located 159 nonprofit (non-FCRC) research organizations that performed at least $100,000 worth of research. Their collective research budget was $361 million in 1969, of which 62 percent came from the Government. A handful of the nonprofits are far wealthier than the rest. The four largest organizations received 32 percent of the total the Federal Government provided the group, and the first eight took 50 percent.[40]

The Stanford Research Institute and Battelle Memorial Institute are probably the two largest private nonprofit research organizations. Both were created to serve private industry, but both are now major Government contractors.

SRI was founded in 1946 by Stanford University academics and West Coast businessmen whose intention was to create a research organization that would "industrialize the West" in the same way that Battelle and Arthur D. Little had helped business in other parts of the country. SRI still has many corporate clients, but its prime client has long been the United States Department of Defense.[41]

Battelle is the giant of nonprofits. As its official biography proclaims, it is larger than any industrial laboratory except for the Bell Telephone Labs, "as active a center of discovery" as the University of Illinois, almost as "big and busy" as the next ten largest independent nonprofits, and "in comparison with most business enterprises, it has been a bonanza." [42]

Gordon Battelle died in 1923 and willed an institute to

perform research in metallurgy. The new institute was located in Battelle's hometown of Columbus, Ohio.

Rather than sit on the endowment, Battelle's trustees recruited new executives from the United States Department of the Interior and adopted Arthur D. Little's practice of selling research to industrial clients on a proprietary basis.

In the mid-Forties Battelle's entrepreneurial instincts led to the most profitable nonprofit venture in history, as the Institute helped develop a new copying technique now known as Xerox. Battelle's interest in Xerox's success has helped place its current assets at close to $250 million. (Battelle maintains an interest in high-risk ventures and has a venture-promoting subsidiary, but no new Xerox is in sight.)

Battelle's first Government contract was signed in 1939. Its metallurgical skills were to be used in the improvement of armor, and the Institute's director was enlisted to head the Army's War Metallurgy Committee.

Since World War II, Battelle, like the profit-making research groups, has both grown considerably and expanded its base of expertise. Battelle's 5,850 employees are located in laboratories in Frankfurt and Geneva, as well as at the Columbus headquarters. The Institute has even received millions of dollars in foreign aid money to establish a Korean "Institute of Industrial Technology and Applied Sciences." Like Westinghouse, Battelle administers one of the Nuclear Regulatory Commission's FCRCs. (The Pacific Northwest Laboratory itself received $56 million in 1970.)

Social science came to Battelle as an adjunct of the firm's charter to study metals. Battelle's economists studied the economics of the metals industry, and its psychologists studied the metals worker. By 1970, these social scientists and other Battelle employers were competing for Government contracts to study housing, education, transportation, and a host of other subjects.

The citizens of Ohio challenged Battelle's growth as a worldwide conglomerate, arguing that it was being financed by "profits" that, according to the terms of the Gordon Battelle will, should have been donated to charity. In a 1975 court settlement, Battelle agreed to contribute $80 million to charity in settlement of past obligations and to make appropriate future donations.[43]

Contracting

There is no coherent body of law or custom that applies to the contracts that are the subject of this book, nor is there a central source of information on the contracts awarded to hundreds of different organizations by myriad Government agencies. Government surveys and texts use an abundance of terms ("professional service" contracts, "research and development" contracts, "management consulting" contracts, "technical assistance" contracts, "study" contracts), all of them covering categories that overlap with vast imprecision.

Like most legal or bureaucratic processes, contracting operates on two levels. There exists an elaborate set of written rules and documents that defines how contracts are to be awarded, written, administered, and evaluated. Central to this formal structure is the individual contract itself. The contract is, in theory, a written agreement that will specify the work to be performed by the contractor, the terms of payment, and the period of performance.

But written contract law represents only a small part of the contract process. The contract itself, as Columbia's Bruce Smith has noted, "is not of decisive importance. The formal contract is merely a step in the process of interaction between agency and contractor." [44]

The contract process is dominated by the network of relationships that exists between contractor and agency, and these relationships are crucial to many decisions in the awarding and administration of contracts. Of equal importance is the division of labor that most agencies have established. "Contract officers" are legally responsible for the administration and enforcement of contracts and may be in charge of dozens of contracts at any one time. They are not likely to have any technical background in the subject matter of the awards they oversee. The responsibility for managing a contract, on the other hand, generally lies with a "project officer," who in turn has little understanding of contract law and who tends to be more concerned with pushing his program along than with following troublesome contracting rules. The division of labor contains a great potential for tense relationships, and the contract officer often finds himself the low man on the totem pole.

Contractors may sue when they feel that the contracting system has operated unjustly, but as for the public interest, there are virtually no instances of taxpayer suits over money that has been spent illegally or wastefully by dint of poor or even illegal Government-contractor performance.

The Armed Services Procurement Act of 1947 established the Armed Services Procurement Regulations, commonly referred to as "Asper," which has become the model for the Government-wide procurement regulations codified in 1949 in the Federal Procurement Regulations (FPR). Both Asper and FPR are weighty tomes—a recent edition of FPR covered about 650 pages—and are supplemented by a wide variety of department and agency rules and guidebooks.

Many full-time contract officers are concerned about and bewildered by these laws. Ralph Howard, former procurement chief of OEO, which made liberal use of research and consulting contracts, lamented: "If you ask me, someone should take the NASA Procurement laws, Asper, and the FPR and chuck the whole goddamn thing. The procurement law is a jungle, and we ought to just throw away these laws. You asked me what are the legal requirements of a contract? When is a contract legally fulfilled? I don't have the slightest idea. These laws keep getting more and more complicated by the day, and the people you are studying continue to complicate the process in their own interest." [45]

Until World War II, there was a strong preference for

competitive bidding to ward off corruption and promote quality and efficiency. Wartime requirements for urgent and flexible procurement, plus the unprecedented purchasing of new technical products, led to an erosion of the practice.

While the procurement laws of the late Forties officially favored maximum competition, they permitted exceptions in times of national emergency and peacetime urgency— that is, when the experience necessary to perform the work is available in limited degree, where contract costs are difficult to determine in advance, or even where the contracting agency can decide that "the contract is for services for which it is impracticable to obtain competition." Given these exceptions, the "negotiated" contract made enormous inroads.

Formal competition requires that agencies place notices of their needs in an official publication called the *Commerce Business Daily*. Respondents may then request further information and bid on the contract. By choosing the negotiated-contract route, an agency is not required to advertise formally its needs and may invite a preselected list of contractors to bid on the job, or may simply award a contract to a "sole source."

The figures are devastating. In a recent survey, the GAO told Congress that about 85 percent of defense contract dollars are not advertised. Of the $7.46 billion in civilian contracts in the fiscal year ending in mid-1968, the GAO found about $1.54 billion related to advertised procurements, while about $5.3 billion were negotiated.

When Robert Finch took office as Nixon's first HEW Secretary, he commissioned a study of the $278.5 million in contracts the Department awarded in fiscal 1968.[46] The study disclosed that 88 percent of awards were negotiated and that, of this total, 82 percent were sole-sourced. Incidentally, negotiations were favored by HEW in its dealings with both profit-making and nonprofit corporations.[47]

HEW's own procurement regulations require that its agencies keep detailed records of each procurement in the files of their contract offices. The study found the Department's contract files "extremely poorly" documented and devoid of meaningful information: "In over 50 percent of the cases examined, justifications in support of single or sole-source procurements were inadequate. In addition, such significant business judgment documentations as cost advisory reports, technical evaluations, and negotiations were conducted informally with prospective contractors." In the Office of Education, where 80 percent of contract files had not been completed, the review found that 90 percent of the sole-source files contained absolutely none of the required justifications for the awards. "OE," the survey found, "was in noncompliance with Federal or HEW procurement regulations and good business practice." In the Social and Rehabilitative Services Agency, 98 percent of the contract files lacked memoranda summarizing the procurement history. In the Environmental Health Services Administration, justifications for negotiation were on file, but "tended to be stereotyped and unsupported other than by a statement from the program officer that the sole source was necessary to get the job done." [48]

The study concluded that the procurement officials were not solely responsible for the failures of competition and documentation. The study found that "procurement personnel are seldom involved in initial decisions that affect the procurement process. Program personnel establish requirements, select the contractor, conduct negotiations, and determine contract price, prior to submitting a request for contract to the procurement activity." The contracting officer is thus placed in an untenable position when he questions after-the-fact program actions, and in most cases he is powerless to remedy improper commitments made by program personnel.

The results of the August 1969 HEW study displeased Secretary Finch, who stated that the procedure of advertised competition should be followed unless it was "absolutely necessary" not to.

But one has only to examine the contracts awarded by

Secretary Finch's office in the year following the completion of the study to discover the discrepancy between rhetoric and action. The Office of the Secretary produced a grab bag of sole-source awards that amply demonstrated the ease with which top agency officials trample on the procurement process.

The 1971 contract log for the Office of the Secretary records that a corporation called the Inner City Fund received no fewer than five sole-source awards from the Secretary's office alone. Inner City Fund was a newly created firm founded by a handful of young men who arrived in the inner city via elite business schools and the Defense Department's systems analysis shop. Founding member Pug Winokur explained that it was patterned after the typical influential Washington law firm.[49] They were not interested in performing mundane studies but wanted to work directly on major policy issues. Within a short period of its founding, the firm was serving in this role at OEO, EPA, the National Security Council, and HEW.

ICF's first award of the fiscal year was OS-71-21. The Assistant Secretary for Population Affairs hired it to develop "meaningful objectives for family planning." HEW requires that sole-source awards be supported by written justifications, and the justification for OS-71-21 was the typical kind supplied. HEW had a "pressing need" to meet the President's promise of adequate family planning services "within the next five years," and the requisite experts had to be "thoroughly familiar" with HEW's management.[50]

Next came OS-71-87, a contract to study criteria for Federal support of higher education. By this time, the young ICF principals had worked themselves up to $254 a day, and the Department worked up a spectacular statement of the firm's unique qualifications which, in addition to the usual time constraints, justified the award.

ICF, said the justification, "has exclusive capabilities to meet the requirements of this study. It is unique in its skills in the management of investigative teams simultaneously seeking program budget data and behavioral data concerning institutions of higher education necessary for interpreting program budget data in the field." This seems to mean simply that ICF was familiar with the current jargon of analysis. But the justification boldly declared that even RAND, the fount of "program budget" study, lacked "the skills to proceed without time-consuming model construction," men skilled in managing investigative teams, and "personnel versed in the behavioral dimensions of institutional behavior." HEW was "aware of no other alternative source of the required combination of skills." The justification is a shocking reflection on HEW's contracting methods, since the "exclusive" skills are scarcely distinguishable from those offered in consulting brochures and college catalogues.[51]

Did HEW really believe that this handful of young men possessed a monopoly of staple technical talent? "There's not very many people around," the young HEW contract officer for OS-71-87 explained, "with the expertise that they have—or at least the ins they have." In any case, Martin Duby confided, "there's no way you're going to open it up to competition anyway." [52]

Contract OS-71-110 turned ICF to national health policy. The firm, the sole-source justification noted, had been "active in preparing the HMO [Health Maintenance Organizations] Act and Family Health Insurance HMO option [*sic*], recently submitted by the Administration to Congress." OS-71-110 provided ICF money for further HMO work. (The only novelty in the file was a program manager's plea that ICF receive at least GS-16 salary for its work.)[53]

OS-71-134 was a continuation of the higher-education work, and ICF rounded out the year with OS-71-180 to study the "integration" of HEW's services. Since the earlier contracts had given ICF work in health, education, and welfare fields, it naturally had "special competence" for the award. The sole-source justification said that HEW Assistant Secretary for Planning and Evaluation Larry Lynn, a former staffer of the Office of the Secretary of Defense, thought very highly of ICF's Winokur. Further, it was felt that much would be brought to the contract by ICF's Steve Smith, who had been with the Office of the Secretary of HEW between 1969 and 1971 and had there been involved with the first ICF sole-source contract of the year.[54]

ICF's gains were losses for the competitive process, but RAND did not suffer from the slight. It received its own $300,000 sole-source contract to study education—with similarly styled explanations of its unique analytical expertise.[55]

The most interesting sole-source award to RAND was a study of the placement of physicians in rural areas. The terms of the contract show that even the most cut-and-dried piece of research can be deemed unique in the fantasy world of contracting. RAND was to study the literature on rural health care, design a questionnaire, analyze its results, and conduct some interviews.

HEW claimed that it was "impossible to describe in precise detail, or by drawing specifications, the exact nature of the work to be done. Only the ultimate objectives and the general scope of the work can be outlined. The precise method for accomplishing the work cannot be established in advance, but is subject to innovation and improvisation during contract performance. . . . As to the essential features of the performance, the best that can be bargained for is the contractor's best effort." [56]

The real defect of the contract was not the feeble justification proffered but the information not offered. Michael Samuels, HEW's first project monitor for the RAND contract, had taken a degree at George Washington University. One of Samuels' thesis advisers was James K. Cooper, M.D., the principal RAND consultant on the study. No one in RAND or HEW thought this relationship unusual. At all events, what happened was that the contract was extended and its cost doubled.

At least one HEW contract was justified because of the friendship between the contractor and Secretary Finch.

Gerson Green was an OEO employee who advised Republican welfare officials in the first months of the Nixon Administration. Green left the Government to work for a social welfare contractor, University Research Corporation. HEW awarded University Research a sole-source contract to study the HEW R & D program. The sole-source justification fixed on Green's unique credentials. Green had served with OEO's R & D program, and "as you perhaps know, Mr. Green was a personal adviser to the Secretary for about three months during the transition period and accompanied the Secretary on his trip to Israel." The justification also contained the usual assertion of necessity. The final report was nearly a year late.[57]

Occasionally, a contracting office was called on to find excuses for particularly poor judgment on the part of top management. Fred Malek, Under Secretary of HEW in 1970, was one top manager who showed a unique disregard for the niceties of the contract law. Malek had authorized Thompson, Lewin, and Associates, a small consulting firm, to help reorganize the Office of Child Development. The basic problem, as a memo in the contract files explained, was that permission "was granted the contractor to perform work outside the scope of an existing contract which committed the Government to an expenditure of funds in violation of the procurement regulations. This situation, of course, is particularly unfortunate, in view of recent publicity that this Department has received. . . ."

To rectify Malek's unauthorized commitment, a statement was created that merely added the new commitment onto an earlier contract. "This hodgepodge of errors," a file note explains, "should not have occurred and should not be interpreted as a deliberate attempt to circumvent the procurement process."

Even with the fudging, the Lewin contract violated HEW's own procurement regulations, which require solicitation of at least three sources for any management consultant contract. Though there are no stated exceptions to this rule, it is honored only in the breach.

The RFP Route

The RFP, or Request for Proposal, is the keystone of competitive contracting. When the Government opens an award to competition, it will normally place a notice of the issuance of the RFP in the *Commerce Business Daily*. RFPs provide a general statement of the work that the agency is interested in and vary widely in content and form. They may have work statements as brief as a page and they may not even give contractors an idea of the experience required or of the "man hours" or dollar value the agency anticipates.

When the deadline is reached, the agency turns the responses over to a review panel or panels.[58] These boards rank bidders according to a variety of criteria—for example, personnel credentials, experience, and cost. The panels make recommendations, which are generally approved by top management.

Available studies indicate that the RFP process is "informal and highly selective." Analyzing the defense and NASA procurement process, MIT's Edward Roberts, of the Sloan School of Management, concluded:

> The real award process is one involving long-term, person-to-person contacts between technical people in Government and industry. They build up common experiences, attitudes, aspirations, confidences. And ideas are generated in this interchange. These are the ideas that later become Government-sponsored R and D projects. When he is convinced that an idea has solid merit, the Government scientist/engineer initiates a Procurement request. He often feels, naturally, that the work should be carried out by the people in whose capabilities he has faith. Acting in what he believes to be the nation's best interest, he tries to secure "his" contractor. (He usually succeeds.) If he is confident of his judgment, he thwarts attempts to saddle his project with another contractor. Only when he regards several companies as being highly qualified does real competition prevail.[59]

At the same time that the procurement regulations try to dampen the importance of contacts, more realistic Government publications explicitly recognize it. For 25 cents, any citizen can pick up a copy of *Small Business and Government: Research and Development*, a little brochure issued by the Department of Commerce. The pamphlet, written on contract by two employees of the Midwest Research Institute, offers helpful tips to businesses interested in entering the "promising field" of the "billions of dollars of research and development contracts":

> Continuous personal contact with the staff of the contracting agency is a means of keeping informed about proposed government R & D contracts. The importance of such contacts is illustrated by a comment sometimes voiced: "You are already out of the running if you first learn of a possible research contract through a proposal request." As in other aspects of business life, personal contacts are important. These contacts should be made not only with the technical liaison and contract relations officers, but with the scientific personnel of the agencies as well. . . . The technical people will make recommendations about proposals and will frequently suggest prospective contractors. Therefore, these people should always be aware of your capabilities. Besides judging your capabilities, the technical staff of a Government agency will provide an excellent sounding board for: ideas that you have originated and that can form the basis for unsolicited proposals; ideas and approaches that you have originated to solve problems that are confronting the agency, and which will form the basis for solicited proposals.[60]

The cultivation of inside contacts does not, of course, assure a contractor that he will win out in competition. There may be many insiders, and they may all have access to helpful information. They may know how much money an agency has to spend—a very important factor in responding to vaguely worded RFPs—and they will also be able to seize on methodologies, problems, or "buzzwords" that the issuing bureau particularly favors.

It is obviously not easy for the outsider to trace the contract process. Occasionally, however, the files shed some light on the procedure.

Peat, Marwick, Mitchell & Co., for example, was one of several Big Eight accounting firms that eagerly sought to produce Office of Education–sponsored handbooks on school accounting. (The handbook contract could lead to many contracts throughout the public school system.) PMM's chief education consultant sent a letter from the Washington office to the Dallas office, with carbon copies to many other PMM offices. "As most of you know," it said, "the request for Proposal from USOE on the Revision of Handbook II will be released shortly. We are a strong contender for this job. Commissioner Hitt of Texas, Mr. Lindman of California, and a number of USOE staff have expressed their confidence in the firm as the best and only logical consultant to do the work." Nonetheless, wrote Perkins, the job was far "from in the bag." Local PMM offices were urged to help coordinate the push for the contract.

Unfortunately for Peat, Marwick, its zeal was not matched by discretion, and copies of the letter were unexpectedly mailed to Office of Education officials. One OE recipient was Dr. Karl Hereford, who found it "grossly inappropriate. It was bad business with us to continue a relationship with a firm that thought it had an inside track." [61]

The letter set off a flurry of memos within OE, and Hereford's view did not prevail. Someone decided that PMM should not suffer for its professional lapses. The firm received a polite enough letter from OE reminding it that the Government did not play favorites. OE then announced its RFP, and PMM received the contract over a handful of competing bidders.

RFPs for consulting work vary greatly in form and substance. "RFPs," explained Clark Abt of Abt Associates, "are generally not sufficiently well defined to lead to good performance. The identification of tasks and the relative emphasis desired and the specific output of each task are rarely sufficiently well specified." [62] One HEW evaluation study found that 63 percent of the bids varied significantly —more than 25 percent over or under the planned costs. The sum of the low bids on $4 million worth of Office of Education contracts was $2.86 million, while the sum of the high bids was $9.81 million. It was not extraordinary for HEW to receive bids for a given contract that ranged from the tens of thousands of dollars to upwards of half a million dollars. [63]

These figures compel an appreciation of the difference between "brains contracting" and traditional hardware contracting. In a mundane hardware contract for, say, $250,000, the difference between winning and losing bids is not likely to be more than a few thousand dollars. HEW could explain its variations only by arguing that Government and contractor had great difficulty communicating with one another or that the substance of the work HEW wanted performed was inherently impossible to specify.

HEW found that its proposal raters were as inconsistent as the bidders, and hypothesized several sources of inconsistency. The RFPs may have been unclear to the raters as well as to contractors; the criteria for rating may have been unclear; raters may have lacked technical competence; some raters may have had special knowledge; and the raters may have communicated poorly among themselves.

In addition, HEW, like most agencies, lacks reliable information on the past record of consulting firms and individuals. Judgment about the capabilities of contenders is often based on firm "name," personal contact, or the great tradition of anecdote—fine ways of doing business in the thirteenth century—or the bloated and yet incomplete brochures produced by the consultants—the twentieth century's contribution to progress.

Why don't agencies keep records of the quality of work done by contractors and use these records as a basis for subsequent contract awards? One of the few agencies that does require formal postcontract evaluations is the Agency for International Development. AID, like many agencies, refused to permit us to examine evaluations, but the late John Curry, procurement chief for the Agency, admitted that the evaluations were rarely relied on in the contract process.

In HEW, the in-house management consulting division compiles postcontract evaluations. This division also refused to permit us to look at these evaluations, and most of the Department seems to be unaware of their existence. Thus, in the course of a discussion about the continual problems HEW has had with "management consultant" contracts, an official of the OS contract office explained that he had continually recommended to higher-ups that they require postcontract evaluations of such contracts.

The consequences of there being no formal, centralized record-keeping can be appreciated only by examining the contract files of several agencies. The contractor selected by one bureau as the sole source for an award may be rejected as patently unqualified for a similar award being made simultaneously by another office.

One by-product of the RFP process is the expenditure of relatively large sums of money for proposal preparation and bidder selection. In a contract study of the program evaluation contracts the Bureau of Social Science Research obtained a series of estimates from fifteen contractors on the amount spent in preparing responses to RFPs for evaluation contracts. The cost of proposal preparation varied from $200 to $16,000, with the median cost at $3,000 per response. Citing a case in which 444 responses were processed by an agency to produce twelve awards for a total of $4 million, the Bureau noted that, at $3,000 a response, the sheer cost of proposal writing could equal one third of the total contract awards.[64]

One major cause of variation is a rapid compression of the entire contract process that might be dubbed the "May–June bloodletting." Congressional delay in approval of agency budgets results in a rushed letting of contracts during the last months of the fiscal year—at which time contracts must be quickly awarded lest the funds revert to the Treasury. "Bloodletting" is also a result of poor planning on the part of agencies. In 1973, HEW revealed that the Office of Education had coped with the 1972 deadline by illegally backdating over $50 million in contracts and grants. The HEW study also offered a case in which the agency was rumored to have begun its RFP on June 29, and by June 30 ten contractors had been solicited, four proposals received, and the contract signed.

The House Post Office and Civil Service Committee's investigation of a Westinghouse contract, the most detailed Congressional inquest into a consultant contract, illustrates the pervasive problem in contracting—that there are no coherent merit criteria by which contractors are selected.[65] The investigation concluded that the contract was awarded to a firm that had literally no experience on the routine tasks involved, and would carry them out at a price substantially higher than that demanded by qualified firms.

Congress had mandated the transformation of the Post Office into a solvent public corporation. One of the first concerns of the new United States Postal Corporation was the status of 750,000 postal employees. In early 1970, a job evaluation study was advertised in the *Commerce Business Daily* to recommend changes in employment structure. Job evaluation studies have long been bread-and-butter work for many business consulting firms. The Post Office study was among the largest such studies ever peformed; the job was a plum.

According to Ann Flory, the postal official in charge of the contract, between ten and twenty firms came forward. Mrs. Flory expected that the contractor would perform the evaluation study, but that postal employees would implement the recommendations. When top management heard that the proposed contract would cost $500,000, they decided to shift to an in-house study. Then Mrs. Flory left the agency and was replaced by a Mr. Eidson, a long-time corporate employee with no particular postal experience. "The entire project," Congress found, "was left in the hands of one man, Mr. Eidson. He had no staff, used no task force, solicited no informed assistants." [66] Eidson paid two individual consultants "ill-equipped by actual experience in this kind of evaluation," and one of the two ended up working on the Westinghouse contract.

Eidson proceeded to contact a handful of consulting firms, including Booz, Allen and Westinghouse, notifying them that bids would be accepted in an impossibly short one-week period. Westinghouse was given the award, even though its bid of $3 million was $300,000 higher than any other, and $1 million higher than the average bid of the four other contenders.

Westinghouse's name appeared at the top of the list when the rater's point total was averaged, but the firm had never before had a job evaluation contract. The Congressional investigation placed on record the list of fifty experts Westinghouse proposed for the study. They included a "senior marketing engineer—TV," an "industrial engineer —dehumidifiers," a "sales manager—soft drink vending equipment," and a "nuclear safety engineer." Not one of the fifty, Congress concluded, had "specific and direct job evaluation experience." [67]

Westinghouse was so bold as to recognize the limits of its staff, and proposed a subcontract to Fry Consultants which would give Fry the job of training the Westinghouse employees in job evaluation. An excited committee counsel revealed to Congressmen the techniques which Fry was to impart to Westinghouse:

> This committee has been hard pressed to gather detailed information. . . . By sheer chance we were approached by an individual late yesterday afternoon who revealed to us that he had been intimately involved with the Post Office-Westinghouse contract. . . . He told us that he had accumulated papers and documents that were extremely sensitive, papers that were given to him in the strictest confidence. As a result of these constraints, he informed us that he had kept them hidden in a copper kettle that was used for making applesauce. After an in-depth study through the long hours

of the night, the staff has extracted some of the more sensitive and exquisite information from which, for want of a better name, I will call the "applesauce" papers. Snugly tucked among the papers the staff was elated to find the training instructions which Fry Consultants found necessary to teach these trained, highly competent, knowledgeable systems-oriented job evaluation Westinghouse specialists. I will read you some of the more earth-shaking passages. On one training sheet entitled "Interviewing Guidelines for Westinghouse-Fry Team Members," and I quote: "In its simplest form, interviewing is the art of asking questions and listening to responses so as to obtain reliable and valid information about a problem." We also find this rather interesting passage: "The interviewer should use continuity words and phrases as 'I see,' 'Ummm,' 'Ah,' 'Isn't that interesting,' or 'Mmmm.' Or he might, as it says here, nod your [*sic*] head "Yes." [68]

Was this, Fry's expert was asked, the kind of pabulum used to teach Westinghouse? "Yes," said the man from Fry.

The Committee concluded that Eidson had chosen Westinghouse before he solicited bids. The Post Office denied this, gamely referring to the terms of the invitation to bid. Westinghouse, the Post Office explained, was the only bidder that understood that 3,128 man hours of work were called for. Booz, Allen's bid was rejected, the Post Office argued, because it had underestimated the time required, though the Booz representative testified that the Post Office had never specified the number of jobs or men to be evaluated. Eidson could not explain where the 3,128 figure came from. "I do not know," he told Congress months after the award, "how many jobs [are to be evaluated]. I do not know today." [69]

The House investigation makes fascinating reading, but was of no consequence. Its conclusions were referred to the Justice Department, which took no action.

II.

PRIVATE MANAGERS OF THE PUBLIC DOMAIN

There are few satisfying and no comprehensive studies of expert contracting. People in government, in the press, among the public, and in the political science profession who are familiar with the subject tend to assume that expert contracting is of limited import. Public interest lawyers who study conflict of interest in government pay limited attention to the contractor work force.

"Ideally," says a report of the Center for Law and Social Policy, "the Government should be able to draw on the best talent available to work on public business. Service rendered should be of the highest quality and, of course, directed toward the public good rather than toward the advancement of private interests. . . . In some time periods, and in some sectors of Government operations, Federal agencies contract for work to be done on the outside. If in-house capacity is lacking, or not present in sufficient quantity, and if the outside contractor possesses special expertise, the arrangements can benefit the public. It may be most justified in nonrecurring situations where the Government agency does not have reason to add to its own staff so as to handle such matters without resort to outside experts." [1]

Discounting lawyerly hedging, the quotation is fundamentally supportive of the practice of contracting for expertise. Its assumptions seem reasonable enough. The Government knows what kind of expertise it needs and how to find bona fide experts. Contracting is a "sometime" affair, done on a temporary basis in "some" agencies. As a corollary, it is assumed that contractors are incidental to the operations of government, not forces in their own right. They do not exercise *de facto* influence by virtue of lengthy tenure, they supplement the civil service and are not used to remold it, they do not advance one concept of government purpose at the expense of another, they do not exercise public authority as private organizations, and, finally, they can readily avoid representing their private interests when they work for the Government. In sum, the contract expert is merely a servant of the civil servant, and the relationship between the two is adequately definable in the contract that binds them.

To subscribe to this picture of contracting is not to claim that the system is perfect. Civil servants will make errors of judgment. An occasional boondoggle will occur as worthless studies are performed or contractors are paid handsomely to do work that civil servants could have performed more cheaply. But given the scope of government these mistakes are considered minor. The recognized exceptions to this rule of benign and limited contracting are the so-called "Government-industry complexes," which exist wherever the public purpose has become inseparably tied to the support of an entire industry. Pre-eminent among these is the defense complex, where the RAND Corporation immediately comes to mind as a typical contract source servicing a Government agency on a recurrent basis. Interestingly, while it is assumed that RAND's permanence has made it highly influential, its image is still that of an academic "think tank." Yet RAND is not a typical contractor. More typical is a company like Peat, Marwick, Mitchell & Co.

PMM, reputed to be the world's largest accounting firm, audits, along with a small number of other accounting firms, the books of most of America's large corporations. PMM, hyperbolized *Fortune* magazine, knows more about American business than the CIA.[2]

In addition to its accounting work, PMM houses one of

the world's largest management consulting organizations, with an income estimated at $35 million a year and a staff of close to 1,000.

PMM's consulting division does extensive and continual work for a wide variety of Government agencies. PMM serves the Government-industry complexes. But the firm is also active at the nexi of state, local, and Federal governments, regulatory agencies and industry, and civilian agencies and their clients. If the diversity of PMM's business calls into question the sole association of heavy expert contracting with complexes, the ubiquity of PMM's contract relationships also does not comport with the assumption that expert contracting is a limited affair.

Cost Control of the Mark 48 Torpedo

The billion-dollar weapons contracts of the early Sixties became multibillion-dollar scandals by the decade's end. While the cost overruns were highly publicized, how they happened to come about was given less attention. In fact, the Defense Department had begun the decade by promising that costs would be controlled, and hired private contractors, including PMM, to serve as the brains and promoters for cost control techniques.[3]

The measure of success of PMM's cost control work is the Mark 48 Torpedo. In 1966, PMM's Sterling Livingston and John Wander, in an article on their work on the Mark 48, co-authored with a professor from Penn State University, noted: "If we could foresee the eventual cost growth of most defense hardware systems, we'd never initiate them." They discussed how the problem has required the "special attention of industrial managers toward developing improved methods of estimating, controlling, and reporting hardware costs," and explained the breakthroughs in cost planning that they had helped produce. Citing a Defense Department survey, the article boasted that the procedure for reporting and controlling weapons costs employed on the Mark 48 Torpedo was "one of the better management cost control plans." [4]

The Mark 48 Torpedo brought together a jumble of private contractors whose accountability to the Navy and to one another was never clear. The Westinghouse Corporation was the prime contractor. It was hired to develop the hardware. The Ordnance Research Laboratory, a private research organization administered by Penn State University, was to serve as the Navy's right arm in the technical problems of torpedo design. Management Systems, a private consulting firm acquired by PMM in 1965, was to help ORL and the Navy. PMM itself was hired to, among other things, introduce a cost control system for the torpedo.[5]

By 1969, Congressmen began to penetrate the veil of secrecy that surrounded defense contracting and discovered, in the words of Representative William Moorhead (D.-Pa.), that the Mark 48 is "not a disaster in procurement like the C-5A, it's an atrocity." While Congress had stood by, the costs for the torpedo had increased from an initial estimate of $680 million to close to $4 billion.[6]

Following the Congressional exposé, the Navy wrote Westinghouse out of the program and brought in a new prime contractor. Because of military personnel rotation policies, at least four project managers and no fewer than ten contract officers served on the program. By 1971, almost all of the official cast for the Mark 48 had completely changed. But PMM and the Ordnance Research Lab remained on the job. Between 1963 and 1973, PMM was awarded close to $4.5 million for its work on the Mark 48, and the firm's contract was renewed again in July 1974.[7]

The Mark 48 contract incidentally disproves the proposition that consultants, unlike civil servants, provide only temporary assistance.

The Defense Department was not the only official agency PMM advised in this matter. The General Accounting Office—Congress's auditor of the Executive Branch—had permitted its defense expertise to atrophy. When Congressmen, appalled by contracting scandals, called on the GAO to make a new foray into the weapons-contracting morass, the GAO was caught shorthanded. Hassell Bell, Associate

Director of the GAO Defense Division, explained that over a dozen private firms offered to help the GAO find its way. The GAO contracted with only one firm—PMM. John Wander, one of the principal people on the PMM Mark 48 contract, was named as the key man on the GAO contract.

The layman might assume that the GAO, by hiring Wander, was passing a favorable judgment on PMM's Mark 48 work. Did this mean that the GAO had on hand an evaluation of PMM's work on the Mark 48, as well as other DOD defense projects? Hassell Bell says he did not even know that PMM had worked on the Mark 48 when the GAO contract was awarded, nor did he inquire. Bell knew John Wander had "gained his background on the subject through several years' employment with a large aerospace contractor and two separate management firms." These were Boeing, Management Systems, and PMM. Only at the prodding of the GAO bureaucracy were these minimal details on Wander's and PMM's record placed in the GAO files.

In short, according to Bell, the GAO made no inquiry into the usefulness of Wander's or PMM's work. Even the lowest-grade GAO employees are required to place more of their background on the record than Wander did.[8]

In a limited sense it was not PMM's fault that its expertise did not control the Mark 48 costs. According to the Navy, the prime contractors failed to foresee technical problems in torpedo development. When problems arose, the Navy decided that it wanted torpedoes at any price. At best, then, PMM's cost control work was a waste of money. At worst, it was a façade that helped mask disaster from Congress and the public.

The Navy, as purchaser of a cost control system, was perfectly satisfied with the firm's work. PMM, said the Navy, had become a fixture on the Mark 48 and was an indispensable source of expertise. The Navy could offer no formal written evaluation of PMM's work, though the contractor had been on the job for close to a decade. This was not unusual. Formal evaluations of expert contract work are few and far between.[9]

As for the public's right to know, PMM partners were clear about their duty to disclose cost problems to the public—"Our answer is, categorically and unequivocally, that we had none at all!" [10]

The value of technical work is, then, frequently a question of political rather than technical judgment. The Mark 48 cost control program was not used and did not perform as promised. This was acceptable to the Navy and its experts, though reasonable men might judge the work a failure.

Ernest Fitzgerald, a former defense official who was fired from the Air Force for exposing $1 billion of hidden costs on the C-5A Aircraft, was a management consultant who worked on the Mark 48 for PMM's predecessor firm. Fitzgerald argues that the excessive costs were known to insiders including PMM, the Ordnance Research Laboratory, and the Navy well before they were reported to the public. Fitzgerald, as well as some other defense consultants, argues that if the consultant is a professional, he is obligated to do his best to prevent the misuse of his product. PMM officials unequivocally reject this view of the consultant's obligation.[11]

John Macy, past chairman of the Civil Service Commission, believes that no one has demonstrated the superiority of private contractors to Government employees. Management consultants, he suggests, have "taken the Government for a ride" at "outrageous costs." [12] It would be hard to argue against Macy, for the Government has failed to develop records that demonstrate the contrary.

One of the least-known regulations in the vast body of contract law urges agencies to keep evaluations of the work of their consultant contractors. This recommendation, appearing in Office of Management and Budget (OMB) Circular A-49, was published in 1959 as the Federal use of consultant contracts was blossoming.

The OMB, the President's central means of executive management, never undertook to administer A-49. By the Seventies, OMB had literally forgotten the existence of A-49. The circular was still on OMB's list of active regulations, but the agency could not produce anyone responsible for its administration. After a series of inquiries, a new recruit to OMB was commissioned to study the matter. "A-49," he concluded, "washes out in the files after 1962." [13]

Executive-Search for OE

In the spring of 1970, the United States Office of Education, an agency in the Department of Health, Education, and Welfare, awarded PMM a contract to help locate top officials. The firm was to report to the Office of Education's William Marumoto and to the office of HEW Under Secretary Fred Malek. As it happened, Marumoto was himself a former employee of PMM. Malek was an alumnus of McKinsey & Co.

What was PMM's task? Why were they hired? What did they do?

In theory, the answer to these questions might be sought in the contract files. The contract should describe the complete dimensions of consultant work, and the PMM contract did call for a weekly written report by the consultants. The official contract files, however, were barren.[14] HEW regulations state that when a contract is modified, in price or scope of work, the contract files must document the reason for the change. The original HEW contract with PMM called for a sum not to exceed $10,000. Although the contract price was raised to $46,000, the files contain no explanation for the increase. Nor did they contain a single weekly written report—something which the initial contract had required.

In March 1972, we asked HEW Under Secretary James Veneman for details of the work performed by PMM. In reply, Russell Byers, confidential assistant to the Under Secretary, explained that HEW had the "good fortune of having established good rapport with several of these [accounting and consulting] firms which, on occasion, refer the names of prospective candidates. . . . With respect to HEW employees who were recommended by private organizations, we regret that our records do not reflect the sources of the candidates' names." [15]

While there was no public record of privately located Government officials, PMM's company newsletter boasted that the firm had located no lesser personnel than HEW's Assistant Secretary for Administration and its Deputy Assistant Secretary for Finance. These were interesting selections, for it is the men who hold these positions who are often responsible for hiring contractors like PMM. According to the HEW procurement regulations, for example, it is the Assistant Secretary for Administration who must approve all "management consultant" contracts.[16]

PMM's choice for Assistant Secretary for Administration illustrates the relationship between management expertise and politics. The outgoing Assistant Secretary was James Farmer. Farmer's credentials as a "manager" were not substantial, but as a leading black "spokesman" he represented the Administration's attempt at conciliating black America. Rodney Brady, the man chosen to replace Farmer, is a business school Ph.D. whose prior work experience had been as a management consultant and in the aerospace industry. Brady's consulting experience, coincidentally, had been as a vice president of the Management Systems Corporation, the firm which PMM acquired in 1965 to gain the Mark 48 contract.

Why and how was PMM selected, what were its qualifications, and what provisions for conflict of interest were made? According to HEW procurement regulations, when management consultant services are being procured, proposals shall be solicited from at least three firms to assure adequate competition. There is no record that this was done.[17]

The justification for PMM's contract states that PMM was a leading practitioner of "executive search" consulting and that PMM was also experienced in educational consultation. The first contention is partially legitimate. PMM has developed a staff that specializes in helping private corporations find new executives. The PMM "search staff" was among the largest in a growing industry. It numbers in the dozens, and PMM told HEW that its consultants, located in many PMM offices throughout the country, would "comb" the country for top talent. HEW and PMM accepted as unquestionable the assumption that PMM's experience in selecting corporate executives qualifies it to select public officials.

That PMM somehow possessed expertise that was uniquely relevant to education did not stand up to independent investigation. In 1970, PMM's largest HEW contract was for the design of a management information system, and Office of Education Management Information Director Robert Kane told us of his disappointment with the firm's work. At the same time that it was receiving the recruiting contract without competition, PMM bid for an OE contract to study the costs of educational Research and Development. The firm was adjudged twelfth or thirteenth of approximately twenty-three competitors, and the OE review panel concluded that PMM personnel were "weak in costing R & D, especially in educational fields" and went on to note "merely adequate plan . . . little substance . . . poorly presented cost estimate." Nor did PMM rate high in the prestigious competition to manage and work for the President's Commission on School Finance. According to the Commission's Steve Sklar, the firm finished third or fourth of four firms that bid for a study of economics of education. PMM, Sklar noted, did not know enough about management techniques in education. Thus Kane's judgment finds confirmation in PMM's unsuccessful bidding record.[18]

McKinsey and PMM Work on the Railroad

In 1968, the Penn Central Railroad was created from the merger of the New York Central and Pennsylvania Railroads. The two old roads' troubles symbolized the decline of the rail industry. Critics doubted that the giant new corporation could improve on the poor record of its constituent parts, but Pennsylvania President Stuart Saunders assured the public that the new venture would succeed by using the tools of the mid-century management revolution.[19]

In 1970, the country was shocked by the announcement that the multibillion-dollar Penn Central had filed for bankruptcy. A parade of studies soon traced the disaster to management failures. One Interstate Commerce Commission brief, for example, concluded that the railroads were not adequately prepared for their merger. The "timing was poor, not because of inflation or tight money, but because Penn Central was unprepared to handle such changes with a minimal degree of efficiency." The ICC "conservatively" estimated that "oversight or mistakes in planning "cost the company $82 million.[20]

Bankrupt or not, the country could not dispense with the Penn Central's rail service, so Congress acted quickly to create the National Railroad Passenger Corporation, known as Amtrak. Backed by Government loans, Amtrak is a private corporation that administers America's dwindling passenger train service through contract with private railroads. The same "management revolution" that was to assure a successful Penn Central merger was promised for Amtrak. The law that created Amtrak stated that it would succeed by employing modern and efficient practices, using "innovative" marketing and operating concepts, and exercising the right to make a profit.

It has been nearly half a decade since Amtrak's creation, and even the energy crisis' unexpected jolt to American automobile mania has not made the corporation a success. "Seldom," headlined a *Fortune* article, "has a company been blessed with such an unexpected opportunity, and seemed so determined to blow it." There might be less surprise over Amtrak's failure if the public knew that Amtrak's success was to be engineered by the very same management experts the Penn Central had called upon. Not only were the trains to be operated on contract by the railroads that had provided inadequate service, but when the United States Department of Transportation solicited bids from private experts to define the new corporation, three of the four bidders—Arthur D. Little, McKinsey & Co., and Peat, Marwick, Mitchell & Co.—had been recent servants of the Penn Central.[21]

In the last week of April 1971, the week before Amtrak began its official life, thirty-three employees were on the payroll. These people had been paid $30,000. But the foundation for Amtrak was not being laid by these stenographers, switchboard operators, and chauffeurs. Close to two dozen law firms, consulting firms, and public relations firms were hired to write the contracts Amtrak would offer the railroads, to recruit future Amtrak officials, to appraise rail facilities, and to serve as Amtrak's liaison with Congress. By April 30, these firms had received commitments for $3,174,000. The most important Amtrak contract called on a private contractor to develop Amtrak's "organizational structure," define the skills needed to fill the organization chart, recommend routes and train schedules, prepare financial projections and marketing programs, and generally ready Amtrak for startup. On December 21, 1970, the DOT hired McKinsey for the work—months before the selection of the Amtrak directors and officers who would bear official responsibility for the success of the new corporation, and even before the corporation's incorporators signed in.[22]

The DOT refuses to disclose the basis for its selection of McKinsey. It must have known, as the public does not, of the firm's role in the Penn Central fiasco. Between 1962 and 1966, McKinsey received $664,315 from the Penn Central. This much about McKinsey's association with the merger can be derived from an obscure form on which regulated railroads are obligated to list payments to contractors.[23]

In March 1965, a letter from the President of the Pennsylvania Railroad and the Executive Vice President of

the New York Central to McKinsey's Jack Crowley discussed McKinsey's work on the Penn Central merger.
McKinsey was working directly for the high-level committee created to plan the merger, and the letter stated that the
firm had helped compile the schedules by which the roads
would be consolidated. "Because of the monumental job
ahead," McKinsey was told, "we understand your principal
role will be that of guide and catalyst to spark timely
actions that must be taken over the months ahead."
Another document explains that McKinsey was to draw on
its wealth of knowledge to ensure the merger's success.[24]

Governmental reports and private investigations of the
Penn Central merger do not even note McKinsey's presence, and their authors are often unfamiliar with the very
name. "McKinsey," said one investigator. "The man
sounds familiar." (James McKinsey died many years ago.)
McKinsey's Crowley failed to respond to requests to discuss
Penn Central work.

When the Department of Transportation hired McKinsey to work on Amtrak, it seemed unconcerned about
McKinsey's responsibility for the Penn Central failure.
McKinsey is the Cadillac of corporate consulting firms. Its
"professionals" continually serve executives in the world's
largest organizations. McKinsey's Washington office provides only a small part of the firm's business, housing
perhaps one or two dozen of its several hundred professional employees, but, from office space adjacent to the
White House complex, McKinsey continually works for the
highest officials.

Probably, as far as the DOT was concerned, McKinsey
had impeccable credentials as adviser to the kinds of
organizations with which Amtrak would deal. McKinsey's
proposal noted, for example, that the firm numbered at
least fifteen railroads and eleven airlines among its clients.
Its reputation in financial circles was solid. During the
Depression, McKinsey had served as adviser to financial
institutions that appraised corporate properties. "Anyone
considering the possibility of joining our staff," explains a

McKinsey recruiting brochure, "should determine our standing by checking our reputation and professional competence with banks and other independent sources." [25]

By 1970, McKinsey had become indispensable to Government managers charged with the creation of new organizations. McKinsey was hired to organize the Equal Employment Opportunity Commission, the Price Commission, the Federal National Mortgage Association, and NASA.

McKinsey's work on Amtrak was extensive. As a McKinsey partner confided, "We virtually for a time ran that thing . . . we were the only people available." [26] Whose views did McKinsey represent? Those of the department that hired it, the Congress that created Amtrak, the railroads that necessitated Amtrak, the financial institutions that hover over the rail industry, or the Amtrak directors and officials? The rail passenger crisis fills volumes of Congressional hearings. Railroad executives, Government officials, railroad lobbyists, rail passenger lobbyists, railroad unions, and many others have made their views known. The testimony of McKinsey is conspicuously absent.

The public record leaves almost as few traces of McKinsey's work for Amtrak, a Congressionally created organization, as it did for McKinsey's work on the Penn Central. The sole official identification of McKinsey with Amtrak appears to be on lists of Amtrak contractors compiled for Congress. The firm's name appeared, for example, in an October 1971 ICC report. By August 1971, the report stated, McKinsey's fees had mounted to $947,320, but the ICC, a Government agency, was "denied access to agreements between Amtrak and the various consulting and professional firms" and denied information on the "types of services performed." McKinsey had, among other things, been hired to develop financial and planning information. Amtrak, the ICC discovered, had been reluctant to provide information "regarding its future financial needs" and "pertaining to future plans." [27]

In 1974, Congress created yet another agency to save

America's railroads. In the confusion of Presidential impeachment, the Executive Branch waited months to appoint the directors of the United States Railway Association. This did not completely frustrate Congress's plans, for McKinsey was long on the job.

The Department of Transportation probably cared little about McKinsey's international business, but the story is equally fascinating. Much of the firm's business is abroad, and many a Harvard Business student has been attracted to McKinsey by the opportunity to spend a summer working in places like Tanzania. McKinsey, virtually unknown to the American public, is the symbol of American management expertise in Europe. The firm has reorganized the leading corporations in Germany, Holland, and Britain, and its work for sacred national institutions like the Bank of England has caused public controversy. The firm has played an important but little understood role in the creation of global corporations. "Our multiple offices," the firm tells prospective recruits, "permit us to serve not only local companies, but also local subsidiaries of worldwide enterprises that are headquartered in other countries." [28]

The Rule of the Interested Expert

The civil servant is a full-time Government employee. A large contractor like PMM or McKinsey may work simultaneously for a Government agency and for private organizations that are subsidized or regulated by the agency. When this happens it may well be by design.

PMM was both auditor for, and management adviser to, the ill-fated Penn Central empire. During the years 1959–70, PMM received over $5 million in fees from the Penn Central and its subsidiaries.[29] While the Penn Central was its largest transportation industry client, PMM had many others, some of whom it advised in proceedings before Government regulatory agencies. Despite, or because of, its industrial clientele, PMM is also an important contractor to the United States Department of Transportation.[30]

When the Federal Government gave the Penn Central monies to run the Metroliner train, it called on PMM to help determine how to account for Metroliner costs. In an August 1969 letter to Clifford Gannett of the Department of Transportation Metroliner project, PMM partner Robert Monteverde proposed for the work a PMM team that included Henry Quinn, "partner in the Philadelphia audit department," and Bernard Kravitz, "partner in charge of the Philadelphia management consulting department." Quinn was the partner "in charge of our audit of Penn Central" and Kravitz was "presently responsible for a major study which we are undertaking of Penn Central's organization, budgeting and accounting systems, and computer capabilities." [31]

PMM, of course, possesses much technical expertise in accounting. The Monteverde letter, however, noted that the proposed study went beyond technical routine. Its author explained that there was no generally accepted formula for determining costs of the railroad service. In fact, there was "public controversy" over the cost of services in the nation's Northeast Corridor.

If there was such a controversy, why should a leading consultant to the private party to the controversy be awarded the key contract to determine the allocation of cost? Monteverde's letter did not ask this question, but assumed that PMM's dual service would assure that a "method acceptable both to Government and to Penn Central be developed." The letter told the Government that PMM was Penn Central's auditor and concluded that this fact would "enhance" the choice of PMM. Penn Central officials with whom this was discussed were, said Monteverde, "in agreement with our position." Not only, then, did the Government have full knowledge of PMM's private work, but it hired PMM because of it. As PMM explains it, it is "transparently ridiculous" to call their dual service a conflict. Both the public agency and the private corporation had an economic interest in the work, and the selection of a consultant that "possessed the mutual confidence of both parties at interest was necessary to an acceptable result." [32]

PMM's dual service for Penn Central and the Federal Railroad Administration (FRA), however, was fraught with conflict of interest potential. PMM was in a position where its private interest—the large Penn Central contract—could very easily guide its public service.

The presumption that a truly independent contractor would have been a better choice to settle a public controversy was, if anything, strengthened by *ex post facto* analyses of the Penn Central bankruptcy that issued from the Interstate Commerce Commission, the Securities and Exchange Commission, and the House Banking and Currency Committee. These analyses, and others, have questioned the objectivity of Penn Central's financial reports. The critics have often been careful to note that although Penn Central's accountants may have technically operated within the bounds laid down by the rules of the accounting profession, the rules were amply flexible. The trustees appointed to run the Penn Central after it went bankrupt testified before Congress that Penn Central's 1969 annual report, for which PMM was the independent auditor, appears to have "reflected a corporate policy of the time of putting the best conceivable face on the facts" to the point that these facts were "dubious allies of the truth." [33]

Some critics went further. Following his committee's investigation, Wright Patman, Chairman of the House Banking and Currency Committee, sent a letter to William Casey, Chairman of the Securities and Exchange Commission, which stated that the investigation had found many of Penn Central management practices to be "highly suspect and in some instances probably illegal." Patman singled out PMM:

> One of the primary areas of questionable activity was the accounting practices used by the railroad in its external accounting firm of Peat, Marwick, Mitchell & Co. In the years immediately preceding the collapse of the railroad, the financial statements of the Penn Central and certain of its

subsidiaries were to say the least very misleading in detailing the true financial condition of the various companies involved. Information in the Committee's possession shows that this policy of "doctoring" the financial statements was done at the direction of the top Penn Central officials. These documents further indicate that Peat, Marwick, Mitchell & Co. played a substantial role in these successful attempts to misinform the investing public.

Patman called on Casey to investigate his charges.[34]

The civil service system has an elaborate set of conflict of interest rules. Executive Order 11222, which prescribes standards of ethical conduct for Government officers and employees, provides, in Section 203:

> Employees may not (a) have direct or indirect financial interests that conflict substantially, or appear to conflict substantially, with their responsibilities and duties as Federal employees.

The order also states, in Section 306:

> Each agency shall at the time of employment of a consultant, advisor, or other special Government employee require him to supply it with a statement of all other employment. The statement shall list the names of all the corporations, companies, firms, State or local government organizations, research organizations and educational or other institutions in which he is serving as employee, officer, member, director, trustee, advisor, or consultant.

By a quirk of law, independent contractors like PMM and their employees are not considered to be within the scope of these conflict rules. This is a real *Catch-22* situation, permitting those organizations and individuals that wish to deal simultaneously with the public agencies and private corporations to do so, as long as they call themselves contractors instead of civil servants.

PMM had the candor, undoubtedly based on its adherence to the American Institute of Certified Public Accountants' code of ethics, to reveal its private clientele to the public. Government agencies, however, rarely require contractors to do this.

The loophole in Federal conflict of interest laws is important. Much more important, however, is the ruling assumption that contractors that work for private clients should serve as brokers between these private clients and public agencies. The dual use of PMM by the private constituency of an agency represents a new kind of conflict that is endemic to the contracting process. This dual use often assumes that the interests of public and private clients are the interests of the public at large. This is not necessarily so.

At the end of 1971 the Penn Central trustees in bankruptcy released PMM as Penn Central auditor. The Government, however, retained its faith in the firm. The PMM Metroliner contract began in October 1969 and was supposed to run only until June 1970. Instead the contract was extended until June 1973, and the contract price increased. Moreover, following the Penn Central bankruptcy, the Federal Railroad Administration hired PMM, on a sole-source basis, to review the cash-flow projections of the trustees in bankruptcy in support of a request to draw against Government guarantees. PMM was also asked by FRA to bid on a contract to serve as the FRA's auditor of the Penn Central.[35]

Freedom of Information

The PMM and McKinsey contracts suggest how important the public's right of access to information about the contract relationship is. It can be seen again and again that the outsider will be denied elementary information about contracting, not only by private corporations but by the Government itself.

In justifying their refusal to discuss their work, private experts often assert that relevant information is available from the Government as "a matter of public record."

In theory this is correct; in practice it is not. An official periodical, the *Commerce Business Daily*, contains a list of Government contract awards. The most comprehensive record available, the *CBD* is useless to the public at large.

While hundreds of awards are listed daily, there are no indexes to contracts, to programs (or even agencies) using contractors, or to the corporations hired to do the work. Nor do most Government agencies prepare such indexes.

In the course of this study requests for information about particular contracts were made of dozens of departments, agencies, bureaus, offices, and divisions. The responses varied greatly, not only among organizations but within them as well. Caprice rather than law seemed to prevail.

A wide range of difficulties were encountered, for example, in response to our efforts to learn more about PMM contracts. The Department of Transportation only grudgingly released information which it had no right, under the Freedom of Information Act, to withhold. In some cases, the contracts proper were made available only after months of exchanges. In other cases, the Department offered to produce contracts only if substantial amounts were prepaid to cover the clerical costs of locating the information. On one occasion, for example, the Office of the Secretary requested an advance deposit of $1,000.[36]

As has been suggested, the contract itself may often tell little about the substance of a Government-contractor relationship. The Department of Transportation denied requests for many other pieces of information which are parts of the contract file. It refused to divulge information on the selection of contractors, evaluations of contractor work, contractor salaries and profits, and the degree of competition involved in awards. The Department denied requests not only for contractually required interim reports by contractors but for required final reports as well.[37]

The arbitrariness of departmental actions was highlighted by the response of the DOT agency which awarded the PMM Penn Central contract. While the Federal Railroad Administration offered copies of contracts without charge, important sections of the contracts had been neatly excised by razor cuts. Paperclipped to the copies was a note which bore the lone word "purged."

To ask for contracts one must know that they exist, and official policies often mask the very use of contractors.

In 1973, for example, Congress required the Secretary of Transportation to prepare two analyses of the financing of transportation. In 1974, these reports were formally presented to Congress. The cover of the reports carried the imprimatur of the United States Department of Transportation, together with the notation that the enclosed material was the work "of the Secretary" of Transportation. A Congressman opening the documents would find introductory letters from departmental officials. He would find no suggestion that these officials had given a private contractor—PMM—$260,000 to do the studies and to write the "official" documents. If the Congressman knew that the reports were but two of seventy-seven reports required of the Department of Transportation, if he suspected that many others were the work of contractors, if he knew that such contractors also did substantial work for private groups with transportation interests—if he knew all of this, then he might suspect that the secrecy attending the Government contract process is more than incidental to the "policies" and "decisions" made by Government officials.[38]

THE REORGANIZATION RITUAL

The men who hold the top management positions in Government—the secretaryships, assistant secretaryships, under-secretaryships, deputy under/assistant secretaryships—shift their jobs far more frequently than the citizen might suspect. One study found that twenty-two months is the average tenure served by assistant secretaries before they hop back to industry or jump to a new Government job.[39]

The Washington headquarters of Federal agencies are squat, monolithic structures that betray little sense of human purpose. It is impossible to tell the front entrance from the back, and inside the corridors of power the titles are designed to thwart any efforts at comprehension. It is quite difficult for the new manager to order a new building, but it is easy for him to redesign the organization chart, rename the titles and titleholders, rearrange desks, and even knock down some of the walls. New managers introduce their new organization charts with the promise that business technique and rationality will save the Government from chaos. Many civil servants find that reorganizations occur with a frequency conducive to disorganization.

In the early part of the century, as the giant industrial corporations struggled with growth, their managers discovered the lodestone of modern managerial wisdom—redesigning the organization chart to turn uncontrollable organizations into sources of profit. Reorganization helped some, like DuPont, to cope with inefficiencies and threatened stagnation, and others, notably General Motors, to sweep ahead of competition. These experiences were chronicled in business lore.[40] While the specifics of the resultant gospel were quite fuzzy, the broad command was not. Corporations could continue to grow and prosper if top management delegated authority and held lower managers responsible for the performance of carefully designed functions. (Thus, each of GM's divisions is responsible for an entire car.)

By the Thirties, the new wisdom was adopted by the management consultants, who had been plying the relatively discreet trade of "efficiency expertise" and personnel counseling. As corporate lawyers and investment bankers tried to cope with the Depression, they called on management consultants to appraise the properties that threatened to fall into their hands. In a demure hardcover brochure published in 1940, McKinsey & Co. announced that it was prepared to study "all phases of a business." These studies "usually are made for commercial banks, investment bankers, trustees, stockholders, and others who have an active interest in the business but are not active in the management." (McKinsey carefully distinguished this work from its more traditional services.) When corporations got back on their feet, the tradition of organizational study had been established. "One major restructuring every two or three years," a McKinsey man explains, "is probably a conservative estimate of the current rate of organization change among the large industrial corporations." [41]

The role that firms like McKinsey play in major reorganizations has become a commonplace, although they are more likely to work directly for management than for outside interests. In the past twenty-five years, McKinsey and a handful of other corporate consulting firms have extended the ritual of corporate appraisal and reorganization to all large organizations in America. If they retain the role of appraisers, it is in Government. There they work for incoming or struggling managers who try to control the public domain that has fallen under their command. The most visible and telling evidence of their role in Government organization is the skimpy record left by a tiny Government program.

In 1953 Congress authorized the Bureau of the Budget (now the Office of Management and Budget) to spend up to $500,000 a year for the improvement of Federal management. In the first fifteen years of operation the fund awarded many contracts to Government agencies as well as private consultants, but only three organizations received more than two awards. These three—Booz, Allen, and Hamilton; Cresap, McCormick, and Paget; and McKinsey & Co.—received a total of fifteen. They were hired to study the agencies that regulate industry (Securities and Exchange Commission, Interstate Commerce Commission, Civil Aeronautics Board, Federal Communications Commission); the agency that regulates labor (National Labor Relations Board); the agency that purchases supplies for the Government (General Services Administration); agencies that subsidize economic growth (Export-Import Bank, Federal Home Loan Bank Board, Housing and Home Finance Administration), and to help create the largest welfare agency (Health, Education, and Welfare). They were also to study Budget Bureau planning and Government manpower.

Booz, Cresap, and McKinsey do similar studies for a variety of special commissions.

The consulting presence for the purpose of reorganization is as secretive as it is pervasive. It is rarely announced to the public, and is often a mystery to Government employees as well. Stanley Ruttenberg, who headed the Department of Labor's Manpower Administration in the Johnson years, wrote a book on his struggle to gain control of his agency. Great Society legislation had created the Manpower Administration to serve as an umbrella over both the New Deal employment programs and new programs directed at minority-group unemployed. As Ruttenberg tells it, the New Deal bureaus enjoyed "more or less autonomous existence within the Department . . . a common position for many of the special interest bureaus that make up consistent elements of Federal Departments." When Ruttenberg found himself thwarted by the state, union, and Congressional lobby that had congealed in support of the earlier programs, he came "to realize the hard way that organizational structure was very important." [42]

Ruttenberg proceeded to reorganize his administration and called in McKinsey to help with the job. During the last half of the Sixties, McKinsey, Booz, and Cresap were continual presences in the Department. As fate had it, Ruttenberg left office on Nixon's election, and McKinsey remained to complete work on reorganization. Despite McKinsey's vital role, the Department's contract files contained only skimpy statements of the tasks it was to perform, and no evidence of the work it did. While Ruttenberg wrote at length of the power struggle, his book fails to mention McKinsey.

Reorganization, whether it takes the form of a quick, often useless study or a marathon lasting years, is a hidden and important part of the political process. The most frequent and subtle form of reorganization is intra-agency reorganization directed by an agency's top management, such as the 1969 reorganization of the Office of Economic Opportunity. One contractor—Booz, Allen, and Hamilton

—had an especially important role in the 1969 reorganization, and their presence raises elementary questions about government. Why was a corporate consultant chosen to reorder the leading "poverty" agency? To whom were they responsible? What kind of expertise did they possess? How did they view the political controversies that were inextricably intertwined with the agency's organizational structure? What work did they do and what did they leave behind? [43]

The 1969 Reorganization of OEO

At 9:00 A.M. on the morning of September 17, 1969, the Office of Economic Opportunity's recently appointed Director, Donald Rumsfeld, ordered the distribution of a new agency telephone directory and an accompanying list of agency personnel and positions. This directory, though labeled "Draft," did more than record the normal changes in the agency work year. It was an announcement to OEO employees in Washington and throughout the country of a "massive reorganization" that had been five months in preparation. The organization chart for the agency was redone, positions were moved about, and some were eliminated.

OEO sat unpretentiously, and somewhat obscurely, above a drugstore and restaurant in midtown Washington. The reorganization of the agency did not change the agency's exterior. In the three weeks following the release of the phone directory, however, the interior resembled a college dormitory at the beginning of a term. The second-floor library and the small cafeteria were among the few places where business proceeded as usual. In faithful execution of the chart, people began to move, and 1,101 bureaucrats spent the better part of a month carting their belongings through the corridors to their new offices.

There were 108 people who did not receive marching orders from the new directory. The 108, or the "cell block," as a Rumsfeld aide called them, were told they were "officially considered part of the agency." [44] Nevertheless, they were not listed in the new directory, did not receive new office space or new positions in the organization chart, and they roamed the halls listlessly.

Among the 108 were between seventy and eighty of the agency's top civil servants, including high-level officials appointed by the Democrats. "Most of the top personnel, not the Presidential appointees, were expected to leave, but the key career people were encouraged to leave," recalls Bertrand Harding, a career civil servant who served as OEO Director in the transition between the Shriver and Rumsfeld administrations. (Harding left OEO to become a private consultant.) "I was not privy to this wholesale reorganization. During my administration as Acting Director of OEO, I decided against such a reorganization. We determined that it would not accomplish anything." [45]

The purge of OEO's upper echelons was not unexpected. Rumsfeld and Nixon had never supported the Democrats' poverty program. As a Republican Congressman from a wealthy Chicago suburb, Rumsfeld had voted against the 1964 Act that created the agency. A sign at OEO's entrance asserted that "this building will self-destruct on January 20." When Rumsfeld was sworn in on May 26, 1969, OEO personnel were sure that "this time the building would vanish."

Nixon granted Rumsfeld autonomy, and the new director took advantage of his freedom. As a career man, Harding said, "I've seen this thing happen before, not quite in the same way. It was a messy job." [46]

The reorganization cost $500,000. Under Congressional questioning Rumsfeld mysteriously revised the figure downward to $40,000. The revised figure was inaccurate. It did not include the money spent by OEO on contractor assistance. Secrecy obscured OEO's use of Booz, Allen and Arthur Andersen, two major consulting firms. To the reader who closely followed Congressional proceedings, to many OEO employees, and even to the inquisitive outsider, the reorganization appeared to be an inside job. No public testimony refers to the role of consultants in the reorganization. The consultant contracts were not recorded on the agency's internal list of contracts; they were not even on the Contract Office's own Rolodex.[47]

When Rumsfeld climbed into his director's chair, OEO had over $500 million in grants and contracts to offer local governments, community organizations, universities, and private contractors, but the money was not all Rumsfeld's to give, for his predecessors, and the recipients, had planned and committed much of it. Still, he found his agency besieged by grantees and consultants in search of awards from the agency. Rumsfeld's administrative assistant, Richard Cheney, recalled: "Don found himself with major problems; he was locked in." [48]

During his campaign, Nixon had singled out OEO as an exemplar of Federal mismanagement. Richard Blumenthal, a White House assistant, recalls that "the President promised better management of OEO, the typical type of issue. They had all those scandals at that time. For instance, the Blackstone Rangers [a black group in Chicago linked with violence] were getting funds, and the President interpreted this to be a major threat. It sounds like a dumb thing for a bunch of scandals to be a major threat. With this type of mandate, of course, Rumsfeld was going to reorganize the agency." [49]

To Rumsfeld's aides, the Blackstone Rangers symbolized the agency's problems. According to Cheney, they believed that if grants to "revolutionary" organizations were weeded out, the agency would be rid of its major problems.[50]

While agencies generally have "management experts" with the same credentials as outside contractors, new administrators frequently call on a contractor to apprise them of their terrain. Why do officials call upon contractors rather than civil service staff? The administrator may claim that manpower from within the agency cannot be spared. He may even agree that the outsiders do not possess unique qualifications, but, more to the point, the new administrator is uncertain of the civil servants under his command. He may be skeptical of their competence, of their loyalty to him, or of their loyalty to a new Presidential administration.

From the new administrator's viewpoint, the "civil service" as a disinterested group of professionals often does not exist. Rumsfeld aide Cheney recalls: "Don found himself with a bureaucracy that hated him." To grab control of the agency and rid it of its revolutionary camp following, says Cheney, "Rumsfeld was forced to seek outside help. I remember Don reciting to me the Al Smith statement, 'If I don't look to my friends for help, who do I look to, my enemies?' " [51]

When Rumsfeld was nominated to head the agency, Daniel Moynihan provided Rumsfeld with a member of his staff, Paul Anderson, a recipient of a White House fellowship. Anderson came to the White House from Booz, where he was Director of Personnel. (Anderson was to return to Booz at the end of his fellowship year to become a vice president and one of the ten directors of the corporation.)

Rumsfeld had specifically requested Paul Anderson's services. The two had met in Chicago, where Anderson was active in Republican politics and Rumsfeld had been a Republican Congressman. In his role as a White House Fellow, Anderson was in turn asked to "specifically finger" the services of Booz for Rumsfeld.[52] Anderson's signature originated the contract that awarded Government money to his once and future firm.[53] Bruce Stevens, a Booz employee, was selected to head and manage the contract for Booz.

When his fellowship ended, Anderson was hired by Rumsfeld as a private consultant. Within a few weeks, he returned to Booz, but continued to work for Rumsfeld. No one at the White House or OEO thought anything was unusual about the arrangement.

When the new directory was published, Robert Cassidy, OEO Director of Administration, met with dissatisfied OEO employees. He explained that Rumsfeld's edict had created two classes of employees—one "tentatively reassigned" and a second that was left "unassigned and available for detail anywhere in the building upon call." [54] An employee asked Cassidy to explain the distinction. Cassidy, who had not been a part of the Rumsfeld inner circle, could not. He called upon one of the few persons who could—Bruce Stevens.

Stevens told those assembled that the unassigned 108 were temporarily "nonpersons," as audience members recall his words. Stevens read a statement which he and Anderson had written for Rumsfeld. "If your name," the statement went, "does not appear on the list, supervisory personnel and representatives of the personnel office will contact you directly and discuss assignment responsibilities." [55] One member of the audience asked Stevens his position, which was not listed on the new charts. Stevens announced that he was a contractor employee.

The American Federation of Government Employees, one of several public employees' unions, had long objected to excessive and possibly illegal contracting. The contractors, the AFGE local of OEO now discovered, were running the civil service system itself. Local 2677 asked the Civil Service Commission to investigate both OEO's personnel decisions and Booz, Allen's role in them. The Commission, the executive agency charged with maintaining the integrity of the civil service, sent over two inspectors, who spent a morning at OEO. "At the meeting," Inspector Russ LeFevre remembered, "we were told that those people, the 'nonpersons,' that have not been placed, will be placed. OEO assured us that they were not on the not-wanted list. That sounded all right to us." As to the allegation that the consultants had usurped official authority, "We did not," said LeFevre, "look into this." [56] OEO had designated three people—Robert Cassidy, Paul Anderson, and Bruce Stevens—to brief the inspectors. The civil service was satisfied with OEO's explanation of the event.

Booz shared the eighth floor of OEO—the headquarters floor—with Arthur Andersen & Co., one of the world's largest accounting firms. Rumsfeld, afraid that Government money would fall into the hands of unacceptable institutions like the Blackstone Rangers, hired Arthur Andersen, at a cost of $25,209, to help OEO purge itself of distasteful contracts and grants. (Grants and contracts are the guts of agencies that, like OEO, do their work by doling out money to institutions.)

Arthur Andersen, like Booz, was given access to documents that were inaccessible to both citizens and Congressmen. Not only was Andersen to review awards to groups that it might deal with in other capacities, but it was also to make judgments about the way in which firms like Arthur Andersen received contracts. Gerson Green was a high Democratic holdover who tried to cooperate with Rumsfeld. "We ignored what they were doing," Green lamented. "But no one blew the whistle. They had leverage over everyone. Our line was to save OEO and not to blow it up. We made a mistake; we should have blown the whole thing at the time." Green recalls that Arthur Andersen was permitted to read agency memoranda containing staff views that were "clearly not for their eyes. Rumsfeld was afraid of a whole series of wild programs, and he used the task force to stifle innovation. The task force used the materials we had prepared to review the political leanings of my staff." [57]

Arthur Andersen took residence in a room whose door bore the legend "Special Review Process of Pending Grants and Contracts, July 1969." Because of his late appointment, Rumsfeld's spending deadline had been extended by thirty days beyond June 30, the end of the fiscal year. As the work of Andersen and Booz progressed, an intense enmity developed between consultants and OEO employees.

Ben Zimmerman, the Director of Program Development and Program Planning, who felt that Booz dismissed him from the agency, recalls that "the Arthur Andersen people were sure that everyone was trying to fund something that was revolutionary. These were politically hot programs during the campaign, and the Rumsfeld consultants were trying to uncover a revolutionary plot in the agency. They actually quizzed everyone to find and get rid of the revolutionaries. It was terrible." [58]

Noel Klores, OEO's Associate Director for Special Projects, felt circumstances dictated a calmer view of the contractor threat. There was, he says, "a general panic over the fact that in the next thirty days Rumsfeld would lock himself into a course for the next year. Rumsfeld was trying to get out one-half billion dollars, and the thought panicked him. He brought in a bunch of guys from Arthur Andersen with no knowledge of the grants and contracts process. It was mainly a holding action. I refused to go up and see them and sent our analysts up there. I knew that time was on our side and that, on June fifteenth, they would start signing the grants out the window." [59]

The last-minute work of the contractor did not change the traditional pattern of money-giving. With the exception of twelve of 400 grants reviewed by the Andersen group, the vast bulk of spending proceeded without Rumsfeld's intervention. In concluding its work, Arthur Andersen submitted a sixteen-page report and expressed its disappointment at being unable to alter the course of funding.[60]

Program reorganization plans anticipated personnel changes by one month. An August 11 memo conveyed the new management decisions in polished bureaucratese. The reorganization, the memo explained, was serving the end of efficiency: "Offices have been combined or eliminated to improve efficiency; activities of the agency will be more thoroughly integrated, without losing the advantages of specific program operations." [61]

Though the reorganization scheme developed by Booz did not differ in form from hundreds of others, it had a clear political cast. OEO's Civil Rights and Inspection Division, for example, was eliminated and placed as an independent division in the General Counsel's office. The Inspection Division was supposed to enforce Civil Rights statutes and regulations and, among other things, check on the compliance of OEO contractors—such as Booz—with the requirements for providing equal opportunity for employment. Its transfer was to "provide for stronger enforcement of the Civil Rights statutes" and "to provide a mechanism for ensuring that the results of inspections conducted by the Inspection Division are translated into meaningful actions by the operating office." [62] Booz's Paul Anderson remembers his attitude: "I wanted to get rid of it [the Civil Rights and Inspections Division] completely. It was only a symbolic gesture. But we decided to put it under the control of the General Counsel instead." [63]

The reorganization decreased the responsibility and independence of the Community Action Program (CAP), which had been the centerpiece of the War on Poverty. "The reorganization should help reduce the abuses that have characterized the past," the official explanation went. "Better control over local Community Action Agencies is built into the new organization." [64]

Evidently, control was to be achieved by giving less money to poverty agencies in order to give more money to consultants. The recommendations cut back on the monies to be made directly available to CAAs (the local community agencies), but increased the monies for "technical assistance" consultants. Paul Anderson claimed responsibility for this piece of management wisdom.

The poor could do little about the proposed changes, but the program changes were most soundly rejected when they conflicted with the interests of the legal profession. In 1966, McKinsey had been awarded a series of contracts to create a regional organization for OEO. (This, the first major reorganization of the agency, was effective primarily as a public relations response to Congressional charges of mismanagement.) When McKinsey recommended that control of OEO's legal services program be placed within the regional offices of the Community Action Program, the legal profession was outraged. As Christopher Clancy, an OEO legal service administrator, explained, the lawyers saw that the change was not "simply managerial." "If," said Clancy, "we integrated Legal Services more fully into CAP, it would have taken away the hiring powers and approval powers on grants and monetary allocations that we had previously. . . . It would have made the regional Legal Services people purely specialists and technicians without the right to set policy." [65]

The National Advisory Committee of the Legal Services Program rallied to the cause, and in a letter to OEO's Sargent Shriver, Jacob Fuchsberg (President, American Trial Lawyers Foundation) explained that the standards of the profession could not be upheld if Legal Services were restructured.[66]

In Fuchsberg's eyes, McKinsey had not intended to "emasculate" Legal Services. "What happened was that McKinsey were making a study in inefficiency and were not sensitive to the problems of lawyers. Theirs was the bureaucratic efficiency approach; our interest was the lawyer's right to make judgment on such legal subjects as individual rights, without having to be responsible to a lay adviser solely interested in the management of the program." [67]

Lawyers are not among the powerless. Shriver returned Fuchsberg's letter, addressing him as a "fellow attorney" of whose "wariness of lay control" he was aware.[68] McKinsey's recommendations were rejected. It remained for Booz to reintroduce them in 1969.

By 1969, the Legal Services Program had become the lightning rod for criticism of OEO. Powerful politicians such as California's Ronald Reagan were eager to bring Legal Services under the control of state governments. Rumsfeld's choice to head Legal Services was a young lawyer who, as a condition to his acceptance of the position, had received Rumsfeld's assurance that Legal Services would remain under central control. When Booz made their recommendations, the new Legal Services head, Terry Lenzner, was anxious and angry. Another internal battle along the lines of 1966 was fought, and Lenzner won the rejection of Booz's proposal. A year later the dispute was renewed, and Lenzner resigned, even though the organized bar again rallied to beat back regionalization.

The reorganization, then, was directed at attaining Republican control over OEO's Washington headquarters and the local OEO programs. The reassignment of old personnel struck a blow at those committed to the programs and, by extension, at the programs themselves. The redesign of the organization chart eliminated some troublesome divisions and placed others under more trustworthy management. The consultants nonetheless insist that they saw themselves as technicians and not as politicians. As Booz's Paul Anderson explains, his work drew first and foremost on the tradition of business management. He and Stevens "started with a blank sheet of paper and began to decide what OEO should be doing. We devised an organizational structure that made sense to us." [69]

The "elimination of specific offices," said Anderson, "was not a conscious decision. An office was eliminated becauuse it did not fit into the new plan. We were not out to remove specific people or, as OEO personnel thought, to get the bastards out." While familiar with the claims of civil servants and OEO's poverty constituency that the agency was dying under Nixon, Anderson claimed: "Our principal objective was not to break up the agency. . . . People were concerned. I was concerned, despite my impeccable Republican credentials. We wanted to extract some sense out of what the hell this agency was doing." [70]

Evaluations of Booz's Work

"The Booz, Allen people," said Padraic Kennedy, former Director of VISTA, "were operating way over their heads." Kennedy formally resigned from the agency in June 1969, but stayed on through the reorganization and was included in the new directory. Kennedy, as well as many others we interviewed, did not find the new reorganization a skillful work of management. "The contractors were poorly equipped to do what they were doing. It was a cerebral exercise on the bureaucracy with no understanding of what the agency was trying to accomplish." [71]

In the fall of 1969, Booz, Allen left the agency. No explanation was given for its departure. William Bozman, the head of the Community Action Program, suggests that "the reason Booz, Allen had to leave was that they were actually making decisions rather than recommendations. The episode represents a case where a person with no Government appointment was making decisions." [72]

Terry Lenzner was harsher. "It was clear that nobody at the agency knew what was happening. It was clear that these peole were circumventing and violating the law. They were hurting morale, and no one except Rumsfeld had any control over them." [73]

White House assistant Richard Blumenthal recalled that "what impressed me about the reorganization was how little it actually was and how ineffectual it turned out to be. There was no conception of management imposed. Rather, there was the appointment of lots of high Presidential appointees." [74]

The purge of personnel was Booz's major accomplishment. In other "implemented" recommendations, funds were increased for technical assistance, and the selection of VISTA volunteers was contracted out to General Electric.

In some cases, firms like Booz leave behind lengthy tomes that offer an abundance of recommendations for management improvement. The OEO job did not get this treatment. In compliance with its $22,769 contract for Stevens' work, Booz, Allen submitted the report reproduced on pages 74 and 75.

The OEO civil servants never understood what Booz was doing. Tom Bryant, Assistant Director for Health Affairs, recalls that the "Booz, Allen people were running up and down the corridors asking questions of everyone. I asked who they were and found out from gossip that they were from Booz, Allen. My first impression was that they were new staff." [75]

File

BOOZ · ALLEN & HAMILTON Inc.

Management Consultants

NEW YORK   WASHINGTON   CLEVELAND   DETROIT
CHICAGO   DALLAS   LOS ANGELES   SAN FRANCISCO
TORONTO   MEXICO CITY   RIO de JANEIRO
LONDON   DÜSSELDORF

135 SOUTH LA SALLE STREET
CHICAGO · 60603
346-1900
AREA CODE 312

July 14, 1969

Mr. John A. Donahue
Contracting Officer
Office of Economic Opportunity
1200 19th Street Northwest
Washington, D. C. 20506

Dear Mr. Donahue:

As specified in our contract with OEO (Contract No. B99-4889), we are
to provide a report summarizing our overall effort, and the results, recommendations and conclusions of the study. This letter report is in response to
that obligation.

Our study has been conducted in two phases:

PHASE I - <u>Assist in a Detailed Review and Analysis of the Present</u>
<u>Organization of OEO</u>

. Over 110 people were interviewed in the Washington
headquarters and regional offices of OEO to determine
the manner in which the present organization operates.

. The functions, staff, discretionary funds and organizational
issues were highlighted for each organizational group.

. The overall major organizational issues for OEO were
presented.

Mr. John A. Donahue
July 14, 1969
Page Two

PHASE II - <u>Develop a Recommended Organization Structure for OEO</u>

A new organization for OEO has been presented to the Director of OEO and is presently under consideration. The recommended organization includes:

- Clear deliniation of the roles of the Director and Deputy Director.

- Functions and reporting relationship for the staff of the Director and Deputy Director.

- The future relationship of current and future national emphasis programs, VISTA, OEO regional offices and community action programs.

- The organizational relationship of activities such as research on poverty issues, experimental and demonstration programs, program operation and evaluation, and operation of agency administrative needs.

Job descriptions have been prepared for the major positions in the new organization.

It has been a great pleasure to serve the Director and agency in this project and we hope to be able to assist in the implementation of our recommendations.

Very truly yours,

BOOZ, ALLEN & HAMILTON Inc.

Gerald R. Riso
Vice President

Since Paul Anderson and Bruce Stevens, whom Booz had detailed to OEO at Anderson's request, served Rumsfeld directly—and no civil servants possessed similar access to the Director—the consultants possessed all the appearances of formal authority. There is, according to law, a profound distinction between consultants and officials. It is that officials can run the Government; consultants cannot. But as a matter of practice it is generally impossible to distinguish an "official decision" from a "consultant recommendation." When pressed, however, consultants gamely try to distinguish their ability to exercise "influence" from their "responsibility" for "official" decisions.

Anderson, for example, tried to distinguish his role in the agency from that of Stevens. Anderson entered OEO from the White House, while Stevens came directly from Booz. "As a Federal employee, I was able to give orders; Stevens only made recommendations. I was able to do things I could not have done if I were a consultant." As Anderson acknowledged, however, by the middle of the reorganization he had returned to Booz and "was already established at the time I legally came under the Booz, Allen contract, and no one knew that my status had changed." While Anderson recalls that he returned to Booz, in actuality he worked as an independent consultant to OEO. Nevertheless, Anderson took full advantage of his earlier status. "There is a distinction," he noted, "between being a known outsider and being someone who is fully part of the power structure. I was looked upon by OEO employees as being part of the power structure, while Bruce Stevens was not as involved with the heads of departments as I was." [76]

In keeping with the tradition of management science, Anderson offered a further explanation of the role of the consultant by distinguishing between the drawing of new organization charts—something within the scope of his work—and the selection of particular individuals to fill the new boxes—a job for officials. He and Stevens "were very careful not to get involved in discussion on individual personnel while under contract." [77]

Bertrand Harding, Rumsfeld's predecessor, saw it differently. "I got the impression that the management consultants were consulting with Rumsfeld on capabilities of people on the job as well as on the organizational structure. Most consultants will deny that this is their role, but in fact they end up doing it. It would not be in the report filed, which is most often meaningless, but it will take place in their private conversations." [78]

While there was no way to determine whether Anderson entered discussions to determine precisely who the 108 "nonpersons" would be, he and Stevens interviewed many agency staff members. Several who were promoted said they felt they owed their promotion to the consultants.

Richard Ottman, who was Assistant Director of Planning and Evaluation, recalls that it was Anderson and Stevens who brought him into the "inner circle" and started "having me work with Carlucci [Rumsfeld's heir]. Whenever we came up with ideas for Rumsfeld," Ottman recalls, "we went to Paul Anderson, who would then take the package of ideas to Rumsfeld." [79]

According to several OEO employees close to Richard Ottman, it was Anderson who informed Ottman that he had been promoted to Director of the Office of Program Development, one of the more prestigious positions in the reorganized agency. Ottman called several more junior people to ask if they would like to join his new staff. "I remember," recalled Donald Wortman, Assistant Director for Operations, "that they were playing around with Ottman, and for a few days he was head of the Office of Program Development. There was even a piece of paper issued on this confirming the appointment." But apparently Anderson had overstepped himself. Ottman's appointment had come while Rumsfeld was away from Washington, and when the Director returned, he rescinded the appointment and placed someone else in the position. Ottman, who left

OEO to become Administrative Vice President of the Institute for Defense Analyses, denies what was understandably an embarrassing situation. "The only thing I was told by Anderson," he claims, "was that they were recommending to Rumsfeld that I be kept as Assistant Director in the Office of Planning and Evaluation." [80]

Anderson had his own office and secretary near Rumsfeld and was essentially incorporated into the agency. He spent much of his time interviewing candidates for the agency's top jobs. Stevens, for his part, interviewed Washington bureaucrats and supervised the regional offices of the agency.

Stevens' profile in the agency was lower than low. Robert Trachtenberg, acting General Counsel of OEO, told us, "I had no idea what Stevens was doing. I was not privy to these discussions of reorganization and did not know he was there for some time." Trachtenberg, in response to our request, searched agency files for a record of Stevens' activity. "The files," he noted with pride, "validate my conclusion. I've looked through them. There is absolutely nothing in them that would tell you what Stevens did." [81]

In the year following Booz's study, OEO increased its technical assistance (TA) budget in accordance with recommendations. Booz's interests were so closely related to technical assistance contracts that it might appear that OEO was redesigned to serve the management consultant.

Between 1965 and 1971, OEO spent $110 million on technical assistance contracts. Don Wortman, who moved up to become Comptroller of OEO two years later, admitted that "all the money we have poured into TA has fundamentally been misspent, and we knew this for some time." [82] Rumsfeld's successor, Frank Carlucci, appeared before Congress in 1971 and stated: "Quite frankly, we have cut down very severely on the number of training and TA contracts. We did not think we were getting our money's worth." [83]

While still in the midst of its reorganization work, Booz

had already received a $300,000 award as part of what OEO called Project Manage, designed to provide technical assistance to local OEO grantees. The Project Manage contract further tangled the conflicting ways in which Booz, Allen was serving OEO. It was reorganizing at the national level; it represented the national level at the local level; and, of course, it sought contracts directly from localities. "There seemed," admitted the project manager, "to be a number of problems with these arrangements. At the same time that we were making additional grants through regions, Booz, Allen had decided to enter into additional contracts with Community Action Agencies. This seemed strange to me, for they were proposing to bid on the TA contracts coming out of the localities at the same time they were working for Rumsfeld." [84]

William Bozman, then head of the Community Action Program, later with the Urban Institute, was another person who found the arrangements a bit curious. "It gave the appearance," he recalls, "of an inside track by having Stevens as a staff consultant to Rumsfeld and having the firm bidding on this contract." [85]

The Project Manage contract, unlike the initial reorganization contract, was awarded after competition, but the competitive process was peculiar. Booz had initially offered to do the job for $380,000. OEO asked for rebids, and Booz lowered its price to $300,000, a price the competition could not meet. The original bids, however, had been produced in response to agency notice that the winning bidder would be obligated to provide assistance in over thirty cities. Once Booz received the award, the number of cities was reduced by six. The contract files did not explain why the number of cities was lowered or why there was no further reduction in Booz's price.

If the competitive circumstances of Project Manage were suspicious, the subsequent history of the contract showed that OEO and Booz had become expert at producing contracts that were gems of imperfection. The contract for

Project Manage specified that Bruce Stevens was to serve as Booz's Project Director on the contract. Stevens, of course, was also working on the OEO reorganization.

On September 30, in the midst of the reorganization controversy, Rumsfeld notified the OEO Contract Office that it would be in "the best interests of the Federal Government" to prematurely terminate both the reorganization contract and Project Manage. No explanation appears in the files.[86]

After dickering between OEO and Booz, it was agreed that Booz would be paid $27,511 as the costs of preparation for the aborted Project Manage contract. The Chicago office of the firm broke down the costs of the contract. The breakdown stated that Stevens had worked for forty-five days at the cost of $315 a day for a total of $14,175. Stevens' billing rate as indicated in the contract was approximately $78,000 a year. (The civil service maximum salary was $36,000.) Included in these figures is the firm's "overhead." However, when a contractor works away from his office and uses OEO facilities and secretaries, the Government should not have to pay to maintain his home office.

OEO's Contract Office did not dispute the amount of time assigned to Stevens on the Project Manage cost breakdown. Yet, according to Richard Cheney, Rumsfeld's assistant, Stevens was preoccupied with his work on reorganization "virtually on a full-time basis, every day until the contract was terminated." [87] Since the contracts ran parallel, it is hard to imagine how Stevens could have worked forty-five days on Project Manage while working full-time on the other. No one in OEO questioned this perplexing circumstance.

We asked the GAO to look into this matter. The GAO, in an August 1972 report, replied that it was possible for Stevens to have worked on both contracts on a full-time basis. (The billing structure for Booz, Allen is that of a seven-hour day, and according to them, Stevens worked for seven hours on the reorganization and also worked an almost equal amount of time on the TA contract. How he managed this feat was not made clear. Nor was his salary explained. If Booz computations on work hours are correct, Stevens would have had an earning of $156,000 a year; yet, according to the GAO, Booz paid Stevens only $24,000 a year.)[88]

Whatever it was that caused OEO to terminate Booz's contract, the firm did not fall from grace. Booz partner Murray Comarow headed the staff of the President's Committee on Reorganization of the Executive Branch (the Ash Council). Booz also received the prime contract to plan the second Nixon inaugural. Booz partner Harry Vincent serves on the board of the Marriott Corporation, and former Booz employee Jeb Magruder served under Willard Marriott as the head of the committee that planned the second inauguration. While Booz was cut off from its OEO contract, the two largest poverty agencies, HUD and HEW, eagerly sought out Booz consultants. Gerry Riso, the Booz partner who oversaw the OEO work, was named to a high-level position in HEW, and Booz also provided the first Nixon Administration FDA Commissioner, Dr. Charles Edwards, who in turn brought Booz alumni to work in FDA.

But a subsequent contract with HUD provides the most interesting comment on the politics of Booz's work for OEO. In mid-1970 Booz, Allen was awarded a $393,000 contract called "A Study and Reports on Issues and Projects of National Interest to Model Cities for Technical Assistance." Booz received the contract, despite the fact that a competing firm was judged technically superior to Booz and underbid Booz's price by $32,000. In answer to an inquiry from Senator Clinton P. Anderson, Assistant Secretary Floyd H. Hyde explained:

> I believe it is important to note that one of the three tasks outlined in the Request for Proposal (RFP) deals with the sensitive issue of citizen participation. . . . The citizen participation study was deliberately placed into this RFP rather than set out separately for bidding in order to gain a

firm with no obvious or apparent commitments to a particular citizen participation point of view.[89]

Hyde felt that Booz had a "neutral opinion" on the problem which Booz's competitor lacked.

Booz may have no explicit commitment to any view of citizen participation, but it is hard to understand how a firm that had just finished reorganizing the prime "citizen participation" agency could be said to have no view of citizen participation. Whether it understood the political implications or not, Booz's reorganization was consistent with the Nixon attempts to lay to rest War on Poverty citizen participation. What, we asked Hyde's assistant Bernie Russell, did Hyde mean? Hyde, Russell answered, simply felt more comfortable with a firm like Booz studying citizen participation.[90]

MANAGED REFORM

The creation of the Interstate Commerce Commission in 1887 signaled a revision in the working theory of American government. The Commission was the first of many that Congress would create and endow with broad and ill-defined powers to regulate major American industries. By the time of the New Deal, the regulatory agency was a dominant organizational form in Washington, and regulatory accountability had become a major problem. In 1946, following years of study by lawyers and administrative scholars, the Administrative Procedure Act was passed by Congress. The Act established the rules of procedure to be followed by regulatory agencies to bring order to the administrative process.

Courses in "administrative law" have become standard offerings in law schools. Twenty or thirty years ago such a course might have equipped the young lawyer to deal with a good part of the Executive Branch. But administrative law was born as the handmaiden of regulatory agencies, and the Government has now come to be dominated by agencies that plan programs and spend billions of dollars. In the spending agencies the administrative process is better defined by the rules of the boardroom than by those of the courtroom.

While the regulatory process is the domain of the legal profession, the spending process has become the domain of the management expert. When the management expert sets about writing his procedures they are often called not rules but "management systems." In every government agency there are "management systems" that govern everything from the organization of agency records to multibillion-dollar agglomerations of contractors.

The "planning-programming-budgeting system," or "PPB," was to be the management system par excellence for the spending agencies. The management experts who developed PPB hoped to regulate Government spending by controlling the budget process.

The management experts, like the New Deal lawyers, came of age in Washington at a time when Americans shared the belief that their kind of expertise marked the path to progress. This faith was officially affirmed in 1965, when President Johnson ordered the Executive Branch to adopt the rules of planning-programming-budgeting. These rules, said the President, would enable America to "identify our national goals with precision . . . choose among these goals . . . search for alternative means of reaching these goals most effectively with the least cost . . . measure the performance of our programs to ensure a dollar's worth of service for each dollar's cost." The new rules embodied "the most modern management tools, so that the full promise of a finer life can be brought to every American at least possible cost." [91]

Systems Analysis

The agencies regulating transportation, communication, public utilities, and financial enterprises have a collective budget of less than one tenth of 1 percent of the Federal total. It is now understood, however, that American eco-

nomic health can be imperiled not only by the infirmities of
the regulatory agencies but also by the coming of age of
"spending" agencies.

Budgeteers distinguish between "controllable" and "uncontrollable" federal spending programs. The uncontrollables are fixed by statute and regulation. By and large, they
involve dispensations to individuals, such as veterans'
benefits, unemployment insurance, medical insurance, and
social security. These programs are often associated with
the New Deal, and budget analysts have noted that they
now represent the largest and fastest-growing component of
the budget. The discovery is shocking, for in the Sixties the
lion's share of expert attention was focused on the glamor-
ous "controllable" expenditures. The controllables were the
creation of the post–World War II welfare/warfare state
and represented the Federal Government's subsidies to new
industries that were supposed to cure vast social ills. The
controllables dispense money, not to individuals, but to
institutions—schools, state and local governments, nonprofits, and industry. The grant and contract gave life to
this relationship. The Defense Department, created by the
unification of the services in 1947, was the gateway to the
New Land. The largest single source of the new spending
dollars, it was there that the masses of experts huddled, and
the more innovative among them developed management
products that became the staples of institutional existence
as the frontiers of Federal spending expanded.

After the airborne delivery of the atomic bomb, the Air
Force quickly acquired the Government's largest following
of industrial contractors. The missile, the jet plane, the
electronics revolution, and the Russian threat were ample
justification for continuing expenditures in the billions of
dollars. The RAND Corporation, created by the Air Force,
made its mark by advising on the management of the new
spending.[92]

The Defense Department parceled off the management of
major new expenditures into distinct organizational units,
known as weapons projects. The novelty of the new form is

best illustrated by comparison with the World War II
Manhattan Project, the super-secret organization of scientists and industry that produced the atomic bomb. While
Manhattan was an ad hoc arrangement that united geographically disparate private individuals and corporations
under military management, it lacked an elemental ingredient of the weapons project of the Fifties. In the jargon, the
bomb was not a "weapons system." It was not planned and
built in conjunction with the "delivery vehicle," the B-29
bomber. The bomb builders had to work around the
existing airplanes, and the bomb's development was limited,
for example, by the size of the available bomb bays. The
postwar projects simultaneously planned and built not only
the instruments of destruction but the facilities needed to
deliver and maintain them.[93]

While the managers of production became "weapons
systems managers," the planners became "weapons systems
analysts." Engineers, economists, and natural scientists by
training, they promise the country efficient production and
wise choices by planning not only the hardware of weap-
onry, but the methods of operating and maintaining the
weapon during its full "life cycle." Planning on a systems
basis, they explain, makes costs and problems more apparent. A weapon that seems cheap to construct, for example,
might have hidden maintenance costs that render it an
uneconomical investment.

The method was not really new. By law, the United
States Government had long been required to examine the
costs and benefits of proposed investments in land reclamation projects, for example. While the defense experts were
aware of the Bureau of Reclamation's cost/benefit studies,
they, like other modern managers, had greater admiration
for the pioneering work of the telephone monopoly.[94]

"Probably the greatest innovations in systems analysis,"
RAND's David Novick explained, "were initiated in the
1920s in the Bell Laboratories. The Bell Labs' method of
analysis then and today bears a close resemblance to what
we called weapons systems analysis in the Defense Depart-

ment or in other organizations such as RAND." The American Telephone and Telegraph Company (AT & T) had created and controlled a nationwide industry through the central planning and development, deployment, and maintenance of incredibly complex technology. It could not develop new telephones without designing sophisticated exchange networks, and neither would be of use without the ubiquitous repair force.[95]

Legend has it that the annual defense budget was an archaic and arcane accounting nightmare until RAND began its studies of defense spending. As traditionally presented to Congress, the defense budget is broken into categories that are called "objects of expenditures." The budget, for example, tells how much will be spent on "military personnel," "procurement," "operations and maintenance," and "research and development"—the largest single categories. These categories identify the recipients of money but not the purpose of the work to be done. There is no indication, for example, how many "military personnel" dollars provide readiness for nuclear war, guerrilla war, or land war. The RAND experts approached the budget as they had weapons spending, and as corporations had long seen budgeting.

RAND proposed a set of functions or "programs" to be the new base of budgetary accounting. Categories like "military personnel" would be replaced by "strategic (nuclear) forces," "airlift and sealift," "general purpose forces," and "guard and reserve forces." In turn, these major functions would encompass numerous components. As Novick explains, "I think this may be made more simple by illustrating it in automobile industry terms. For example, at General Motors it means not only dividing up between Chevrolet and Cadillac divisions and the other major lines that GM produces. It also means, within the Chevrolet line, identification of objectives in terms of price classes, categories of cars that they are trying to sell, and setting up specific programs for each of them. Then they calculate the resources required and the potential profits and losses under various conditions." [96]

The old defense budgeting operated on yearly plans. "One of the major features of the system that was introduced in Detroit was the fact that they were not planning just for next year's automobile. . . . In other words, Detroit continuously has five model years in planning, as well as one model in production." [97]

Along with five-year plans, a final promise from the experts was their broad vision in deciding on investments. In considering alternative expenditures, the analysts promised to take into account not only the tangible costs of production but the less tangible political, economic, and social ones. Where General Motors planned with an eye on competition, the Defense Department would plan with an eye on the communists. The country was to be assured that today's costliest investment, in mere dollars and cents, might be the wisest means of meeting the foreign threat.

General Motors symbolized the spirit of reform, but Ford was its exemplary practitioner, and in 1961 President Kennedy named Ford President Robert McNamara as Secretary of Defense. McNamara appointed Charles Hitch as Defense Department Comptroller. Hitch had co-authored at RAND *Economics of Defense in the Nuclear Age*, a book that the press called the "Bible of Defense Management." As the Department's chief accountant, Hitch, an economist by training, was authorized to introduce the RAND budgeting ideas throughout the military and he created an office of systems analysis with the help of contract employees from RAND and the Stanford Research Institute. By 1963, the Department codified the "programs" and required the submission of budget materials according to their rules. Each year, the services and systems analysts would exchange "program" budgets, and the analysts would also prepare special studies and annual five-year plans.

Everyone knows that bureaucracies suffer from an overabundance of rules. The management experts solved this problem by eliminating them. The new budgeting rules were a management system dignified with the brand name "planning-programming-budgeting system," or PPB.

While the new rules were inevitably justified in the rhetoric of efficiency, the PPBers could not ignore their potential for conflict with the relatively well known power interests that have a stake in the Defense Department. Thus the PPBers cast themselves not only as innovative managers but also as crusaders for political reform. At the same time that they promised to end the inefficient purchasing habits of the competing services, they linked their own rise with the ascendancy of central civilian control over the services and, in the grand style of the American tradition of "good government reform," promised to save the country from "vested interests."

> The fundamental idea behind PPB was decision-making based on explicit criteria of the national interest in defense programs, as opposed to decision-making by compromise among various institutional, parochial, or other vested interests in the Defense Department. . . . It is the Secretary of Defense who is charged with ensuring that the interests of the nation take precedence over the special institutional interests of the military departments, the defense contractors, the scientists, the localities, and other groups that make up or depend on the Defense Department.[98]

The PPBers contrasted this prospect with the traditional view that "once the President and the Congress have determined how much money can be spent on Defense, the job of the Secretary of Defense is to allocate the money among the services, to see that they live within the financial limits, and to arbitrate disputes. But basically it is the joint Chiefs of Staff and the services who should decide how the money is spent, with minimum civilian supervision."

PPB is the archetype for the successful practice of expertise. The PPBers spoke the language of industrial efficiency, but they were also capable of disarming displays of political awareness. Before the military's Congressional defenders they ate humble pie, defusing their arsenal of expert techniques. Systems analysis, they continually explained, was simply "applied common sense." Above all, it was not to be confused with the use of the computer or the practice of higher mathematics. In the end it was impossible to know with certainty whether the PPBers thought they were saving the country from the military or building the world's largest industrial monopoly.

The Resistible Rise of PPB

In 1965, the Federal Government acted to create a vast market for PPB. By executive order President Johnson announced that almost all civilian agencies, as well as the Defense Department, would be required to adopt the new rules. Federal recognition in turn provided the PPBers with easy entry into all institutions that trucked in Federal spending. What did state highway departments, public schools, city governments, state governments, and foreign aid programs have in common? By the late Sixties, they all had become purchasers of PPB.[99]

As of 1968, Federal civilian agencies alone employed 1,000 PPB analysts, many of whom had been hastily trained by the defense experts to occupy newly created civil service positions. Special offices were created to direct PPB work. The more notable were headed by alumni of the private research organizations. HEW's Office of Planning and Evaluation, for example, was directed by Alice Rivlin, a Brookings economist, and Bill Gorham, who had come to HEW from the Defense Department and RAND and who later left the agency for the Urban Institute, the Ford Foundation/Government–funded "RAND for the cities." The OEO Office of Research, Program Planning, and Evaluation was directed by a series of RAND alumni who staffed it with their protégés.[100]

Because of the importance that was attached to PPB, the existence of large civil service staffs did not stand in the way of procurement of contractor assistance. Old defense hands were signed on to explain systems analysis to civilian staffs. Systems analysts who knew nothing about health or housing or transportation were paid to study the ways in which systems analysis could be applied to "social problems." Finally, new organizations were created to provide the "research base" for planning. OEO, for example, created and funded the Institute for Research on Poverty, another "RAND for the poverty program." [101]

PPB was marketed swiftly and widely to eager Government officials. If these officials often bought PPB because they were required to, many undoubtedly were also excited about their purchase. Within a short time PPB became the new rage. In the newly created Department of Transportation, where Planning Research Corporation was hired to teach PPB, the first Secretary of Transportation told the press: "We haven't figured out how it works, or even what it means, but we're still trying . . ." [120] It was purchased not only by the new departments but also by the old ones that already had comparable management systems.

In the early Sixties, the Department of Labor (DOL) hired a contractor to create a Departmental Management System (DMS). Management insights being finite, DMS sounded very much like PPB, providing for the collection of new kinds of information about newly defined departmental functions. With the master blueprint of the DMS in hand, the Department hired Booz, Allen, and Hamilton to study data needs for all its management systems, and McKinsey & Co. to study the computerization of information. (In the jargon, McKinsey was to do a "feasibility study" for a departmental "management information system.") Booz discovered that the DMS was already being ignored. Supervisors did not "plan, program, account for, and review their work in accordance with DMS guidelines, but rather would prepare additional reports for management. These reports, moreover, lose their value, since the fact-gathering or data collection does not adhere to DMS procedures." [103]

Along came the new PPB regulations on top of DMS.

Planning Research was hired to teach DOL "cost/benefit analysis" and to spell out new categories and rules for PPB. The civil servants in DOL's own management office were utterly confused by PRC's work. "Our problem with PRC," wrote one man in the office of the Assistant Secretary for Administration, "is its apparent basic assumption that the Department has done nothing whatever to embark on PPB." Why, the staffer complained, did PRC want to replace existing program categories with new ones entitled "psychic," "structural," "aggregate," and "poverty"? What did the contractor mean by these terms, and how were they any better? [104]

Already confused by PRC's work, the civil servants could not understand why the Department was awarding yet another multiyear contract to Systems Development Corporation that called on SDC to perform "systems analyses" of the labor market. As a major Air Force contractor, SDC had no credentials in labor economics. The civil servants in the management office, on the other hand, were themselves management experts. They were irritated less by SDC's lack of expertise than by the redundance of the growing number of "systems analysis" contracts. The contracting division offered the Assistant Secretary for Administration a line-by-line exegesis of the proposed SDC award. If there appeared to be no redundance, he concluded, it was only because the contract was so vague. "No matter how we slice it, systems analysis is still the application of management information and cost/benefit studies aimed toward analytical attempts designed to help a decision-maker identify a preferred choice among possible alternatives." Wrote the Assistant Secretary: "Systems analysis is systems analysis is systems analysis."

In 1968, the Department commissioned yet another contractor (this time an individual consultant) to study the DMS-PPB agglomeration. This consultant concluded that while the Department led Washington in the design of PPB, the system was not working "in the sense that effective management actions proceed from or relate to a functioning DMS. In a very real way, people support the DMS system, but it is not yet the case that the DMS system supports the people." [105]

By 1968, management inability to implement PPB was self-evident. Not even the Bureau of the Budget, which directed agencies to produce PPB studies for the Bureau's use, could understand PPB. An in-house study determined that PPB was a "source of disagreement and confusion." Some Bureau officials saw PPB as "an entirely new approach which will soon replace the old system. Others describe it as a repackaged version of activities which have been performed for years. Most views are less than clear, because the system is changing rapidly." The future "is not seen with clarity." [106]

The Demise of PPB

In 1968, the Bureau of the Budget hired McKinsey to do a grand study entitled "Strengthening Program Planning, Budgeting, and Management in the Federal Government." As Bureau insiders saw it, the managers were being called on to save PPB from the economists. The economists who created PPB could create accounting categories and play with numbers, but they were not very good at teaching the game to middle management. [107]

As the first stage in the reformation of PPB, McKinsey told the Budget Bureau that it would "pilot test" the "building block" idea. The Bureau's management experts applauded, and its economists and lawyers scratched their heads.

The "pilot test" has become a reliable weapon in the expert's arsenal of scientific-sounding jargon. Everyone knows that a "test" has something to do with technical rigor. Unfortunately, McKinsey's "pilot test" proved about as useful as licensing a blind man who says he would like to drive. The firm agreed to test its new system in segments of the Departments of Commerce, Labor, and Agriculture. By reading Government manuals and interviewing agency officials, it traced programs down through the chain of command, then renamed activities so that the "building blocks" at each level appeared to be components of the box on top of them. In theory, the managers at each level would agree to the definition of their activity and "contract" with the next level to perform the work defined by their "building block." Top management would then be in control of the classic pyramidal organization.

The remnants of the study left in the contract file show that it was a slapdash affair. McKinsey buzzed through agencies, offering superficial suggestions. A meeting with Commerce Department weather bureau officials, for example, led to the conclusion that its activities were mistitled. The Department of Labor proved most difficult of all for McKinsey. Even though the firm, under contract to the Department's Manpower Administration, had been at work on agency organization, it suddenly discovered that program categories were vague and that it was hard to improve on them.

McKinsey marked the end of its "pilot test" by submitting its study to the Bureau. The study said that programs could be renamed. It concluded that the "pilot test" was successful and recommended an investment of hundreds of man hours to "implement" the new system throughout the government. The success of the "pilot test," then, had little to do with reality. What difference the name changes might make was not tested.[108]

McKinsey's study, as the Bureau's Jack Carlson put it, "did not set the world on fire." While the office that commissioned it minimized the failure, no one acted on the million-dollar recommendations. The surest sign of the study's demise was the decision of McKinsey's study director, Robert Fri, to leave the firm for a sojourn in the upper echelons of the Environmental Protection Agency.[109]

By 1969, PPB's period as a panacea had passed. It died officially when the Bureau of the Budget changed the regulations that required hours of useless PPB paperwork. The Bureau had little control over the Defense Department's budget, and other factors doomed PPB there. With the exit of the Democrats, Nixon promised to restore defense decision-making to the services. The "downgrading" of the central systems analysis office received much publicity, but the ascent of Henry Kissinger was more important in shifting defense–foreign policy decision-making to a new center of power.[110]

PPB fared even less well outside the Federal Government. Allen Schick, then at Brookings, assessed PPB's value to state government. "It wouldn't be hard for you," he explained, "to find that the payoff is microscopic." [111] (A later chapter will sketch the failed ambitions of McKinsey and the New York City Budget Bureau.)

PPB's life cycle had ended, and few but administrative scholars mourned it. Certainly not the confused careerists. As for the contractors, they had profited from PPB, and they remained at the center of budgeting. If PPB failed, there were soon to be new generations of management products. The Nixon Administration's Ash council proposed reorganization as the cure-all for Big Government's ills. While the Ash council left the Defense Department untouched, the Fitzhugh Commission, drawing heavily on the Defense Department's stable of management contractors, found a thousand and one ways in which its management could be improved. The Budget Bureau, itself renamed the Office of Management and Budget following an early Ash council recommendation, had a ready successor to PPB. "Management by Objectives" (MBO) was a clever strategic retreat from PPB. MBO did not call for the grand recategorization and systematic analysis of spending, but simply asked managers to set a few measurable goals and "manage to the objective."

The new concepts, like the old, brought corporate technique and technicians to the aid of government. With the exception of corporate lawyer John Connally, the six Ash council commissioners were famed management experts, including Richard Paget of Cresap, McCormick, and Paget, the former Dean of the Harvard Business School, and the former Chairman of AT & T. The council was directed and staffed by men from places like Booz, Allen, and Arthur D. Little. As to MBO, Budget Deputy Director Fred Malek told the press that it was a technique he picked up in his days as a corporate consultant with McKinsey & Co.[112]

BUSINESS IN THE
HUMANE SOCIETY

While the management expert operates largely out of public view, the trained eye can capture glimpses of his presence. McKinsey, for example, encourages its personnel to speak at conferences and to contribute to professional journals. Still, the public presentations of management experts are couched in generalities, conveying an impression of wisdom without betraying many names and facts. The reader is referred, for example, to the management classic produced by the man most often associated with McKinsey's rise. Marvin Bower's *The Will to Manage* might have been written by Billy Graham or Woody Hayes.[113]

If Marvin Bower is McKinsey's patron saint, John Corson's career was most closely associated with the growth of McKinsey's Government business. Corson's career stands out, if only by contrast to the scarcely perceivable activities of his peers. His pursuits illuminate much else. His life touches America's organized centers of culture and power, and he has preached a gospel of progress, a view of the American system that continues to serve as the "boiler-plate" preface for studies, speeches, and reports on America's crises. At the height of his powers, Corson opened the Government market for McKinsey and worked to integrate the interests of McKinsey's established private clientele with its expanding public clientele.

Corson's background stunningly complemented McKinsey's. He was by training an academic and a welfare administrator, not a businessman. Born in Virginia in 1905, he studied economics at the University of Virginia, then made his way through positions of increasing responsibility in New Deal Social Security programs. Corson left the Government for a stint as an executive at the *Washington Post* and, in 1951, joined McKinsey's nascent Washington office.[114]

While there, Corson continued his affiliation with the private nonprofit organizations whose seed money and influence shaped America's welfare programs. He recognized and encouraged the role of the nonprofit organization as a complement to the profit-making corporation. As a longtime adviser to the Carnegie Foundation, for example, Corson had a perch from which to view the mid-century expansion of American education, and he used his position to ensure consonance between the management tradition and the educational tradition. With Carnegie money he helped found the Institute for Educational Development, a nonprofit that promised to "close the loop" and bind together industry, government, and education. Corson served as a trustee of the Educational Testing Service, a nonprofit familiar to all students. The Corson presence was ubiquitous, yet unobtrusive. It was Corson's associate at Carnegie, John Gardner, who would acquire true public eminence, first as a spokesman for educational reform, then as a voice for institutional reform.[115]

Corson and McKinsey opened doors for one another. "John," sighed a McKinsey partner, "liked to serve on committees." McKinsey's growing involvement in the management of the welfare state is evidenced by the variety of advisory positions Corson acquired. He studied the organization of the Army with the Davies Commission, Federal grants-in-aid with the Kestnbaum Commission, the Russian nuclear threat with the super-secret Gaither Commission. He served on commissions to study higher education, the Public Health Service, air traffic control, and municipal personnel. "John Corson," recalled Johnson Civil Service Commissioner John Macy, "was on almost every Government pay review committee." [116]

Corson was a member of a private, profit-making consulting firm, but continually had his hand in the evolution of the governmental personnel system. Corson worked for a profit-making firm, but was an ardent promoter of the nonprofits. Some might see conflict in the simultaneous service of Corson (and McKinsey) to private organizations and the agencies that subsidize and regulate them, to the contractor system and the civil service system, to the industrial system and the welfare system created to mitigate the industrial system's failures. Corson saw not conflict but opportunity for reconciliation. If he recognized any threat to this opportunity, it was only from businessmen who mistakenly feared the growth of Big Government. It was Corson's mission to bring these businessmen to their senses, and this was the message of his magnum opus, *Business in the Humane Society*.[117]

The book, published in 1971, received little public attention, but it is an outstanding catalogue of the operations of Big Government. Even readers familiar with the Washington scene, Corson notes, will be "impressed with the magnitude and scope of the subsidy, contract, grant, and regulatory processes as they have evolved in recent decades." The "humane society" which is emerging "is not to be an elaboration of the Welfare State against which businessmen railed in the 1940s and 1950s. Indeed, in contrast, the Welfare State will be viewed in retrospect as a pinchpenny conception of what society is obligated to do for all of its members, not merely for those who are poor." "Americans," Corson explains, laid the groundwork for the "humane society" by "redefining what is the responsibility of all of the people, as distinguished from what is the responsibility of the individual and his family." These Americans "pushed Government into assuming an ever-increasing role. They were then confronted with the choice of steadily enlarging the Government or giving private groups the responsibilities of government. They chose the latter course." [118]

If "Americans" indeed made such a choice and agreed to pay the price, it is men like Corson who supplied the ideological lubricant that made the private sector acceptable as the manager of Big Government.

John Corson arrived at McKinsey just as the Republicans were returning to the White House after an absence of two decades. As Corson retells it, the party's elder statesmen feared that the Democratic appointees who managed the Executive Branch would frustrate Republican attempts to control government. The Republican patronage machine had become a vestigial organ, and Republican leadership doubted their ability to find their own managers. So it was that the Party of Business called on the elite business consulting firm for help. No note was taken by either that they were placing their trust in a man, John Corson, who had once been a proud New Dealer.

"We are," says a discreetly hardbound McKinsey brochure, "prepared to assist our clients in locating candidates for executive positions. To that end, we maintain confidential files of the names of men who are doing outstanding work in various fields." The brochure appeared in 1940. Today, the firm formally denies that it performs "executive searches." Thus, when Republican Party Finance Chairman Harold Talbott approached McKinsey, the firm was "somewhat skittish." The job, recalls Corson, was an incredible plum, but McKinsey was not in the "headhunting" business. McKinsey resolved the dilemma by redefining its charge. It promised the Republicans a broad survey of Federal management—"If you really wanted to be in charge, what were the key jobs?" Once this question was asked, McKinsey could help, as a courtesy, to find men to fill the jobs.[119]

In October 1952, Talbott received a series of folders from McKinsey. Each bore the title "Restaffing the Executive Branch of the Federal Government," and one folder was devoted to each major agency. The folders contained primitive intelligence. They told the Republicans the purpose of each agency, the key positions, the incumbents in these positions, and the qualifications required for these positions. The State Department folder, for example, revealed that David Bruce was Under Secretary of State, that he was an attorney, banker, and career foreign service officer, and that his successor might well have experience in foreign affairs. This type of material all but concealed the kernels of real information. While over 2 million people were employed by the Federal Government, McKinsey had discovered that "through staffing a maximum of 610 executive positions in the Federal Government, the new President can make the will of the people effective. . . . Full control of policy and programs can be obtained through proper restaffing of no more than this number of positions —and probably fewer." McKinsey suggested that 204 positions be restaffed immediately.[120] (The positions under study did not include professional positions, such as attorneys, and mundane patronage posts, such as postmasters.)

When Eisenhower met with his newly appointed Cabinet, Sherman Adams, his ill-starred aide, gave each Cabinet officer a personalized copy of the folder for his department. The folder explained that McKinsey would be "pleased to answer questions about any of the positions in this section and otherwise to assist any user of this report in making it of greatest value." [121] According to Corson, about half of the Cabinet officers availed themselves of McKinsey's search services. As in all subsequent uses of consultant recruiters, there is no public record of the men selected in this way.

Since 1883, the civil service system has placed the selection of most Government officials beyond the direct control of the President and his Cabinet. There are many exceptions to this rule, and the most important concerns the selection of higher Government officials. Many top positions are reserved for political appointees. The party in power not only may exercise its rights of political appointment, but also contrives to control indirectly those positions which it cannot directly control. The private management expert has become adept at devising means of aiding the latter activity as well as the former.

The McKinsey study paid deference to the importance of the civil service, then explained that "individuals who have gained positions through the civil service system are not invulnerable to change." Civil servants, offered McKinsey, could be transferred elsewhere in the agency, asked to resign "for the good of the service," or simply severed from any tasks of importance. For legal reasons, qualified McKinsey, it would be difficult—though "not impossible" —to tamper with veterans; but, while "civil service employees cannot be dismissed without cause . . . they can be removed from specific positions where their services are not useful." [122] Since 1952, Government managers and their experts have honed the ploys and techniques of dealing with the civil service system. They employ them not only on the election of a new President but also in the continual reorganization of individual agencies. (See, for example, Chapter II.)

During the 1960 campaign, consulting firms soldified the role of private experts in the Presidential transition. The Brookings Institution offered to educate both parties in the problems the new President would face. A special panel was created to advise the competing camps, and one of the panel members was John Corson. The financial support for the program was provided by Corson's Carnegie Foundation. Each candidate sent a representative to the meetings held by Brookings. Candidate Kennedy chose Washington lawyer Clark Clifford. According to Corson, Clifford asked McKinsey to provide him with a study quite similar to that the Republicans had received in 1952. Corson delivered the McKinsey report to Brookings' Robert Calkins in November 1960. [123]

The Nixon Administration's central recruiting office was organized by Fred Malek, who had worked in McKinsey's Los Angeles office. He staffed the Nixon personnel office with men from places such as Peat, Marwick, Mitchell, & Co.; Cresap, McCormick, and Paget; and Headrick and Struggles, one of the largest firms devoted primarily to recruiting. [124]

Government by the Talented

In 1962, following the requests of "officials of the Kennedy Administration and former officials of the Eisenhower Administration," the Committee for Economic Development (CED) established a group to study the "improvement of management in government." The group was chaired by Marion Folsom, an Eisenhower Cabinet member, and included three other former Cabinet officers, three former under secretaries, other former officeholders, and CED members from McKinsey (Marvin Bower) and Booz, Allen, and Hamilton.

In 1966, the Committee published *Men Near the Top.* "There are," the book began, "near the top of the hierarchy that runs this country's Federal Government, about 5,000 men and women whose activities vitally effect the lives of every American." With "few exceptions," the report went on, "their names are unknown to most Americans . . . yet this relatively small group of men and women occupies a critical place in the management of our Government. If only by their location near the top of the most powerful government in the world, they can (and do) exercise considerable and increasing power." Ever since the days of Frederick Taylor, Folsom's preface explained, management experts had asked what it was that people in industry do. Few, however, had asked, as *Men Near the Top* did, what top civil servants do. Not surprisingly, Folsom failed to ask what high-level governmental contract experts did, even though their power sounds suspiciously akin to that of the "men near the top." [125]

The co-author of the CED report was John Corson, who relied on data provided by McKinsey. The Bureau of the Budget had hired McKinsey to study Federal pay scales, and the firm, which is the established authority on corporate pay scales, was on its way to becoming a basic source of information on Federal practice.

Corson's report came to some interesting conclusions. The "men near the top" had risen from within the civil service. They had spent their careers in a single agency. Above all, they were not dilettantes or generalists at management. The CED lauded the way these men had progressed, but characterized them as a generation in need of replacement. The Federal Government required more dynamic men, men able to deal with a wider range of issues and programs, men of the kind found in consulting firms like McKinsey.

The theme of the study was familiar: Bureaucracy atrophies and does not breed the source of its own reform. (As John Gardner would have it, bureaucracy lacks the capacity for "self-renewal.") Bureaucracy needs stimulation from outside. Nowhere has this need for privately induced reform of public management been more clearly spelled out than in a 1951 study, *Executives for the Federal Service*, also funded by the Carnegie Foundation. That study was also written by John Corson.[126]

In *Executives for the Federal Service* Corson directed his attention to the management of the cold war. For "as long as we can see in the future," Corson claimed, "the country would be faced with the overwhelming threat of war," and top talent would be needed to manage the "emergency agencies." As he would in *Men Near the Top*, Corson expressed a qualified admiration for civil servants, but found the civil service service fundamentally deficient. There are good civil servants, but their place is limited to their current jobs, "where they are needed and usually well satisfied." Corson, the former civil servant, had little faith in the career system. Those civil servants who had come to serve in the "emergency agencies" had not been selected on merit. Some were transferred in large reorganizations. For the most part, Corson held, the civil servants in the new agencies were "drifters" and "opportunists" who "grasp the opportunities by the needs of the new agencies." The nation, Corson argued, had to lure businessmen to serve in the "emergency agencies." Corson gave no consideration to potential conflict between public service and private interests. His only concern was the reluctance of businessmen to temporarily forgo private advancement. He proposed to solve this problem by methods that drew less on management technique than on the traditions of Tammany Hall.[127]

Personal acquaintances, Corson explained, are crucial to the location of talent. Government managers just did not know enough talented businessmen, and, conversely, dynamic men were none too eager to work for officials they did not know. Corson called on major organizations of labor, media, and management to create the climate of opinion that would convince businessmen "of both the nature of the current emergency and the need for executives to manage important public functions." This country's business leaders had to recognize the "necessity of making available for civilian public service some of their ablest executives. . . . Relatively few business jobs now yield their aides because they are already concerned about the current emergency." Business leaders must realize that "Government efforts to build our national defense and to control inflation are of such consequence to the business community that they should loan some of their most talented aides." [128] The Fifties were exceptionally kind to McKinsey. The firm worked for between "twenty-five or thirty" Federal agencies, getting "more than its share" of the prestigious contracts awarded by an Administration that it helped create. Corson had ample opportunity to promote, by private action and public testimony, his theme. In 1960, when Senator Jackson and the Senate Democrats focused pre-election interest on the growing Russian nuclear threat, Corson testified as an expert on personnel policies and urged the Government to "enlist a larger proportion of society in the cold war." Corporations, he pronounced, should take a more self-interested view of public service: "It seems to me, the one lacking ingredient which we have to somehow create is a recognition in American business that an understanding of the function of the Federal Government is valuable to the guy who winds his way up in the corporate structure. It is valuable in a society in which 20 percent of all goods and services produced by private business are purchased by the Government. It is a valuable understanding of an important customer.[129]

"If you analyze," Corson helpfully pointed out, "how many corporations are doing business with the Government in one way or another, such experience in government has practical, selfish value within the corporation. If we can get that idea better established in the corporate enterprises of this country, they then will see a reason, and the young man working up can see a reason, for having this particular understanding as well as what he has to have to get ahead in his company; then we will hope to get a goodly number that will be made available." [130]

Corson did more than testify and write books. In 1958, McKinsey and Brookings cosponsored a study of the growing role of the corporation in Washington, and in 1963, Corson drew on this seminar and his experience with the Presidential transition project to create a novel venture in Government-corporate relations. With the assistance of an AT & T executive and Elmer Staats, then a Budget Bureau official and now Comptroller General of the United States, Corson invited high-level corporate and Government officials to join in periodic off-the-record exchanges on basic issues. The "seminars" were funded by the Carnegie Foundation, and Brookings eventually took over their administration.[131]

The business-Government gatherings eventually led to the creation of the President's Commission on Personnel Interchange, a permanent agency that annually sends several dozen Government managers to business and several dozen bright businessmen to Government. Brookings, which administers several training programs for industry and Government officials, administers the personnel exchange program's orientation sessions.[132]

The personnel exchange commission was almost the last creation of the Johnson era, but it was readily accepted by the Nixon Administration.

George Graham, Director of Brookings' Government

Studies Program during the 1960 Presidential transition project, is one long-time public administration scholar who sees the 1952 "purge" by the Republicans and McKinsey as the first wave in a "constant purging of the higher civil service that is destroying it." In Graham's eyes, distrust of the higher civil service shown by each new Presidential administration borders on paranoia. After all, why should civil servants be any less capable of bipartisanship than John Corson or McKinsey? [133]

One measure of the damage of political purge and corporate buddyism may be a decline in the competence of Government officials. "In the still of night," wrote the late Clinton Rossiter, "and with the eyes of his mind, Mr. Eisenhower must have often looked back sheepishly to his campaign promise of 1952 to 'mobilize the best brains of America.' . . . It seems plain that Eisenhower will not be especially remembered for the talents he assembled about him." [134]

Independent journalists and social scientists have largely ignored the subtle game of personnel selection. By default, the only studies are those sponsored by institutions with a direct involvement in the personnel system—for example, McKinsey and Brookings. A Harvard Business School survey performed in the mid-Fifties found that businessmen were "summer soldiers." The median stay in government for one group surveyed was only one and a half years. Treasury Secretary George Humphrey supplied the survey with an explanation for this figure—the businessmen he recruited soon parlayed their leave into corporate promotions. In 1960, Corson testified about the rapid turnover of businessmen in Government, and in the late Sixties the talk of Washington management was a study that found that the average tenure of the high-level manager (assistant secretary) was only twenty-two months.[135]

A brief turn at being an assistant secretary may do wonders for a career, but as Dr. Charles Edwards, a Booz, Allen medical manager who was named Commissioner of the Food and Drug Administration, discovered, a new

Government executive must stay on the job for at least two years in order to manage a budget he has prepared. The impossibility of short-term control is matched only by the chaos created by continual efforts to establish it. To "hit the ground running," as a career management official put it, the anxious and eager new appointee will call on the ever-ready contractor to tell him about his agency—and help "reorganize" it.[136]

Like the management system reformers, the personnel reformers draw first their strength, then their alibis, from the alleged bankruptcy of the official bureaucracy. Dr. Edwards, for example, said of Nixon's Ash council for a super-reorganization of government: "I thought when I first read the plan, it made sense. But the longer I've been in Government I'm absolutely convinced it's wrong. Yet I also think one of the great disaster areas in Government is the civil service."

With the help of the unseen hand of free enterprise expertise, the civil service has become a chronic disaster area. At the most superficial level, the manipulation by profit-minded experts of Government pay scales has made the Federal pay system comparable only to the tax laws in terms of inequity and inefficiency. The rise of the highly paid Government contractor and the desire to make Government office more attractive to businessmen pushed up pay scales throughout the Sixties. Unfortunately, the drive to parity with the private sector was strong enough to create inflation, but hardly made it possible to raise salaries anywhere near those offered by industry. This dilemma was pointed out by the President's Advisory Commission on Executive Level Compensation, a group headed by Arch Patton—McKinsey's expert on corporate compensation.[137]

The real crisis is spiritual, not financial. As C. Wright Mills has pointed out, Americans have never really taken their civil service seriously. The Senate Watergate committee uncovered a document that revealed the working assumptions behind two decades of "government by the talented." The document was found in a study of the activities of the Malek personnel office and appears to have been an introduction and guide to Nixon Administration personnel managers.

The "Federal Political Personnel Manual" assured its readers that the "merit system" is a fraud:

> Because of the subjectiveness of the certification process with respect to midlevel and senior level positions, there is really no "merit" in the "merit system" save the minimum qualifications that a candidate be eligible. The bureaucrats operate their own patronage system while telling the politicians to "keep their hands off" so as not to interfere with the "merit system." [138]

In detailing the "rape of the merit system," the document cited the culpability of politicians and private experts. While politicians cited by the manual were Democrats, the private experts were people much like the Nixon personnel men.

A subsequent section on removal, reminiscent of the McKinsey appendix to its "Restaffing the Executive Branch" folders, explained that "you cannot achieve management policy or program control unless you have established political control." The "facts," the manual stated, "were not lost on John and Robert Kennedy."

> Shortly after Kennedy's nomination, the Kennedy campaign reportedly hired a management consulting firm which made a review of the Executive Branch of Government. In that survey they pointed out every position, regardless of whether it was career or noncareer, which was thought to be an important pressure point in the Executive Branch. They did a thorough research job on the incumbents occupying these positions. After Kennedy's inauguration, they put Larry O'Brien in charge of the effort to "clean out the Executive Branch" of all those incumbents of those positions whom they felt they could not rely upon politically.[139]

If the Nixon Administration had any failing, the manual argued, it was its incompetence and naïveté. Too many holdovers retained their jobs. So the Nixon Administration

began, under Malek, an ambitious effort to centrally direct
the recruitment and location of officials throughout Government. Malek placed management experts in key administrative positions throughout the Executive Branch, and
they would be supplemented by outside help:

> Recruiters to the nonpolitical sector, again, need have little
> knowledge of personnel or government in general, but
> should have a thorough knowledge of the agency and the
> sales techniques involved in executive recruitment. The best
> place to find these people is in commercial executive search
> and placement firms.[140]

Contracting Out

Of all the techniques used to control the civil service
bureaucracy, contracting out is certainly the most subtle. As
the ever-helpful "Federal Political Personnel Manual" explains:

> In 1966, Johnson offered legislation, which Congress passed,
> called the Revenue Expenditure Control Act. It required the
> Executive Branch of Government to reduce itself in size to
> the level of employment in fact existing in 1964. The
> cosmetic public theory behind the Act was that the reduction of, and stabilization of, a personnel ceiling for the
> Executive Branch would first cut, and then stabilize, Federal
> expenditures connected with personnel costs. . . . What the
> Johnson Administration simply did after passage of that Act
> was to see to it that "friendly" consulting firms began to
> spring up, founded and staffed by many former Johnson
> and Kennedy Administration employees. They then received fat contracts to perform functions previously performed within the Government by Federal employees. The
> commercial costs, naturally, exceeded the personnel costs
> they replaced.[141]

By the Sixties, the practice had, of course, become
bipartisan. When John Corson was asked by the Jackson
subcommittee whether he would advise contracting out
even where the Government lacked the expertise to oversee

contracts, he replied, "I would not deny to this Government the capability that we have in this country in areas where we desperately need them, because we are unable to meet the first [governmental expertise to oversee contracts] problem." [142] McKinsey's work for NASA provides one of the most revealing episodes in the "desocialization" of government through contracting out, incidentally placing billions of dollars in corporate treasuries.

America responded to Sputnik by creating a new agency to house the American space venture. The National Aeronautics and Space Administration (NASA) was superimposed on the old National Aeronautical Control Administration (NACA), which had been created during World War I to guide air technology development. NACA spent its research dollars in Government laboratories rather than with private industry, and its record seems to contradict the contemporary credo that private industry is an inherently superior spender of the Government research dollar. According to Senator Stuart Symington, former Air Force Secretary, NACA was "probably one of the most successful Government organizations of all time."

In the event, Keith Glennan, a university president, was named to head NASA, and Glennan immediately called on Corson and McKinsey for the development of NASA's official organization chart, which was issued in January 1959. NASA's official administrative history records that McKinsey merely rubberstamped the plans of the civil service. Thus, at best, the task afforded McKinsey an opportunity to familiarize itself with NASA.[143]

Having made its formal contribution to NASA's creation, McKinsey's assistance became more substantial. Corson provided Glennan (on an "informal" basis) with candidates for three NASA positions—general counsel, business administrator, and assistant to the director. John Young, who worked on the project for McKinsey, calls the assistance "informal" in the sense that it was not a "billable" item, but it was a "natural thing that goes on. A guy asks . . . you know a lot of people." [144]

Glennan accepted Corson's recommendations. One of Business Administrator Siepert's first official acts was the selection of McKinsey for the job of transferring defense laboratories to NASA.

In late 1959, Corson wrote an article in a management journal that called for the "redesign of the free enterprise system for the space age." The article promised business space-age profits if it would join Government in a "partnership" to beat the Russians and thwart socialism. Not long after Corson's article, NASA Director Glennan called for a revaluation of NASA's contracting policies, and NASA hired McKinsey to perform the analysis. Fearing perhaps that McKinsey's word alone might not suffice, Corson prodded Glennan to create a citizens' committee to also evaluate NASA's policies. The membership, selected with Corson's help, was to be "experienced in large-scale organization for research and development activities and in Government operations." Government, of course, could not provide this kind of expertise, so the Kimpton Committee was set up, headed by an oil company executive who was joined by five other industrialists and the Carnegie Foundation's James Perkins. Like all such Blue Ribbon panels, the Kimpton Committee needed a staff. It naturally needed an independent staff, so McKinsey got the job.[145]

NASA's historian records that McKinsey produced a study of contracting for NASA that substantially overlapped the report of the Kimpton Committee. And while McKinsey was placing its imprint on NASA's contracting policy, NASA kept Congress at bay. Drawing on the legal advice of McKinsey's choice for General Counsel, Glennan told the General Accounting Office that Congress would not get access to information on NASA contract awards. The refusal, the GAO complained, was unprecedented.[146]

The McKinsey studies considered whether NASA should build its own R & D facilities, rely on other governmental facilities, or turn to industry. McKinsey concluded that NASA should contract out as extensively as possible, retaining only the minimal staff necessary to conceptualize programs, or, at least, to "effectively review and approve conceptual and preliminary design elements of projects submitted by contractors." [147]

The report was an exercise in blandness. "There is no doubt," recorded the NASA historian, "that its recommendations were cautious and conservative and in most cases advocated the continuation of the status quo." The report provoked controversy in only one area. "Most NASA officials felt that in-house activity had to be more than the minimum necessary to keep tab on out-of-house efforts." [148]

NACA, NASA's predecessor, had a budget of less than $100 million a year. It used this money to conduct research, largely in Government laboratories. By 1960, NASA's budget was $1 billion and climbing quickly. In contrast to NACA, however, 85 percent of NASA's money was spent on grants and contracts. And so, as Corson boasts in *Business in the Humane Society*, Americans had "chosen" to place their faith in free enterprise. By 1969, a number of governmental agencies, such as NASA, were spending more on contractors than on Government employees. Indeed, each of a dozen private corporations received a larger portion of the Federal budget than each of a dozen Federal agencies. One example, cited by Corson, was North American Aviation. A major McKinsey client, North American and three other corporations ate up no less than one third of the $24 billion expended on NASA's Apollo program.[149]

McKinsey, however interesting and influential, is nonetheless only one contractor among thousands. It is to the growth and management of the contract bureaucracy itself that we now turn.

III.

THE PROLIFERATION
OF THINK TANKS

Since World War II, the contract bureaucracy has grown like Topsy, but its heritage is not quite such a mystery. At the turn of the century, administrative reform goals of efficiency and economy, to be achieved by the application of business methods, made the businessman's participation in government respectable.

THE NONPROFITS

In the first quarter of the century, private money financed private nonprofit corporations that were to provide the levers for reform of the Federal government.[1] Thus were founded in Washington the Institute for Government Research (IGR), which promised to pursue "scientific investigations into the theory and practice of governmental administration"; the Institute for Economics, which expected to "aid the public in making decisions in the light of knowledge"; and the Robert Brookings Graduate School, which hoped to provide future official managers with "professional and cultural training in the studies which have to do with the control of a developing society." In 1926, these institutions merged to form the Brookings Institution, now a venerable Washington think tank.

The reforming Progressives hoped that corruption-proof accounting mechanisms could end municipal scandal, and Progressive administrators hoped that management expertise could help curb the evils of industrialism. If there is a difference between then and now, it is that the Progressives had greater hopes for local reform.

In 1910, President Taft called on leading municipal reformers to serve on his commission on "efficiency and economy in government." The commission urged the Federal Government to adopt reforms made by municipal governments. It recommended that Congress create a central agency which would serve as the President's bookkeeper for Federal funds. The commission's report was ignored by Congress, but the idea had staying power. In 1916, partisans of the commission organized the Institute for Government Research to promote budget reform. The Institute helped draft the Budget and Accounting Act of 1921. The latter authorized the creation of an Executive Branch Budget Bureau, and, by requiring the President to present his own version of the annual budget, turned the Presidency into a primary force in the determination of the budget. The Act also created the General Accounting Office to serve as Congress's auditor of the budget and to prescribe accounting standards. The GAO's bureaucracy is far larger than the Executive Budget Bureau's, but the latter's ability to dispense monies has made it the most powerful Executive agency.[2]

If there is any task that is supposed to be an "official" and nondelegable executive function, it is the preparation of the budget. The liberal (and often illegal) *de facto* delegation of authority to contemporary contractors is seen in a new perspective when it is realized that, half a century ago, private citizens helped write the first Presidential budget. According to the Brookings official history, when the 1921 Act was passed, President Harding turned to the Institute for Government Research for the preparation of his budget. The delegation of authority to the Institute was sweeping:

> Institute staff had been conducting the detailed studies needed to put the budget into operation. When Charles G. Dawes came to Washington as the first Budget Director, he maintained his office for a time at the IGR, where he called on the staff for help in determining the form of the budget, installing proper accounting procedures, and working out many of the technical questions involved in inaugurating the

new system. Willoughby loaned Dawes a team of IGR technicians headed by Henry Seidemann. Dawes said later that their efforts determined "the whole form of the new budget, of all the general tables setting forth the condition of the treasury, financial operations in the past, and estimates for the future.

Seidemann was largely responsible for the presentation of the budgets in 1921 and again in 1922.[3]

The timing of the delegation anticipated another aspect of today's common practices. Now as then, private corporations direct the initial operations of Government agencies, marking their course before permanent official management is even recruited.

Of course, the successful corporate adviser does not thrive by ideas alone. Brookings succeeded because it was staffed by men experienced in bureaucratic politics, and supported by the cream of the new industrial elite. Among its supporters were Presidents Taft and Hoover, representatives of the Carnegie and Rockefeller fortunes, the presidents of Harvard, Yale, Wisconsin, and Johns Hopkins, and future Supreme Court Justice Felix Frankfurter. Private funds guaranteed Brookings' existence, but Rockefeller support had to be withdrawn when the robber-baron taint proved still too strong. Robert Brookings, a St. Louis businessman, became the Institution's primary fund raiser.

World War I mobilized business and Government in an unprecedented fashion as corporate officials flowed into Washington to organize wartime management. Robert Brookings, for example, chaired the "price-fixing" commission of the War Industries Board. Economist Wesley Mitchell came to Washington to head The Board's "price section." The war gave Mitchell, and American economists in general, their first opportunity to collect information about America's rapidly growing industrial base. Mitchell tried to gain official acceptance for a postwar data-gathering bureau. When the government turned him down, he found private support.

The National Bureau of Economic Research (NBER)

was founded in 1920 by economists who believed that economic progress depended on the systematic collection of economic information. The founders of NBER did not assume that the Federal Government would, or should, direct the economy. On the contrary, they believed that free enterprise was a sufficient guarantor of progress. If the national economic data they sought was of any use at all in the Twenties, it was to the planning departments of General Motors, DuPont, and other "national" economic institutions, not to the Federal Government.[4]

NBER economists set out to find certain yardsticks, the better to understand the economy. One such, for example, was the concept of Gross National Product (GNP). And their comparative studies of "business cycles" led to the official definitions of terms like "recession," "inflation," and "depression." [5]

The NBER, like Brookings, had a three-cornered relationship to government, whereby the Government accepted private advice from them as its own, but the private advisers relied on private profit for their subsistence. Still in the Twenties, for example, Secretary of Commerce Herbert Hoover called on Mitchell to direct major studies of unemployment. The Government placed its imprimatur on the studies, but the Carnegie Foundation paid the bill. President Hoover commissioned social scientists to assess American progress. Mitchell chaired a study called "Recent Social Trends," and the Social Science Research Council, another private nonprofit corporation, administered it. The Rockefeller Foundation paid the bill for the Council. President Roosevelt called on the Council to coordinate his Committee on Administrative Management. The Committee's work, a sequel to Brookings' Budget Bureau studies, recommended the consolidation of Federal agencies and the centralization of power in the Presidency. The Committee's work was reflected in Roosevelt's decision to create the Executive Office of the President in 1939, a crucial step on the road to the "Imperial Presidency." [6]

During the New Deal the NBER worked closely with the

Treasury Department and the Department of Commerce. NBER employees, and NBER employees temporarily ensconced in the official bureaucracy, helped transfer NBER's information-gathering techniques and categories to the Government. NBER economist Simon Kuznets has since won the Nobel Prize for his work in the creation of National Income Accounting. Wesley Mitchell's protégé Arthur Burns worked on the Bureau's famous business cycle studies. He now manages the business cycle as Chairman of the Federal Reserve Board.[7]

Brookings, for its part, has been the alter ego for the official Budget Bureau, serving as a breeding ground and retirement home for budget officials. Brookings' President Kermit Gordon directed the Bureau in the Sixties, as did Brookings economist Charles Schultze. When, in 1975, the Congress opened its own central budget office in an attempt to regain control over spending, it chose senior Brookings economist Alice Rivlin to head the staff.

Brookings, its President explains, operates in the "conviction that policy studies by an independent staff of highly qualified specialists—if they are timely, disinterested, and conducted in a setting close enough to the center of decision-making to enable the author to distinguish the attainable from the visionary—stand a good chance of turning the course of policy thinking in a desirable direction." (In the jargon of "independent" expertise, politics has been replaced by "policy" and politicians by "decision-makers.")[8]

Brookings is, of course, attuned to the political winds, or at least to the sentiments of the "decision-makers." While NBER's board has included labor representatives, Brookings has been filled by men from the leading corporations, financial houses, law firms, foundations, and universities. Sometimes they do mistake last year's attainable goal for the current "policy-making" climate. During the Nixon Administration, for example, Brookings welcomed former Democratic officials to its staff. As a result, the Nixon Administration viewed Brookings as a hotbed of sedition and placed its president on the "enemy" list. Watergate conspirator Colson even suggested that the Institution be firebombed. Four decades earlier, Brookings, similarly suffering from a cultural lag, had been a bastion of conservative opposition to the New Deal. New Dealer Hugh Johnson voiced a sentiment that was only slightly more moderate than that of the Nixonites: "That crowd," he declared, is "one of the most sanctimonious and pontifical rackets in the country." [9]

But, as noted earlier, the founders of the nonprofits had faith in the essential justness and wisdom of capitalism. They believed that, with a few modifications, progress could be "managed" in the "public interest." Progress "by agitation or class struggle," Wesley Mitchell told fellow statisticians in 1919, "is a jerky way of moving forward." The evils of industrial capitalism can be alleviated, he said, through "the acquisition of knowledge" toward "steadier and more certain" progress.[10]

Robert Brookings also hoped that management technique could be used to steer American capitalism away from socialism and communism. He argued that "little or no thought has been given to an analysis of capitalism as practiced, which would enable us to correct its injustices and thus bring about the more equitable distribution of wealth." Brookings believed that wealth could be more equitably distributed, not by a redistribution of wealth, but by the promotion of progress in which all could share: "The problem of continued improvement in the living condition of the workers is not a problem of the redistribution of present production, but a problem of *increased* production per capita." Big Business and Big Business management techniques were the chosen tools:

> "Big Business" is in the public interest because, by largely segregating management from ownership, it places management in the position of a trustee, whose duty it is to develop that efficiency which promotes maximum production per capita . . . because through the magnitude and diversity of

its operations it lends itself best to the adoption of labor-saving devices, mass standardized production, and other recognized elements of efficiency.

The country, Brookings argued, had to understand that conflict among the classes had to be replaced by cooperation. It would be necessary to create consensual national policies to "promote the greatest good of all." [11]

The men who founded the nonprofits had a very clear vision of the "public interest" which they were designed to serve. This vision is hardly the only reasonable definition of the "public interest," but if it appears so unexceptionable today, that is, at least in part, due to the successes of the nonprofits.

The role of Brookings and the NBER is essentially similar to that of hundreds of other contemporary nonprofit corporations that help the Government deal with industry, occupational groups, welfare, and social problems. While they may lobby Congress, the nonprofits usually work more intimately with the Executive Branch. They are private engines of information and influence that guide the Federal bureaucracy's efforts to expand into, regulate, or subsidize the private sector.[12]

The public knows little of the "voluntary" contributions of the nonprofits. The alleged energy crisis, for example, has revealed the startling degree to which the Government has delegated energy policy-making and administration to industry associations like the American Petroleum Institute, the American Gas Association, the Atomic Industrial Forum and the National Coal Association.[13]

The American Petroleum Institute, the oldest of the major oil associations, emerged from World War I's National Petroleum War Services Committee. The API has thousands of members from all segments of the oil industry, but the giant integrated oil companies have had a dominant role in its operation. The API was chartered to "afford a means of cooperation with the Government in all matters of national concern." While it produces much research of interest primarily to the industry, there is also, Professor Robert Engler has noted, "a continuing concern with fundamentals of national oil policy and the behavior of Government agencies in Washington and in state capitals." API executives and experts have long been an adjunct of official oil agencies. During the New Deal the organization worked closely with the Government in the administration of oil industry codes. During the New Deal and World War II, the Government created numerous industry advisory committees that provided further linkage between public administration and private expertise and interests. Nonprofits like the API helped staff such committees and provided them with basic sources of information and expertise.[14]

In the Seventies, the country discovered that the Government had abdicated its right to collect information. The natural gas shortage, for example, found the Government with no independent knowledge of the amount of gas available to the country. The Federal Power Commission and the Department of the Interior had effectively delegated to the American Gas Association the task of collecting estimates of gas reserves. In doing so, the Government had permitted the industry to withhold raw data from the public. As debate on gas supply raged, the nation's regulators lacked the basic information necessary to determine whether shortages were due to genuine declines in supply or to the industry's determination to withhold supply until the Federal Government decontrolled the price of natural gas.[15]

The experience of the energy crisis is hardly unique. Harried Government officials continually call on nonprofit expertise to supply them with information necessary to administer hurriedly mandated regulatory schemes. The Cost of Living Council, created to administer the wage-price freeze, called on Battelle Memorial Institute and the Stanford Research Institute to provide data and analysis on which industrial regulation could proceed and employed them on a paying contractual basis. With the onset of the contract revolution, of course, the Government can afford to hire profit-making corporations as well. The Cost of Living Council, for example, employed Arthur Andersen & Co., a Big Eight accounting firm, to structure the questionnaires it would submit to industry. The Department of Labor hired Arthur D. Little to work on standards for the industrial use of asbestos, even though (perhaps because) Arthur D. Little had private clientele that were interested in lenient standards. The Department of Transportation, as discussed elsewhere, hired firms that served the railroad industry to structure the information base for railroad regulation.[16]

The Government relies on nonprofit expertise to regulate nonprofit agencies as well as industrial firms. HEW, for example, reimburses hospitals that participate in Federal medical care programs on the condition that their operations are accredited by a private nonprofit hospital association.

Technicians of Growth

During World War II, Federal spending accounted for as much as 40 percent of the Gross National Product. The researchers and sponsors of the elite nonprofits were not socialists, but they feared that a postwar depression would occur if the Government were permitted to abandon its new role in the economy. The nonprofits heavily influenced post war legislation—the Employment Act of 1946 and the Marshall Plan—which stabilized the free enterprise economy.

The Employment Act of 1946 declared it to be Federal policy to maximize employment and obligates the Government to stimulate the economy to this end.

The Act created the Joint Economic Committee to provide Congressional oversight for the economy and a parallel Council of Economic Advisers to serve the President. These agencies have no formal authority to effect legislation or spending, but give the stamp of officialdom to the macro-economics developed by the nonprofits and universities. Staff members are frequently drawn from the nonprofits. Brookings' Edwin Nourse was the first Chairman of the Council of Economic Advisers, even though the Institution itself was a conservative opponent of Federal intervention in the economy.

The National Planning Association (NPA) filled the need for "nonpartisan" economic advice left by Brookings' opposition to the New Deal. NPA was founded during the Depression on the wave of popular support for national planning. Even amid the ruins of free enterprise, NPA's founders hoped to build national planning on the tradition of "management engineering." The NPA, like Brookings and NBER, is a private nonprofit corporation, governed by trustees who approve staff reports. The NPA's Board reflects its New Deal origins. Representatives of labor and agriculture sit alongside academics and executives. And it linked the economic theories of Keynes to postwar American policy. (Harvard economist Alvin Hansen, Keynes's primary American exponent, served as an NPA trustee.) [17]

The creation of the Committee for Economic Development (CED) marked an important turning point. This purely private corporation was created at the behest of a Government agency, as were many postwar contract research corporations. In 1933, the Department of Commerce called on sympathetic businessmen to advise the New Deal as members of the Business Advisory Council. During the war, the Department asked the Council to organize a new advisory body that would give the Department leverage in the battle for postwar planning. The arrangements resulted in the CED, which has long outgrown its initial purpose.[18]

The CED is composed of 200 "trustees" selected from the pinnacle of corporate and nonprofit management. CED trustees frequently serve as board members on other government-related nonprofits as well. The trustees empanel ad hoc groups of private experts to study selected issues of national concern. The work usually results in a series of scholarly monographs and a thin volume for public consumption. The summary volumes are given wide circulation. "I pay attention to them," reports the Director of the

Joint Economic Committee of Congress, "but they are not in a class with Brookings and do not have nearly the clout." What the reports may lack in scholarship they compensate for as concise statements of establishment consensus.[19]

CED's views parallel and often anticipate official thinking, for it has always been close to the official policymakers. Its first executive secretary was a Commerce Department official, on a paid leave of absence, and its first office space was located inside the Department of Commerce. The Business Advisory Council, from which the CED emerged, enjoyed an even more curious proximity to official status. In 1955, Congress was denied access to departmental information on the Council on the grounds that its activities were an internal matter of government. The cozy arrangements made it impossible to determine whether the Council was technically a public or a private organization. The Council subsequently declared its independence from Government, but its periodic retreats continue to attract high Government officials for convenient off-the-record discussions.

CED has been credited with providing the corporate support and compromise necessary to the passage of the Employment Act. As initially drafted, the Act was termed the "Full Employment Act." In order to assure passage, the word "full" was deleted. The change, according to Herbert Stein, a long-time CED economist who graduated to the Chairmanship of the Council of Economic Advisers, embodied the "central agreement upon which all postwar economic policy has been based. To keep unemployment low is accepted as a national goal of very high priority, but full employment is not accepted as an absolute goal overriding all others." [20]

While the nonprofits promoted postwar planning, the official planning agency was put out of business. The National Resources Planning Board, a New Deal agency headed by a former Brookings Board Chairman, recommended postwar actions far beyond those embodied in the Employment Act. The Board's final proposals, issued in

1943, urged that the Government guarantee "full employment" and "guarantee and, when necessary, underwrite . . . equal access to education for all, equal access to health and nutrition for all, and wholesome housing conditions for all." These ends were too much for Congress, which cut off the Board's funding. With the official agency dissolved, Congressional committees concerned with postwar planning retained the advice of Brookings and of Marion Folsom, a Kodak executive and CED member.

The nonprofits believed that further Federal spending would be required to stabilize the postwar economy. Debate centered on its purpose. Domestic welfare spending, it was feared, would compete with free enterprise. Foreign aid, on the other hand, would permit corporate expansion. During and after the war, the nonprofits prepared proposals for foreign aid that were drawn upon in the formulation of the Marshall Plan. When the Plan was announced, the primary source of controversy concerned the location of the agency that would administer foreign aid. Republicans hoped that it would be administered by an agency friendly to business interests, while Democrats pushed for the State Department. The Chairman of the Senate Foreign Relations Committee called on Brookings to study the matter and credited it with the compromise that was reached. The Economic Cooperation Administration was created within the State Department, and its first Administrator was businessman Paul Hoffman, a CED trustee.[21]

The Marshall Plan underwrote the foreign division of the contract bureaucracy. Aid funds employ contractors by the dozen to help plan and manage American spending and to provide "technical assistance" to foreign recipients. Private beneficiaries of aid moneys include nonprofits like Brookings, NPA, Stanford Research Institute, Battelle Memorial Institute, dozens of universities, numerous profit-making consulting corporations, and assorted organizations created primarily to receive foreign aid contracts. The postwar spending programs opened the floodgates for Federal contract dollars. The contract spending did not create fundamentally new arrangements among private corporations and public agencies, but it did provide Federal funds for the expansion of established relationships.[22]

The FCRCs

In his farewell address President Eisenhower warned of the "military-industrial complex," whereas, as Army Chief of Staff, he had encouraged its development. (In a 1946 memo General Eisenhower urged the military to continue its wartime practice of contracting civilian expertise to guarantee the "close integration of civilian talent with military plans and developments." [23]

When the military continued to fund university and corporate administered laboratories after the war, the Office of Naval Research became the sponsor of a wide variety of projects. It was the RAND Corporation, however, that captured the spirit of the new age.[24]

RAND

While RAND now calls itself an "independent nonprofit corporation," it was conceived as a joint venture of the Air Force and the aerospace industry. Following the war, Arthur Raymond and Franklin Collbohm, two engineers who had worked in the military's wartime Office of Scientific Research and Development, sought to continue their wartime work. The Air Force was still a ward of the Army, but its leaders perceived that the development of aerospace technology could lead to a powerful and independent service. Collbohm and Raymond found a powerful and eager patron in General "Hap" Arnold. In late 1945, Arnold met with Donald Douglas and told the executive that the Air Force was willing to award Douglas a multimillion-dollar contract to the Douglas Aircraft Corporation for the study of German rocketry. Douglas accepted the contract and established "Project RAND." [25]

Both the Government and industry understood that the contracting out of work would alter the distribution of power in the nascent defense complex. The Air Force bureaucracy was opposed to the delegation of vital planning work. Curtis LeMay, the champion of technology appointed by Arnold to oversee the RAND contract, was dispatched to quell an incipient rebellion. As RAND biographer Bruce Smith recounts:

> There was a good deal of opposition to the Douglas proposal expressed at the meeting, as expected. Particularly sharp opposition came from the delegation of material and procurement officers from Wright Field. They objected that what was being proposed was civilian assistance in military planning. They also expressed opposition to bringing the Air Force planning process into the research and development area. . . . The Wright Field delegation proposed instead a tightly controlled program telling the contractor what it should do and specifying in rigid detail [a research program]. . . . Fortunately for the future of Project RAND, General LeMay exercised the prerogatives of his office and overruled these objections. He pointed out that the purpose of the project was not to state a requirement and tell the contractor what to do. Rather, the contractor was to perform long-range research that might form the basis for a future military requirement.[26]

It was hoped that awarding the contract to an established corporation would shelter RAND from bureaucratic sniping. Donald Douglas, for his part, saw in the contract future profits, not a sacrifice of Douglas' interests. At its inception, then, the Project RAND contract represented a delicate and deliberate balance of interests—a balance that proved untenable when it failed to meet industry expectations.

Douglas began to feel that the RAND contract hurt its competitive position against other airframe manufacturers, but the tension was temporarily alleviated when certain of the firm's competitors were included in a RAND oversight board. Ultimately, however, the solution proved unsatisfactory, and Collbohm asked Douglas to let him take the remainder of the $10 million contract elsewhere. Douglas argued that he could not lawfully terminate Douglas' role in mid-contract.

To gain its independence, RAND needed to assure the Air Force that the contract would not collapse if it left Douglas. To achieve the proposed change, RAND needed the same two things that had made the early nonprofits possible. "One was a board of trustees; the other was working capital," recalled RAND Vice President J. R. Goldstein. "It was hard to get one without the other and relatively easy to get one with the other." Collbohm was able to acquire both with the help of Rowen Gaither, a San Francisco lawyer. Gaither, the scion of an old American family, had attended Harvard Law School and served as business manager of the MIT Radiation Laboratory during World War II. The Radiation Laboratory bred a host of men who became leading "administrators of science," and Gaither's acquaintance with them proved helpful.[27]

Help was obtained from the Ford family, which was transforming its small family foundation into the major national resource that the Ford Foundation has become. The RAND Board of Trustees was chosen from the ranks of the same establishment that sits on other nonprofit boards. As Collbohm told Congress, RAND set out to select board members "one third from industry, one third from the academic field, and one third which we call the public interest, like foundation presidents, and so on." The Gaither law firm serves as RAND's counsel, and helped in the creation of the Air Force's further nonprofits, including SDC, ANSER, Mitre, and Aerospace. Gaither's ability to assist nonprofits was measurably enhanced by his selection as Chairman of the Board of the Ford Foundation.[28]

RAND did not, as is often implied, propound heretical military policies. It accepted the "technology race" as given and influenced policy only by channeling technology spending in new and costly directions.

The late Mendel Rivers, Congressional advocate of unlimited arms spending, attributed the credo of the "technology race" to RAND sponsor "Hap" Arnold. "Nobody, but nobody," paraphrased Rivers, "can take credit for or stop the state of the art. It is something that will move, and it just pours out of the head of people and it is unconscious and it will go ahead and those who get on the saddle can, and those who can't leave." [29]

RAND acquired fame as a source of "policy analysis," and "systems analysis" is frequently cited as RAND's contribution to the modern discipline of "policy research." We have already considered the corporate origins of systems analysis and of the "planning-programming-budgeting system" (PPB) which RAND designed to aid defense policy-making. The limits of systems analysis are highlighted by the RAND "basing study" of the very project continually used by RAND and its publicists as an example of highly successful analysis.

In 1951, the Air Force asked RAND economist Charles Hitch to study the most efficient means of spending money on European bases. Hitch, the story goes, turned the apparently routine study over to young analysts Albert Wohlstetter and Henry Rowen. Wohlstetter mulled the problem over, then considered it in the context of the Russian-American "system." Bases located simply with a concern for efficiency, Wohlstetter suggested, might be a ready target for surprise attack. The truly efficient arrangement, he concluded, would be a design that could withstand Russian "first strike" and then provide the base for an American "second strike" response. RAND's promoters considered this "systems analysis" of base location a *tour de force*.[30]

Yet the basing study was essentially only a traditional efficiency analysis, and RAND's assumptions were hardly as revolutionary as its promoters imply. In accepting the possibility of Russian attack, RAND merely gave expert credence to hard-line cold war assumptions about Russian motivation. Moreover, the basing study folklore oddly fails to note the derivative nature of the assumption. Pearl Harbor was fresh in the military mind, and it did not require genius to consider the possibility of surprise attack. General Arnold himself had suggested such a scenario for World War III. On VE Day, Arnold proclaimed that

America would be the first target of the next war and argued that it must guard against surprise attack by learning how to strike back with "three-thousand-miles-per-hour robot atom bombs launched from space ships." [31]

The story not only reveals the limited intellectual contributions of systems analysis but places success in its political context. Anyone can produce a study, but only those with privileged access are likely to know how and where to sell it.

As RAND Trustee Edwin Huddleson, Jr., explains, "There are a dozen Air Forces. . . . If you're knowledgeable and competent there are bound to be people who agree with you." Communication with decision-makers is essential, for the delivery of a printed report alone does not eliminate the possibility that "no one has the time to read it and make it usable." [32]

RAND spent months selling its work to Air Force officials and gave over ninety briefings throughout the bureaucracy. "You have to get invited to those briefings," notes RAND Vice President J. R. Goldstein. "You don't create large changes without an awful lot of arm-waving. . . . You just have to go over everything." The systems analyst must not only possess a fundamentally acceptable political viewpoint, but must be skilled in bureaucratic politicking. The nonprofit may tell the public that, because it works for official government, it works wholly in the public interest, but the expert knows that the Government is not monolithic and that there are many competing official views of the public interest. The successful expert must have sufficient access to the bureaucracy to drum up support for his views or to build alliances for views he is commissioned to represent. In its prime, if not today, RAND had greater and freer access to the Air Force bureaucracy than most Air Force officials and, as long as it did not question basic assumptions, it was assured of some form of support. The basing study also illustrates what precautions RAND took. RAND, records Bruce Smith, was careful not to "end run" the Air Force. It sold its ideas hard within the Air Force, but did not bring its recommendations to central defense

authorities or to competing services. The Air Force paid
RAND, and, explains Goldstein, RAND tries to maintain a
"lawyer-client" relationship with its prime source of support. The RAND–Air Force relationship changed in the
Sixties when RAND was closely associated with the office
of the Secretary of Defense. In supporting the Secretary,
RAND actively threatened particular Air Force expenditures. The Air Force termed RAND's dual role a "conflict
of interest," and RAND agreed to change its practices.
While such conflicts are well understood by bureaucrats
and consultants, they are glossed over in the myth of the
independent nonprofit.[33] The kernel of insight in the basing
study blossomed into a "theory" that helped win a Presidential election and allocated billions of dollars to defense
spending.

The concept of "second strike" became the touchstone
for deterrence theory, the alternative to "massive retaliation." The theory, which provided the official rationale for
nuclear arms spending, was developed by a handful of men,
most of whom were civilians and affiliated with RAND.[34]

While RAND may present itself to the public as an
organization without profit motives, it tells industry that its
work is highly compatible with profit motives.

In 1960, for example, an industry-Government conference was convened to discuss aerospace planning. RAND's
Gene H. Fisher told the corporation why they should have
their own planning units. It might, he hypothesized, be
argued that "everybody nowadays understands the concept
of strategic deterrence." Not so. "Careful examination of
the stability of the 'delicate balance of terror' would yield
interesting and often somewhat subtle results." Many of
these results "have future weapons systems hardware implications that long-range corporate planning activities can ill
afford to ignore, especially during the 1960s, when it will be
all the more important to explore the numerous subtleties of
deterrent situations." Hughes Aircraft's Harold Linstone
seconded Fisher's argument. Linstone explained that a
Hughes study, "Mirage 70," had projected a policy of

military flexibility for the Sixties and had recommended that the company schedule guerrilla warfare into its business future—"a potential gain of at least one year in company lead time was possible." [35]

RAND was as devoted to the technology of deterrence as to the theory and helped convince the Air Force that it was technically feasible to build a nuclear warhead that could be borne by a missile. The deterrence theorists also argued that highly sophisticated communications networks were needed to control American response to provocation and to assure the enemy of the credibility of our capability. This "need" justified billions of dollars in "command and control" technology. The role of Mitre, another nonprofit, in the stimulation of command and control spending is discussed later in this chapter.[36]

Herbert York, who served as Director of Defense Research and Engineering under Presidents Eisenhower and Kennedy, was one scientist-administrator who concluded that the technological enthusiasm of his peers was a prime cause of the arms race. In the Fifties, he wrote:

> The breakthrough, or the "quantum jump," became not only the expected norm, but also the desideratum. . . . Many weapons scientists and engineers also believed that such a situation was normal and desirable. They virtually promised their military and Congressional supporters that the future would be as glorious as the present, only more so. Thus we have Herman Kahn in his book *On Thermonuclear Warfare*, written in 1959 when the rate of breakthroughs still seemed to be rising, making a whole set of extrapolations which turned out to be false. . . . Every one of these errors in prediction arose out of the twin false assumptions that the immediate past was typical and that the technological future could be predicted by simple extrapolation. . . . Unfortunately, many technologists as well as laymen don't realize this, and they are repeatedly fooled by the apparent sophistication of efforts like Kahn's 1959 predictions.[37]

The Role of Rowen Gaither

When the 1957 launch of Sputnik intensified the cold war, President Eisenhower empaneled a group of citizens to study the crisis in national security. It was chaired by Rowen Gaither, who, by 1957, was Board Chairman of both RAND and the Ford Foundation. Gaither worked with the cream of the consulting establishment. Fellow panel members included McKinsey's John Corson, Brookings' Robert Calkins, and present and future consulting-firm board members James Perkins (IDA and RAND), William Webster (RAND, Mitre, Arthur D. Little), Hector Skifter (RAC Board Chairman), and Robert Sprague (Mitre Board Chairman.) The Institute for Defense Analyses, RAND, and McKinsey provided staff support.[38]

The Gaither panel was given unique access to official information and reported directly to the President and the National Security Council. Its creation was not publicly announced, and information on its work was publicized only through leaks. Eventually, political scientist Morton Halperin, currently at Brookings, pieced the leaks together in a monograph on the Commission.

The Gaither panel was supposed to consider a Federal Civil Defense Agency recommendation that $40 billion be spent for fallout shelters. Instead, it turned to a broad analysis of defense. It concluded that the Eisenhower Administration grossly underestimated the Russian threat and was not spending enough to meet it. Influenced considerably by a classified Wohlstetter report, the Commission discovered the "missile gap." The briefing to the President, records Halperin, "dwelt at length on the problem of maintaining an effective second-strike force. . . . What must deter the Russians was not the force which the United States had, but the force which was capable of surviving an all-out Russian attack. . . . the planes of America's strategic forces were exposed and concentrated in a way that made it extremely unlikely that they could survive a nuclear attack. The committee warned that by the early 1960s, when Russia had an operational ICBM, she would be capable of destroying the American retaliatory force." The United States, argued the Commission, should spend enough to develop an "invulnerable second-strike force." It was not enough to have weaponry sufficient to "kill" Russia once over.

Eisenhower was not moved by the Commission. In 1953, he had expressed the fear that defense spending might become "an unbearable security burden leading to economic disaster. . . . Communist guns in this sense have been aiming at the economic target no less than the military target." The Gaither panel was no help. "You fellows," the President was said to have told the panel, "are working on the wrong problem. Why don't you help me with some of the disarmament measures I am interested in? I can't get any help from the Government agencies which should be helping me." [39]

The Gaither conclusions, although kept secret, fueled the 1960 election. Senator Jackson turned a Senate subcommittee into a mouthpiece for Gaither panelists, Robert Sprague argued that even conservative Republican businessmen should favor defense spending, McKinsey's John Corson called for businessmen to come to the aid of the cold war cause, and RAND studies were placed in the hearing record. In a 1959 article for *Foreign Affairs*, RAND's Wohlstetter gave the elite public a full-blown definition of deterrence theory. The article, entitled "The Delicate Balance of Terror," explained that deterrence required an immense and multipurpose military force.[40]

Senators Kennedy and Johnson were among the most vociferous Democratic critics of Eisenhower defense spending. Kennedy, in particular, had lamented the decline of conventional forces. In his 1960 campaign, Kennedy made a major issue of Republican responsibility for an alleged "missile gap" and promised to revive the defense budget.

President-elect Kennedy named Ford Motor President Robert McNamara to the position of Secretary of Defense. McNamara in turn appointed RAND employees to high official positions. Shortly after the inauguration, McNamara reported to Kennedy that Eisenhower frugality had left the Defense Department in a sorry state. The lines of analysis borrowed heavily from the deterrence theorists.

The Defense Department, McNamara wrote, possessed "(1) a strategy of massive nuclear retaliation as the answer to all military and political aggression, a strategy believed by few of our friends and none of our enemies and resulting in serious weakness in our conventional forces; (2) a financial ceiling on national security, making military strategy the stepchild of a predetermined budget; (3) a strategic nuclear force vulnerable to surprise missile attack, a non-nuclear force weak in combat-ready divisions."

These conclusions were the predicate for an abrupt increase in defense spending. As Presidential adviser Theodore Sorensen boasted, "in three years Kennedy's buildup of the most powerful military force in human history—the largest and swiftest buildup in this country's peacetime history, at a cost of some $17 billion in additional appropriations—provided him, as he put it, with a versatile arsenal ranging from the most massive deterrences to the most subtle influences." [41]

For his part, RAND Vice President Goldstein proudly noted in the early Sixties: "To the growing extent that informed public opinion in this country appreciates that there are deficiencies in our strategic posture which will require a lot of budget to fix, I think the writings and speeches of the RAND people have played a major role." RAND's analyses, however, were much more valuable as propaganda than as science. The "missile gap" never materialized. William Kauffman, head of RAND's social science department in the early Sixties, provided a convenient rationalization for the failure of prediction. "Exactly why the gap did not materialize," he wrote in an analysis of McNamara's "strategy," "remains something of a mystery. . . . Crying wolf for once had a salutary effect . . . the greater part of the explanation lies with what the Soviets had not done. In a word, they had not built as many ICBMs as they were thought capable of doing. Everyone has reason to be thankful." [42]

The lesson the experts learned was that it paid to cry wolf. The McNamara systems analysts conjured up the specter of another missile gap to justify further missile spending. The second gap did not materialize either, and at the end of the decade, RAND analysts and defense officials offered similar rationalizations.[43]

The deterrence theorists not only brought questionable assumptions to their systems analyses but promoted defense spending without giving critical thought to its effect on the economy. As theorist Bernard Brodie noted in 1959, "few professional economists" doubt that the defense budget could be substantially increased. To support this point, he cited studies by the Committee for Economic Development and the National Planning Association. The 1958 CED statement on defense spending illustrates the unequivocal professional support for the growth of the defense complex. "We see," stated the report, "no need to be apprehensive about whether or not the American economy can stand the strain of this [1959] or even a considerably larger budget. The risk that defense spending of from 10 to 15 percent of the GNP, or if necessary even more, will ruin the American way of life is slight indeed. It is even less likely that there is some magic number that, if exceeded, would bring economic disaster." The Vietnam defense budget, a principal source of current economic ills, did not exceed the "safe" percentages. The CED, to be sure, did not conclude that increased spending was necessary. This task was left to another spokesman of the expert establishment—the Chairman of the CED, who also happened to be the Ford Foundation Vice Chairman, Rowen Gaither.[44]

Mitre

Mitre, a private not-for-profit corporation created in 1958 to help the Air Force promote and manage technology, was born at the juncture of the cold war and the computer. Its septic headquarters in suburban Boston and Washington house close to 1,000 members of the nation's "technical elite." Mitre's annual income of close to $50 million is quite large for a professional services organization. It is only a fraction of the millions spent on private contractors under

Mitre's direction. Its technical work force is composed primarily of electrical engineers, mathematicians, and physicists. Mitre now works for a wide variety of defense and civilian agencies, but its prime source of income remains the Air Force. It is classed by the government as a "Federal Contract Research Center." As discussed in Chapter I, this appellation has been applied to nonprofit corporations created to contract with particular governmental agencies. The Atomic Energy Commission, the Defense Department, and NASA have been the primary supporters of the FCRCs. The Office of Education has funded two dozen or so small nonprofits, and the National Science Foundation supports several FCRCs engaged in "basic research."

In 1951, the Air Force awarded MIT a contract to study American defense against nuclear attack. In 1952, a study group of private experts concluded that the United States should construct radar and communications networks to provide warning against such attack.[45] The design of the North American Air Defense Network was contracted out to Lincoln Laboratory, a nonprofit managed by MIT. The work proceeded rapidly, and by the end of the decade acronyms like the "DEW (Distant Early Warning) Line" were part of every schoolchild's cold war lexicon.

In 1958, the Air Force and MIT agreed that universities should not acquire permanent responsibility for America's air defense, and Mitre was created to take the job over. In early 1959, 500 Lincoln employees moved into the new Mitre buildings in Bedford, Massachusetts. Mitre was located next door to the headquarters of the Air Force's Electronics Systems Division (ESD), and much subsequent electronics spending became joint ventures of public agency and private corporation.

The air defense network and the missile were the major Department of the Air Force programs on which contractors were put to work. While Lincoln-Mitre managed the former, the Aerospace Corporation was created for the latter.

In the early Fifties, a committee of private experts told

the Air Force that the Intercontinental Ballistic Missile was as feasible as it was necessary. The committee, headed by John Von Neumann, showed that it was possible to design a nuclear warhead capable of being carried by the missile. A parallel recommendation was offered by RAND. The Air Force decided to hire private contractors to build the missile, and the management work was assigned to two young engineers who had staffed the committee. In 1954, the Ramo-Wooldridge management contract began with ten employees. By 1957, the Ramo-Wooldridge Corporation was grossing over $50 million.

The initial Air Force contract with Ramo-Wooldridge included the so-called "hardware ban," a clause that precluded the managers from bidding for hardware contracts that they planned or managed. The Ramo-Wooldridge Corporation, however, merged with a manufacturing company and became the TRW Corporation. Just as the industry had pressured Douglas Aircraft to divest itself of the RAND contract, TRW was urged to divest itself of its management contract. Congress held hearings and was told (and told itself) that the missile program was a technical wonder, but that TRW was guilty of excess profit-taking. In 1960, the Aerospace Corporation was created to take the missile management contract from TRW. The new corporation also followed the RAND pattern and immediately adopted the image of the "independent nonprofit" organization.[46]

HOW THE PUBLIC INTEREST
IS DEFINED

"Aerospace," the major government-sponsored study of nonprofits' records, "was formed in June 1960 to serve the public interest through providing leadership in the advancement of science and technology for the United States Government." While the Air Force retained official responsibility for missile production, *de facto* authority passed to

Aerospace. As one student of weapons management summed up, "acting as the Air Force's technical staff in the highly technical development effort . . . it [Aerospace] obviously gained substantial influence over dollar allocations and contractor selection."[47] Aerospace's relationship to the Air Force Systems Command (AFSC) parallels Mitre's relationship to the Air Force's Electronics System Division. The AFSC has general responsibility for major aerospace programs.

The FCRCs may well have been created in violation of the Government Corporation Control Act. Passed in 1945, the Act prohibits the creation of Government corporations without the approval of Congress. As administrative scholar Harold Seidman comments:

> In many respects the not-for-profit corporations are indistinguishable from early Government corporations chartered under state law. Seemingly, the Government Corporation Control Act provision that "no corporation shall be created, organized, or acquired by any officer or agency of the Federal Government . . . for the purpose of acting as an agency or instrumentality of the United States, except by or pursuant to an Act of Congress specifically authorizing such action" would apply to not-for-profit corporations.

Seidman notes that when, in 1962, the House Government Operations Committee held the first hearings on the proliferation of the FCRCs, Committee counsel questioned the applicability of the 1945 Act but, as Seidman notes, "did not press his question." The Comptroller General, Seidman adds, "has been discreetly silent on the subject." [48]

The Comptroller General did question the legality of the delegation of management implicit in the modern "systems management" contract. A 1960 General Accounting Office document concluded that there was no legal basis for this degree and kind of delegation. The GAO's opinion was lost on Congress. By 1960, contracting out was a *fait accompli*. In 1962, a special Presidential panel on contracting out concluded that the country, through benign neglect, had begged the profound legal and philosophical questions that contracting raised. "No Congressman," records Don Price, "chose during the Fifties to make political capital out of an investigation of the interlocking structure of corporate and Government interests in the field of research and development." [49]

Conflict of Interest

Mitre was shaped by the handful of men who also founded the other Air Force contract research centers—Systems Development Corporation, Lincoln Laboratory, RAND, Aerospace, and ANSER. The legal work for Mitre's incorporation was done by Rowen Gaither. When Gaither died in 1961, his protégé Ed Huddleson, now a senior partner in Gaither's San Francisco law firm, donned the mantle of legal godfather for nonprofits. Huddleson has served on the boards of RAND, SDC, Mitre and Aerospace, and his firm has long been RAND's counsel.

William Golden, an investor who served for many years as trustee of Mitre and SDC, explains that the management of the nonprofits was carefully placed in the hands of interlocking boards of trustees, but Huddleson dismisses the idea. Mitre's board (drawn from the organizations at work on Air Defense—MIT, RAND, SDC) is, he says, the only instance of interlock by design. Huddleson, however, defines design narrowly. He is a member of the Aerospace Board, not by design, but because lawyer friend "Ros Gilpatric called me up and asked me to be on the board." [50]

The governing boards represent a very limited range of interests. These interests were almost completely covered, for example, by the three incorporators of Aerospace. One was a Wall Street lawyer and former defense official whose clients included Boeing and General Dynamics, a second was a research administrator in an organization that relied on contracts, and a third was a career air industry executive.

The link between nonprofits and industry is as solid at the bottom as at the top. "A near replica of Government,"

Aerospace told Congress in 1972, "was neither desired nor created." Eighty percent of Aerospace's management and technical staff comes from industry, 10 percent from recent college graduates, and only 10 percent from other sources. Those who leave return to industry, and "the sentiment is strong for industry among present employees." [51]

Nonprofits had been a pronounced presence on Mitre's board, but the board chairman has consistently gone to corporations that rely on defense electronics spending. Two chairmen, James Killian and Lloyd Brace, served as directors of AT & T while serving Mitre, even as AT & T's Western Electric subsidiary was a major beneficiary of spending overseen by Mitre.

Robert Sprague's career best illustrates how narrow a conception of conflict of interest holds sway. In 1953, Sprague was nominated by President Eisenhower as an Assistant Secretary of the Air Force. The nominee for Defense Secretary was General Motors' Charles Wilson. Wilson's equation of the good of the nation with the good of General Motors led the Administration to require its appointees to divest themselves of holdings in defense-related corporations. Wilson did so before taking office. Sprague declined to give up his interests in the Sprague Electric Corporation, then a small manufacturer of electrical components. Sprague was not appointed to the Air Force position, but, as a private citizen, he served for years as an important adviser on air defense spending and as a trustee-chairman of Mitre. There was probably no political appointee whose influence on the Department outlasted Sprague's, but Sprague's activities were never subject to Congressional approval, and his private interests in a defense-dependent corporation were never subjected to public scrutiny.

There are no effective conflict of interest "rules" for the selection and behavior of trustees. If trustees had to be disinterested in defense spending, hardly any present trustee could retain his position. Thus Mitre, for example, may oversee the work of Western Electric, and Western

Electric may inevitably buy parts from Sprague Electric, but Mitre is not being construed to be directly overseeing the work of Sprague Electric, and Robert Sprague can be a Mitre trustee. And AT & T's Western Electric subsidiary is a major ABM contractor, and Mitre oversees Western Electric's work, yet Mitre Board Chairmen James Killian and Lloyd Brace simultaneously serve on the board of AT & T. Because AT & T is so big and powerful, it seems, no conflict is seen in this dual service. "If," explains Ed Huddleson, "there are going to be these major communications systems, these organizations [AT & T] will get their due regardless of Mitre's role. . . . These systems exist because of the way the world exists." But the world does not just "exist." People cause it to exist.[52]

Trustee William Golden gives some hint of the way things work. Golden was certain that the Mitre–AT & T interlock was no cause for alarm, because "First, Lloyd Brace is an honorable man. Second, because Lloyd Brace doesn't have the slightest idea of what he is doing—he's not a man of technical knowledge, he never got involved in technical things." What, Golden was asked, of scientist James Killian? "Killian," granted Golden, "would know what is going on." But "I know James Killian as well as I know Lloyd Brace. He is also an honorable man. I would think that an honorable man would be able to keep out of conflicts which would work to the advantage of each of the companies. The man has to be honorable. I grant you that there are circumstances from which AT & T could benefit if they knew what Mitre might recommend," but apparently the "minitude" of Mitre's influence is nothing when compared with the "magnitude" of AT & T. Golden, eager to be more than a character witness, tried to explain that "it is important to have a well-connected board of trustees. Killian's being on the board has helped Mitre get business." Was "good business" for Mitre good for AT & T and for the country? Killian, Golden answered, "is an honorable man." Golden also saw no problem in Mitre's dealings with Brace's Boston Bank, from which Mitre's mortgage came.

"Where else would you go? I realize that the bank got the business, and this certainly appears to be a conflict of interest, but where else would Mitre go?" [53]

Nonprofit trustees are as candid as the officials of any other group of consulting firms. They are proud of their creations and feel no need to defend them. "Trusteeship," explains Huddleson, "is a public interest outlet for men and women who otherwise would be contributing time to organizations like the opera or the Boy Scouts or a museum or a children's hospital. You want to do it with competent guys that can work effectively. It is not a citizen participation activity." [54]

Not that the creators of the nonprofits do not have their own vision of integrity, but it is a fact that many, if not most trustees have a strong private interest in corporations (profit-making and nonprofit) that are dependent on the Government dollar, and also that the possibility always exists that the actions of particular trustees may directly benefit particular corporations with which they are also affiliated. The existing conventions of governance call the first evil a virtue and deny the possibility of the second. Both positions are contrary to our legal, as well as moral, tradition.[55]

Conflict of interest laws exist at every level of government to guarantee that public servants embody the "appearance of integrity," above and beyond its substance. As the Supreme Court has stated, the Federal conflict statutes are

directed not only at dishonor, but also at conduct that tempts dishonor. This broad proscription embodies a recognition of the fact that an impairment of impartial judgment can occur in even the most well-meaning men when their personal economic interests are affected by the business they transact on behalf of the Government. To this extent, therefore, the statute is more concerned with what might have happened in a given situation than what actually happened. It attempts to prevent honest Government agents from succumbing to temptation by making it illegal for them to enter into relationships which are fraught with temptation.[56]

The court has made clear that conflict law is not a product of the scholastic mind but is to be applied to the world as it is. Conflict law recognizes the fact that indirect influences may be as damaging as more formally direct influences.

> To limit the application of the statute to Government agents who participate only in the final formation of a contract would permit those who have a conflict of interest to engage in the preliminary, but often crucial, stages of the transaction, and then to insulate themselves from prosecution under Section 434 by withdrawing from the negotiations at the final, and often perfunctory, stage of the proceedings.[57]

The Court has commented with even greater precision on the kind of relationship involved in the Government-industry complex. It has explained that private actions which appear to be consistent with Government interests are no more acceptable than private actions that are clearly inconsistent. The "more evidence an agent gives of agreement with the policies of the Administration, the more responsibility he is likely to be given, and in case of a conflict of interest, the greater is the possible injury to government." Governmental acquiescence in the *de facto* delegation of authority will not excuse:

> The prohibition was therefore designed to protect the United States, as a Government, from the mistakes, as well as the connivances, of its own officers and agents. It is not surprising therefore that we have consistently held that no Government agent can properly claim exemption from a conflict-of-interest statute simply because his superiors did not discern the conflict.[58]

The principle is fundamental, and cannot be voided by the assertions of consultants or officials, that the advisers are honorable men.

The arrangements by which the nonprofits are governed clearly violate the spirit of the law. Yet trustees do not violate its letter. The nonprofits are purely private organizations, in the technical legal sense, and their trustees are exempt from laws governing public service. The arrangement is a brilliant legal evasion at the center of the management innovation that is the Government-industry complex.

Public Accounting for Mitre

The defense contract research centers allegedly "operate in a goldfish bowl." The nonprofits, boasted Mitre's chief management scientist, "have no secrets," they have been reviewed by the staffs of Congressional committees, by the General Accounting Office, by ad hoc groups set up by the Defense Department, by the latter's internal audit agencies, and by the Internal Revenue Service. If the nonprofits have indeed been "studied to death," few studies are public, and the ones that are are pabulum. "What," asked Ed Roberts, an MIT expert on research management, "has Mitre got written about them that's meaningful?" [59]

The governors of Mitre, and other nonprofits, may know how, and how well nonprofits work. They are vague about such things in public, and they have ensured that hard information is made available only to those who stand to benefit directly from defense spending. Mitre excels in the production of public annual reports, house organs, and brochures, but these materials can be considered informative only by reference to the greater obscurity in which comparable profit-making contractors are permitted to operate.[60]

Qualitative evaluations of the Federal Contract Research Centers are performed only by the agencies that rely on them and by "independent" review panels that replicate the nonprofit boards of trustees. A 1966 "Board of Visitors" study is the primary publicly available "independent" analysis of the Air Force's relationship with Mitre. Who were the "visitors"? They were men who worked down the block in the aerospace industry.

A 1972 Aerospace "independent" evaluation by aerospace industry executives offered Congress this nugget: "Since Aerospace necessarily gets deeply involved in the affairs of these companies, one need not fear any undue bias toward Aerospace by these gentlemen." Congress, which often gives the nonprofits opportunity to place unquestioned justifications of their existence in the public record, accepted the logic.

Mitre's board of trustees, Congress was told, "keeps its own books on the Corporation's performance, as it were." Congress played the sphinx to this statement, but inquiry turned up no Mitre official who knew of such books. Trustee Golden, for example, could amplify on the Congressional testimony only by explaining: "I have been a member of the Board of Trustees of Mitre for fourteen years, and it is my impression that Mitre is good." Could he document this? No. As a businessman, he lacked technical expertise, but he had confidence in Mitre's management. Golden could not single out specific examples of Mitre's work for commendation.[61]

In the summer of 1970, President Nixon's "Blue Ribbon Panel" on the Defense Department concluded that "there is no adequate mechanism to evaluate the performance of the numerous [defense] research groups. The dissipation of research, exploratory development, and management and support categories on R & D funds on unproductive work in contractor and in-house laboratories . . . occurs all too often." [62] The Defense Department met the charges with a study of the nonprofits.

It was performed by defense employees, who assumed that the work performed by the nonprofits should continue, and continue to be done on contract. The conclusion was that the close relation between nonprofits like Mitre and the military should be maintained.

The study team found scarcely any evidence of a wasted dollar. The twelve-page appendix on Mitre catalogued its functions and concluded that it performed "efficiently and economically." [63]

The General Accounting Office has confined itself to financial audits for the nonprofits. Its lone effort to study the substance of nonprofit research ended in limbo. In 1971,

GAO employees proposed to study a series of Mitre's projects to "obtain an insight as to the quality of Mitre's work performance through ascertaining the degree of customer satisfaction, accomplishment of project goals, and the ultimate use of the project." A consulting firm could have parlayed the idea into years of work. The GAO was incapable of self-deception. It found the relationship between Mitre and the Air Force's Electronics Systems Division to be closer than that normally present between Government and contractor. When the relationship approaches "joint project management," it declared, "customer satisfaction" is not a reliable measure of contractor performance. The GAO lacked the expertise to offer any other measures. It shelved the project, issuing no final report.[64]

Congress has consistently been less than critical of complicated defense spending projects. Its periodic concern for the nonprofits has become a ritual without substance. The form of the ritual was established in the early Sixties, when Congressmen, for the first but not the last time, were amazed to discover that "nonprofits" which look like private profit-making corporations are doing "public" work. Congress managed to ignore the effects of contracting on government and concluded that, if there is anything wrong with the nonprofits, it is the threat they pose to profit-making contractors.

For some time Congressional inquiry was fixated on the high finances of the nonprofits. Congress discovered that the nonprofits not only paid attractive salaries but also used contract money to seek new business. The Aerospace Corporation provided a field day for Congress, for its executives happily testified to their entrepreneurial ambitions. In the early Sixties, Aerospace executives received considerably more than Government executives, and Aerospace had a $250,000 contract with a public relations firm.

Congress placed a ceiling on nonprofit salaries, but has not successfully prevented the abuse of fees paid to nonprofits. In lieu of profits, the nonprofits receive an award that is to be used as a financial reserve as income from contracts varies. The fee is calculated as a percentage of contract award and is also to pay for self-generated research. (The research provision is to permit the attraction of talented employees and is comparable to the Independent Research and Development awards received by profit-making defense contractors.) Aerospace was also a leader in the abuse of the fee. A General Accounting Office study found that in its first five years, Aerospace spent only $411,000 of $16 million in fees on independent research. A large sum was spent on the acquisition of new facilities. Congressional criticism caused the Defense Department to change its rules on the fee. A "needs" policy was adopted, by which the fee was keyed to the Department's judgment of the nonprofits' "need." In effect, the policy should have made it impossible to question fees. As a GAO study found, the Department could not document the basis on which needs were determined. In 1969 and 1971, the GAO reported the continual abuse of the fee, citing the Department's failure to follow its own regulations. By 1969, the nonprofits were, illegally, using the fee to market themselves to civilian agencies.[65]

Command and Control

By 1964, Mitre's reputation exceeded public documentation of its work. SAGE (a "command and control" system using computers to communicate information) was completed with much fanfare and gave rise to several mythical management products that permitted Mitre to prosper well beyond its original "mission." As the "systems manager" for SAGE, Mitre had command and control credentials that opened the door to an inexhaustible bureaucratic market.

The *Armed Forces Journal* offered readers a sample of the variety of startling deficiencies that require the attention of the command and control expert. For example, it takes thirty-two hours to produce a tabulation of the status of United States forces in the Pacific; it takes the Air Force all night to produce a four-inch-thick book that details the daily status of its forces; Secretary of Defense McNamara had to speak to fourteen officers on the telephone in order to get an estimate of the bombs available for an escalation of the war.[66]

The number of command and control problems, or pseudo-problems, is endless, and the remedies themselves are continually rendered obsolete by changing organizational structures as well as by changing technology. Command and control has been Mitre's meat and potatoes. It has worked on the supersystems—SAGE, NMCS (National Military Command Systems), and WWMCCS (Worldwide Military Command Control System).

The 1969–70 debate on the funding of the Anti-Ballistic Missile (ABM) is the only instance of serious public consideration of defense electronics spending. The debate occurred at a transition in Presidential administrations, and Congressional opponents of ABM were aided by experts who had worked closely with the Democratic defense program.

The workability of the ABM hinged on the reliability of electronic systems. "It is," explained MIT's J. C. R. Licklider, "now part of the common wisdom of many scientists, engineers, and administrators of technology that, particularly for a certain class of [electronics] systems, costs and time tend to be grossly underestimated and performance mercifully unmeasured." To demonstrate the improbability of a workable ABM, anti-ABM experts pointed to the record of the Air Force's "L" systems. "L" was the symbol assigned to "two or three dozen" electronic systems planned by the Air Force, and Mitre has worked on at least sixteen Ls. Most of the Ls, Licklider asserted, "were never completed. None was ever completed on time or within the initial budget." Unfortunately, Licklider qualified, his knowledge was based on "common wisdom" rather than sound documentation. Someone, he urged, should write a history of the L systems. Neither Licklider nor Mitre knows of such a history.[67]

Unbelievably, it is impossible to obtain the grossest of estimates on the dollars that Mitre has helped the military spend. "I couldn't even guess," said a Mitre vice president. It requires considerable sleuthing and speculation to match the material in Mitre's brochures with the truncated public record.[68]

When DOD proposed an expensive computer purchase to support its Worldwide Military Command and Control System, a GAO investigation found that DOD was not merely proposing to replace perfectly adequate computers, but that it held the purchase to be the solution to "communications problems" that may well have had other remedies. If, as the GAO suggested, the communications problems were caused by "organizational problems" or personnel incompetence, high-priced computers would have made for an even more unmanageable situation. The GAO, however, did not link poor planning to Mitre's work as the systems planner.

The fount of command-control spending was 416L, the SAGE system. It is now part of "common wisdom" that SAGE itself had feet of extremely costly clay. SAGE, RAND's Malcolm Hoag told Congress, "was a very bad system," and the defense community well understood that SAGE was not capable of performing as promised. Going the auto industry one better, an electronics system need not work at all before it is replaced. It merely must "advance the state of the art" sufficiently that a new and unworkable design can be conceived. No sooner did work on SAGE peter out than Mitre got to work on its successors—BUIC (Backup Interceptor system) and AWACS (Airborne Warning and Control System).

Charles Schultze, now at Brookings, was Budget Bureau Director during the early stage of AWACS's development. The Bureau, Schultze later told Congress, bought the Pentagon's line that AWACS could warn of a bomber attack as SAGE could not. But what the Bureau "did not look at so closely was, do you need an air defense system of this magnitude of all?" In the early Seventies, the Air Force

changed its tack on AWACS. Granting the limited usefulness of AWACS in continental air defense, the military
stressed its usefulness in limited wars. As Richard English
and Dan Bolef wrote in *Scientific American*, "Thus as a
component of the Aerospace Defense Command, AWACS
seems relatively harmless, if also relatively useless. In its
tactical role, however, it could facilitate the prosecution of
limited, non-nuclear wars." Thus the first adage of military
spending: Military plans are never killed, but live to be
funded under new rationales.[69]

A curious Congress could find ample evidence that
electronic systems are often little more than multimillion-
dollar style changes; that they do not work as promised;
that there are cheaper solutions to the legitimate problems
they are supposed to solve; and that the political and
economic implications of high-technology electronics
spending cannot much longer be ignored. Mitre, and other
nonprofits, are not the prime cause of the failings, but they
are central to them.

As long as citizens believe that technical decisions are
forbiddingly complex and the technicians, in the words of
Mitre Vice President Charles Grandy, rationalize that they
are merely "a simple group of systems engineers and
scientists doing systems engineering work . . . we are not
running the Government, we are not making policy," then it
is fine enough to assume that the system works as Mitre's
clients say it does.[70]

Organizational Conflict of Interest

Within the defense complex, concern for the hardware
contractor led to imposition of the hardware ban, which, as
we have seen, hardly protects the public interest. It recognizes a limited form of organizational conflict of interest to
insulate the hardware contractor from competition with
firms that plan and manage weapons projects—provided
these are FCRCs. To all other nonprofits and to profit
corporations, the ban applies only when it is accepted
voluntarily. Nor has the hardware ban been interpreted to

cover software (computer) firms, with the result that they are free to recommend information-processing methods and receive highly lucrative awards emanating from their recommendations to perform the processing. Thus, the concept of organizational conflict of interest has been limited to the conflict between preliminary research and subsequent hardware contracts. It has never been broadened to separate preliminary research from service contracts that may flow from the research.

Firms whose main product is "professional services" are subject to no conflict of interest consideration whatsoever. Government agencies commonly rely on contractors who already serve the industries to be regulated for the development of policies. The arrangements become visible only when contractors associated with particularly disastrous policies are hired to point the way to reform.

In the late Sixties, for example, the decline in America's rail passenger service prompted Congressional interest in the methods used by the Interstate Commerce Commission to grant the abandonment of passenger service. Railroads were permitted to abandon passenger services if they petitioned the ICC and demonstrated that substantial savings would result. The petitions were accompanied by "avoidable cost" studies performed by private consulting firms. The House Interstate Commerce Committee, noting the ease with which abandonment requests were granted, wanted to know more about the "avoidable cost" method. While the railroads continually produced studies that showed ample future savings, there were no studies that examined the accuracy of the predictions made. Chairman Harley Staggers requested a study that tested the abandonment methods, and the Federal Railroad Administration hired Wyer, Dick & Co. to do the work.[71]

Wyer, Dick not only had prepared studies of the sort under question, but was on retainer to two of the eight railroads the Federal Railroad Administration promised to study for Staggers. Instead of the study requested, the Administration had Wyer, Dick perform a study that showed that further savings would flow from further discontinuations.

Staggers was infuriated by the Administration's abuse of Congressional intent, its choice of a railroad advocate, and the shoddy documentation behind the choice. The Government's reaction was telling. It conceded the shoddiness of the contracting process and hedged its failure to perform the study requested. But the Administration was shocked at the objection to Wyer, Dick. All qualified firms, the Government explained, worked intensively for the railroads.

In 1966, the Food and Drug Administration's Bureau of Regulatory Compliance hired Booz, Allen, and Hamilton for the first phase of a "long-term improvement effort." For $350,000, Booz was to conduct an "across-the-board analysis of field activities, goals, objectives, organization, and opportunities." The firm was to be given access to "all activities of the Bureau." [72]

The Bureau's duty was to regulate the food and drug industry. Booz had, and still has, connections with that industry. James Allen, the Allen of Booz, Allen, was on the Board of Directors of Abbott Laboratories, one of the nation's leading drug producers. He also served with Jewel Companies, a major warehouser and distributor of drugs, groceries, and similar merchandise. Booz has a division that specializes in health services consulting and, in 1965, it purchased Foster D. Snell Co., a biological testing laboratory. Snell advertises that it has considerable experience in the preparation of "new drug applications" for the FDA. Snell also provides marketing and "general business analyses" to its clients and promises clients that its services "are supported as required by the experience and assistance of other parts of Booz, Allen, and Hamilton." [73]

At just about the time that the FDA was hiring Booz, the Pharmaceutical Manufacturers' Association, a major drug industry lobby, hired the firm for a highly confidential study of its own organization. Booz's public work dovetailed neatly with the private interests served. Booz's study told the FDA that it had relied too heavily on legal action to produce industry compliance—it had acquired the image of the "cops on the beat"—and urged the FDA to follow a different path. "Industry self-regulation and other voluntary efforts within established guidelines," it told the FDA, "are expected to increase in significance as the FDA places greater reliance on cooperation by state agencies and industry." Booz's conclusions were doubly curious. The firm was hired to study the Bureau of Compliance, and the FDA possessed a distinct bureau for voluntary compliance. Booz not only offered an undocumented industry position, but it offered a position not called for by contract.[74]

The true relation between Booz's work and industry interests is a subject for conjecture. Booz itself refuses to volunteer the names of its clients, much less the work it performs. The drug lobby was similarly reticent. The FDA contract files reveal no record of the firm's private clientele, and FDA officials assert that Booz was never asked to reveal them. Even so, Booz earned the FDA's trust. It received a $300,000 contract to implement the "management system" it called for in its first contract.[75]

Harbridge House

Nothing is sacred. The Government hires contractors to design contract laws and to teach contract officials how to administer contracts. Harbridge House, a Boston-based firm of close to 200 professionals, is one of a handful of consulting firms that specialize in the Federal procurement process. Harbridge House has written Government procurement regulations; Harbridge House alumni have become leading Federal procurement officers; and Harbridge House has become a famed source of the very texts, seminars, and training courses by which corporate and public procurement officials are taught the changing rules of the contract game.

Harbridge House advertises itself to be a "creative interpreter" of the rapidly changing procurement regulations. The $1 million it received from the Social and Rehabilitative Services (SRS) administration over a decade illustrate its creativity. The sum represents four sole-source awards, three awards received under highly peculiar competitive circumstances, and two awards whose bases the files do not reveal.

SRS administers a variety of welfare programs for the aged and the handicapped. Harbridge House became a welfare consultant in the Fifties. It sold a package of services—research, seminars, and handbooks—to state and local welfare administrators. In 1961, Harbridge House received its first contract with SRS.[76] The firm was to study the Office of the Commissioner and to prepare detailed plans for merging components of the organization. The explicit terms of this contract and other contracts to Harbridge House required an illegal delegation of public authority. Harbridge House was not only to "provide the goals" for the new organization but also to "write the necessary statutes and legislation and to fully justify any need for an increase in staff." [77]

Harbridge House's second contract (for $67,915) is an extraordinary example of improper coaching of the governmental agency involved.

In March 1963, Harbridge House's Vice President, H. M. Temple, sent a detailed letter to SRS's Mary Switzer.[78] The first part of the letter told her how to justify the contract to her staff. The second part told her how to justify a sole-source award for the record. Temple suggested that no qualified competitors existed for the job. As an alternative, he suggested, the Harbridge House award might be viewed as an extension of work performed earlier. Temple proposed that the bureau rationalize the firm's close ties with the welfare program in precisely the fashion that procurement regulations advise against. He suggested that each future Harbridge House contract be viewed as an extension of previous work. Finally, Temple suggested that the bureau needed the study immediately.[79]

The Temple letter and the sole-source justification both found their way into the contract file, the letter being neatly excerpted by the bureau to produce the justification.

In January 1969, Aubrey Villenes, Chief of Procurement for HEW, wrote a memo to the SRS contract office about the Harbridge House relationship with SRS:

> A review of the justification and simultaneous review of past management consultant awards to Harbridge House by the Social and Rehabilitation Service and SRS organization elements prior to the activation of SRS would, in my opinion, result in severe criticism by the General Accounting Office. There are several established capable management consulting firms in the immediate Washington area with a capability of performing these services. If the SRS continues to award "sole-source" contracts of this nature to Harbridge House, we shall (if we are not already) be in violation of both Federal Procurement Regulations and Federal Statutory Law, as we have, in effect, ignored the requirement for competition and have placed Harbridge House in a preferred position. I strongly urge that this be brought to the attention of all concerned and that every effort be extended to give the Procurement Board the next management consultant requirement early enough to permit full competition as directed by law.[80]

Villenes' memo had no effect. Shortly after it was written, Harbridge House received a sole-source to study SRS's "manpower needs." It concocted a dazzling justification for the award. As rubberstamped by SRS, the justification stated that Harbridge House had a "proprietary model for program analysis which will greatly expedite the work. Proposals had not been solicited from other firms, since Harbridge House is the only firm known to have the capability of being able to perform the required work within the specified period of time. It possesses a unique knowledge of this agency." [81]

What, the official author of the justification was asked, was a "proprietary model for program analysis"? "I guess," ventured Lowell Genebach, "it just means their techniques

—the fact that they have been in a developmental role all along in this organization. As I recall, they built up their proprietary model by working in their various functions within the agency." [82] This explanation, Genebach granted, was merely a rationalization.

SRS did not realize the legal predicament it posed. If there is such a thing as a "proprietary model," Harbridge House's "development" of the model on SRS money made the model a public and not a "proprietary" model. The sole-source justification was a contradiction in terms, and Harbridge House must have known this. The firm is an expert on rights in Government-funded invention. It was hired by the government to do a major study of patent policy and taught seminars to private industry in the "maximization" of proprietary rights stemming from Government contracts.

In 1970, Harbridge House participated in yet another misapplication of contract law. SRS invited several firms to bid on a contract. Harbridge House was not among these. The firm nonetheless submitted a proposal. The evaluation panel rated Harbridge House and Booz, Allen equally competent to perform the study. Booz proposed $179,408 for the work. Harbridge House proposed $276,190. Harbridge House received the award. The files naturally contain no explanation for the award, nor was there evidence of flaws in the Booz, Allen proposal and no evidence of attention to the Booze price advantage.[83]

Mary Switzer, who was SRS's administrator in the Sixties and who saw nothing special in the work of Harbridge House, had this to say about her experience with consultants: "Harbridge House generally told us what we knew. I admit there was a minimum of competition, but when a firm like Harbridge House starts something, it seems uneconomical to turn it over to another group." [84]

The Harbridge House experience cannot be dismissed. Harbridge House remains a trusted source of procurement expertise and continues to teach procurement officials, including those in HEW, how to administer contracts.

IV.

EFFICIENCY IN GOVERNMENT:
Private Control of Public Spending

EDUCATION

When the new Senate Budget Committee wants to "go to the top" for quick and expert advice on Federal spending, a young staff economist explained, it calls on Brookings' Charles Schultze. Schultze directed the Budget Bureau during the Great Society, and, on leaving the Government, helped Brookings produce its own commentary on the annual Federal budget.

In 1970, Schultze, appearing on an American Economic Association–sponsored panel, joined in the critique of a recent survey of the state of economics. The survey, said Schultze, while technically competent, did not show that economics was relevant to pressing social problems. Economists, he told the meeting, can no longer complacently concern themselves only with the big picture of the American economy. Federal grant and contract dollars have come to provide basic capital for industry—ranging from hardware industries such as aerospace to social industries such as schools and hospitals. Public managers must know more about the details of the industrial growth they are increasingly responsible for. Schultze stated:

> Public decision-makers did need estimates of production functions in the aggregate for devising stabilization and growth policies. But they did not need that information in the detailed and operational form which individual industrial managers require in order to produce output. But when the Government itself is the producer of output, then it should act like any other producer and at least acquire knowledge of its own production function! . . . Yet we know shockingly little about social production functions.[1]

The Government, Schultze suggested, would have to rely on experts to tell it how its money is spent. To the "extent that the public authorities themselves must choose the function, as in the case of public programs, detailed knowledge of input-output relationships becomes critical." True, Schultze acknowledged, centralized "Federal command and control" of local health, welfare, and educational industries would not be possible the way it is in the defense business. Decentralization of social decision-making is not only desirable but necessary. "But decentralization per se solves nothing. Decentralized decisions must somehow be made compatible with central goals. And that in turn requires a system of organizational structures, performance measures, and penalties and rewards which induce decentralized decision-makers to act in ways consistent with overall national plans and objectives." The experts must create the "definitions and measures of performance" from which "a system of institutions and incentives to channel individual decisions toward socially desirable performance" can be "designed."

The social welfare programs of the Great Society provided a great challenge for America's management experts, and the challenge was particularly great for spending directed at America's elementary and secondary schools. It is always common wisdom that America's schoolrooms are ripe for innovation, and the first great outflow of Federal dollars provided a unique lever for central direction of change. The Office of Education, Commissioner Sidney Marland told Congress, would test "educational products," and products "stamped OE" would become schoolroom staples. With careful deference to the politically powerful forces of local education, the experts hoped to bring the assembly line to the schoolroom.[2]

The flow of education dollars helped pay for new management systems called "evaluations," and Congress soon wrote requirements for "evaluation" into authorizations for further spending. The techniques of evaluation emulated earlier practices. Evaluators sought to combine the national data-gathering ambitions of the statisticians of the American economy with the micro-analyses that efficiency experts and social scientists had long performed in the individual factory. A long-term study of Head Start and Followthrough was one of the experts' most ambitious experiments in evaluation. It incidentally demonstrates the difficulties inherent in the application of managerial insight to social spending.[3]

The Need for Evaluation

On November 30, 1967, Alice Rivlin of HEW's Office of Planning and Evaluation sent co-worker Bill Gorham a memo entitled "What Next in Education?" [4] Rivlin's memo reflected on the plight of the "policy analyst." "To put it bluntly," the memo began, "almost nothing is known about what works well and what does not in education." The PPBers had talked of comparing investments in alternative programs, but since it now appeared that "it cannot be demonstrated that smaller classes, newer buildings, different methods of curricula, more experienced or trained teachers—or any combination of these—would enhance the effectiveness of the American schools," how was the Federal Government to write guidelines that would recommend "good practice" to schools using OE money? [5]

The memo considered the means by which good practice could be discovered. It rejected as politically unpalatable carefully controlled experiments that would be dictated to states and localities by the Federal Government. Something more than the traditional survey of schools was necessary, however. HEW had sponsored contractor surveys of compensatory education programs, but these, said Rivlin, had not provided sufficiently detailed information, or tracked the lasting effects of spendings on what the experts called the "target population."

So Rivlin singled out a third approach, "planned variation." As the memo put it, the government would fund projects "which differ in substantial ways from one another

. . . fund enough of these projects so that differences in other variables can be controlled statistically, and . . . evaluate the results in uniform fashion, following the same children over several years."

A Candidate for Analysis

In 1967–68, a prize candidate for "planned variation" was placed at OE's doorstep. Followthrough, which had been administered by OEO, was transferred to the agency. (The program serves the disadvantaged after their graduation from the better-known Head Start program.) Head Start and Followthrough both owed their existence to the prevalent social scientific opinion that the earlier years of life are crucial to subsequent educational attainment, and Followthrough came into being when studies suggested that the gains of Head Start would be dissipated unless money was spent to "follow through."

In an effort to rein in the War on Poverty, Congress refused to increase the Followthrough budget as planned, and left it at less than $20 million for 1968–69.

Faced with the budget cut, OE reclassified Followthrough from a dying welfare program to a "research and development" program and said that Followthrough contractors were performing a "longitudinal evaluation" of the spending. In the Federal budget, Followthrough was listed as an "experimental" program.[6]

One useless evaluation preceded the variation study. In 1967, OE awarded $146,000 to the University of Pittsburgh for an "evaluation" of Followthrough. A 1971 GAO investigation revealed that the report for the project was of such low quality that it was never released, and a July 1967 memo from the Deputy Commissioner of Education explained that the entire contract had been a mistake. The award was "not based upon the quality of the Pittsburgh proposal, but primarily upon the basis of an oral commitment made to Pittsburgh in violation of internal proceedings."

The Associate Commissioner for Elementary and Secondary Education pronounced that the "difficulties experienced in this particular situation are unlikely to reoccur [*sic*]." [7]

In the spring of 1968, a year after the program was transferred, amid rampant disorder, from OEO to the Office of Education, the Followthrough staff began to prepare for the planned variation study that would begin with the fall term. It asked the American Institutes for Research (AIR), the Educational Testing Service (ETS), and the Stanford Research Institute (SRI) to chat with it about the prime contract.

AIR and ETS had impressive credentials as educational data-gatherers. AIR's psychologists had coaxed OE into a major collection of data called Project Talent, and AIR spent years mining the resulting data bank. ETS, of course, produces and administers a wide variety of tests. SRI, one of the largest nonprofits in the country, had virtually no experience with education programs. Its prime claim to competence was a large contract from OE for the operation of an "educational policy research center," using systems analysis.[8]

On May 31, 1968, representatives of the three firms arrived at OE. Although the Followthrough contract became one of the largest the agency has awarded, the gathering was so informal and hasty that one competitor did not present a written proposal, and OE prepared no written record of the basis for its award. According to Dr. Richard Snyder, the first OE director of the project, SRI was the unanimous choice. It had the "most imaginative proposal . . . and showed superior organizational commitment." [9] (Snyder had come to OE from HUMMRRO, an Army-sponsored social science research organization.)

The contract award did not conform to the Federal Procurement Regulations, which provide that the minimum time to be allowed for the submission of bids, when the bids are not for standard commercial articles, should be not less than thirty days. The three firms were told about the contract in early May, and Stanford Research Institute, the winner, was formally invited to bid eleven calendar days before the deadline for bidding. Both the Federal Procurement Regulations and HEW's own rules required that when, as in the Followthrough case, a contract is negotiated, the contract files must contain data to explain the negotiation. Further, they must explain the reason for the choice of negotiation, the extent of competition involved, and "other essential information bearing on the actual negotiations." This information was not prepared for the files.

Nonetheless, the consummation of the SRI contract caused bells to ring in OE. According to a rhapsodic OE interoffice memo, the planned variation experiment would mark a new era "in which the knowledge and technical expertise of the educational specialist, the systems engineer, and the behavioral scientist are brought into harmony with the pluralistic value structure of the society."

With the prime contractor on board, OE invited nonprofits, schools of education, and its contract research laboratories to offer their wares to the nearly ninety locations that would receive Followthrough funding in 1968–69. The number of schools involved would rise from 29 serving 2,400 children in 1967–68 to 120 serving 60,000 children in 1970–71. Each locality was to be matched with a sponsor. Ideally, the localities and sponsors should have been chosen according to some objective criterion. OE, however, was compelled to defer to political reality. State education agencies nominated local participants, and the locals chose their favored form of innovation, ranging from Skinnerian psychology, the computer, "affective learning," and the use of parents as teachers, to the "flexible" curriculum, in which "the classroom is the child's workroom, where he is free to investigate objects and explore media." If all went as planned, the variations could be mechanically transferred from the laboratory to the Followthrough schoolroom and from there to the schoolroom at large. (SRI lumped the approaches into five categories—"the structured academic, the discovery, the cognitive discovery, the self-sponsored, and the parent-implemented.")

The initial Followthrough contract with SRI, contrary to Federal Procurement Regulations, did not define the subject of study or SRI's role in the study. And it failed to allocate responsibility for the project between OE and SRI. The contract, flexible and pragmatic, seemed to have been drawn up on the assumption that the funding would last for several years—time enough to define the ends of the study. SRI assumed a primary role in defining its own work and the purpose of the Followthrough evaluation.

It is clear in retrospect that SRI lacked the expert knowledge or concern necessary to make judgments about poverty education.

SRI decided that an understanding of Followthrough could be gained only by tracing the program from the Economic Opportunity Act "through the Executive Branch and into the community." If one does this, "a context has been established, but this context is largely doctrinal, legalistic, and administrative. An important missing element is a perspective on poverty in the United States that could clarify, unify, and guide the evaluation of legislation in community action."

What was SRI's perspective on poverty? "It is clear," stated the corporation's 1970 proposal for contract renewal, "that the vicious cycle by which poverty is perpetuated from generation to generation is difficult to break out of. Just why this is, is less clear. Poverty may be best defined, for our purposes, as inability to cope with one's overall environment, accompanied by a consequent inability to provide an adequate income." Elsewhere, SRI placed a more positive cast on the ambiguous specter of poverty. "One thing is perfectly clear," the firm offered. "Poverty, however defined, is a result of many personal, social, and political and economic factors interacting in complex ways." What were the implications for Followthrough? "A full understanding," said SRI, "of the changes wrought thereby [through FT] may not be possible for years, but the task of the evaluation is immediate for the social and educational problems demand solution."

School for Contractors

SRI was the primary management contractor, and the local variations involved contracts with local sponsors, but there were numerous other participants. OE contracted out shamelessly. On one occasion it paid over $2,000 for a sketch of the legislative and administrative history of Followthrough, a topic Followthrough officials should have been intimately familiar with. The price worked out to $200 per double-spaced, wide-margined page of publicly available information! [10]

In May 1968, Henry Riecken, President of the Social Science Research Council (SSRC), proposed that its Committee on Learning and the Educational Process be given a $150,000 grant. SSRC represented the kind of "new educational expertise" that OE actively courted in its effort to divorce itself from the "teacher's college" tradition of research. SSRC's scholars were affiliated with the best universities and dealt with the better R & D agencies, as well as OE. SSRC itself was created with Rockefeller funds and had long served as social science's broker-spokesman in the government-academy-foundation interlock. The organization, for example, was engaged with the National Academy of Sciences in a series of surveys for the social sciences, a venture supported by HEW, the NSF, and the Russell Sage Foundation.

Riecken, presumably knowledgeable in proposal writing, offered a brief and authoritative justification for an OE grant to SSRC. "There is," he explained, "a growing body of opinion that success in school is a critical determinant of opportunity in adult life." Riecken stated that SSRC would hold three conferences on educational evaluation. The first would explore the rationale behind funding early childhood programs, the second would get at the "critical" dimensions of evaluation, and a third would tell how OE could make use of the knowledge produced by the first two conferences. Riecken proposed to involve a *Who's Who* of childhood development experts. "If," he asserted, "the various aims of compensatory programs and the assumptions underlying them can be explicated, it should be possible to reach some agreement on appropriate means of measuring the success of the programs." These propositions sounded strikingly like the assumptions Rivlin had offered as underlying Followthrough itself.[11]

In a 1970 letter to OE, Riecken traced the subsequent history of the grant. Apparently, SSRC had made a curious mistake. It had underestimated the interest of minority groups in compensatory education and was forced to revise its first conference to include social scientists from minority groups. Riecken saw no need to explain why, well into the second half of the twentieth century, eminent experts on compensatory education could have been so imperceptive. After accommodating the race problem, SSRC discovered that social science was not up to the task proposed. The grant money was running out, the business of the second conference was completed three months after the date of grant termination, and Riecken announced that SSRC would not get to the part of the project that would render the first two conferences useful.[12]

Followthrough was becoming an academic bureaucracy in its own right, training cadres in the arts of bureaucratic experimentation. SRI freely employed numerous academics as consultants, including some who participated in the SSRC grant. (In several cases consultants were paid thousands of dollars, one of them receiving a fee of at least $14,000.) And the SRI stable of high-powered senior academics was augmented by a "Junior Fellows" program. Junior Fellows were to receive money from the Government and divide their time between SRI and local project cities. The National Opinion Research Center, a survey research firm, received hundreds of thousands of dollars on subcontract to SRI to interview thousands of parents, teachers, and students; a firm called Bio-Dynamics was employed to study the medical care provided by Follow-through; Educational Testing Service supplied advice on tests. Finally, the National Training Laboratories, an organization noted for its sponsorship of sensitivity training, received a grant to travel around to the local Followthrough sites.

The first two years of the Followthrough evaluation were disasters. The program at large repeated the failings of the SSRC grant. As fall semester 1968–69 began, the Follow-through administration discovered that it had underestimated the ambitions of its subjects. Though the program had hired minority group members to serve as "general consultants" at local projects, "unfortunately," as an OE staff memo explained, there was "relatively trivial" minority staffing of the sponsor contractors and a "notable absence" of minority employees in "senior decision-making positions on our USOE Followthrough staff." When OE's minority employees actively protested the imbalance, a Howard University official was called upon to mediate the grievances.

In the spring of 1969, OE, SRI, and the sponsors met in Pajaro Dunes, California. A representative from OE summarized the meeting, reporting that the notable aspect of this "quite unstructured" gathering was the "lack of consensus at this relatively late date." The local program sponsors "seem not to have really accepted the idea that there will be a nontrivial evaluation in the near future."

The upshot was that the first year of planned variation was being written off as a break-in period, and the data gathered that year were not to be used. Nevertheless, in 1969–70, the Followthrough bureaucracy was expanded, the monies for the program doubled, and seventy new locations were added.

The spring 1970 SRI proposal lamented that the ability to develop complete and reliable descriptions of local variations represented the most important weakness to date. The programs were the central "independent variable" of the project. In layman's terms, SRI was saying that it did not know what the subject of the experiment was. SRI further explained that it had little idea of how the "planned variations" actually varied from one another. Without adequate description of the variations, SRI explained, it would be hard to compare their effects on education. SRI promised to learn to describe the variations.

Again in the spring of 1970, OE commissioned two teams of half a dozen experts to appraise SRI's activities. Three reported on the financial and administrative details of the contract, the rest on the substance of SRI's contribution to Followthrough. In May 1970, written reports from both teams recommended that the SRI contract be continued.

Marvin Alkin reviewed the program as director of an OE-funded Center for the Study of Educational Evaluation: "The greatest deficiency of the SRI project," Alkin's memo began abruptly, "is its failure to provide adequate specification of the kind of study it is intended to be and the functions it proposes to serve." Alkin tried to distinguish between what he called a flexible "research" effort—which Followthrough might be—and an evaluation which, in Alkin's mind, implied a predetermined specification of the subject of evaluation and of the likely outcomes. "If," said the evaluation expert, "one is to take seriously the title of the [SRI] proposal, 'Longitudinal Evaluation of the National Followthrough 1970–71,' then one must be dismayed at what is proposed. . . . I cannot vouch for the worth of the approximately $4 million already expended."

In May 1970, written reports from both teams recommended that the SRI contract be continued. OE accepted the conclusions of the review panel and kept the SRI contract in force.

Head Start Loses Ground

In July 1969, Head Start was moved from OEO to the new Office of Child Development (OCD) in HEW. No sooner had Followthrough struggled through its first year than Head Start also adopted planned variation as its motif, and, in June 1969, SRI received a contract to manage a Head Start planned variation.

The HEW contract file does not record the basis for the SRI award, but there is little doubt that HEW was banking on the experience SRI had with Followthrough.

Unfortunately for SRI, OCD had staff with expert—and relevant—credentials. Dr. Lois Ellin Datta, in charge of the Head Start Evaluation Branch, for example, is a psychologist who had written on Head Start and its evaluations—in contrast to Richard Snyder, the initial R & D director of Followthrough, with his defense background.

A child completes Head Start in one year, while the Followthrough cycle runs three years. Because of this difference, SRI had to act for Head Start much more quickly than for Followthrough. An interim report on the fall 1969 semester was due in January 1970, and a final report, to be used in planning the next school year's program, was due in June.

The SRI interim report did not arrive at OE until June, and Dr. Datta deemed it unacceptable. It must, she insisted, have been the work of graduate students, not education experts. In August 1970, SRI requested permission to skip the interim report. "Extraordinary efforts," they said, were being invested in the final version.

In September 1970, Datta began to receive the reports, and she was appalled. She found not only that the work was poor, but that SRI had plagiarized, from among all possible sources, her own work.

In its introduction, the SRI report tried to sum up the course of prior evaluations of Head Start, in order to place the planned variation in context. "What is present," wrote Datta to SRI, "looks as if someone abstracted the Hypotheses, Designs, and Major Findings of a few studies, plus several pages of Direct Quote Without Ascription from a 1969 paper I wrote, which is outdated in light of 1969–70 reports, and is calling this a review of the literature and background." The section on prior evaluations of Head Start, wrote Datta, was "lifted almost word for word from my 1969 paper. . . . Can't your staff think for itself?"

Datta soon discovered that SRI had a difficult time even

explaining planned variation itself. "The objectives of planned variation and what we are trying to do," she wrote, "deserves far more than two or three inaccurate paragraphs." To help SRI along, she sent them some brochures on the program.

By spring 1971, SRI had yet to produce its report, and OCD called in a review panel. Dr. Datta and the panel concluded that the current SRI report would have to suffice. It was "only marginally satisfactory," acceptable only because of "time pressures" and not because of quality of the analysis. The report was the product of a contract that, by June 1971, had cost $1.8 million.

In their brief review, Datta and the panel were critical of SRI's staff and resource capabilities. A U.S. Department of Health, Education, and Welfare audit, *Review of Head Start and Follow Through Evaluation Contracts with Stanford Research Institute*, provided confirmation in a finding that:

> Despite our most vigorous efforts, over almost the entire period of the contract, to get SRI to strengthen their staff, the overall staff picture remains one of shallow resources, with almost no capability in areas critical to this evaluation effort—including the areas of early childhood education and child development.

In a rebuttal to Datta's panel's conclusions, SRI acknowledged the "serious gap" in its staffing.

After two years in which HEW had spent close to $2 million on SRI for Head Start, three years in which $7 million were spent on SRI-Followthrough, and four years in which close to $2 million were spent building an "educational policy research center," SRI still lacked bona fide expert staff.

As a result of its panel's findings, OCD began to cut bait. SRI was to be relegated to the role of data collector, and the data was to be shipped elsewhere for analysis.

Subsequent to the review of Followthrough in the spring of 1970, OE management expert Karl Hereford dashed off a memo. Followthrough, he noted, was spending $4 million with SRI in 1970–1. Just as Datta had grown anxious about obtaining reports from SRI, Hereford suggested that OE begin to think about obtaining the bare data that SRI possessed. It was clear that "this is not likely to occur without an especial effort on our part." OE received SRI's promise that before the end of the year it would account for all the data and analysis OE had paid for.

On December 30, 1970, SRI sent Snyder a letter in partial compliance with the contract requirement for data. "If USOE desires," SRI wrote, "filled-in instruments [interview and test forms] will be shipped. Based on a visual inspection of the quantity of cartons containing original data, this material will weigh several tons and will require substantial storage space (e.g. several thousand square feet)." SRI had placed the data on computer tape, and it was natural to expect that OE preferred the tape to the raw data.

SRI offered to send the agency computer programs written for its B5500 computer. The relevant programs, however, were not written for the agency's B5500. "Needless to say, SRI cannot provide proprietary software that has been used extensively on this project. . . . Most of the computer programs . . . have been implementations of larger programs such as SRI's MTP . . . a larger SRI proprietary program that was not developed on Followthrough funds." In other words, SRI would not give OE information it had paid for, because it was locked into programs developed on other SRI monies.

In August 1971, the General Accounting Office issued a report on OE evaluation contracts. The GAO report, which did not name contractors, concluded that the $7 million spent on Followthrough, the largest contract studied, may have been wasted. The report blamed OE—for poor monitoring of the contract!

Endgame

The GAO report was officially released in August of 1971. As is GAO's custom, the public report contained an exchange between GAO and agency officials. In a letter dated June 1, 1971, HEW assistant comptroller James Cardwell promised GAO that, as of that date, the SRI-Followthrough contract would be modified to provide for orderly completion.

Nothing of the sort happened. Inside OE the Follow-through leadership was changing hands, and SRI was given until September to produce materials to try to demonstrate its competence.

SRI's materials duly arrived in September, were shipped to a group of OE staffers and outside experts, and were found by them to be unacceptable.

On October 1, 1971, the Followthrough staff met on the contract. Those at the meeting agreed that the "deliverables received from the contractor to date have been valueless and that future deliverables under the contract will continue to be valueless." Robert Mintz, special staff assistant to the director of the OE Contracts and Grants Division, predicted that OE would renew the SRI contract: "Follow-through personnel are reluctant to terminate the contract, because (1) they want to save face, and (2) they want to avoid 'losing' the $6.2 million balance of contract funds by having it revert to the Treasury."

True to Mintz's prediction, in the last month of 1971, the SRI contract was renewed. Six million dollars were tacked on—bringing the SRI-Followthrough total to over $13 million, of which over $857,000 represented their "fee" (i.e., profit). Although the $6 million represented the largest annual award for SRI, the Followthrough division had decided to do what Head Start had done—remove SRI from all tasks but data collection.

A December 1971 memo by new Followthrough director Gary McDaniels summarized the limits of SRI's competence. SRI's spring 1970 report, said McDaniels, had precipitated a "crisis of confidence in the contractor." When the September 1971 submittals were found unacceptable, the November resubmittals "hardly erased concerns."

In the spring of 1972, we sent a letter to HEW Secretary

Elliot Richardson, arguing that SRI's performance on Followthrough represented a blatant example of irresponsible performance by a major national contractor. The facts indicated that OE clearly bore a large share of responsibility for the confusion. OE's irresponsibility, however, did not excuse SRI, which was taking millions of dollars without claim to even elementary expertise. Federal Procurement Regulations provide that agencies may penalize contractors who fail to perform according to contract, and SRI had not performed. On this basis, we requested Richardson to debar SRI from further contracting with OE.[13]

In response to our letter, Secretary Richardson commissioned three studies of Followthrough—by the HEW Office of Planning and Evaluation, by the Followthrough branch, and by the HEW audit agency.[14]

The audit agency report was due in August 1972. When it was finally completed (in March 1973), it verified the disastrous maladministration of the SRI contracts. The release of the report was delayed, in part, because SRI was given a chance to comment on the "draft" of the report. We asked for access to the draft on the same terms as SRI. HEW denied the request. The agency explained that the "draft" was an intra-agency document and therefore could be withheld from members of the public. Presumably, then, SRI was considered part of HEW. While audit agencies have made "drafts" of their reports available to contractors under study, they have not made "drafts" available to the public at large. The significance of this practice was highlighted by a GAO report on defense contractor profits. Congress discovered that the final version, made public, had been altered at the behest of defense contractors.[15]

The HEW audit progressed slowly on account of the poor quality of the contract files. The audit confirmed that OE had failed to follow official regulations and that the agency had been guilty of poor administration. It also confirmed SRI's responsibility for illegal contract activities and poor performance. SRI had not only plagiarized in one of its reports to the Head Start division, but had failed to produce progress reports as promised and had failed to give Followthrough the specific expertise it had promised in its first Followthrough contract.[6]

The auditors did not attempt to make their own evaluation of the work performed by SRI. Instead they relied on the reports of the review panels and the comments of officials. The closest that the audit agency would come to judging SRI's work, then, was a comment on the competence of the SRI staff. While SRI performed satisfactorily as a data-gatherer, its "limited staff capabilities" were not adequate to produce the data design and analysis and test development required by OE.

The audit work demonstrates the limited usefulness of traditional audits. The auditors verified the existence of testimony that condemned SRI's work, attempted no independent evaluation of the work, and failed to draw any conclusions on the issue before them. The audit, for example, verified the existence of the Mintz memo, adding that audit agency "discussions with the special staff aide and others who participated in the meeting indicate that the tone of the meeting was as he [Mintz] described it in the memorandum." If SRI's work had been useless, what justification was there for renewing the contract? The audit accepted OE's justification for renewing the contract. It cited without qualification OE's statement that "it was not deemed prudent at that point in the study to change contractors."

The audit begged the ultimate question it was commissioned to help resolve. The contract law provides for debarment, as well as lesser penalties, in cases of nonperformance. The audit verified uncontradicted evidence of nonperformance. Yet the audit came up with no legal conclusion. What is more, it claimed that only general conclusions could be drawn and offered up the ritual recommendations for better contract management.

The upshot was that Followthrough lumbered on, while SRI, though dropped from all tasks but data-gathering, at which it appears to excel, was not penalized for poor performance. In fact, it was invited to bid when OE decided to invite bidding for the completion of the other tasks.[17]

THE IRRELEVANCE OF MANAGEMENT CONTROLS

The Great Society's administrators promised that sophisticated analysis and controls would be applied to social spending. Ironically, no Great Society program was as frequently evaluated as its education spending. As a history of the Elementary and Secondary Education Act records, the "legislative mandate for formal reports and evaluations of programs was loud and clear." Evaluations were to be performed by every level of the program's administration. Federal monies flowed to state agencies, and state grants to localities were conditioned on local assurance that "effective procedures of educational achievement will be adopted for evaluating at least annually the effectiveness of the educational programs in meeting the special educational needs of educationally deprived children." The states in turn had to supply their own evaluations to Washington. Finally, the Act was amended to require annual Federal evaluation reports to Congress.[18]

The resulting evaluations provided only fragmentary evidence of the quality of Federal spending. "There really has been no decent evaluation of Title I," stated OE's evaluation director John Evans in 1973. "Attempts to measure the impact of the program on educational achievement," OE told Congress, "have been less than satisfactory in that no nationally representative data can be reported." Nor could adequate local data be found. OE hired the Research Council of the Great Cities Schools to survey local Title I evaluations. The report found that local efforts had been doomed by poor planning, politicization, inadequate technical skills, and general confusion over "who was to measure what for whom." Evaluation, the contractor concluded, would improve with age.[19]

The waste produced by evaluation is still greater when what economists call the "opportunity cost" is considered. Evaluation was promoted at the expense of more feasible and necessary alternatives. It did not require computers or Ph.D.s to know that the education dollar was not effective because money was abused by its recipients.

OE hired the American Institutes for Research to summarize the fruits of its evaluations. Their most striking conclusions were evident without subtle analysis: numerous states and localities received Title I monies in continual violation of the rules.[20]

Title I improprieties were brought to public attention, not by a contractor report, however, but through the independent studies of a small civil rights research group. The Washington Research Project put together its own observations and data collected by HEW's audit agency. "Many of the misuses of Title I funds," the Project found, "are so gross that even nonexperts can readily spot them," but "the accepted experts have failed to inform the public honestly about the faulty and sometimes fraudulent" operations of education programs. The Government responded to the furor caused by the Project's report in predictable fashion. It commissioned a "Title I Task Force," which soon buried the controversy beneath mounds of contractor-performed studies.[21]

The Task Force was headed by Tim Wirth, then an HEW official, now a Congressman from Colorado. Contractors were employed liberally. Macro Systems, a firm founded by Booz, Allen alumni, studied the organization of Title I administration. The Urban Institute studied the evaluation of Title I. The Inner City Fund summarized the Task Force's work. Fry Consultants composed a master plan for the Task Force, and Thompson, Lewin, and Associates performed a similar function. Persistent inquiries to OE produced a copy of one Macro Systems report and several documents from the Urban Institute. No further evidence of work could be provided. The Washington Research Project's Michael Trister complained of lack of access to

Task Force work, and the Task Force's efforts petered out when Wirth left HEW.[22]

Even some supporters of evaluation are troubled by the uselessness of the spending. The Urban Institute concluded that the evaluation system is "being built piecemeal with every contractor doing his own thing on most of the bits and pieces." What is the Government getting for its money?

> The program models developed differ from study to study and have little operational meaning to program managers. The data collected are specialized and unique to each study. Differences in definition, sampling, technique, timing, content, make it impossible to relate the data of several independent collection efforts.[23]

The Institute urged agencies to clarify the purposes of particular studies and to administer the studies with a view to their ultimate usefulness.

Evaluation was flourishing without rational controls. In 1971, following a study of the Department of Labor's evaluation system, the Institute team concluded that "after investment of significant resources and effort, not one Federal agency (including the Department of Labor) has an overall evaluation system, and few programs are able to make any use of the evaluation produced. On the whole, Federal evaluation efforts have not been cost-effective."

Weapons and Management Consultants

Sterling Livingston graduated from Harvard Business School in 1940, one year after Robert McNamara. Livingston's current grandfatherly demeanor is at odds with his reputation as "probably the world's greatest salesman." McNamara followed a more conventional path to the top of defense management. While McNamara labored in Detroit, Livingston used his faculty position at the Harvard Business School as home base from which to embark on consulting ventures.

During World War II Livingston worked on a Navy team that rewrote the Department's procurement regulations, an experience that put him on the ground floor of a major postwar growth industry—Government contracting. The Navy, Livingston recalls, "absolutely decimated its procurement system" after the war and called on Livingston to help rebuild it. Livingston was asked to write the procurement manual for the Navy's Bureau of Aeronautics and was soon employed to train users of procurement manuals. The Navy offered to channel contracts to Livingston through the Business School. When Harvard vetoed this, Harbridge (Harvard plus Cambridge) House was born.

Harbridge House was only the first in Livingston's line of defense-oriented consulting firms. It would be followed by Management Systems, which in turn was acquired by Peat, Marwick, Mitchell & Co. (PMM turned Management Systems into the firm's Washington office.) Livingston eventually sold his interest in Harbridge House and currently uses the Sterling Institute as his Washington base. (The Institute's Watergate suite is a training center for public and private managers.)[24]

The brochures produced by the various Livingston firms suggest that very little in contract administration is left to official imagination. Harbridge House, for example, not only works for all the services, but "drafted, compiled, and edited the first publication of the NASA procurement regulation and, in follow-on work, performed studies and submitted revisions of selected parts." PMM says it helps the defense complex with "program management systems designs and implementation, research and development management, cost effectiveness studies, RFP preparation assistance, defense marketing strategy, proposal preparation assistance, integrated logistics support, contractor performance evaluation, Government-contractor negotiation assistance, and renegotiation assistance." [25]

It was the touch of the master salesman to design management products for the field workers in the contract bureaucracy. As soon as the bigwigs accepted Livingston's advice, he would explain it to those who had to administer contracts. In this way, the consultants expanded their market by socializing bureaucratic underlings in management techniques. The packages of manuals, seminars, and training courses that became a Livingston trademark were soon offered throughout the consulting business. In 1959, for example, Harbridge House joined with the National Security Industrial Association, a contractor trade association of which Livingston was a director, to establish the National Defense Education Institute. The Institute was the Association's "teaching arm." In 1969, Congress was told that the Army and the Air Force had finally acquired their own procurement faculty, but the Navy still contracted out to Harbridge House and others for procurement instruction.[26]

The military places responsibility for "procurement policies and procedures" in the offices of Assistant Secretaries for Installations and Logistics (I & L). Each service has its own I & L office, and there is one for the Department as a whole.

For many years, service with Livingston seems to have been the basis on which the Army chose its I & L Assistant Secretaries. Four men held the position for the bulk of the period between 1961 and 1973. Paul Ignatius was one of Livingston's first recruits to Harbridge House. Ignatius' successor at I & L was Robert Brooks. Brooks came to the Army from Harbridge House and returned to head the firm. Brooks was followed by Ron Fox. Fox was employed by Livingston at Management Systems and left the Army to continue as a contract expert at the Harvard Business School. Dudley Mecum also worked for Livingston at Management Systems and came to the military from its successor firm.

Livingston was also quite close to the men who served as I & L Assistant Secretaries for the entire Department. Tom Morris, the first McNamara I & L Assistant Secretary, relied on Livingston for advice and hired his consultants to study the organization of the military's procurement offices. (Morris himself had worked for Cresap, McCormick and Paget, another consulting firm whose roots are traceable to the World War II Navy Department.) Ignatius served for a brief period as Department-wide Assistant Secretary. Barry Shillito, the I & L Assistant Secretary during the bulk of the Nixon years, owed his rise to early help from Livingston. Shillito became Assistant Secretary after serving as President of the Logistics Management Institute (LMI), a contract research center created in 1961 to serve the I & L office. Livingston had stimulated the creation of the Logistics Management Institute, was one of its incorporators, and helped recruit employees, including Shillito.[27]

Livingston's firms and their alumni are not the only constitutents of the weapons management culture, but they are an important part of the structure of connections that have defined the meaning of procurement expertise and determined who gets hired as management expert. Under Livingston's guidance, for example, the Harvard Business School became a gathering place for defense management officials and private management experts. The Business School's weapons studies, for which Livingston was an adviser, were only a fraction of the defense management activities carried on at Cambridge. Business School faculty members developed a curriculum on defense management, and promising defense officials were continually being sent there to study. The Business School in turn enrolled Ph.D. candidates whose defense-related theses provided further content for the curriculum. The brightest candidates were offered jobs in Livingston-related enterprises and soon made their own way as defense experts.[28]

The system has been so successful that it even breeds the handful of informed critics of weapons-contracting management. Ernie Fitzgerald, the courageous official dismissed unlawfully by the Air Force for his exposure of billions of dollars of waste, came up through the Cambridge-Livingston school. Fitzgerald's formal schooling was at the University of Alabama, where he received a degree in industrial engineering. He was hired by Arthur Young, a Big Eight accounting-consulting firm, and served on the Lockheed account. Livingston found Fitzgerald at Lockheed and brought him to the Cambridge-based Management Systems firm for acculturation. Fitzgerald was subsequently promoted to an official position in the Air Force, where he violated the golden rule of the consulting culture by publicly revealing the ineffectual and fraudulent practices engaged in by defense contract managers.

Cost Control in Defense Contracting

In 1957, the Harvard Business School, advised by a committee of aerospace executives and funded by the Ford Foundation, undertook a study of a dozen major weapons projects. In 1962, the study reported that the final costs of the projects averaged 3.2 times the original estimates and ranged up to seven times those planned. This finding destroyed the contract mythology of the Fifties, which held it unacceptable to bind contractors to initial estimates for complex and uncertain projects, so that the major weapons of the day were produced under "cost reimbursable" contracts.[29]

The Harvard findings were the springboard for the contract policies of Robert McNamara, the Kennedy choice for Secretary of Defense. He declared the eradication of the "cost overrun" to be the major management challenge faced by the Department. New management techniques conceived and administered with ample consultant assistance would win the war on waste.[30]

The "incentive contract" was the major cost control reform of the Sixties. "Essentially what Secretary McNamara sought to do," Congress reflected in 1970, "was harness the profit motive for cost reduction."

It is, Assistant Secretary of Defense Tom Morris told Congress in 1962, "the judgment of our best informed policy executives that a significant part of these cost overruns [of the Fifties] are a direct result of the fact that risks are not being shared equitably by the Government and the contractor—because such contracts provide a fee which does not vary, and thus fail to discriminate (1) between good performance and bad; (2) between early successful completion and protracted failure; or (3) between tight management control of costs and wastes." [31]

With the incentive contract, government and contractor would negotiate specified cost, performance, and time goals, and the contractor would be rewarded for surpassing these goals. The contractor would agree to share a certain percentage of the excess costs, if there were any. This meant "more risk for the contractor, but also the prospect for greater rewards. This was the very essence of the American enterprise system." [32]

In 1962, the Department of Defense revised the Armed Services Procurement Regulations to favor the "incentive contract." By 1969, defense and NASA had awarded 5,000 incentive contracts, including most major weapons systems contracts, placed at $53 billion.

The consulting culture produced leading promoters of the incentive idea. Paul Ignatius, the Livingston protégé serving as Army I & L Assistant Secretary, was reported to have influenced McNamara's acceptance of the concept. The promotion of incentive contracting was one of LMI's first projects. It subcontracted to Harbridge House the task of writing the official Defense Department guide to incentive contracting.

The incentive contract happened to come along just when the aerospace industry was discovering that its growth rate of the Fifties could not be sustained. Industry-sponsored studies, such as that performed by SRI for the Aerospace Industries Association, were one response to the crisis. As Professor Murray Weidenbaum, then an industry economist, wrote in 1964, "the defense market over the long run seems to be no longer a major growth area of the American economy, but one characterized by continued instability and fluctuation." Arthur D. Little responded to the call with a booklet entitled "Strategy for Survival in the Aerospace Industry." [33]

The promise of incentive contracting soon proved to be another mythical construction of management's intellect. The correlation between profit and efficiency never materialized. Incentive contracting spawned mountains of paperwork and continually increasing contract costs. By 1969, there had been 45,000 modifications in incentive contracts. Each modification made a mockery of the promise of "fixed" agreements.[34]

In 1966, RAND analyst Ivan Fisher produced a paper on incentive contracting which concluded that the "incentive effect on cost and efficiency may not be as important as customarily believed." Fisher found that it was impossible to relate risk-sharing to the outcome of the contract. He made the further subversive suggestion that any apparent savings on incentive contracts were not due to greater efficiency but were the combined product of initial underestimations of cost and free revisions of estimates.

The Defense Department suppressed Fisher's study, eventually releasing a watered-down version. Embarrassed, RAND curtailed its study of defense incentive contracting.[35]

The Fisher study was followed by a steady trickle of skeptical analyses of incentive contracting. In 1968, LMI, an early promoter of incentive contracting, admitted it had made a mistake. Most analyses of incentive contracting, it declared, had failed to view profits in perspective. The assumption that contractors attempt to maximize profits on a contract-by-contract basis is unfounded, "for whether management is operating in the company's interest or for personal gain . . . the drive for profit is not absent, but it is constrained by aims which ultimately are more consequential." [36]

In 1969, the Democrats left the Defense Department, and Congress dragged some of the Pentagon's scandals into the sunlight. When the cost overruns again became a public issue, the Nixon Administration and its Blue Ribbon Panel responded by changing the rules. In 1969, the Armed Services Procurement Regulations were rewritten to eliminate the preference for incentive contracting.

Friends of management provided the usual eulogy. The incentive contract was said to be a fine idea that produced unexpected consequences. No one was at fault. "It is less the logic of the concept," intoned the House Military Operations Subcommittee, "than the results of its applications, as shown by hindsight, to projects of unexpected complexity and subsequent criticism of the McNamara policies in weapons acquisition." [37]

PERT

The guided missile was the super weapon system of the Fifties. "I was astonished," recalls Sterling Livingston, "at how terribly primitive, how poorly designed for control" the Air Force missile program was. "I don't think that the TRW [the private management contractor] control system was knee high to the Polaris." Livingston shares with other management aficionados the belief that the Navy's Polaris submarine program was the most exceptionally managed weapons program of the Fifties. The manager for Polaris was not a private corporation but the Navy's Special Projects Office (SPO).[38]

In the course of its work, SPO commissioned the development of a battery of management techniques. The most famous of these was PERT—the Program Evaluation and Review Technique. Shorn of its celebrity, PERT is simply another management system.

A turn-of-the-century management expert gave his name to the Gantt chart, a simple graph on which the sequence of construction tasks is ordered. The chart was introduced into military arsenals before World War I. But the Polaris submarine system is composed of thousands of complicated components which are impossible to graph on a simple Gantt chart. The Polaris not only contained thousands of components, but required simultaneous work on numerous tasks. So, in 1957, SPO commissioned Booz, Allen, and Hamilton to modify the Gantt idea. The result was PERT, which replaces the bar graph with a network. The computerization of data, the head of SPO told Congress, was the most novel component of PERT:

> The principles of PERT have been known for a number of years and applied in a gross way for a number of years. It is

only since the capabilities of computers [became] available for general use that PERT system or PERT-type system has become feasible.

The PERT system allows you to go into great detail, far greater detail than you would ever be able to do without the use of computers, to store the knowledge and to manipulate the information so that you can manage it, put it out for humans to manage.[39]

Navy management of Polaris was so successful that even Lockheed performed well. Praise for PERT, however, was greater than praise for the weapons produced. In 1962, the Defense Department revised its procurement regulations to require the use of PERT on many large weapons contracts. By 1964, management experts could choose among 1,000 books and articles written on behalf of the new wonder, and consultants did a booming business with corporations that had to comply with PERT regulations.

New models of PERT were rolled out. The initial PERT was designed to control time and schedule. SPO followed this with a system designed to control cost. Livingston's Management Systems was hired to write the official DOD-NASA PERT/Cost Guide.[40]

The consulting culture was flushed with success. A 1962 Booz, Allen pamphlet portrayed PERT's future with unqualified optimism. A Booz survey found that PERT was being used by sixty-nine military contractors, fifteen firms engaged in both military and commercial work, and nineteen commercial firms. PERT, Booz boasted, is a "management breakthrough," and, "originated on the Polaris project, is now recognized as a thoroughly proven technique. . . . Results have been uniformly good." The Defense Department dubbed 1962 the year of "management systems," and Sterling Livingston received the annual merit award of the Armed Forces Management Association.[41]

The Management Systems Reality

Frederick Scherer studied Polaris in his work for the Harvard Business School's weapons project. PERT/Polaris,

Scherer recalls, was a "big façade in the public relations sense. The fact is that the Navy was not using it." The Harvard reports did not consider PERT's usefulness. In 1972, MIT political scientist Harvey Sapolsky produced the first public account of PERT's actual role in the Polaris program. The famed Polaris management techniques were, Sapolsky found, "not applied on a significant scale in the operations of the SPO until after the successful test and deployment of the initial FBM [Fleet Ballistic Missile] submarines, or they were applied, but did not work, or they were applied and worked, but had a totally different purpose than that officially described." [42]

Sapolsky says that the Navy's technicians were eager to use a new scheduling technique, but resisted PERT because they doubted the reliability of the information it produced. Their doubts proved correct. Contractors readily designed methods to render PERT toothless. Lockheed, a major Polaris contractor, helped the Navy and Booz develop PERT and received permission to process PERT information before it was relayed to the Navy. The company created a separate staff for PERT, isolating PERT from the "bench engineers" who were supposed to make the crucial estimates for the PERT network. Corporate management took PERT away from the technicians.[43]

Army I & L Assistant Secretary Ron Fox told Congress in 1969 that PERT became an independent source of contract waste:

> PERT/Cost groups were naturally considered a legitimate overhead charge to the Government. Consequently, many contractors viewed PERT/Cost as a "make work" type of operation that did little more than provide additional information for Government personnel to study. Many contractors also viewed PERT/Cost as the rationale to negotiate higher overhead rates and thereby provide a larger base for negotiation of profit on programs.[44]

If PERT was useless, it was an immense public relations coup. "The people in DOD and Congress," Sapolsky was told, "had to be impressed. PERT made us okay with the people who had the money. We did it in spades, computers, the whole bit." The management innovation did not control costs, but it loosened Congressional purse strings. The "fact that not one of the participant groups claimed to have benefitted directly from the installation of PERT did not prevent unanimous agreement that PERT was of great benefit to the [Polaris] program as a whole." [45]

How was Polaris managed? The answer is simple. Polaris management was extremely competent. It relied for information on extensive visits to contractor plants, telephone calls, and regular management conferences. It did not need computerized information.

"Who," asked Harvard computer expert Anthony Oettinger in 1964, "has objectively investigated the dynamics of the PERT reporting process? or the need for it? . . . Why should the data be gathered at all?" Consultants succeeded nonetheless in "installing" PERT in schools, city governments, poverty agencies, and even, Sapolsky found, barber shops.[46]

The consulting culture was not unaware of the continual misuse of its invention. The consultants rationalized reality in a familiar manner. First, they argued that someone had oversold PERT. "When you really get to know such a system," Livingston explained, "you have to know how limited it is." Then they argued that inherently valid management techniques are subject to misapplication. People, not systems, control costs. "We designed information systems," continued Livingston, "and would turn them over to the military. The military would not have people who knew how to work them. It was too complex for them to run. When we designed a system and turned it over to the military, it would never work." [47]

Their premises blissfully unexamined, the experts went on to create new models of cost control systems. The idea was to "improve" PERT. The Air Force Systems Command, for example, created a special Cost Management Improvement Program. McKinsey & Co. ran the program and brought all the cost control requirements up to date. The PERT requirement was replaced by a "Cost Planning and Schedule Control Specification" requirement. On the valid assumption that the old PERT directive had caused great confusion, the new rules permitted contractors to build their own systems in accordance with general "specifications." The change, it was hoped, would bring PERT in "through the back door." McKinsey then helped the Air Force introduce efficiencies in the abuse of the incentive contract. It wrote a manual to guide the modification of contracts whose terms were supposed to be fixed. To top this off, McKinsey created a grand "cost information reporting" system (CIR). It was to gather information on contract costs for use in the refinement of future cost estimates. Ernie Fitzgerald, who was involved in the Air Force's cost control program at the time, was particularly critical of the new cost reporting system. McKinsey's system was to collect "historical costs." Past practice, it was well known, was extremely wasteful. Future estimates based on historical costs would build waste into the system forever.[48]

The improvements did not impede the accretion of defense waste. The C-5A disaster, for example, was concealed from defense officials as well as the public, despite Lockheed's deployment of cost control information systems. The Defense Department, as Fitzgerald told Congress in 1969, had an inventory of close to 700 management systems to control the contract bureaucracy. "Despite this," he concluded, "our formal reporting systems do not tell us objectively where we stand on any major program despite literally hundreds of pounds of monthly reports on some programs. We cannot determine objectively how much work has been done, what the planned cost for the work was, or the amount of overrun or underrun on work done so far. Nowhere can we find in the formal reports any indication of what items we are buying should cost. Worst of all, there is no formal requirement or provision for corrective actions in existing cost control systems. Without such provisions, the most elaborate of management systems can do little except convey the bad news." [49]

The road to ignorance was paved with information. SRI's 1963 report to the aerospace industry stated that it already suffered from overmanagement. The industry wanted the Government to move from "its position of overmanaging industry by developing and suggesting simpler, more effective, and less costly surveillance techniques." The incentive contract was supposed to be a major act of "disengagement." "Paradoxically," the Fitzhugh panel observed, the era of the incentive contract was "marked by a multiple increase in the number and detail of management control systems contractually imposed by the Defense Department." And, sadly enough, they were wasteful and irrelevant. "The sheer volume of reporting requirements exceeds, by a substantial margin, the review capabilities of managers within the Department of Defense. More significantly, the increase in management control systems contractually has not cured the cost overrun or schedule delay problems." [50]

In 1974, the Harvard Business School published a sequel to its earlier studies of weapons systems. The new volume, taking the story through the Sixties, was authored by Business School Professor Ron Fox, former Assistant Secretary of the Army's I & L office. In 1971, however, Fox returned to the academy, overwhelmed with frustration. It was, he recalled, "like pushing a wet noodle up an incline." [51]

The Fox book, like the earlier Harvard studies, assumes that the defense complex needs only enlightenment to reform itself. Journalist Robert Sherrill points out that the book documents maladminstration and corruption, but suggests melioristic reform instead of drawing obvious conclusions about responsibility and blame. As a Fox student put it in his Ph.D. thesis, "cost overruns, schedule slippages, and performance degradations continue to occur. Whether it is because of or in spite of the requirement management systems is unknown." [52]

In 1972, Ernie Fitzgerald, who served with Fox in the Management Systems Corporation and at the Pentagon, wrote another major inside account of the defense management. Fitzgerald's populist style contrasted with Fox's scholarship, but both books told similar tales of foolish waste. Fitzgerald, however, saw no mystery in the source of waste. Management experts, civilian and military defense officials, and contract executives are the *High Priests of Waste* of the book's title.

The official response to Fitzgerald's book was revealing. Aerospace executive David Packard, who, as Deputy Secretary of Defense, served as the Nixon Administration's spokesman for weapons procurement, declared that there was no need for Fitzgerald's "kind of 'expertise' to unearth the cost overruns. . . . They were painfully visible to all of us.' " [53]

The cure was obvious. The Defense Department should get rid of "Monday morning quarterbacks like Fitzgerald [and] put officers with professional management training and experience in charge." What did Packard do? The Defense Department rewrote its procurement regulations to eliminate "cost overrun" from the official vocabulary. Billions of dollars of waste were eliminated with a stroke of the pen.[54]

Packard did try to procure trained military managers, and the Department dusted off a moribund institution called the Defense Weapons System Management School. As the *Defense Management Journal* noted, the school had been languishing in Ohio, where "one could easily get the impression that the school's function was of minimal importance." The Department changed the school's mailing address to Fort Belvoir, near Washington, D.C., but it still needed a faculty and a curriculum. The Department promised to "select outstanding men in applicable management and educational fields not only to teach students and the newly assembled faculty, but also to demonstrate new and proven educational techniques." A curriculum committee, chaired by Ron Fox, was established. With the committee's assistance, the school hired PMM to produce the "long course" curriculum and the Sterling Institute to develop an "executive refresher course." [56]

Packard's tenure was a boon to the consulting industry. Harbridge House received $1,324,000 from DOD in fiscal 1969, $1,964,000 in fiscal 1972. The Sterling Institute received $525,000 in 1969 and $231,000 in 1972. PMM, according to the Department's computers, received nothing in 1969, $1,771,000 in 1972.[55]

If there is anything more profitable than a new management technique, it is the cure for the waste caused by old ones.

TECHNICAL ASSISTANCE FOR THE LOCALS

In 1948, the Federal Government awarded $2 billion in grants-in-aid to state and local governments. In 1974, close to $40 billion was available to an organizational zoo of nonprofits for purposes so varied that a contractor was paid $200,000 to catalogue them. America's foreign aid programs fund pays American contractors to teach foreign countries how to spend American money, and manage their societies. Federal monies now permit local government to employ "technical assistance" contractors to the same end.

It was the wisdom of the day that the Eisenhower Administration would turn back the tide of Federal grant spending. Instead, an Eisenhower Commission on Intergovernmental Relations endorsed the grant economy. The Commission hired McKinsey & Co. to track Federal dollars down to the grassroots, and the corporate consulting firm reported favorably on the local use of Federal funds. McKinsey was "impressed with the influence of the grant-in-aid device, over a period of time, in lessening the power of the executive heads of state and local government." Local power, McKinsey predicted, would shift from politicians to "program professionals" and "professional groups" as the flow of grant dollars proceeded.[57]

McKinsey was correct. Decades of Federal highway programs have produced a rich and established highway planning industry. The Housing Act of 1954 has been a continual lease on life for urban planners. Great Society legislation underwrote the "poverty consulting industry."

The experts fueled the politicians' faith that states and localities could be incorporated into the "Federal system," much as large corporations merged newly acquired subsidiaries. The experts promised that the methods used to control the outflow of the Federal dollar would, by the same token, solve the local crises of the time.

Management Comes to the Urban Crisis

Model Cities, conceived in 1965 and located in the newly created Department of Housing and Urban Development (HUD), was the Great Society's showcase solution to the urban crisis. While the Economic Opportunity Act of 1964, creating the Office of Economic Opportunity, mandated the "maximum feasible participation" of the poor in Federally funded programs, the Model Cities Act called for maximum feasible participation by experts. Local programs were to "include to the maximum extent feasible (1) the performance of analyses that provide explicit and systematic comparisons of the costs and benefits . . . of action designed to fulfill urban needs; and (2) the establishment of programming systems designed to assure effective uses of such analyses." [58]

Local City Demonstration Agencies (CDAs) were to be located, geographically and politically, somewhere between City Hall and the ghetto to plan and coordinate the Federal, state, and local "resources" that can be applied to the "social, economic, and physical problems in slum and blighted areas." The CDAs were to be purely managerial creatures, contracting with other agencies for the administration of social services. Terms like "delivery of services, decentralization, coordination, local initiative in planning, comprehensive planning, and target area" became major weapons in the War on Poverty. "The more controversial and/or ambiguous the phrase," noted political scientist Judson James, "the more important its manipulation by the contending interests." [59]

The formal title of the Model Cities legislation is the Demonstration Cities and Metropolitan Development Act, and the term "demonstration" implies, of course, that the Government is eager to show the taxpayer how his money is being used. It is also supposed to convey an aura of technical control. The Government hires experts to scrutinize the use of "demonstration" dollars. When the demonstration proves successful, the experts have learned enough to help the Government "transfer" the success to other needy areas. Political reality pierced the "demonstration" veil early in Model Cities history. Local pressures caused the reallocation of Federal grants and destroyed the spirit of careful control. Instead of twenty demonstration cities, there would be close to 150. Worse, the title "Demonstration Cities" was itself changed to "Model Cities." The President, rumor had it, could not approve of any war-related "demonstration."

Federally funded local planning was to be a central feature of Model Cities. The planning, in keeping with the management spirit, was to be "comprehensive" and would consider all components of the "urban system." Further, the legislation tried to simulate a profit motive to stimulate creativity. Cities were to compete for the planning grants, and their success at planning would determine their receipt of subsequent funds. With so much at stake, the locals eagerly called on experts who professed familiarity with Federal requirements. The experts, for their part, battled to convince the Federal Government that their breed of expertise had a unique purchase on planning wisdom.

The Planners vs. the Managers

A 1969 Federal study found that the Federal "planning assistance" budget was approaching one quarter of a billion dollars. This money was provided by no fewer than three dozen distinct laws, whose haphazard origins had fostered

Model Cities: Some Contracts and their Official Descriptions

TITLE	CONTRACTOR	AMOUNT	DESCRIPTION*
Modification and Installation of CDA Information Systems (CDAIS)	Consultec Fry Consultants Peat, Marwick, Mitchell & Co. Transcentury Corp. Training, Research, & Develop. Inc. Westinghouse PMS BASYS (a division of Booz, Allen)	$531,986 $1,054,525 $713,258 $538,277 $779,975 $349,560 $340,680	These seven contractors have provided the same type of assistance to model cities in 7 geographic regions. They have worked with the staffs of 144 cities in developing and installing project performance information systems and evaluation programs. This type of information is a vital input to the management of the program so that program weaknesses can be corrected and resources employed in the most effective projects.
Management Improvement: The Management Assistance Project (MAP)	Arthur D. Little Booz, Allen Public Admin. Westinghouse PMS Thompson, Lewin, Inc. Training, Research, & Develop. Inc. Jacobs Co. (a division of Planning Research Corp.) Fry Consultants	$262,533 $158,706 $267,761 $230,426 $265,793 $168,666 $368,265	To provide continuous on-site assistance to MCAs in building increased management capacity to identify local problems, establish priorities, develop strategies for addressing problems, allocate resources, monitor performance, and evaluate impact of local efforts to improve living conditions in blighted areas of the cities.
Management Information System (CDAIS): Auditing System	The Systems Discipline Inc.	$449,900	Once the basic information systems are installed, the responsibility for their continued operation will remain with local agencies. Many such agencies have requested periodic assistance in evaluating their needs. This contract is providing that assistance. The contractor has completed the first phase of the work

	Management Assistance	The Jacobs Company (Division of Planning Research Corporation)	$424,478

program by developing and testing procedures for analyzing the strengths and weaknesses of a model city agency's system for identifying, collecting, storing, and using information needed in the management of its program.

The Model Cities Program has presented local governments with relatively new and unique management problems, due to the nature of the program and certain legislative mandates, which the governments involved felt its traditional management structure inadequate for their solution. This contract is an attempt to assist cities in strengthening their existing management capacity to meet such problems. The contractor has developed six management assistance bulletins. In addition the contractor has provided extensive on-site management to 11 cities, each of which had serious difficulties requiring immediate attention.

	Planning Process	Marshall Kaplan, Gans & Kahn	$1,791,530

The Planning Process Study has led to the intensive study of: (1) methods of planning in 21 Model Cities, (2) the roles of key actors including citizens and chief executives and their staffs, (3) the environment in which the planning took place, (4) the resulting plans themselves, and (5) some implementation of the plans during the "first action year."

* Descriptions taken from 1972 HUD Appropriations submissions.

parochial planning "constituencies" and "duplication, conflict in goals, and wasteful expenditures of public monies."

The oldest and largest planning funds go to a particular "function"—the highway. A percentage of Federal highway monies is allocated to planning assistance, and in 1969 the sum represented one quarter of Federal planning dollars. Section 701 of the 1954 Housing Act was the largest single source of "urban planning" funds. The Act allocated monies to "facilitate urban planning for smaller communities lacking adequate planning resources," and "701 monies" were used to pay for land use studies, the preparation of urban renewal plans, and other surveys of the urban scene.

The "need for professional planners," noted Ernest Erber on the fiftieth anniversary of the American Institute of Planners, "became insatiable. The program doubled every few years." [60]

HUD set out to redefine urban planning. Model Cities officials felt that "701 comprehensive planning" had simply not been "comprehensive" enough. They stereotyped the "701" planners as graduates of university planning departments who were "physical planners," primarily interested in land use. The planners that HUD wanted to fund would be concerned with action. They would understand "social, political, and economic processes" as well as urban geography.

HUD needed funds to promote its image of the planning ideal. The available planning dollars were concentrated in 701. In addition, legislation permitted assistance only to cities with populations of less than 50,000. HUD needed a justification to open the 701 budget to management-conscious planners.

In 1967, HUD commissioned four contractors to evaluate the effectiveness of 701 spending. Arthur D. Little, the corporate consulting firm, had written a highly critical report on the narrow preoccupations of the District of Columbia's highway planners. Marshall Kaplan, Gans & Kahn was a young firm formed by refugees from the physical planning establishment. Bob Hammer, of Hammer, Greene, Siler Associates, was a leading protagonist of social planning. Anthony Downs, of the Real Estate Research Corporation, had helped officials formulate Model Cities. These consultants appeared to share HUD's critical view of the planning establishment. Since they were potential recipients of planning dollars in their own right, they could be trusted to conclude that planning assistance should be cured and not eliminated.

The contractor reports were so important that HUD marked them "administrative confidential" and withheld them from the public. In March 1969, a watered-down version of the "principle findings" was released.[61] The first finding was that millions of 701 dollars had "stimulated" local planning. Further findings held that the "stimulation" had been a boon to consultants, but not to the public.

The contractors confirmed the scuttlebutt about 701 plans. Planners used the money to produce predictable and useless plans. "Some professionals have tended to 'boiler-plate' basic materials in several reports—revising generally identical material with only the names of the towns changed. Frequently this involves only the presentation of descriptive material such as the rationale for a capital improvements program, while other consultants use identical formats for all studies, so that it is necessary to change only the figures in tables and key parts of the text." [62] Since the consultants were not obligated to ensure the usefulness of plans, they were hardly ever useful.

As the Marshall Kaplan, Gans & Kahn report told HUD:

> At its narrowest, citizen participation has accordingly meant manipulation of comprehensive planning to serve the most parochial interest of a carefully defined and tightly knit power structure whose short-range goals are almost clearly at variance with the long-range problems and needs of the community. At its broadest, citizen participation has meant the . . . establishment of business leaders more concerned with commercial than human problems. Thus, in a sense,

comprehensive planning has frequently tended to further the alienation of the least vocal and effective elements of a community.[63]

George Raymond, president of the American Society of Consulting Planners and head of a firm heavily engaged in 701 studies, saw the HUD studies as a direct threat. In a letter to Hammer, Greene, Siler Associates, Raymond complained:

> I was also much surprised to hear that the revision of the 701 program, which is about to be instituted by HUD, is based in large part on the four-consultant study. . . . [We] find that many of its recommendations will be implemented without our knowing anything about them. How all this complies with HUD's professed belief in involving the constituency is certainly not very clear, unless, of course, the professional planner in private practice is not accepted as a member in good standing.[64]

Squabbles among competing professional groups are frequent and not normally noteworthy. But Raymond's allegations of discrimination made a point of public import. The HUD studies had indicted old-style planning, but they had not made a case for further planning spending. On the contrary, they implicitly suggested the irrelevance of all planning spending. "I believe," he wrote, "these reports to have addressed themselves to the problem of evaluation of 701 planning in the small community in an incredibly indirect way—as a matter of fact, in a way which was bound to confirm many of the prejudices with regard to 701 planning. . . . I believe the entire orientation of the conclusions of this study to be misguided because of the lack of understanding of the fact that this report turned out not to be discussing the 701 program but the state of planning in the United States." [65]

The reports served their purpose. Congress amended Section 701 to permit assistance to the larger cities served by Model Cities. HUD issued guidelines by which Model Cities could qualify for 701 funds, plus further guidelines that encouraged local planning agencies to use funds to purchase new management techniques. HUD also issued a statement that urged the locals to use "private consultants where their professional services are deemed appropriate by the assisted government." The 701 program flourished again, and for fiscal 1973 HUD asked Congress to provide $90 million for "planning assistance."

In the first year, Model Cities plans did not deviate from tradition. Alan Pritchard, reviewing them for the National League of Cities, recalls:

> I remember one city, Atlanta, proposed eighty-five programs for the first year. Obviously something too big to be planned, funded, or administered in any sort of rational way.
>
> Oversell like this at the local level worked to get the whole program out of scale all around. . . . The Johnson Administration told the cities to plan comprehensively. It told them to be imaginative, to think not about what the neighborhood is but what it should be. Most of all the Johnson Administration urged them to be comprehensive. As a result, the cities developed wishbooks rather than feasible plans.[66]

The Nixon Administration's task force on Model Cities, headed by urbanologist Edward Banfield, concluded that planning had been a waste.

> Instead of letting the cities proceed in their own way, the Model Cities administration persistently has substituted its judgment for theirs, thereby causing delay and uncertainty and eventually waste, confusion, and frustration . . . enormous amounts of time have been spent collecting and arranging facts and figures to be sent off to Washington under the label "plan." (The Chicago plan, for example, ran to 2,500 single-spaced legal-sized pages.) We will not say that none of the cities have gained anything of importance from this planning (or "planning") but it seems clear that the amount gained has not been large in relation to the time and money spent. We are inclined to think that many of the cities would have done more and better planning if the Model Cities administration had left them alone.[67]

A report by Westinghouse to HUD provided a traditional management analysis of the disaster. HUD's new ideas were valid, but the locals did not appreciate them: "The Model Cities process, in its literature, is heavily tied to policy planning as it is now taught in many planning schools. Cities, however, still have not accepted city planning. . . . If city governments were unable to accept completely physical planning in the past, they cannot be expected to accept social comprehensive planning under Model Cities." [68]

Only consultants benefitted from the confusion. According to HUD, "residents of designated Model Cities areas as well as other interested citizens are involved in the planning" of Model Cities. In practice, the locals had to rely on the experts.

Cities relied heavily on consultants in the first planning year. In some cases up to 5 percent of the budget went to local universities, planning firms, and national consulting firms. Prince Georges County spent $71,000 on contractors; Newark spent $370,000; Honolulu spent $100,000; and Wilmerding, Pennsylvania spent $150,000. The Hoboken, New Jersey budget illustrates the liberal dispensation of contracts. The Hoboken Development Corporation requested $148,000 for the first year of a housing program, from which consultants received $123,000 for feasibility studies. Consultants received $25,000 for "employment research, industrial development and marketability research, and fiscal capacity research." By contrast, no funds were allocated to the citizens group affiliated with the employment program or the local agency that administered it. Hoboken was obligated to prepare a physical plan, for which consultants were to receive $35,000, and was required to evaluate Model Cities, $40,000 of the $75,000 evaluation budget going to consultants. "CDA evaluation staffs, in many cities," Westinghouse told HUD, "are little more than contract managers, doing little in-house evaluation themselves." [69]

After the first year, Model Cities planning funds decreased, but consultants took their cut of the "action" money. In New York City, McKinsey became *de facto* Model Cities administrator. The firm, complained an angry city employee, occupied Model Cities office space, and its "contracts with New York Model Cities total $320,000." (A McKinsey interoffice memorandum expressed it: "We have all found it rewarding and educational to become so deeply involved in turning around the Model Cities program here in New York." [70])

Washington, D.C. also bore a heavy contract burden. City Council Chairman Sterling Tucker complained that "for every dollar spent in the model neighborhood, at least 50 cents is spent on professional services." [71] HUD did not try to monitor, evaluate, or otherwise comprehend the role of contractors in Model Cities. It did hire the National League of Cities to serve as a center of Model Cities information, and the League, said HUD, had information on consultant use. The League, however, merely offered locals the names of consultants and did not try to evaluate their use. The Model Cities contract to the League was valued at $36,000. The Office of Management and Budget was aware of consultant waste, but did little about it. Thomas Ubois, the budget examiner for Model Cities complained:

> We asked a lot of questions about the funding of consultants but never could find even approximate answers. . . . The question was one of accounting. How do you count these things? For example, you would separate money for education and find that the money was not going to education but rather to the overhead costs for consultants. We talked about this a number of times, but nothing was done about it.[72]

The Safe Streets Act of 1968 marked Federal entrance into another sacred preserve of local government—law enforcement. The Act created the Law Enforcement Assistance Administration (LEAA) to dole out grants to state and local agencies. The House Government Operations Subcommittee on Legal and Monetary Affairs examined the administration of LEAA funds, the hearings being the only significant Congressional analysis of the "comprehensive planning" spending of the Sixties.[73]

The law provides that states may receive "block grants" of money to use as they choose. The only requirement is that the states prepare "comprehensive plans." The "block grant" would guarantee traditional local autonomy, and the comprehensive plan would guarantee the integrity of local spending.

"Probably the best evidence" of LEAA's failure, Congress found, "is the comprehensive plan annually submitted by each of the fifty-five state planning agencies. Intended to fill a void in criminal justice planning, the comprehensive plans . . . have, on the whole, been too much the products of outside consultants, too much in the nature of shopping lists for hardware items, and too infrequently a 'comprehensive' blueprint for action."

The subcommittee concluded that in the years 1969–71 an average of 17.5 percent of planning grant monies went to consultants. Virginia contracted out over 60 percent of its funds during the three-year period, North Carolina over 40 percent, and California close to 25 percent. "In most cases, outside consultants were hired without competitive bidding. Sometimes their qualifications in criminal justice are minimal or nonexistent. Often," Congress found, "their work products are superficial and of little value."

The firms that received the largest shares of LEAA planning monies were not traditional planning firms. The Congress found that seven firms received a total of $11 million. Three of the seven—Touche, Ross; Peat, Marwick, Mitchell; and Ernst & Ernst—are Big Eight accounting firms. One, Booz, Allen, is a major management consulting firm. The others included two computer software firms and an industry trade association—the International Association of Chiefs of Police. The largest award was the $2 million Detroit paid Touche, Ross for training courses and information systems design.

The Successful Urban Consultant

If the Government wanted to know about the usefulness of its contractors, it could have asked them. "Twenty years of Federal planning assistance programs," wrote Marshall Kaplan, "have not visibly 'built up' the planning capacity of local governments or improved the quality of life. Indeed, the prime beneficiary of such aid seems to be neither local governments nor local residents, but local and national consultants." [74]

Kaplan was a partner in Marshall Kaplan, Gans & Kahn (MKGK), the San Francisco-based consulting firm that received $1 million to do a major "evaluation" of Model Cities for HUD. The Model Cities evaluation permitted Kaplan to update his bleak image of consulting. "I think," he wrote HUD's Donald Dodge (head of the Office of Community Development), "it is astounding that the industry has contributed so little to an effort that supposedly had a public interest concern. As you know, our chronologies [studies] contain a hell of a lot of evidence concerning the failure of technical assistance and the reasons for it." This failure, Kaplan said, "can be supported by reams of data. . . . Many times Technical Assistance, particularly some of the exotic information systems (the specialty of management firms) is a rip off." [75]

MKGK was itself a primary consulting beneficiary of Model Cities monies. Founded in the mid-Sixties, it soon supported fifty professionals on $2 million annual gross income.

The appearance of MKGK was a contrast to the stodgy planning firms that had served the cities, and the slick corporate firms that were also to serve them. MKGK thrived on the contrast. Kaplan, a university planner by training, cultivated the image of the professional rebel. He spoke out against the limited preoccupations of established planners and argued that planning had to be made "relevant" to the poor. He was in consulting by choice, not as a career.[76]

But if the MKGK style differed from its corporate competition, the practices were similar. The Kennedy Democrats of MKGK succeeded in the Republican HUD because both parties shared a fundamental faith in management expertise. MKGK not only knew something about the city—which the corporate consultants did not—but it excelled in recommending managerial solutions to social problems.

Kaplan had directed the "Oakland Task Force," a group of Federal and local officials commissioned to study the administration of Federal grant money in the City of Oakland, California. The Oakland study was recognized by scholars and administrators as a model of its kind, and an early Nixon Administration directive reorganized regional offices in accordance with its recommendations.

The Nixon Administration, if it cared little for the ghetto clientele served by Model Cities, was quite comfortable with the rhetoric of management that promised to regulate Federal aid. Kaplan served as a consultant to Nixon's Council on the Organization of the Executive Branch, which shifted the management framework of Model Cities funding to local Community Development Agencies (CDA) instead of City Demonstration Agencies (CDA). The new CDAs would serve, and be controlled by, the "community" rather than the ghetto.

Kaplan's influence reached its apex when he was called on to serve on a HUD Task Force to study the transition from Model Cities to revenue sharing. The final report, known in HUD as the "Kaplan Report," was a technician's guidebook to the "consolidation and simplification" of grants-in-aid.[77]

Good management may have something to contribute to the solution of urban problems, but, as Kaplan's own studies show, promises of good management have rarely borne fruit. Kaplan's sympathies may have been with the ghetto, but his feet were firmly planted in HUD. His ability to influence Model Cities policy was derived from his friendship with Floyd Hyde, the former Mayor of Fresno,

California, who was the Assistant Secretary in charge of
Model Cities. While MKGK was performing contract work
on Hyde's program, Kaplan also worked directly for Hyde
as a personal consultant.

Neither HUD officials nor the public at large could
distinguish Kaplan's private actions as consultant from the
official acts of HUD. Further, while Kaplan acted as a
high-level Model Cities adviser, his firm was receiving
hundreds of thousands of dollars in Model Cities contract
monies.[78]

The HUD-MKGK relationship violated elementary rules
of public management and created the same bureaucratic
jungle that the MKGK reports condemned. As Hyde's
adviser, Kaplan appeared to be a Model Cities "official."
He flew regularly to Washington from MKGK's San
Francisco office, and when Hyde sent a task force to
examine the New York City Model Cities program, the *New
York Times* identified Marshall Kaplan as the "Federal
official" in charge of this group.[79] HUD, of course, offered a
different version—Kaplan was traveling with the New York
Task Force "in his capacity as project director for Marshall
Kaplan, Gans & Kahn." New York was being studied
under contract. "Mr. Kaplan traveled with the HUD
employees to do personal research under the contract, not
as a Task Force leader." [80]

HUD had more difficulty explaining the "official" role
taken by Kaplan in the Hyde-convened Task Force on
grant "simplification and consolidation." The Task Force's
work bears all the earmarks of a *de facto* delegation of
authority to a consultant whose firm was intimately concerned with the Task Force's recommendations. The Task
Force members included over two dozen HUD employees,
plus Marshall Kaplan and MKGK's Howard Kahn. The
summary of the Task Force Report issued by HUD,
however, bore the Kaplan firm's imprimatur on the cover.
The first page was headed:

To: Floyd Hyde, Assistant Secretary for Community Development

From: Marshall Kaplan
Subject: Summary of Task Force Report

The Report itself carried the same identification and was commonly called the Kaplan Report.[81]

HUD contends that the work was done by a "HUD Task Force" headed by a HUD employee:

> Mr. Kaplan did not head the task force Report on Program Consolidation, Mr. Joseph Crane [a HUD employee] did. He advised and gave direction to that report, since this was in the area of the contract on which Marshall Kaplan, Gans & Kahn were working, but all assignments of personnel and work were made by HUD-employed personnel.[82]

Crane, by his own admission, gave nominal direction.[83] The real direction came from Kaplan.

The Model Cities evaluation was MKGK's prize contract. In Kaplan's eyes, the study of the Model Cities experience was itself a contribution to social scholarship. Kaplan rolled out the term "holistic evaluation" to define his creation. The "holistic evaluation," it turns out, is nothing more than what experts used to call a case study. Kaplan's case studies are certainly more interesting than most of the evaluations produced by HUD, but they are equally well suited to the needs of the bureaucracy. While Kaplan candidly condemns the bankruptcy of consulting, Arthur D. Little's Arnold Schuchter singled out the MKGK Model Cities evaluation as evidence of the common failings of supposedly critical evaluations.

The Kaplan study, Schuchter pointed out, managed to obscure truths that were evident even to lay observers of Model Cities. The report stated, for example, that "residents' needs were so great and problems so large that priority determination was more an art than a science." In other words, noted Schuchter, planning was a mess. "Federal agencies," said the report, "could not in most instances give cities a guarantee of the future availability of categorical program funds, or even a precise handle on the Federal funds flowing into the respective cities." In other words,

Model Cities was a nice façade superimposed on the usual tangle of bureaucratic red tape. Finally, "resident involvement," said the MKGK document, "while an objective of each of the cities, was never an easy part of the planning process." In most cities, said Schuchter, "this means the lack of significant and widespread citizen involvement from the lower-class poor and a struggle by middle-class oriented citizens to become power brokers or get the relatively high-paying jobs. . . . Even when outright censorship is avoided, evaluation documents conceal criticism in clichés and commentary." [84]

Management expertise, Kaplan's success shows, is not always the same shade of grey, but an iconoclastic reformer who turns into a successful Government consultant will very likely become a very traditional management expert.

Information Systems

The presence of Marshall Kaplan did not overshadow that of other consulting firms at HUD. In September 1969, HUD sponsored a program called Community Demonstration Agency Information Systems (CDAIS). Over $4 million in contracts was awarded to seven consulting firms, including PMM, Westinghouse, Fry, and Booz, Allen.

The purpose behind CDAIS was to gain Federal control over local CDAs by increasing Federal reporting requirements. The HUD program was modeled after a 1967 OEO-sponsored program known as a Community Action Program Management Information System (CAP/MIS). CAP/MIS was designed by McKinsey. The Urban Institute evaluated this system in 1969 and concluded that it was one of the most unutilized reporting systems in the Federal Government, "an acknowledged failure by OEO officials." CAP/MIS was discarded.[85] CDAIS fared no better. According to HUD officials, to contractors who evaluated the program, and to the CDA directors, the systems were worthless.[86]

In an attempt to make CDAIS work, HUD again hired seven contractors, including Arthur D. Little, Booz, Allen,

Westinghouse, and Planning Research, and sponsored a program called the Management Assistance Program (MAP). Over $2 million worth of contracts were awarded. The purpose of MAP was to offer technical assistance to CDAs in using CDAIS and other information systems. The contractors involved concluded that information systems were a disaster and that the MAP experience "suggests that local governments are not too receptive to consultants who have been selected to serve them by higher levels of government." [87] In their opinion, these failures indicated that "additional technical assistance will be required to establish and install those aspects of the model cities process which will be necessary for development of a comprehensive local management process." What did "comprehensive management" mean? Westinghouse stated that "it remains unclear just what comprehensive local management is." [88]

V.

EFFICIENCY IN INDUSTRY:
Public Funding of Corporate Growth

In February 1961, shortly after the inauguration of the President, John Kenneth Galbraith and Jerome Weisner, Kennedy's top science adviser, drafted a memo to the President. Its subject was "pockets of poverty" in America, but not of the kind that Michael Harrington's *Other America* was later to bring to the attention of President and country. These other "pockets of poverty" were "backward industries" which lacked "organized stimulus to change."

Kennedy formed a committee to study "civilian industrial technology." Heading it were Jerome Weisner, Secretary of Commerce Luther Hodges, and one of Kennedy's economic advisers. Michael Michaelis, on leave from Arthur D. Little, served as Weisner's executive secretary, while Robert Stern, a Little alumnus, became the responsible Commerce Department man. Arthur D. Little was itself commissioned by the National Science Foundation and the Commerce Department to study innovation in civilian industries. J. Herbert Holloman of General Electric was made Assistant Secretary of Commerce for Science and Technology and assigned to the job of promoting the Administration's Civilian Industrial Technology Program (CITP) proposals before Congress.

Initially, the textile and housing industries were designated as backward. They were cottage industries in an industrial age, and "research and development" was to remodel them into modern, efficient corporate systems. Soon the idea was extended to the social services, and R & D dollars began to buy the technology and expertise necessary to transform the social bureaucracies into profitable social industries.[1]

HOUSING

At the end of World War II, Congress directed (through the Veterans Emergency Housing Act) that certain surplus production facilities be converted to the manufacture of industrialized housing. As a result, the Curtis-Wright Aircraft plant in Columbus, Ohio, became the Lustron Corporation. The Government loaned the corporation $15 million. With this, Lustron devised a prefabricated industrialized housing system—the Lustron House, a pastel-colored, porcelain-enameled steel house. After production cost overruns and a doubling of the loan, Lustron requested yet another $50 million to produce its first house. The costs were becoming astronomical, and the corporation folded. The Lustron Corporation ended by owing the Government $37 million. In exchange, the Government became the owner of the longest pastel-colored-steel assembly line in the world.[2]

Lustron was a new way of organizing the housing industry. The Government was subsidizing one particular company, giving it preference over the rest of the industry; knowledge acquired in the defense sector was to be transferred to civilian programs; and the Federal Government was to act as a "market aggregator," providing demand for the product, especially if the consumer should not initially want it. These ideas reappeared in the 1960s, when the technology reformers took on the housing industry.

The original postwar subsidization of private industry was labeled "national capitalism" and was strongly opposed by independent home producers. In 1949, when the Emergency Housing Act was up for renewal, the director of the Prefabricated Home Manufacturers Institute told Congress that the Government should not pay for start-up costs, research and development costs, or advertising and public displays of a private firm against which other corporations must compete.[3] The independent producers successfully opposed a Government marketing guarantee which had been suggested to justify the investment in factory equipment when Lustron was set up. Nor had labor a more positive response to Lustron. Walter Reuther of the United Auto Workers made a counterproposal to convert war production facilities into publicly owned and publicly run corporations for the mass production of housing.

The housing shortage has been an issue on Capitol Hill since World War II. In the Housing Act of 1949, Congress set a goal of 810,000 Federally subsidized units and established the urban renewal program. Twenty years later, the Government had still not reached its goal, but had created new subsidy programs and a whole new administrative agency—the Department of Housing and Urban Development (HUD)—to deal with the problem.

The failure to supply housing for America's poor has been blamed on many things. The experts of our study have favored as their explanation the "irrational" nature of the housing industry. Their solution is to replace the industry with one that could use the technology of the twentieth century. They have viewed housing simultaneously as a social problem of the poor and as an opportunity for "technological innovation."

By the end of the Sixties, the sole accomplishment of HUD's R & D program was a scattered collection of housing sites, and Milton Semer, a lawyer for one of the nation's largest building firms and formerly President Johnson's housing adviser, likened it to "a car show that won't go away," not the beginning of an answer to the housing problem.[4]

CITP

The Civilian Industrial Technology Program (CITP) singled out housing as a backward industry worthy of its attention and, in 1963, created a special panel to study the industry. Robert A. Charpie, then a Union Carbide executive, was chosen as its chairman. (In 1967, the year that the Mitre Corporation was to become a vital organ in the embryonic HUD R & D program, Charpie joined Mitre as a trustee and, in 1972, was elected Chairman of the Board.) The Charpie panel "thoroughly studied" its problem and produced an eleven-page public report that found the housing industry was making an inadequate contribution to the nation's economic growth. The problem was to be solved through the introduction of new technologies and new methods of industrial organization. The problem with housing, said Charpie, was not that it failed to serve the poor. He, in fact, went so far as to mistakenly credit the industry with helping alleviate most of the "pent-up" needs of the poor.[5] Clearly the technology reformers had loaded their guns for different bear: the transformation of the housing industry itself.

What were the technical failings of the industry? The major evidence of backwardness, not surprisingly, was the low level of R & D the industry was paying for. This low level was associated with the industry's fragmentation. The housing industry, unlike other basic American industries, is not dominated by a handful of giant producers. One commission on housing later determined that the fifty largest producers of housing in the country produced less than 15 percent of the annual housing output. The nation's largest housing producer, Levitt, erected less than one half of 1 percent of all housing units in 1970.[6]

There has always been, in America, a popular concern with industrial concentration and the evils of bigness. The reformers augmented the antimonopoly repertoire with a twist of their own. They argued that it was precisely those industries in which markets were dominated by small local companies that bore the taint of monopoly. This attack on the "monopoly of smallness" was made in the case of the housing industry and on an industry of comparable dollar volume, the "education industry." These industries' fragmentation, they argued, made it possible for local firms to live without the threat of competition from innovative firms that might break into the local market. None was forced to innovate to meet competition, and, as long as they were small, none had the capital or the desire to do so.[7]

Among the barriers to innovation cited by the Charpie report were zoning laws, building codes, land development policies, and the vested interests that supported them, such as local builders. Also cited were the unions, whose jobs were written into the building codes, and citizens and other businessmen who used them as devices to enforce aesthetic, racial, or commercial predilections. Thus, while housing innovation was advocated in the name of a commonly accepted goal—"progress" through new technology—this innovation would require changes which might be political liabilities to the groups to whom the program had to be sold.

Nevertheless, the Charpie panel concluded that "the stage is set for a further significant rationalization of the housing industry during the next decade or so." What did "rationalization" mean? The report expressed a desire to avoid "prejudging" the changes that might do the industry good at the same time that it offered the automobile industry as an example of an "innovative" industry and indicated that the housing industry should increasingly rely on prefabricated buildings and mobile homes in preference to on-site construction.[8]

It was the Government's role, said the panel, to subsidize those "willing to experiment with new ideas and concepts." The mechanism of innovation would be the contract. The Defense Department, a major purchaser of civilian goods and services, including housing, education, and health care, should become a testing laboratory for "both large and small-scale experiments in technological innovation." The panel singled out the "cost-reduction" techniques being developed in DOD as an appropriate take-off point for housing experiments.[9]

The Charpie report was the first of a series of Government-sponsored reports that considered industrialization as the solution to the housing problem. A later (1967) Presidential Report[10] came to the conclusion that the problem with the housing industry was not a technological one. To the surprise of many, the housing industry was more innovative than anyone had previously suspected. Materials and product changes were constantly occurring, but because of the local nature of the industry, these could not be measured against a national standard. It was believed that the only way costs could be brought down was through standardization of design, a solution that appears unacceptable to the public. The industrialized housing process has yet to prove that it can reduce costs, and the free market capabilities of industrialized housing producers have yet to demonstrate any such capability.

The Charpie report was followed by a CITP recommendation that the Commerce Department fund several millions of dollars' worth of housing research. This recommendation was promptly attacked by hostile Congressmen. Herbert Hollomon and other CITP spokesmen were subjected to name-calling (Secretary of Commerce Luther Hodges was called "Mr. Hodge podge") by Appropriations Committeeman John Rooney (D-N.Y.), who objected to these "intellectuals" and their alleged noninvolvement in the housing industry and to the political "amateurs" in CITP. Hollomon and other CITPers saw Rooney as not only a representative of parochial views but a man of Neanderthal mien. Behind the name-calling, however, this was a highly symbolic battle. The most articulate anti-CITPer in Congress, Congressman Bow of Ohio, attacked the proposal for interfering with the free enterprise system. The proposal was, he said,

> an ill-conceived and ill-defined research program that would tamper with the delicate free enterprise mechanisms of the highly competitive $80 billion per year [housing] industry, undercut that industry's own substantial research and development efforts, create a costly and self-perpetuative program that offers little prospect of benefit, set up a new era of political patronage, and would introduce to the American taxpayer a new brand of Government bureaucrat and technocrat.[11]

A good percentage of Bow's remarks were, as we shall see, not far from the mark.

Congressional reactions confirmed the CITP reformers' impressions of the obstacles to change. Donald Schon, who had moved from Arthur D. Little into the Department of Commerce, found that Congressional resistance "revealed a great deal about the complex and dynamically conservative [*sic*] building industry system." CITP had "lift[ed] the . . . web," and it was possible to see the "connections between apparently separate elements of the system. It turned out that building suppliers, craft unions, code inspectors, purchasers, contractors, and virtually the whole array of building industry units make up a coalition of shared interests built on prevailing technologies." [12] Research threatens these interests and causes them to link up with their Government representatives to fight change.

The CITP battle confirmed for Schon that the housing industry, as well as many other "fragmented" industries, was a "system" whose own "dynamism" sometimes worked on the level of "unconscious activity" and was sometimes a "conscious conspiracy to employ the web of building industry connections to maintain the industry's stable state." [13]

Schon, as an employee of Arthur D. Little, had written studies for the Department of Commerce and the National Science Foundation (NSF) which called for invasions of backward industries.[14] It was gratifying to discover that the industry was eager to strike the pose of the antagonist. The battle, says Schon, even as it was being lost, showed that the cause of the technology reformers was just and the techniques of systems analysis appropriate.

A 1966 NSF–National Planning Association Conference on Technology Transfer provided CITP protagonists with an opportunity to speculate on the road ahead.[15] They argued that the usual market is not big enough to make a profit in industrialized housing. Individual sites are separated by many miles, and the additional travel costs make the expense of the industrialized housing process too high.

In addition, each locality in the country wishes to set its own standards as to how its communities should look and to write zoning laws and code ordinances which prohibit changes in the type and style of the housing.

Hollomon suggested that the Government had offered insufficient incentive to entrepreneurs to counterbalance these problems, and he established himself as an early protagonist of Government-sponsored "market aggregation." Charpie proposed that Government R & D money be used to stimulate the formation of consortia, groups of private companies with a common purpose.[16]

The Charpie recommendations represent the beginnings of what might be called "corporate liberalism" in the housing field—the belief that Government funding of large corporations will rationalize the structure of the housing industry.

The National Academy of Engineering (NAE) noted in its 1972 report on industrialized housing that there were five markets that appeared to be particularly suitable to exploitation by large corporations.[17] One of these was the military construction market. The Defense Department buys a large number of homes for its employees, and in the late Sixties it began to call on companies like General Electric to produce industrialized housing on military bases.

A second and third market, said the NAE, lay in the multifamily (as opposed to single-family) detached housing and the anticipated boom in vacation homes.

The other two markets were tied into expanding Federal programs, to which the technology reformers linked their cause. These were "New Towns" and Federally mandated subsidized housing for low- and moderate-income families.

The Woods Hole Phenomenon

When the Department of Housing and Urban Development (HUD) was created in 1965, its administrators and Congressional supporters had faith in the ability of technology to solve HUD's problems. The first Secretary of HUD,

INDUSTRIALIZED HOUSING—PEOPLE AND DEMONSTRATIONS

CIVILIAN INDUSTRIAL TECHNOLOGY PROGRAM
(subpanel on housing) (1963)
Director: Robert Charpie (Mitre Director—1967;
Chairman of the Board—1972)

WOODS HOLE (1966)
Hortense Gabel (Ford Foundation; Institute of
Public Administration)
Thomas Paine (GE Tempo-NASA-GE)
Ezra Ehrenkrantz (Building Systems
Development Inc.)
Donald Schon (NBS-OSTI)
Lyle Fitch (Institute of Public Administration)
Edward K. Rice (T.Y. Lin Associates)
James Simpson (HHFA-Abt Associates)
Anthony Downs (Real Estate Research)
Jack Ruina (Institute for Defense Analyses)

KAISER COMMISSION (1967)
Edgar Kaiser, *et al.*
Walter Reuther
Landmark 26,000,000
estimate GE Tempo

**URBAN SERVICES
CORPORATION**
Walter Reuther
Thomas Paine
Hortense Gabel

DOUGLAS COMMISSION (1967)
Paul Douglas *et al.*
Ezra Ehrenkrantz
Anthony Downs

SCSD PROJECT (1961–65)
Ford Foundation, EFL
Ezra Ehrenkrantz

HUD'S RESEARCH AND TECHNOLOGY PROGRAM (1966)
Thomas Rogers—Director (1966–68) (DOD-HUD-Mitre)
Harold Finger—Director (1968–72) (NASA-HUD-GE)

INSTANT REHAB (1967)
IPA
Hortense Gabel
T.Y. Lin Associates

BUDGET PREPARATION
Mitre, IDA, Kaiser

DEPARTMENT OF DEFENSE
General Electric

MDCDA (1966)
Walter Reuther
Donald Schon
Hortense Gabel (Center for Community Change)
Ezra Ehrenkrantz

IN-CITIES (1968)
Kaiser Engineers
Donald Schon
Abt Associates
Ezra Ehrenkrantz
Westinghouse Electric
Battelle Memorial
Mitre
Anthony Downs

OPERATION BREAKTHROUGH (1969)
Mitre
Ehrenkrantz
Levitt, GE, TRW, Boeing *et al.*

Robert Weaver, solicited advice from administrators of the big R & D agencies on how to get monies for R & D. Alain Enthoven, chief systems analysis whiz kid in McNamara's Defense Department, urged the use of systems analysis as a key to Congressional purse strings.[18] Several others recommended that he align himself with the proper people, such as the National Academy of Sciences (NAS), to create the necessary aura of expertise.

In 1966, at the initiative of Weaver and Presidential science adviser Donald Hornig, HUD and the White House Office of Science and Technology (OST) sponsored a month-long summer study conference at Woods Hole, Massachusetts. In addition to the fine marine biology laboratories, the National Academy of Sciences facilities at Woods Hole are a traditional gathering place for beneficiaries of Government R & D largesse and a summer home for the Defense Department's scientific elite. A Woods Hole conference is a normal part of the R & D process.

The gathering at Woods Hole brought together Government officials, systems analysts, self-styled, "space types," and representatives of private companies and nonprofit groups with their eyes on housing monies. HUD Secretary Weaver was a participant, as were his Under Secretary, Robert Wood, and the science adviser Donald Hornig. Donald Schon attended in his capacity as Director of the Institute for Applied Technology of the Department of Commerce. Others of the nearly 100 participants came from nonprofits like Stanford Research Institute, Midwest Research Institute, MIT, Aerospace Corporation, and Systems Development Corporation;[19] industrial corporations like Ford and General Electric; and profit-making consulting firms like Building Systems Development Corporation and Real Estate Research. The construction industry was conspicuously absent.

The conference was to determine how HUD could apply to the cities "the kind of forced-draft technological effort that has characterized space and defense." [20] Though it dealt with a fundamental issue of public policy, the Woods

Hole gathering for the cities was as secretive an affair as many a Woods Hole conference for the Defense Department. For one thing, it was closed to the press. According to one participant, the secrecy was intended to create a mystique: "Walter Rosenblith [the conference chairman, an MIT biophysicist] wanted to design [another] Manhattan Project. Putting a small group of people together and insulating them would ensure the strong possibility that out of this would come a social invention." [21] On orders of the President, the papers produced by the conference were kept secret. The public was left to view the Woods Hole discussions through HUD's public relations office. A pamphlet on the conference,[22] released six months later, failed to mention Woods Hole's most prominent recommendation—the call for the creation of a "Comsat for Housing," which emanated from a panel on housing rehabilitation consisting of four representatives from industrial and consulting firms, four representatives from HUD and the White House, and the Ford Foundation's Hortense Gabel, who chaired it. The panel, echoing the Charpie report, charged that the construction industry was "a closed system profiting from the maintenance of obsolete technology" and called for the funding of "efforts to coordinate different products, particularly when they are manufactured by other firms" through a "Comsat for Housing." [23]

(Comsat was one of the most popular models for change in the mid-Sixties. In setting up the Comsat Corporation, the Government had entered into a joint venture with AT & T to control communications satellites technology. Comsat turned the development of a "system" over to a quasi-public monopoly and provided Federal R & D money to private industry with a minimum of bureaucratic strings.)

The new housing Comsat was envisioned as a procurement and management office which would eventually create an entirely new housing industry. Its first task would be to fund "user and performance criteria studies." "User studies," the poverty war's equivalent of a market survey, would determine the housing needs of the poor. "Performance criteria studies" would develop industrial standards for housing producers. The setting of performance standards was crucial if a housing industry based on "systems" was to replace the traditional industry. Producers would not be required to use any particular materials or techniques, as long as the standards were met. In theory, this would encourage producers to innovate to meet standards in the most efficient manner possible. The use of performance standards would also help break down the patchwork of local practices and building codes that prevented efficient mass production of housing.[24]

The Rehabilitation Panel's late June "debriefing" letter to HUD was written by Hortense Gabel and Dr. Thomas Paine, a panel member and head of General Electric's Tempo Division,[25] and proposed that $5 to $10 million be allocated initially for the purpose of starting up the corporation and funding the proposals for user and performance standard studies. The new corporation could then ask for bids from "systems companies new to the housing field such as Litton Industries and Lockheed." [26]

In the first stages, the new corporation would focus on rehabilitation, but new construction would be increasingly mixed into the market. And the corporation would purchase property to ensure markets for the new housing producers. The panel saw a great possibility for market aggregation in recapturing acres of unused city property where homes for the poor could be built. The corporation would negotiate labor issues with unions and zoning and building code questions with state and local officials.

The Gabel-Paine proposal was unusually specific in its estimation of the cost savings that could be expected from the new approach. "The aim," said their letter, "is to build housing better, cheaper, and faster"—at half the traditional cost and in half the time. This claim was clearly beyond the wildest expectations of any real housing expert, and later studies show it to have been completely unrealistic. Donald Schon, who was instrumental in the "calculation" of this figure, explains that exaggeration was a necessary tactic to attract public attention.[27]

According to Schon, Hortense Gabel emerged as Comsat's "product champion," willing to push new ideas until they overcame "institutional obstacles" to acceptance. "She argued her cause formally and informally through successively higher levels of HUD, organizing presentations and reviews for the Under Secretary and Secretary. She presented the idea in its most favorable light, talked to each advocate or defender in terms of his greatest interest, built alliances, made judgments about the timing of confrontations." [28] Clearly, her access in the agency was greater than that of any average citizen.

Weaver asked Gabel to discuss the new Comsat with other experts. In August, as a HUD adviser, she began formulating a proposal for the President and, in that capacity, met with Paine and others at Paine's offices in Santa Barbara, California. Other Woods Hole carryovers included Ezra Ehrenkrantz, Donald Schon, and James Simpson. Ehrenkrantz, the head of Building Systems Development Corporation, was an architect whose interest in "systems building" quickly made him one of the most influential of consultants, as well as one of the most successful of businessmen. Schon, who had represented the Government at Woods Hole, had left the National Bureau of Standards to form his own consulting firm, the Organization for Social and Technical Innovation (OSTI), which also became a direct beneficiary of the new systems building fad. Simpson left HUD shortly after this meeting to serve as a consultant to Clark Abt's Boston firm as it made the move from DOD–NASA into civilian systems consulting.

The Santa Barbara group reiterated the earlier proposals, affirming again the ability of private enterprise, with enough public support and financing, to solve the housing problems of the poor. As precedent for the new organization, the group cited AEC and NASA and, in deference to political reality, the Federal Housing Administration. FHA, said the group, had promoted the extension of credit to the poor. Just as Charpie had patted the housing industry on the back for helping the poor, so the Gabel-Paine panel congratulated HUD for something it never did. By 1970, even government-sponsored studies recognized the racial imbalance of FHA funding.

The new organization was to be christened the Urban Development Corporation, a corporation "in the best American tradition of creating new institutions to serve national purposes." It was to "develop performance specifications and design criteria to attract the research and development capacity of large-scale industry; provide a national market for improved and less expensive systems, materials, components, and construction tools; develop a major information center to assist municipalities, industry, labor, sponsors and cooperatives, and the public in rebuilding slum neighborhoods." [29]

The Federal Government was to "acquire and rehabilitate dwelling units and facilities in target areas of selected cities." The corporation would also "provide incentives for labor to increase productivity and integrate work forces through continuity of operations and expansion of employment; provide similar incentives to assist general contractors to modernize scheduling, bidding, and construction practices." And the new corporation would "receive public and private funds; acquire land and buildings; mortgage property; contract for construction and management; train personnel for itself and others; transfer, lease, or sell buildings and facilities to nonprofit, limited profit, and profit organizations." [30] How the corporation would accomplish these monumental tasks was not made clear.

The Santa Barbara group reported to HUD in September 1966. For the next two months, HUD leaders discussed the proposals with spokesmen for all the relevant interests. They talked to NASA about the use of its facilities for testing new technologies and its negotiating skills for systems contracting, and also talked to DOD about similar proposals.[31]

In early November, Secretary Weaver transmitted to President Johnson the proposal for a corporation whose life was to begin on January 1, 1967 and which would be empowered to spend $50 billion in a decade to buy up slum areas and renew or replace 5 million buildings.[32] On November 26, a *New York Times* headline, "A Company Like Comsat To Battle Slums Is Urged," was the first public mention of the proposal.

On January 6, 1967, the *Washington Post* reported: "White House Kills Urban Housing Plan." What had happened? Some stories suggested that the President was angered by the *Times*'s premature disclosure of the proposal, because White House "sources" at the time claimed that the proposal had "bugs" in it. Milton Semer, President Johnson's White House adviser on housing, points to the naïveté of the proposal that said housing costs could be reduced by 50 percent. Semer called the propagandizing of the ideas of Woods Hole "the product of the mind that set us back a generation." [33]

Woods Hole was the high-water mark of success of the technology reformers. It demonstrates the ease with which the technology reformers would prefabricate facts to conform to a theoretical bent. It had many accepting the premises of "experts," who simply projected their vested interests. Unlike the Charpie panel, the participants at Woods Hole hid their corporate ambitions in the rhetoric of social reform.

The Douglas Commission
and the Kaiser Report

Though the ill-fated "Comsat for Housing" was the Woods Hole group's special favorite, the conference's other recommendations became the base of HUD's research program. HUD, in fact, received Congressional permission to form a research office of its own, and it was created with none of the fanfare that attended the CITP proposals. Though its object was to spur the housing industry, as the CITP had proposed, its location in HUD instead of the Department of Commerce permitted it to be sustained on the backs of the social-problem constituency, shifting attention away from an antagonistic industrial community.

The Congressional authority for housing research is found in Section 1010, a little-debated part of the Metropolitan Demonstration and Development Act of 1966. Better known as the Model Cities Act of 1966, it was the vehicle for continuing the Model Cities program begun in 1965.[34] A showpiece of Johnson social legislation, the Model Cities were regarded as laboratories for urban experimentation.

The R & D Section of the Model Cities Act presented an anomaly. The Act called for citizen participation in the development of programs, but its research component did not break stride with the elite tradition of research programs. Decision-making would involve business, academic, and nonprofit representatives in partnership with Government officials. Citizen representation would exist only by proxy. Program design might be based on surveys of the local population, and program implementation might require the approval of local officials, but in the end the R & D establishment would control the choice of programs.

The initial funding for the HUD R & D effort, called Research and Technology, was a paltry $500,000—just enough to hire a staff and contract for the first few studies. By 1972, the Research and Technology budget had increased to over $50 million. At the beginning, the new office was overshadowed by special commissions created to study urban problems. One of these, the Kerner Commission, established in the aftermath of the 1967 riots, examined housing as a component of racial violence. Two other commissions focused more directly on the housing problem.

In June 1967, President Johnson announced a commission that would study "every possible means of establishing the institutions to encourage the development of a large-scale efficient rehabilitation industry." [35] Johnson appointed as head of the Commission on Urban Housing Edgar Kaiser, Chairman of the Board of Kaiser Industries, one of the nation's largest construction firms. UAW leader Walter Reuther, an early proponent of industrialized housing, was a key member, together with the AFL-CIO's George Meany and the International Electrical Workers' Joe Keenan. In addition to Kaiser, the committee contained executives of other large corporations with housing interests, plus a handful of representatives from the traditional housing industry. Whitney Young of the Urban League provided respectable black representation.

Not surprisingly, a dispute arose between the big builders, who favored the development of a new industry, and the smaller builders and their labor allies, who favored the traditional industry.[36] The divergent commissioners produced an assessment of the housing industry that significantly modified the interpretation developed earlier by the technology reformers. Consultant studies for the committee demonstrated that the housing industry was indeed fragmented and subject to the vagaries of local markets and building and zoning codes, but did not support the argument that the industry was technologically backward. "Contrary to widespread belief," states the introduction to the commission's final report, "homebuilding is not a technically stagnant industry, resistant to new ideas." The document warned the public not to expect quick results, in cost reduction or otherwise, from the promises of systems building. Still, while denying their basic premise, the Kaiser Commission did endorse the idea of Government support for innovation, and made obeisances to the rhetoric of the technology reformers. It was in the nation's interest, it said, that the Government should support activities to identify, study, and remove "existing constraints" to the "implementation of technological advances." [37]

An immediate result of the Kaiser report was the revival, in 1968, of the Comsat formula, in the form of the National Housing Partnership, a Congressionally chartered nonprofit corporation that raises money through stock sales and FHA grants and offers funding for low- and moderate-income housing. It remained a modest effort, rehabilitating or building 2,793 units during its first two years.[38]

As the work of the Kaiser Commission proceeded, so did that of a National Commission on Urban Problems, headed by former Senator Paul Douglas (Anthony Downs of Real Estate Research and Ezra Ehrenkrantz of BSD were two commission members.) The Douglas Commission had been mandated by Congress to study building codes, tax policies, federal regulations, and housing practices. Its report came out in December 1968, recommending housing experimentation and suggesting the prospect of "substantial" cost reductions.[39]

The sustained influence of the Woods Hole crowd was again evident in a General Electric Tempo study for Kaiser and in the testimony of Tempo's chief, Paine, before the Douglas Commission. The Tempo-Kaiser report put the number of units that had to be built in the next decade at 26 million.[40] Housing expert Henry Aaron of Brookings Institution, writing later on the national goal figures, stated that "public awareness of the housing problem is shaped by statistics that are conceptually inadequate and empirically inaccurate. . . . The national housing goal that is based on these figures . . . is itself an expression more of political commitment than of realistic forecasting." [41]

The acceptance of the Kaiser Commission figure became a significant factor in today's housing crisis. According to Miles Colean, a housing economist, "This arbitrary requirement, which was readily assumed to be beyond achievement by the forces of the market place, changed the rate of subsidization of new housing from glacial to avalanche proportions." [42] What was needed in the ghetto was the rehabilitation of homes, not the building of more, as FHA scandals well demonstrate. Tempo created an illusion, a statistic. Without this arbitrary target, there would have been no justification for creating a new housing industry.

"Instant Rehab"

Thomas Rogers, recruited from the Defense Department's Office of Defense Research and Engineering, where he was Director of Electronics and Information Systems, became the first director of HUD's R & D program. How did his previous experience relate to his new job? Rogers candidly admits:

> I had no idea of what I was getting into. Nobody quite understood that you couldn't make money off of poverty. We hadn't gotten to the moon yet, and we knew we were in trouble in Vietnam. But we knew God would provide. In the cities, we didn't know what we were doing. I didn't want the job, but my friends encouraged me by telling me, "Why not do something besides killing people?" [43]

Rogers' candor might have been unusual, but his ignorance of the city was not. It was to be a precedent for the selection of other defense-NASA men to head civilian research programs.

In theory, of course, the R & D background was supposed to give men like Rogers the means by which they could solve some of the agency's problems. In fact, with his lack of relevant experience, Rogers relied on the advice of "outsiders" who were often equally ignorant.

The first Research and Technology money repaid the debts of Wood Hole. Rogers doled out a $77,500 contract to MIT's Walter Rosenblith, chairman of the Woods Hole conference,[44] to fund fifty "hardware" researchers in the "search for simultaneous equations to locate and remove the sources of urban discontent." [45] The study is not available at the HUD library, program offices, or distributing agency.

More important, HUD made $85,000 in awards to the National Academy of Sciences and the sister National Academy of Engineering to map out the strategy for HUD's research program.[46] Their reports questioned the program's ambitions. HUD was cautioned by the academics against overdoing the systems approach. If the reports did not produce particularly novel advice, neither was the advice heeded by HUD; it went right ahead with its planned systems studies.

HUD was told by the NAS that the systems approach could be useful in organizing the HUD R & D program itself. HUD contracted with the RAND Corporation to sponsor a conference to lay out the "agenda" of urban problems to be studied. RAND suggested, though with apparent misgivings, the appropriateness of the defense-NASA model:

> We do not expect that the technique and format of military program analysis will survive unmodified in the environment of HUD. They were developed in the context of a strongly hierarchical organization, a narrowly construed (if rather fundamental) mission, fewer intergovernmental transactions, greater internal fungibility of resources, and greater insulation from Congressional pressures. Yet, it is sensible, we think, to build on this military experience.[47]

HUD followed this advice.

RAND was accompanied into HUD by two other defense research organizations, Mitre and the Institute for Defense Analyses. The two groups were called on to assist in writing the research budget for HUD (from which they were to be paid) and to write the justifications that would get HUD its first R & D funding from Congress.[48]

With study contracts awarded to the appropriate think tanks, HUD, in a moonshot for the city block, placed all its resources behind the "instant" rehabilitation of a slum tenement and successfully rebuilt a Harlem apartment in forty-eight hours (exactly forty-seven hours and fifty-two minutes). Unfortunately, the cost was astronomical, and HUD refused to release figures.[49] One HUD official described the bill as "close to the cost of furnishing a Hilton Hotel." [50] Under Secretary Wood granted that the effort was both the "most intensive and expensive effort to date to apply space engineering techniques to a key housing problem in our older cities." If, admitted Wood, the impact of the experiment were limited to the one tenement, "we will have provided very expensive housing indeed, and we might better have bought each family a home on Long Island." [51]

The principal R & D contractors for "Instant Rehab" were the Institute of Public Administration and T. Y. Lin Associates. T. Y. Lin received the $1.3 million contract (R & T and FHA monies) to restore the demonstration building, and IPA, the nation's oldest policy research center, received $340,000 to "evaluate" and "test" the construction. Lyle Fitch, the president of IPA, was one of the Woods Hole conferees. Hortense Gabel, who is credited with having generated the concept of "Instant Rehab" while she was Rent and Rehabilitation Commissioner of New York City, is a trustee of IPA. Edward K. Rice, the president of T. Y. Lin Associates, also was at Woods Hole.

While HUD balks at releasing a cost analysis of Rehab and states that none is available, IPA's evaluation report (which is absent from the physical premises of HUD) found the costs of the effort to be $45 per square foot, as compared with $14.37 per square foot for conventional rehab efforts. IPA concluded that "no data have yet emerged . . . to indicate that costs per usable square foot can be lowered enough to make them comparative with conventional rehabilitation or new construction." [52]

IPA, however, blamed the failure not on the systems techniques ("the demonstration project was brilliantly successful in demonstrating that a systems approach using critical path scheduling and suitable materials can cut the time required for the main physical work of rehabilitating an old-law tenement"),[53] but on the inability of the city to modernize building codes. When the technical aspects of a project fail, shifting the blame to social problems is a device commonly employed by the technology reformers. HUD was unable to offer any evidence that the "brilliantly successful" systems approach was ever used again.

The failure of HUD to provide precise cost figures on the

experiment was an unhealthy sign. The commissions and studies that advocated new technology had emphasized Research and Technology's benefits in reduced costs. If experiments were to be anything more than extravagant giveaways, cost data, however revealing, would have to be gathered and subjected to public disclosure. Some of the studies and commissions recognized this and called for the creation of oversight groups to monitor the experiments.

The School Construction Systems
Development Project

Ezra Ehrenkrantz enjoys the reputation of having been responsible for one of the few successful civilian systems ventures. He is an architect and chief executive of Building Systems Development Corporation, a consulting firm with offices in New York and San Francisco, and the root of his success lies in his association with the School Construction Systems Development Project (SCSD).

The story of SCSD began in 1953, when Ehrenkrantz was awarded a Fulbright fellowship to study the use of prefabricated building components in the postwar construction of British schools. In 1958, the Educational Facilities Laboratories (EFL), a Ford Foundation beneficiary that provides seed money for the study and design of school facilities, produced an Ehrenkrantz report praising the British experience with prefabrication. Together they then successfully solicited the interest of a number of California school districts and, in late 1961, EFL gave Stanford University's School Planning Laboratory, the Western center of EFL, $50,000 with which to begin planning. Ehrenkrantz was named architect for a new group, the School Construction Systems Development Project, organized to direct the program.

SCSD proceeded according to standard operating procedures for systems development projects. Consultants entered the schools to determine the needs of school-building users. The survey of "users needs" laid the groundwork for the development of "performance specifications" for new schools. These standards were then made available to bidders. The project did not specify components or materials to be used, but "merely specified the problem to be solved and left the solution itself to the manufacturer." SCSD asked for separate bids on groups of components, or "subsystems," so that the makers of individual components had to work together, "a simple idea, to be sure, but one," says EFL, "that had been little tried before on projects the size of schools." [54]

To entice manufacturers to bid and to do the retooling required by SCSD, the project had to guarantee a sufficiently large market to ensure volume production and a net profit. Initially, the group aimed for the construction of twenty-two schools and a guaranteed market of $30 million. By 1966, although it was engaged in producing only thirteen schools, EFL expressed satisfaction with the results.

While the image of SCSD is one of success, it is difficult to ignore the fact that EFL funded the papers that judged the experiment a success, and EFL itself has been cautious in its estimate of the project's success in reducing costs.

The actual costs of the schools were always hidden, but an investigation conducted by Senator Proxmire, through interviews with California education officials, discovered the costs to be far beyond the expectations of the state when the experiment began.[55] Karl Justin, an architect with the New York firm of Max Urbahn Associates, suggested in *Technology Review*, the MIT alumni magazine, that there was a dearth of independent evaluations of SCSD and felt the project planners had been blowing their own horn for too long. His analysis suggested that the overall costs of the schools are not necessarily reduced by reducing costs of components, and he pointed to the propensity of SCSD projects to sprawl and produce high land costs.[56] Another "independent" review of SCSD was written by the National Bureau of Standards. The NBS review cited figures which would indicate that SCSD was a success in cost-reduction technique. When we questioned the accuracy of these figures, Donald Schon, the author of the report, conceded that the figures in the report were those of Ehrenkrantz and that NBS had not performed an independent study.

Nevertheless, the SCSD idea spread quickly, and Ford and Ehrenkrantz continued their roles as catalysts and consultants.

The Detroit Experiment

The city of Detroit provided the setting in which the Comsat idea was first tried out by its leading advocates, Ehrenkrantz, Gabel, Schon, and Walter Reuther. (Motor City's role as manager of an automobile empire has not exempted it from ghetto problems rivaling those of other major cities.)

In 1966, a mixed private-public housing authority had been incorporated by Walker Cisler, Board Chairman of the Detroit Edison Company, Detroit's Mayor Jerome Cavanaugh, and Walter Reuther. The Metropolitan Detroit Citizens Development Authority (MDCDA) was a non-profit organization whose purpose was to build low-cost housing and rehabilitate houses in low-income neighborhoods and to "bring about changes in the housing industry's techniques." [57]

Reuther was the driving force in the creation of MDCDA. He relied for advice on Gabel, on Ehrenkrantz's Building Systems Development Corporation, on Schon's OSTI, and on the Ford-funded Center for Community Change. MDCDA set for itself goals that were a combination of social, economic, and technological purpose. It would guarantee community participation in planning the new neighborhoods by working with nonprofit sponsors of housing projects and other community groups. It would stimulate the introduction of black construction workers into local union and contractor organizations. And it would sponsor the development of new housing systems and supply a market in which they could be demonstrated.

Building Systems Development, Inc. received a contract to advise on MDCDA strategies for attacking the problems of low-income housing. When MDCDA awarded the contract for the actual construction of Detroit's major low-income housing complex, it was the firm of Leefe and Ehrenkrantz which received the design contracts for the homes.

The Martin Luther King homes do not represent one of Ehrenkrantz's prouder accomplishments. Constructed of some prefabricated modules and embodying the kind of "systems" thinking Ehrenkrantz had been advocating, the homes are described by high-level MDCDA officials as being an unmitigated disaster. Local architects consider the project an aesthetic failure. To the tenants, who talk unlovingly of "the Project," the planning deficiencies are the most obvious.[58]

Another MDCDA project was that of developing new interest groups among the poor to help the Authority fight Detroit's vested interests that oppose housing reform. Donald Schon's OSTI was called upon to develop strategies for this endeavor. A New Detroit, Inc. (a Ford Motor-sponsored good-city group) analysis and the head of MDCDA's Community Relations Department agree that the strategies failed.[59]

MDCDA's final goal was to create a housing market for the developers of innovative housing. It decided to create a model new community near Novi, a Detroit suburb, to provide the necessary market for the winner of an industrialized housing competition organized by Ehrenkrantz and an erstwhile British associate of his, Sir Richard Llewellyn Davies. The MDCDA contracted with the Center for Community Change for advice on site selection. The Center is a Ford-sponsored organization; Mrs. Gabel was Vice President of the Center, and its President, Jack Conway, was a trusted assistant to Reuther and a former HUD executive. On the Center's (i.e., Hortense Gabel's) recommendation, the MDCDA purchased 546 acres of land near Novi. The land was purchased before the MDCDA had completed its plans and without informing the surrounding community of the intended use of the land. The planners thought they could easily overcome any resistance that might arise, just as they assumed that other "vested interests" could be swept aside.

According to the New Detroit report, the Center and Reuther both spurred the quick purchase of the land on the assumption that nothing would be lost in purchasing first and studying later. Any increase in land value while the new town was under study would accrue to the corporation. If the studies were negative, the land could be sold without problems.

The land was purchased in August 1969, but the suburban community was not informed of the new project until the following March. According to the New Detroit study, "The way the news came to the community, mostly in the form of a HUD leak to a resident (according to press reports), was designed to make tempers flare to a fever pitch." [60] The local citizens did not want the low-income project, and local politicians would not support it. As MDCDA prepared to make its formal presentation to them, the community rezoned the land to block the plans of the reformers. MDCDA decided to sell its land, but, in the worst of possible outcomes, the land had to be sold at a $500,000 loss.

A series of further misfortunes hit MDCDA. It went into a rapid decline and eventually died out altogether. A 1971 report on MDCDA for New Detroit, Inc., described the MDCDA's efforts as a "good social goal gone awry." [61]

In-Cities

HUD's first large-scale "demonstration project," begun in 1968, was called In-Cities. Funded under the Model Cities legislation, which required "citizen participation," In-Cities was "designed to develop an objective and, where possible, quantitative understanding of the constraints that inhibit the introduction of innovations into the production of housing for lower-income families." [62] A consortium headed by Ehrenkrantz's Building Systems Development, Inc. (BSD), in association with Kaiser Engineers, Donald

Schon's OSTI, Turner Construction Company, General Research Corporation, and Anthony Downs's Real Estate Research Corporation, won a large contract for the "systems requirements" phase. "It was all a coincidence" explained Mrs. Gabel, that "Don, Tony, and Ezra were awarded In-Cities contracts." [63] Abt had a joint venture with an architectural firm, and Westinghouse Electric was an independent contractor.

In Phase II, the consortium, with Battelle Memorial Institute replacing OSTI, was supposed to apply the Phase I information in the building of "a multiplicity of variegated low-cost" houses.

In-Cities was to build housing in fifty-six "inner" cities selected from 144 candidates. On-paper success was a foregone conclusion. The Kaiser Commission cited In-Cities as an example of the kind of contracting effort it was recommending. HUD told the Senate in 1968 that "it is already apparent that the In-Cities experiment is having a strong impact on the housing industry and generating a great deal of innovative thinking." [64] This was not apparent at all.

According to the Phase I contractor report, the contractors accumulated a "truly significant body of information on user's needs, constraints, building technologies, and city-specific data." [65] At a cost of over $200,000 the "user needs" section presented the following "major findings" of the housing requirements of the poor:

> A range of different family types (in terms of configuration, age, race, or customs) requires internal space that is flexible and adjustable as the age, configuration, values, and other needs of the family change. Large families (including nuclear, extended, and single-parent families), small families in the early, childbearing stage of the life cycle, families that frequently have roomers or long-term visitors, or families that vary radically in size and/or composition, all require space flexibility.
>
> The manner in which services (the so-called helping and supportive services and management, and other services

related to housing) are delivered to lower-income families is often in conflict with their life styles, needs, and expectations. More services seem to be required, along with more appropriate and sympathetic delivery systems.

The need for security and safety is physical and psychological. In addition to physical security, there is need to know who "belongs" (and therefore is nonthreatening) and who is an intruder.[66]

It then described some of the problems that the poor face in finding decent housing:

Generally the poor are greatly limited in their range of choice of housing; however, for the most part, they live where they prefer within this limited range.

The twin constraints of too high prices and too few rooms are implicit in poverty housing.

Although public housing tenants appreciate low costs, they resent being subject to a variety of institutional restraints, including invasion of privacy by management.

Inadequate recreation facilities for children and teenagers cause complaints by many occupants of lower-income housing about other people's children and concern for the safety of their own.[67]

This invaluable information on the needs of the poor was supported by a theory of "human needs." The systems men seized on the texts of human "specialists" to provide technical support for their own social analysis. Among the most favored of authorities found in systems reports is the late psychologist A. H. Maslow. As a founder of "humanistic psychology," Maslow argued that humans have a "hierarchy" of needs that must be fulfilled. Maslow had provided a convenient theory of needs that could be simply expressed and, equally importantly, could be reduced to the pleasing diagram style of systems management reports.

The In-Cities user needs study produced a flow chart of human needs and told HUD that, if the basic human need of survival were not achieved, the result would be "death, retarded development, or disease." Housing would have to provide for self-esteem as well as mere shelter, for if the human need of self-esteem were not met, the result would be "self-degradation, inefficiency, or antisocial behavior." [68]

The researchers also brought back some helpful insights about data-gathering among the poor. They found that

> paper and pencil tasks posed real problems for the function-
> ally illiterate; language barriers can be expected with some
> poor people of foreign extraction; in sample interviews,
> persons were encountered who appeared to have personality
> problems or were under the influence of alcohol or drugs;
> brainstorming sessions were difficult to conduct successfully
> because many respondents simply could not be induced to
> shift quickly from one topic to another, and too often
> individuals insisted on elaborating on their problems; the
> elderly posed problems caused by a short attention span and
> a lack of ability to grasp and relate to special research
> techniques. [69]

The study produced housing designs to match the needs it found. In defining the "minimum space requirements" in a bedroom, the study concluded that, in a room with two beds, there should be a space between the beds. The report also recommended that, in constructing eating facilities, HUD should be primarily concerned that there be ample room to move around the table while serving. Diagrams were employed to illustrate each of these "essential points."

A separate study was devoted to constraints in the housing industry. Here it was discovered, as "another major finding," that blacks and the poor have difficulty in obtaining monies from lending institutions and that the construction industry is "clannish" and discriminates against blacks. [70] Reflecting on this section of the report, an embarrassed Harold Finger, Rogers' successor, commented: "The code problem is one of the major areas I think we have to work on because it is a major constraint. Basically, we didn't have to go through an In-Cities type of program to define codes as a restraint. It was known before." [71]

The section of Phase I entitled "Technological Innovation," written by Kaiser with help from BSD, was intended to be the highlight of the report. It was, in fact, just a Yellow Page compendium of industrial firms from which HUD could purchase building materials. It contained a diagrammed list of building components, including a host of "useful" definitions for those new to the housing field:

> Ceiling—ceilings as a subsystem may provide a source of light, acoustical modification, fire protection;
> Fixtures—fixtures are the terminal devices in the utility subsystem. Some of these devices may also be part of another subsystem, such as burners or lights;
> Doors—doors can be a component of an interior partition subsystem;
> Hinge—a hinge is an example of a part.[72]

If the study was worthless, as even Schon and Ehrenkrantz themselves admit, the reward for the contractors was ample. Phase I, HUD stated, extended over a forty-five-day period, from May 1, 1968 through June 15, 1968. The payments to the contractors for this short period were listed as follows: Abt Associates and Daniel Mann, Johnson and Menedenhall (a joint venture): $378,671; Building Systems Development Corporation (in association with Kaiser Engineers, Real Estate Research Corporation, General Research Corporation, Turner Construction Company, and OSTI): $298,178; and Westinghouse Electric Corporation: $398,750. The grand total for Phase I was $1,075,599.[73]

The contractors recall Phase I with difficulty. BSD and Kaiser had a falling out at the beginning of the project. Ehrenkrantz's Building Systems did its own users' needs study, but it was not published and is retained as the sole property of BSD. The study which HUD distributed appeared under Kaiser's name. William Meyers of BSD recalls: "I was called in at the last moment to help write the technologies section. Kaiser Engineers knew almost nothing about new technologies, and that might explain why the report was so poor." [74]

Other contractors are reluctant to talk about the report.

Clark Abt does not remember much about the report or the circumstances surrounding it; he recalls only that "we did not do very much." [75]

The Phase II contract carried a face value of $4,952,085. The design of the new "low-cost" housing revealed an estimated cost to HUD of $28,000 per unit, substantially above prior expectations. HUD officials realized that the projected cost, including site development, land, and other factors, would go over $50,000—far above the means of most poverty families! HUD never released estimates of the costs.[76] (Those given here come from Milton Semer, the White House adviser on housing.)

The project was canceled, but not before several million dollars more were spent. The only site selected for development was Dade County, Florida. The Dade County Authority tossed away the systems approach and based its design on the conventional concrete-block-and-stucco materials used in that area. The demonstration showed only that houses could indeed be built in Dade County!

The amount paid to Kaiser and BSD is unknown. As of January 1972, HUD had not completed its audit of the contract, and it refuses to explain why any money was given at all.[77] HUD insists that a substantial reduction in award was made, even though, by April 1969, the Department had already reported expending $1.5 million.

If it was impossible to determine the costs, it was just as difficult to find out what work the contractors performed. In December 1971, we wrote HUD asking for a detailed analysis of contractor work. HUD did not provide the information.

The "market aggregators" and evaluators for the In-Cities project were the Mitre Corporation. As the brain trust of the Air Force's Electronic Systems Command, Mitre could be considered *the* systems expert, but its representatives who acted as evaluators of other contracts had no previous experience in the housing area. William Meyers of BSD found the level of knowledge among Mitre analysts "disastrously low. The guys from Mitre would come in and sit in the conference rooms without saying much and simply be observers. They knew little about what we were doing, but they were very interested in learning." [78]

Mitre was to develop a yardstick by which the costs of systems-built housing could be compared with that of conventionally built housing. They never did this; they merely estimated that costs of the systems-designed homes would be triple the amounts BSD-Kaiser had originally estimated.

For this, Mitre received $137,286. It received an additional $104,000 to evaluate In-Cities. The firm submitted a seventy-three-page history of In-Cities that complemented the Phase I reports. The report explained that, unfortunately, "to date no construction has taken place and, therefore, no constraints have been encountered to the use of industrialized prefabricated technology." [79]

Harold Finger saw that In-Cities was useless and canceled it. David Moore, the Government Technical Representative on the In-Cities contracts, summed up: "It's hard to say whether it was worth it, or not worth it. I guess we might call it a moderately expensive learning process." [80] HUD's "contract sheet" bore a short epitaph for the program: "Review of the project showed the high cost of the project was not justified by the benefits to be gained. Scope of the work was reduced to construction of housing using innovative program financing in Dade County, Florida, only." [81]

The new administration at HUD did not find the In-Cities studies to be of any use. No copies were printed for public distribution. HUD's Dave Moore was "hesitant" to give us his copy, and we obtained the loan of the only copy in the possession of the HUD dissemination center.

Thomas Rogers resigned as Director of Research and Technology on May 16, 1969. He left HUD to become Executive Vice President of the Mitre Corporation for Urban Affairs. On June 1, 1969, the Mitre Corporation received an additional contract of $165,096 to begin the task of designing HUD's next large R & D project—Operation Breakthrough.

Breakthrough

At his first appropriations hearing, George Romney, Nixon's HUD Secretary, sought to disassociate himself from the work of the Democrat R & T program:

> If you want my impression of the research that has been going on, the bulk of it has not been very productive in terms of what we are charged with as a department. As far as I am concerned, it has been largely in the area of making it available for planners and thinkers. . . . Now we are talking about getting into the real problem—of undertaking to get an application of modern management and modern technology, to develop some housing that will take advantage of all the scientific and technological knowledge we have in this country, and that is quite a different thing.[82]

Romney appointed Harold Finger as Assistant Secretary of Research and Technology. Finger had advanced degrees in aeronautical and mechanical engineering and came to HUD from NASA, where he had headed the NASA Technology Utilization Program, a program concerned with the transfer of NASA technology to civilian uses.

Finger's task at HUD was to direct Operation Breakthrough. Announced in May 1969, Breakthrough was a slightly restyled version of the model for housing reform that the R & D consultants had been trying to sell throughout the Sixties. The sales pitch included "market aggregation," [83] "performance criteria," "cost reduction," and, of course, "systems building." Building codes and zoning laws were "institutional obstacles" to be broken down.

Breakthrough was to be a $120 million venture that offered a role in the housing field to virtually any firm that could sign its name to a Government contract. If familiar management consultants like McKinsey; Peat, Marwick, Mitchell & Co.; and others did not become part of

Operation Breakthrough, it was not for want of trying. Almost every group appearing in this book tried to come down with a piece of the action.

Breakthrough had one other unique feature—it would "certify" contractors as "housing systems producers." In theory, the opportunity for Government certification would be a carrot to lure firms into the housing systems market.

The Breakthrough concept went far beyond the 1962 CITP housing research program. The Government was not simply sponsoring the development of information. HUD would be underwriting the actual production of houses.

The program revived the dream of industrialized housing in its pristine form, shorn of Great Society pretensions of solving the housing problem of the poor. As MIT economist Stegman pointed out, even though the legislation under which it was proceeding mandated the search for less expensive housing for low- and moderate-income families, "The ultimate sayings, when translated into reductions in monthly rates, would be negligible." [84] HUD now admits the costs were, in fact, so high that Breakthrough was not serving the poor.

HUD had two possible sources of funds for Breakthrough. It could use Model Cities money and build the housing in low-income neighborhoods or it could use the authorization in Section 108 of the Housing and Urban Development Act of 1968, entitled "New Technologies in the Development of Housing for Lower-Income Families." This section permits the Department to "encourage large-scale experimentation with new technology" in national efforts to solve the housing crisis of the urban and rural poor—and does not require citizen participation. HUD chose the latter course.

Romney seldom referred to Breakthrough as solving the problems of the poor until later speeches, including one at a NAACP convention.[85] In an unprecedented action, *House and Home*, a housing industry journal, charged the Administration with "effectively obscuring the fact that we as a nation have made almost no commitment to helping our low-income families. Our total commitment to helping our poor get decent housing is a measly $375 million. So the first step out of our low-income housing crisis would be to face the fact that we'll have to spend more money." [86] But HUD continued to act as if technology could substitute for money.

Congressional hearings on Breakthrough revealed the continuing doubling of contractors as HUD's R & T program planners. Finger went before the Subcommittee on Urban Affairs of the Joint Economic Committee, accompanied, not by HUD civil servants, but by Ezra Ehrenkrantz and Charles Biederman, both of whose companies were to be Breakthrough winners. Biederman told the committee:

> I hope that I am not putting Mr. Finger in a compromising position, because we intend to be one of the bidders of Operation Breakthrough. . . . We urge Congress to thoroughly support and encourage Operation Breakthrough, because we think it is going to be terribly effective in developing innovative building techniques, and a response to the need for industrialized housing.[87]

Biederman's apology was quite appropriate; he was a Vice President of Levitt, the nation's number one housing builder. (He complained to the Congressional committee about the problems of being a "small builder"—an appellation Levitt applied to itself.)

How, asked Congressman Clarence Brown (R.-Ohio), could the committee be sure that HUD would not bring about another Lustron experiment, in which Congress would commit itself to a program and develop a market, only to find that people did not want to live in the homes? The Congressman was apparently unaware of the "user needs" study HUD had performed for In-Cities. Finger asked Biederman to reply for him. Biederman hesitated and said he knew of no Government study on users' needs and that Levitt normally conducts its own. Chairman Richard Bolling (D.-Mo.) asked Ehrenkrantz whether he knew of any study. Ehrenkrantz replied that with "five hundred thousand to a million dollars" he could do a national users' needs study that would determine what the public wanted in the way of housing.[88] Again Finger was silent. No one dared pull out the In-Cities project.

Did HUD really expect anyone to believe that its program could "solve the housing crisis in two years," "turn the home-building industry into a modern assembly line," "break forever the power of the union, zoning, building codes, and other special interest lobbies"? The new salesmanship was described by economist Stegman:

> Breakthrough is consistent with the American ethic that says the assembly line can do anything: It provides an opportunity for defense-and-space-oriented industries to capture a larger share of the nation's housing budget at a time when defense and space budgets are being bitterly contested and possibly reduced; and finally, the program is designed to encourage the production of better and less expensive housing for all income groups and not just for those families unable to afford decent housing. As a program aimed at helping "middle America," its political appeal is substantially greater than it would be if it were billed as a new attack on the nation's low-income housing problem.[89]

Mitre assisted in preparing the invitations to bid on Breakthrough. In early 1970, "research and development" contracts were awarded to twenty-two consortia of Housing Systems Producers, groups of management firms, and the building contractors assembled together for the Breakthrough experiment. Among these were Thompson Ramo Wooldridge (TRW), Republic Steel, and General Electric. (TRW's Vice President, Reuben Mettler, had previously headed a Nixon Task Force that recommended market aggregation for civilian areas such as housing and transportation.) Other contractors included some of the largest home producers and conglomerate corporations—for example, Alcoa Construction, Boise-Cascade, ITT-Levitt, and National Homes Corporation.

Each of the prime contractors had a coterie of consultant

and architectural subcontractors. Ehrenkrantz's BSD, for example, was in the TRW group.

HUD had announced that Breakthrough would award two types of contracts, for "study" as well as for production and site development. When it saw that the proposals it had received contained little in the way of innovation, however, the agency changed its plans and awarded less than a handful of study contracts. Ehrenkrantz's firm took one of them, making it the only recipient of both types of awards.

Breakthrough placed HUD's R & T program close to the shoals of antitrust violations. The Government was consciously enticing large corporations into the housing industry, permitting flexible arrangements among them, and providing government "certification" for privileged winners.

In HUD's eyes, the industry was so fragmented that there was no need to worry about the dangers of monopoly. In addition, HUD assured its critics, at least five or six producers would be given the opportunity to attack each local market.

The experimental apparatus of HUD rested on a bedrock of secrecy. Closed to the public and the press, Room 7223 of HUD headquarters sheltered the panel reviewing the contract proposals for Breakthrough. "The whole program," said a *Business Week* reporter, "was negotiated like the planning for a CIA overthrow in Latin America. There was nothing you could find out; everything was behind closed doors. There were periods when they wouldn't even let me in the building, and I even liked Finger and what they were doing. I supported them." [90]

When we requested access to contract files, HUD informed us that it would cost $100 per contract for HUD to purge the files of proprietary information and permit us to see publicly available material.

There was good reason for HUD to withhold data. The designs were more often a source of embarrassment than of new ideas. Nevertheless, the public paid for the production of reams of worthless publicity on them. HUD contracted with NAS, at a cost of $90,000, for a brochure containing the proposals of the Operation Breakthrough bidders. The resulting 590-page book contained only the sketchiest details from the proposals of over 236 groups that bid on the contracts.[91] The Red, White and Blue Breakthrough book printed the barest details on the proposals; HUD officials—for instance, OB Director Arthur Newburgh—admit it was a waste of money.[92]

Robertson Ward headed a panel of the American Institute of Architects (AIA), which had long supported the Breakthrough concept. Ward himself had served as a prominent member of Ehrenkrantz's SCSD project, but the AIA panel's 1970 report expressed disappointment:

> Many of the systems had already been developed or were on an existing noninnovative technological base where final results could be predicted. In quality, many range from the mediocre to the dismal.[93]

In August of 1971, HUD released some of the costs in Breakthrough. These represented only the Government's contribution, not the real costs to the contractors or the costs incurred in building. More than $70 million of Research and Technology monies went into the program. Sixty-five million dollars of mortgage funds were also provided, most of this under special Government loan incentives. Special FHA subsidy promises were given to the Breakthrough contract winners: if market aggregation fell through, the Breakthrough contractors would be guaranteed this special source of funds to help keep their factories in production.

If costs are analyzed using only HUD's funds, the construction cost of a unit averages $23,000—only a few thousand dollars above the average cost of $21,000 for conventional housing. (This is slightly less than half the full cost of a home, which must also include the purchase of land, site development, and planning.) Contractors who produced at lower cost generally were experienced prefabricated home producers. It was the larger corporations, new to industrialized housing, who showed the higher cost averages (using their own money to supplement Government funds, when these proved insufficient). TRW, the Air Force's missile manager, and Republic Steel produced homes that cost at least $40,000 and $50,000, respectively, for construction alone.[94] The former editor of *House and Home* "guesses" that the units are in the neighborhood of "well over $100,000, on the average." [95] Breakthrough's director added that "every day the costs are increasing. We will not know for some time what the costs to the Government in extras, unrecorded as yet, will be." [96]

Ezra Ehrenkrantz felt no need to apologize. "You can't innovate cheaply," he asserts.[97]

If the costs for construction greatly exceeded anticipation, site development was equally expensive. The "prototype site developers," those groups that would ready the land to accept the new homes and bring consensus in the affected communities, included Boeing, Volt Information Sciences, Urban Systems Development, and the Alodex Corporation. On-site development cost another $15 million and off-site $22 million, or $7,100 per unit. HUD personnel took over the task of site development, since the contractors performed ineffectively.[98]

HUD contends that, with volume production, it will be possible elsewhere to realize a significant decrease in costs. But by the end of Breakthrough, Republic Steel had yet to fully assemble a factory to put out units, and TRW, according to Ehrenkrantz, would require a very large market, the size of which he would not venture, to move to efficient mass production.[99]

The central performance standards devised under a $4 million contract were just "pulled out of the air," said the head of an NAS review panel.[100] "The standards are so flawed as to make building in accordance with them nearly impossible," said a builder in *Business Week.*[101] Ezra Ehrenkrantz refused to use them, because the costs would have been even higher.[102]

What about the quality assurance that Breakthrough was

to provide? HUD paid Computer Sciences Corporation $880,921 to review the quality control that went into Breakthrough homes. CSC produced a summary report which concluded:

> There was no evidence that Quality Assurance practices were initiated to ensure quality products and minimize the cost of reject or rework. In many instances, that Quality Assurance function is actually accomplished by the same supervisor that is responsible for production. This approach does not ensure objectivity. Many of the forms associated with almost complete production units were observed to be either blank or only partially completed.[103]

In 1972, the National Academy of Engineering (NAE) held a symposium on its year-long study of industrialized housing. Clarence Broley, who had left Arthur D. Little to become executive secretary of the HUD-sponsored study group, concluded: "In the opinion of the Committee, the assertion by individuals that industrialized housing is a panacea and an easy solution to the nation's housing problems is fallacious." [104]

Broley explained that, when NAE began its study on "this highly emotional subject," all of their biases would have led them to believe that Breakthrough would offer "technological innovations" and be a successful experiment in market aggregation. The "popular wisdom," Broley said, pointed to success. The popular wisdom, though, was "myth." [105]

The new Director of Operation Breakthrough, Arthur Newburgh, admitted: "We learned that you cannot apply the dicta of NASA to the housing industry. Applying lavish spending techniques had no application to this industry. The Government is a bad buyer of construction. We didn't know what we were doing." [106] In private, Newburgh said, "I am vexed that the NAE took on their study the way they did. It was a waste of time and money. The fact that Breakthrough was a hardware technological failure was obvious." The claim that "market aggregation" would

encourage a capital-intensive industry was, admitted Newburgh, a "fraud." [107]

THE HIGHWAY INDUSTRY AND
MASS TRANSIT

The nation's highway system is the most spectacular
example of the power of Federal subsidy. The Federal
Government began to subsidize highway construction in
1916, but the real acceleration of highway buildup came
with the growth of the suburbs after World War II and the
Congressional creation of the Highway Trust Fund in 1956.
The highway system, conceived in 1956, was to have been
completed in 1969, at a cost of $27 billion. More recent
estimates place the completion date closer to 1980, at a cost
of close to $70 billion.

While the highway complex is at no loss for members
who are political and economic heavyweights (including
state and local highway agencies, construction companies,
truckers, tire makers, and oil companies), its rise has been
greatly facilitated by private research organizations in the
highway promotion business.

The Highway Research Board (HRB) sits atop the
pyramid of highway experts. The Board is an affiliate of the
prestigious National Academy of Sciences, a Congressionally chartered organization of America's scientific elite.
Established in 1920, the Board's competency extends from
roadsigns and roadbeds to the "social and economic"
aspects of highway building. Directed by state and Federal
officials, who help initiate research, and private citizens who
sit on panels and committees, the Board sponsors a highly
visible program of contract research, for which the National
Cooperative Highway Research Program's *Summary of
Progress* volumes provide convenient abstracts.[108]

Quasi-official groups like HRB work in tandem with
more purely private research associations. The auto manufacturers, for example, created the Automotive Safety

Foundation to provide state and local officials with their expert view of highway safety. In 1969, General Motors commissioned Cresap, McCormick, and Paget to turn the Foundation into a more effective public relations vehicle. The Foundation was merged with two other associations and became the Highway Users Federation for Safety and Mobility. In 1970, D. Grant Mickle was serving as Chairman of the Highway Research Board and President of the Highway Users Federation.[109]

The livelihood of highway planning and engineering experts has been ensured since 1934 by the provision that up to 1.5 percent of Federal highway funds can be earmarked by states for surveys and planning. Among these experts, the name of Wilbur Smith stands out.

Wilbur Smith and Associates employs over 500 people. Smith, a young Phi Beta Kappa graduate of the University of South Carolina, joined the South Carolina Highway Department in 1933. In the next decade he organized the state's Traffic Engineering Department, taking time off to work at Harvard's Bureau of Street Traffic Research. In the early Forties, the Harvard traffic group moved to Yale, and in 1943, Smith became a faculty member of the Yale Bureau of Highway Traffic, where he remained until 1968.

Smith's rise was enhanced by a wide variety of public service, trade association, and professional activities. He served as a board member of the American Roadbuilders' Association and the Executive Committee of the Highway Research Board. The HRB commissioned Smith and Associates, along with Bertram D. Tallamy and Associates, to produce a broad study of "Research Needs in Highway Transportation." As President and Board Chairman of the Eno Foundation, Smith also has a hand in the foundation-sponsored *Traffic Quarterly*. Under commission from the Automobile Manufacturers' Association, Wilbur Smith and Associates produced a series of texts which, a Smith brochure advises, "have become classical textbooks for studies in Transportation Science at universities throughout the United States and most other English-speaking countries." [110]

The Smith brochure calls the development of arguments for highway construction "research and development."

With abundant funding, the highway planners developed sophisticated quantitative techniques and formulae to plot and justify the creation of future highways. Alan Voorhees, a student at the Yale traffic school, modified "Reilly's law of retail gravitation," which hypothesized a relationship between the size of a retail store and its ability to attract customers, to produce a "gravity model." The gravity model's bedazzling array of formulae and numbers quickly became a standard tool for the rationalization of highway expansion. Voorhees himself graduated from Yale to the Automotive Safety Foundation, then formed Alan Voorhees and Associates, a transportation planning firm that is now a subsidiary of the Planning Research conglomerate.

In the Sixties, the first wave of antifreeway protests swept the country. In such major cities as Boston, San Antonio, Cleveland, Baltimore, Memphis, and New Orleans, citizen opponents of the freeways attacked the planning studies.[111]

The District of Columbia spawned one of the longest-running antifreeway battles. Wilbur Smith; De Leeuw Cather; J. E. Greiner; and Howard, Needles, Tammen & Bergendoff; and other planning firms had been commissioned to route highways in and around Washington. When the threat of litigation stalled construction, President Johnson turned the problem over to a committee of Federal and local officials. The committee turned to the District Highway Department, and Arthur D. Little was hired.[112]

Little was asked to determine whether the studies performed on District of Columbia transportation in the 1955–65 period had considered such effects of the proposed freeways as the relocation of families, neighborhood dislocation, the aesthetic qualities of the city, and accident rates, and effects on the tax base of the city and city parklands.

Little found that "present plans for freeway extensions in the District are based on insufficient data and on questionable assumptions and forecasting techniques" and criticized the weighty planning studies submitted by Smith and other firms for not including calculations of the effect of new freeways on land use, or any formulae that related decisions to build schools or shopping centers to the locations of proposed roads. Smith's methods, the Little report concluded, were "naïve." The "available evidence" universally demonstrated the interdependence of transportation and land use.[113]

Peter Craig, a former Assistant General Counsel for the Department of Transportation, performed similar studies for a citizens' group that opposed the District's transportation plans. Craig concluded that Washington's experience with planners was not unique. He found similar patterns in Boston, New Orleans, San Antonio, Memphis, and New York. In each case, planning studies were commissioned to justify spending once local and Federal agencies had agreed that money would be forthcoming. Because the Federal Government promised to pay the overwhelming portion of the bill, plans quickly won the support of local Chambers of Commerce. The agencies that commissioned the required plans made no effort to verify the predictions and conclusions they contained and, naturally, no alternative to highways was considered.[114]

In 1962, Congress proposed to blunt the damage by amending the highway laws to require states and localities to engage in "comprehensive" transportation planning. Transportation was to be studied as a "system" that included consideration of alternatives to the automobile. The new law required not only a new kind of plan but a continuous "planning process." It was a boon to consultants. Wilbur Smith experienced its greatest growth with the influx of "comprehensive planning" monies.[115] Anything could be planned, but, in practice, monies were available only for more roads. At decade's end, a Department of Transportation survey found that the new planning had produced no change. Typically, the study found, the law inspired the creation of large committees, with representatives from bus companies, transit and conservation districts, port authorities, and planning commissions, all of whom endorsed existing highway plans. There were new and more sophisticated plans, but the sophistication was "technical, rather than institutional." [116]

The comprehensive planning funds allowed transit planning firms to broaden their expertise. Smith, for example, began to hire social scientists, systems analysts, and "public administration experts." It was now prepared to boast that it, like Arthur D. Little, possessed "unique multidisciplined capability." When, in 1970, the Office of the Secretary of Transportation's brand-new division on urban and environmental affairs called for bids on a series of studies of transportation planning, Smith told DOT that the typical comprehensive plan of the Sixties "examined transit as an element of the transportation system of the community, but typically saw highway problems and sought highway solutions because of institutional and legal constraints on transit development." Smith, on the other hand, was prepared to "search for public transportation solutions"—if the Government saw fit to provide the seed money.[117]

New Systems

The aerospace mystique was at its peak in the mid-Sixties, and the Federal transportation agencies hopped on the bandwagon. The Kennedy Administration responded to pressure for increased funding of Northeast railroads with a major "systems analysis" of the "Northeast Corridor." Peat, Marwick, Mitchell & Co., Mitre, Resource Management, TRW, and numerous other contractors were given several million dollars to design a grand scheme to renew transportation in the Boston–Washington corridor. Other firms received further millions to promote civil aviation (notably the vertical short take-off and landing airplane) as the solution to the middle distance intercity commute, and the Federal Railroad Administration bankrolled TRW to bring aerospace technology to the railroad. Urban mass transportation had its own "systems" study.[118]

Representative Henry Reuss, a liberal Democrat from Milwaukee, introduced an amendment to the 1966 mass transit legislation requiring the Federal Government to study improvements in transportation. The study was to supply the design for a research program and the vehicle by which "technological breakthroughs" in mass transit could be achieved. The name "New Systems" was given to the entire project.[119]

The direction of the study task fell to Charles Haar, a Harvard law professor working in HUD as Assistant Secretary for Metropolitan Development. (UMTA had yet to be created.)

Haar hoped that innovative hardware could solve the transportation problem and sought ideas from contractors. Seventeen contractors, including some of the large non-profits—Battelle, Stanford Research Institute, and Midwest Research Institute—received awards. Peat, Marwick, Mitchell & Co. developed projections of travel demand. North American Rockwell, the prime NASA contractor, wrote up aerospace technologies. Large industrial firms, including General Motors and General Electric, received contracts to write about their work. Finally, the Institute for Public Administration, which had authored a standard work on mass transit needs, was paired with Wilbur Smith and two Westinghouse subsidiaries for a study of innovations that could be introduced in between three and eight years.

Dozens of volumes of New Systems studies issued forth. While the contractors considered nearly 300 specific proposals for new technology, the studies also contained a litany on political and social factors pertinent to the introduction of new technologies.

A summary of the effort was packaged by HUD in a brochure, "Tomorrow's Transportation," whose theme was familiar: Urban transportation was a backward system lacking "change and the capacity for change."

"Tomorrow's Transportation" was a pitch for R & D subsidies. "Under our system of government," it explained, "private enterprise bears the primary responsibility for research and development in the transportation field. But the Government can help. It can plan and fashion research and development for a total transportation system which is beyond the responsibility and capability of private industry." The New Systems study was conceived to provide the plan by which Federal funds would stimulate private innovation. By 1970, the study was a dead letter.

Paul Sitton, the first administrator of the Urban Mass Transportation Administration, recalls that he acquired his volumes of New Systems studies when he saw cartons of studies being carted away for incineration. They lacked indexes, Sitton discovered, and were not very useful. Tom Floyd, who worked under Sitton at UMTA, concluded that "for the amount of money, the study was a very disappointing thing. I don't think the results were that successful." The work did not gain Congressional attention, nor even attract debate at transit industry gatherings. When the Institute for Defense Analyses (IDA) held a conference for the New Systems contractors, participants concluded that their work had been neglected. "The New Systems study," explained UMTA's Franz Gimmler in 1971, "resulted in reports, and it was over." [120]

The Urban Mass
Transportation Administration

When a new Federal Department of Transportation was created in 1966, not only did New Systems Director Haar leave HUD (for Harvard), but the mass transit program departed as well (in 1968), leaving HUD to become part of the Department of Transportation. The Federal Highway Administration (FHWA) is the heart of the new Department. It dwarfed the two agencies—the Urban Mass Transit Administration (UMTA) and the National Highway Safety Bureau—that were created to counterbalance the impact of the automobile. The new agencies tried to compensate by heavy reliance on consultants.

The National Highway Safety Bureau called in Booz, Allen and Arthur Young to scout out the auto industry's production method. System Development Corporation was hired to prepare a "documentation center"—the agency's one-room library. Booz was hired to survey "safety manpower" and SRI to write about training safety manpower. Peat, Marwick, Mitchell & Co. developed management brochures and training courses for several governmental levels of the program. Operations Research Inc. helped with PPB and wrote an academic treatise on cost-benefit analysis and auto safety. Most of these studies—standard contractor fare—left few traces.[121]

Paul Sitton professed a passionate distaste for the "consulting racket." The gravity model, he claims, "set back American transportation for decades." [122] His disdain for contractors did not outweigh his need for them, however. In 1969, UMTA administered $180 million with a staff of approximately fifty civil servants, and Sitton turned to the systems analysts for help. The Applied Physics Laboratory, a Johns Hopkins–administered FCRC, was hired to study corporate hardware schemes. The Urban Institute was hired to perform systems analyses of transportation. Sitton laid out several hundred thousand dollars more for quantitative model builders. He did not believe in models, Sitton recalled, but he hoped to use the contracts to establish a dialogue with systems analysts in DOT.

As in HUD, IDA and Mitre were relied on to perform the basic tasks of R & D planning and management. IDA had no more experience with transportation than with housing, and its presence was short-lived. (When UMTA pressed IDA to prepare an R & D presentation for Congress, for example, the Institute warned UMTA that it lacked necessary competence. "IDA agreed to do what it could," but the effort was quickly canceled.)[123]

Mitre also had no experience in urban transportation, but it had solid ties to the Department of Transportation. Its work for the Defense Department on the Air Defense network had led to a long-term contract with the Federal Aviation Administration for computerization of civilian air traffic control. Mitre established another long-term relationship with the Office of High Speed Ground Transportation, a component of the Federal Railroad Administration. It has provided the Office with "technical support" in the continued quest to build high-speed trains. Finally, Mitre was a major contractor for the Department's Northeast Corridor Transportation study.[124]

Frank Hassler, Mitre's first director of the UMTA contract, was an aerospace technician. He was succeeded by Reed Winslow, who came to Mitre from Wilbur Smith and the Automotive Safety Foundation.[125]

Mitre's work for UMTA soon ran the gamut from the "quick and dirty studies" that serve bureaucrats in crisis to the design and management of "demonstrations" and "experiments." A Mitre annual report boasted that the corporation's "plans serve as major technical backup for UMTA's research and development program presentation to Congress." One Mitre contract proposal offered UMTA help in preparing the R & D budget, even though such sensitive activity cannot be delegated to private corporations.[126]

In November 1969, as UMTA was about to add $361,000 to Mitre's contract, UMTA Assistant Administrator for Administration Boswell dashed off a skeptical memo to Carlos Villarreal, the Nixon appointee to head UMTA. Boswell pointed out that Mitre's contract would cost close to $1.4 million for the year. "When it is realized," wrote Boswell, "that all of UMTA will be run this fiscal year for less than $1.5 million, I have problems." The Mitre contract, Boswell asserted, was loosely administered: "Once the Administrator approves this $361,000, he will have no knowledge as to how it will be allocated between tasks." Boswell pointed out that such funding of Mitre might bring criticism from Congress. Ignoring the memo, Villarreal approved the increase. Its civil service employees now joked

that UMTA meant "Urban Mitre Transportation Administration."

Center Cities

Mitre and other aerospace consultants provided UMTA
with sound ties to the technical and industrial elite, but
UMTA wanted to reach the grassroots of urban transportation politics. It needed to stir the enthusiasm of local
political and civic powers to gain local support, and it
needed to show industry that there was a market for new
transit products. Its solution was the Center Cities Transportation Project (CCTP), officially a "research and development" program.[127]

On one level, Center Cities represented the systems
analyst's redefinition of the transportation problem. The
crisis in transportation, UMTA explained, existed because
components of the "transportation system" had evolved in
isolation, and local political entities had not coordinated
developments. Center Cities would view transportation
functionally. Rather than impose one mode of transportation as a solution to urban problems, contractors would be
free to recommend whatever combination was necessary.
Solutions would not be confined by arbitrary political
boundaries, but would be designed to serve the "center
city."

On a second level, CCTP was a Government-sponsored
lobby for Federal spending. Center Cities, explained Harry
Broley, director of Arthur D. Little's Center Cities team,
would "aggregate markets in such a way that the private
sector could say, 'Here is ten to twenty billion worth of
hardware coming down the line.' " [128]

As an employee of the Budget Bureau during the
Johnson years, Paul Sitton had become acquainted with the
concepts of civilian technology reform. He discussed them
with Michael Michaelis, a staff member of the White House
Office of Science and Technology. Michaelis had been
employed by Arthur D. Little and left the White House to

return to Little, where he continued to crusade against "institutional obstacles" to civilian reform.

A number of consulting consortia bid on the proposal, but the group headed by Arthur D. Little seemed to know UMTA's desires best. In February 1969, a $2.5 million contract was signed. Arthur D. Little headed a team of contractors that included Real Estate Research Corporation, the architectural firm of Skidmore, Owings & Merrill, and Wilbur Smith and Associates. Michaelis was named to chair the contractors' "management steering committee." Mitre, UMTA announced, would monitor progress, and IDA would evaluate CCTP's success.

The Center Cities contract was an extraordinarily vague and ambitious document. Not only was the "center city" not defined, but there was no specification of the cities in which the consultants would go to work. There were no explicit limitations on the contractors' authority to represent UMTA in dealings with cities and no specification of the local authorities with whom they were to work.

UMTA's Gordon Murray saw the concept as a cloak for a "mercenary" and hastily conceived public relations venture. The ambiguous Request for Proposal, Murray concluded, betrayed ignorance, not expertise. Others feared that UMTA and Little had not considered the relation of center-city planners to the myriad state and regional planning agencies to which DOT already owed a confused allegiance. The critics were dismissed as representatives of vested interests, or transit officials who did not appreciate "systems" thinking.[129]

According to the contract, CCTP would be conducted in three phases. In Phase I, contractors would develop "analytical techniques" for coping with consumer preference, traffic flow, financing, and technical innovation. The consultants were to ensure "a soundly based concept of effectiveness criteria." The contractors were also to develop "criteria" for selecting cities to receive CCTP attention and money and to organize "interdisciplinary research teams" to work in each city. Finally, the contractors were to "identify individuals and groups whose support is needed for approval of mass transportation proposals or for usage of mass transportation and tentative development of means of obtaining participation in Phase II."

Phase II called for the contractors to "work in close cooperation and liaison with appropriate institutions and groups," presumably the interests contacted in Phase I. Phase III obligated the contractors to turn plans into "demonstrations." CCTP cities would receive top priority among competing applications for demonstration grants. This priority would be the incentive necessary to assure that cities would choose to turn the Phase II plans into operating R & D demonstrations. Once the demonstrations were adjudged successful, they would be ready for replication throughout the country.

The Little consortium chose to set their "interdisciplinary teams" to work in Dallas, Denver, Pittsburgh, Seattle, and Atlanta. UMTA moved to placate cities excluded from CCTP monies. The National League of Cities was given funds to study "nontechnological barriers to change" in eight other cities. Urban America, a liberal research and lobby organization, received $250,000 to hold conferences at which twenty-one further cities could hear about or, in the jargon, "receive the technological transfer" from the five-city and eight-city contracts.

Shortly after the Little contract was signed, Sitton, a Democrat, left UMTA for the National Academy of Sciences. The Nixon Administration replaced him with Carlos Villarreal. Villarreal came from the aerospace industry, where he had worked on the rocket control systems for the Apollo spacecraft. His résumé said that he had "extensive experience in organizing and managing research and development programs in Government and industrial contracting." Villarreal's aerospace background was not coupled with any experience moving earthbound people. This naturally made him an attractive UMTA administrator; as he told Congress, he had "no preconceived ideas or prejudices about the solutions to existing problems." [130]

Despite the Democratic origins of CCTP, the Nixon Administration quickly endorsed it. DOT Secretary Volpe kicked off CCTP with a March 1969 address to a major transportation convention in Pittsburgh. Systems thinking came easily to Volpe. If America could send a man to the moon in seven days, he declared, it could move people to the Pittsburgh airport in seven minutes. Volpe, whose construction firm had prospered from road contracts, acknowledged that the excesses of the automobile had to be redressed. "We have concluded," he said, "that the real transportation problem in the center cities is not congestion, parking, and air pollution per se. Rather, the problem is that no one has been successful in *solving* the problems of congestion, parking, and air pollution. . . . This nation has the technical capability. What we haven't had is the effective implementation of this capability." Volpe claimed that the reason for the lack of effectiveness was the absence of an "action" program for implementation. "You know and I know," he told his audience, "that the filing cabinets in mayors' offices are filled with unrealized plans." The plans were unrealized, not because of infeasibility, but because they had failed to get the many varied interest groups in the cities' power structures to work together. UMTA's consultants would bring together the cities' warring factions. With five cities selected to share in "development, expertise, and information, the manufacturers of transit equipment will have delineated for them a much more positive market potential." Buyers of bonds issues would know what rate to offer. Labor, "in helping plan new systems, can be expected to work with us for the common good." Center city businessmen would know what to expect in terms of economic growth. And last, but, of course, not least, "the people, the ones who really are the 'life blood of urban society,' will help these cities create central transportation systems that blend rather than clash with the human environment." Volpe vowed that he personally would not be satisfied with the consultants until they lit "the spark of community involvement in each of the participating cities." [131]

Volpe's speech did the full-time technology reformers proud. Their major themes—market aggregation, consensus building, the promise of NASA-like action, and the ready dismissal of the dismal past—were all present.

Phase I was an exercise in ambiguity. What was the center city, why were the five chosen cities selected, and what was being learned from studying them? The experts commissioned by UMTA to review Little's Phase I report could not answer these questions.

The choice of the five cities seemed, in retrospect at least, uniquely irrational. IDA found that Dallas needed no planning help. The city's leaders wanted money for projects that were already planned; Denver had no major transportation problems. Atlanta had already engaged in a decade-long debate on transit planning. It needed more consultants and studies, noted one reviewer, "like a hole in the head." In Seattle, the Center Cities contractors had thrown their support behind a bond issue which was supported by "numerous, comprehensive transportation studies" that belied the Little report's implication that Seattle did little planning. (The bond issue was defeated, and the downturn in Seattle's economy caused by aerospace unemployment relegated transportation planning to the bottom of Seattle's crisis list.)

There were other problems with the CCTP concept. The Little report, one reviewer pointed out, identified approximately thirty-five plans and planning agencies in the five cities. Why, he asked, should CCTP add another layer of planning bureaucracy? Lee Huff, of the Office of the Secretary of Transportation, charged that, in Denver, the contractors had met with a small group of businessmen and officials to produce plans that would not "upset the apple cart."

"The contractor," wrote Huff, "speaks favorably of his ability to develop cooperative business relationships with private business interests in the city. This is not so surprising, since the contractor represents a Federal program promising money for central business districts, convention centers, and sports arenas. There is much less information about solicitations of other interests, e.g., the poor, labor, etc." Huff found Little's puffery insufferable. Little told DOT that the CCTP "can create in the five cities institutions capable of dealing with the problems of CCTP on a continuing basis, leaving them with a broad capability not only to plan for year 2000, but to plan for tomorrow." This statement, wrote Huff, "strikes me as naïve, presumptuous, or both."

The Mitre review of Phase I took the contractors to task for failing to provide the expertise promised. Little, said Mitre, had not collected enough data—especially data on "institutions" and "transportation" in the cities. Missing data, said Mitre, would have to be collected if CCTP was to produce "national guidelines" for center city transportation, and the failure of Phase I meant that UMTA would have to sacrifice either its pursuit of national guidelines or its action projects.

A November 1969 IDA memo summed up the confusion. "There are," it said, "many unresolved questions about the entire program, including the Federal role, the implementation process, future transportation requirements and guidelines. Moreover, there are no Federal standards for CCTP; in fact, there are few standards for any mass transportation programs."

An UMTA consultant sympathetic to CCTP tried to rationalize the apparent failure of Phase I. Sumner Meyers, of the Institute for Public Administration and a frequent spokesman for technological reform, admitted that the Little report was disappointing. The solutions proposed to the five cities' problems were "extremely conservative," and the data base on which the proposals rested "leaves quite a bit to be desired." "To put it bluntly," Meyers explained to

UMTA, "I think we have to recognize that it would be impossible for Little to deliver everything promised in the Center contract. Much of what is in that contract represents puffing—the promises that innovators traditionally make in order to get the chance to do anything at all."

But Meyers saw the "flaw in the report itself rather than in the thinking behind it." He said, "Like many students of innovation, I believe that transportation improvements are bound up in institutional, not technical, constraints. I also believe that the key to unlocking these restraints is good personal relationships. From what I know about the program, the ADL report considerably underestimates the power of the relationships they have formed. In that sense, the report is much more conservative than real-life circumstances warrant. . . . The temptation is overwhelming, especially for those without extensive first-hand experience in urban work, to evaluate the ADL reports in academic rather than action terms." [132]

Meyers' reassurances were short-lived. The issues reappeared at a meeting midway through the second phase. Was CCTP to introduce new technologies, build rapport with powerful interests, or boost the image of the Department? Meyers suggested that the program tie itself to corporations that had equipment to sell. (As the record of the meeting explains it, CCTP should demonstrate new technologies—"put new artifacts on the shelves.") Others pointed to the need for "quick action projects with ribbon-cutting ceremonies within six months" and some to "the identification and solving of institutional problems." To do everything at once, the conference recorder wrote, seemed impossible.

The dilemma was compounded by the aimless drift of the eight-city and twenty-one-city projects. Urban America's conferences merely opened UMTA to noxious criticism. Piqued by their exclusion from the pot of gold that appeared to be the property of the five cities, the representatives of the twenty-one cities attacked CCTP and UMTA in general. City spokesmen criticized UMTA's interposition of consulting firms between the Federal Government and the cities. CCTP was another "consultant bonanza." The demonstrations in the five cities had introduced no new ideas. A representative from Minneapolis–St. Paul, for example, argued that UMTA had ignored similar proposals for years.

UMTA decided to cut its losses. Phase III was eliminated, and cities were urged to action in Phase II. The killing blow was a decision to deny funding priority to CCTP-generated demonstrations. Without guaranteed funding, cities' incentives to participate quickly dissipated. In the summer of 1970, UMTA prepared CCTP for burial.

Howard Merritt, Villarreal's special assistant, wrote a memo to Little summing up UMTA's comments on their "draft guidelines on transportation concepts and innovations": "I am most disappointed. From these guidelines I am led to believe that our center cities, five, ten, twenty, fifty years from now will still be laced with urban freeways, hemmed by ever larger parking lots, congested with automobiles, served by diesel shuttle buses, and fed by express buses or steel-wheeled rapid transit. And they will be if this is the best guidance we can provide."

After two years of sharing in the tough rhetoric of action, UMTA hypocritically termed Little's efforts unrealistic. The draft did not guide the "systems developer" and "transportation innovator" to a future real-world application:

> The guidelines do not provide a market focus on the kinds of concepts and innovations on which federal research and development should concentrate over the next few years. The draft does not suggest where the private investor may find a market in urban transportation. It does not suggest that planners—by incorporating the bolder concepts and innovations in their longer-range plans—can create the market and can spur the public and private investments necessary to make them happen within the planned time.

CCTP not only failed to build support for itself, it ignored UMTA's supposed concern for minority groups, ghetto dwellers, and unaffiliated consumers. While Villarreal told an Urban America conference that mass transit success depended on grassroots support, and while Little's contract included a blank check to organize local power, Urban America's Larry Stinchcombe was formally and bluntly notified that the Urban America contract did not call for the stimulation of citizen support for transit.[133]

Gerald Anderson, a black consultant from Cleveland, was hired to review citizen participation in CCTP. In none of the cities did he observe programs that provided for citizen participation. In Pittsburgh, where the program was to link up with Model Cities efforts, Anderson reported on "the sad state of affairs with regard to whatever it was, if anything, that went on in Pittsburgh with the code name of CCTP. There is no evidence that anyone was maintaining official liaison with the program. Worse, no one seems to give a damn." [134]

The locations selected as Center City sites managed to exclude ghetto areas. Pittsburgh was an exception; provision was made to work in the Hill, a ghetto model citizen neighborhood. There a mass of blank paper was spread out for residents to draw in their image of the neighborhood transportation system. According to UMTA's Franz Gimmler, one of the findings on the Hill was that residents would like to commute to a community away from the center-city area. This was not considered an appropriate CCTP project, so residents were given the opportunity to have another bus within the ghetto. "Quite frankly," explained Gimmler, "the center of the city is 'different from the downtown ghetto.' " [135] Had the program tried to aid the ghetto dwellers instead of businessmen, it might have been open to the charge that UMTA was "phonily" embracing minority groups.

UMTA's official brochures single out "the elderly, the handicapped, and the poor" as the main sufferers from the absence of adequate mass transit.

In late 1970, over a dozen volumes of CCTP reports were

issued. (The citizen would probably find it impossible to obtain copies of the reports from a local library. By late 1972, he would not find the reports in the Department of Transportation's own library.) They harped on "institutional obstacles" to be surmounted before UMTA could bring decent public transit to America. These, of course, were the obstacles that CCTP had promised to overcome.

Of seventeen "action projects" planned for Phase II, only a few got off the ground. The prize was a "bus-intercept," by which commuters could park their cars at the Atlanta stadium and be shuttled downtown. The CCTP reports implied that the project was revolutionary, yet the idea had been around for years and had been tried in several places, including Washington, D.C.

People-Movers

The Democrats had grouped UMTA's R & D spending into geographic service areas. There were contracts, for example, to study the problems of the center city, the airport, and the suburbs. The Republicans reorganized the "R & D matrix" by grouping contracts according to vehicular modes—bus, rail, and "new systems." The reorganization permitted UMTA to plump for further funding, and UMTA officials rushed off to tell Congress and transit associations of their new and exciting designs. The new "matrix," they pronounced, would emphasize "action" and "demonstrations," not the unproductive paper research that characterized the old plan. The Democrats had, of course, made the same promises.

Superficially there was little change. "Systems managers" were selected to administer major projects. Mitre received a contract to sell local bus companies on new management techniques. Booz, Allen was given $4.5 million to manage the design of new buses. Boeing received $10 million to develop a new rail car. Three million dollars worth of contracts were given to TRW, Planning Research, and Peat, Marwick, Mitchell & Co. to "systems manage" the design of new transportation planning techniques. (Subcontractors on the planning project included such firms as SRI, Voorhees, and Wilbur Smith.)

One qualitative change did, however, occur. While the Democrats' definition of the "center city" had excluded the ghetto, the Republicans' definition of "urban transportation" excluded the city altogether. If CCTP demonstrated anything, the new UMTA R & D staff observed, it was the difficulty of staging successful demonstrations in complex urban environments. There was, said Franz Gimmler, no point in "influencing and encouraging events as if you could control them." So UMTA decided to sidestep urban congestion. The Villarreal administration's blue-ribbon demonstrations would not be located in major cities, but in small cities, airports, and isolated testing grounds.

Once it decided to forgo urban reality, UMTA was free to plan the production of sophisticated and costly technological solutions. In Robert Hemmes, Villarreal found an ideal administrator for this approach. Hemmes was a Naval Academy acquaintance of Villarreal and taught engineering at Stanford. He believed that R & D could succeed through the application of the "scientific method." He proudly showed visitors the latest treatise on "social evaluation," explaining that he would apply the method to UMTA's demonstrations. Hemmes's systems analysis staff manfully outlined the scientific design of major UMTA demonstrations and produced pamphlets on the purpose of the demonstration.[136]

Hemmes and Villarreal placed their bets—and up to two thirds of UMTA's R & D budget—on people-movers—basically, highly automated bus-like vehicles that run on tracks. This "new system" was the most costly and sophisticated concept available, and UMTA hoped to provide the country and the aerospace-transportation industry with a speedy demonstration success that would justify larger budgets. (The Department itself hired Sperry Rand, an aerospace corporation and major DOT contractor, to tell it how to reorganize its R & D and management.)[137]

UMTA offered money to corporations that promised to install people-movers in airport settings, but the lion's share of the people-mover budget was put to work in Morgantown, West Virginia, which has a population of some 30,000, rising to 50,000 when the University of West Virginia is in session.

"Personal rapid transit" had initially been promoted by a number of small corporations, most of which operated with little or no Federal funding. UMTA asked the Applied Physics Laboratory to evaluate the private designs. Meanwhile, UMTA awarded grants to a West Virginia University professor who proposed to demonstrate people-movers in Morgantown. The proposal was supported by the university, and, most importantly, by Harley Staggers, Morgantown's Congressman and a senior member of the House Interstate and Foreign Commerce Committee. So, as Hemmes explains, the scientific method was "telescoped." Instead of choosing an ideal urban locale to demonstrate personal rapid transit, UMTA chose Morgantown. "All I can say in defense of Morgantown," he explained weakly, "is that I believe, of the three candidates, problems would have been worse elsewhere." [138]

To the world of high-technology R & D, the University of West Virginia did not present a reassuring prospect. The university had proposed to manage the Morgantown demonstration, but UMTA took it off the job. The task of systems manager was delegated to the Jet Propulsion Laboratory (JPL), a NASA FCRC which had acquired renown for its work on the Mariner flights to Mars.

Once the demonstration was placed in the hands of national experts, the troubles began. The university, relying on a study by the Alden Self-Transit Company, had proposed to bring people-movers to Morgantown for $13 million. JPL quickly placed the cost at $37 million. The new estimate caused a crisis. UMTA was willing to spend $20 million, but not $37 million. It threatened to cut costs in half by reducing station stops and equipment. Staggers, recalls Hemmes, wanted to hold UMTA to the facilities promised by the initial press release. Following frenetic discussions, a modification in costs was agreed to. JPL "refined" its estimate to $28 million. "We don't," sighed Hemmes, "try to write predictive press releases any more."

Unfortunately, $28 million was itself only a station stop. As the demonstration encountered technical difficulties, UMTA called on new managers. A member of the Federal Aviation Administration's ill-fated SST task force was assigned to head a special Morgantown project office in UMTA, and Boeing was hired to replace JPL as systems manager. Boeing shortly produced a revised cost estimate. If the demonstration were pared to its essentials, UMTA explained, it would cost only $55 million.

Morgantown blew apart. By 1974, $57 million had been spent, and it was estimated that it would cost $125 million to complete the full three-mile, six-station system as planned. UMTA and the University of West Virginia engaged in heated debate over the Government's obligation to fulfill its obligations to the people of Morgantown. Without further funding, both parties suggested, the existing construction may have to be ripped up and removed—at a cost of millions of dollars.[139]

In 1975, the Office of Technology Assessment, a Congressional office whose creation was inspired at the high tide of systems analysis, prepared a study of UMTA's people-mover funding. The $95 million spent by UMTA, the office concluded, produced little of value. Morgantown was the sole significant "accomplishment," but no further funds should be spent for Morgantown extensions until the system is actually demonstrated to be operable.[140]

Morgantown has been UMTA's most costly effort to find an alternative to the automobile. Its failure was paralleled by failure elsewhere in the Department of Transportation. The vertical/short take-off and landing planes touted by the DOT-NASA Civilian Aviation R & D study have not begun to develop as the study suggested they might. In early 1975, there were reports that the Ford Administration was shutting off funding for the high-speed train research that was to revolutionize intercity commutation. One hundred million dollars and nearly a decade of study had not produced success. The high-speed train, lamented the head of the Mitre research group which had received a dozen contracts to bring it about, "had great promise as an R & D project and for economic viability." [141]

In a pleasingly simple series of charts, produced every so often for Congress or interested citizens, successive incarnations of the Federal mass transit agency have explained the "demonstration program." According to the simple model, the Federal Government funds research and demonstrates the workability of a new idea or product. Localities can then buy into a demonstration success through mass transit capital grant monies. "Demonstrations" are supposed to be learning experiences for the nation and the bureaucracy.

The 1961 Housing Act authorized the first trickle of demonstration monies—$25 million. This money, along with a small sum for regional planning, was seen by the authors of the legislation as basic to long-range solution of the transit problem.

In the early years, money was used to subsidize existing systems starving for cash rather than to demonstrate luxurious new approaches. R & D became an accepted cloak for subsidy.

The record was not impressive. "I'm afraid," sighed Tom Floyd, Sitton's assistant in the Johnson years, "there has been little learned from the first decade of demonstration programs." [142]

In later years, a handful of demonstrations captured national attention. Minibuses were introduced in the Washington, D.C. business district and became highly popular. The freeway leading from suburban Virginia to Washington was the site of another touted demonstration success, an "express bus" lane that offered commuters an alternative to their cars.

Successes like the minibus and the express lane were technically simple. They required no computers and no hardware innovation. The minibus demonstration cost UMTA about $150,000. When UMTA R & D tried esoteric approaches, it failed. Half a million was spent on a disappointing effort to convey Los Angelenos to the airport in helicopters. MIT was given $800,000 to computerize bus routing—until UMTA decided that computers were not necessary. Over $1 million was given to the University of Pennsylvania to develop a "minicar," until managerial troubles and political pressures caused the "phaseout" of the program.

The above successes and failures were relatively well publicized by UMTA. Most demonstrations never made a ripple. As Sitton explained, "project reports have never gotten to the cities. There was never any evaluation of them. It was often only by chance that information developed for one project was ever used again. There was no follow-up." The prime beneficiaries of the demonstrations were the contractors that attached themselves to demonstrations as planners, managers, or evaluators. (UMTA even hired a contractor—Mitre—to compile the public list of UMTA demonstrations.)

It takes a minimum of intelligence to see beneath the fraudulent rhetoric of demonstrations. Nixon appointees to UMTA were, in this respect, no less perceptive than their Democratic predecessors. Robert Hemmes was distressed to discover that most demonstrations paid for the placement of hardware in a city, but did not demonstrate that the hardware would be useful elsewhere. (Hemmes singled out a highly touted grant of over $4 million to support Westinghouse's "skybus" in Pittsburgh as just "an exhibition.")

"These projects," said Franz Gimmler, "didn't have transferability. They made sense and were interesting, but they were inherently parochial." Even where reports were produced and distributed on time, "only by the greatest stretch of the imagination could you read an Oakland report and transfer it to Philadelphia." [143]

Congress periodically gives transit R & D the roasting it deserves. But, while calling for a change of course, its critiques have always placed transit R & D back on the same old track. The 1975 study by the Office of Technology Assessment, if press reports are to be believed, would be no exception. The office condemned waste—and who would not? It concluded that progress could come about if UMTA gave industry a stronger voice in R & D planning and management.[144]

THE HEALTH AND HOSPITALS CORPORATION

Research, development, and innovation are words whose appeal to Americans is matched only by the looseness with which they are used. In the health sector, R & D conjures up the image of a medical researcher or a doctor conducting an operation with little precedent. The New York City Health and Hospitals Corporation was a different kind of innovation—one which promised to care for patients by caring for their hospitals.

The New York City Health and Hospitals Corporation (HHC) commenced operation on July 1, 1970, with a budget of over $620 million. The HHC was sold as "a research and development demonstration" that would take over the management of eighteen New York City hospitals.

According to HHC promoters, the problems that beset the municipal hospitals arise from limited resources, low productivity of personnel, and their dependence on New York's bureaucracies. These promoters include consultants, and it was consultants who ran the HHC in its first days. As a 1969 grant application written by McKinsey for the HHC put it:

> The implementation of the New York City Health and Hospitals Corporation will be an event without precedent for its potential impact upon the organization of total health services in a large urban area. While it ostensibly only involves reorganization of public hospitals and health facilities, it has great implications for future development in

the private health sphere. . . . As an experiment in reorganization of total community health services, it will be the most
expansive and total effort ever undertaken in the United
States.[145]

Management reforms were certainly essential. The old
New York City hospital system was not even able to keep
track of its debts. In practice, management reform meant
something more, and less, than it should have. It meant
ignorant action, false promotion, and byzantine politicking
that brought no benefits to those to be served, and as a
result, it meant a good deal less innovation and efficiency
than promised. In these respects, HHC is a model deserving
of attention.

In 1967, the corporation idea was called, by its author,
the "greatest promise the city has to offer—private management would bring profit to the health sector." [146] In 1969,
the city's Mayor and the Corporation's authors called it a
model for the nation.[147] In early 1972, McKinsey's HHC
project leader called it a proven "research and development
success." [148] In 1972, New York State and New York City
opened investigation into the failure of HHC. In 1974, the
HHC hired new administrators to reorganize the Corporation, by then on the verge of insolvency.

Mayor Lindsay's Entry

In 1965, Congressman John Lindsay ran successfully as a
reform candidate for Mayor of New York. Lindsay outlined
his program in a series of "White Papers" written by the
staff of the Ford Foundation–sponsored Institute for Public
Administration (IPA).[149]

The mid-Sixties were the heyday of the belief that
manipulation of organized structure could cause change.
IPA saw New York City as ripe for management reform. In
an "Agenda for the City," IPA President Fitch stated:
"Practical organizational and staffing aspects of the current
city functions, mundane as they may appear, are probably
the most important challenge confronting this administration." [150]

Following the campaign, the new Mayor asked Institute staffers to join him in the Roosevelt Hotel to formulate the first measures of his administration. The major product of the meeting was a report known as the Craco Commission Report. It called for the creation of ten superagencies, which would reorganize old bureaucracies along new functional lines, breaking up old fiefdoms and placing control in the hands of an entirely new set of administrators. (The call for "superagencies" anticipated by several years the Ash council's call for similar superagencies at the national level, and IPA's agenda for the city set the pattern for Brookings' Agenda for the Nation.)

The Institute picked up a plum of its own as the new plan created "fiscal agents" to circumvent the established bureaucracy. Mitchell Sviridorff, a Ford Foundation official chosen to head "the first poverty superagency," appointed the Institute as fiscal agent for Federal manpower grants. IPA received the city's Federal funds before they became part of the regular city budget. For four years, the Institute was handling the money for the city's manpower programs.[151] Ultimately, the City's Counsel and Controller questioned the curious practice of contracting out financial management and program direction, a central function of the city, and the IPA arrangement was canceled.

This was the first in a string of exceedingly close relationships between consultants and Lindsay's New York City government.[152] IPA was just one of several well-established consulting groups called in by the Mayor as he tried to counter the dead weight of the bureaucracy with cadres of consultants.[153]

Mayor Lindsay created an Operations Research Council to bring to the city "scientific techniques" and "high efficiency management methods." The picture of the city as a system was to be tested in style in New York City. In the mid-Sixties the City called on RAND to form a New York City RAND Institute to systematically study city problems.

But Lindsay's power base was to be the city's Budget Bureau. In his first four years in office, the Bureau's staff doubled to about 200 professionals. About thirty-five made up the "program, planning, and analysis division," modeled after the Systems Analysis Office in the McNamara Defense Department. It was in the Bureau of the Budget that McKinsey carved out a place for itself.

Chairman of the Council's Management Information Subcommittee was McKinsey's David Hertz, who brought management science to the firm and was a leading member of the Operations Research Council. When Hertz's subcommittee on management information caught the fancy of the Budget Bureau's Policy Planning Council, McKinsey was formally contracted to work for the Bureau.

The head of McKinsey's team was an ambitious young man named Carter Bales. About Bales and McKinsey the aura of indispensability grew rapidly. It was Bales who was the model for the bright young people from Princeton and Yale who were hired to staff the Bureau. The recruits were often new both to the city and to systems analysis, and Budget Director Fred Hayes recalls that the best training to be had was offered by Bales: "When he approached a project he conveyed both a strong conception of what the output was going to look like and a sense as to how to go about getting there." [154]

Early on, Lindsay decided that the New York Budget Bureau should have the PPB that was the rage in Washington. Frederick Hayes, the new Budget Director and the city's "first modern budget manager," came from OEO, where he had used McKinsey to design a management system for Community Action Programs. Lindsay wrote proudly of the management capabilities of his Budget Bureau:

> One of the most important things my administration has done is to gain central control of decisions that were previously made with no controls at all. The Policy Planning Council and the PPBs that we established in the Budget Bureau gave the city, for the first time, information about exactly where money can be most effectively used. We know specifically what it costs to implement new programs and

whether new alternatives will give us a better run for our scarce money. We know what services we can trade off for new programs and whether inefficient efforts can be salvaged or must be abandoned.[155]

The enthusiasm of the McKinsey team gave the ambitious attempt to systematize urban life a bureaucratic reality that bore little relation to urban reality. The magic of PPB and management science would wear off, but, in 1968, the Mayor was not alone in believing that the city needed, and was getting, better management.

The PPB work drew Bales and McKinsey into the vortex of the growing Budget Bureau. In June 1968, the Budget Bureau was reorganized and, in violation of the canons of government, McKinsey was given an official position in the city's government. Hayes divided the Bureau into six divisions, each to be headed by an Assistant Director of the Budget. Five were civil servants; the sixth was Carter Bales, who was to head the new Division of Program Budget Systems. "At that time," recalls Hayes, "the division was a shell without a staff. Its only resource was the contract with McKinsey and Company. The responsibilities assigned to the Director were, in fact . . . virtually identical to the work performed in the McKinsey contracts." [156]

McKinsey obtained a privileged position with few parallels in our investigation—it was, in title and in fact, both a public and a private organization.[157]

Health Services and Efficiency

The city's health bureaucracy received the medicine that management habitually prescribes—massive reorganization. A new Health Services Administration (HSA) boldly hung out its management reform shingle and proclaimed the dawn of a new day. Dr. Howard Brown was HSA's first administrator.

The millstones around HSA's neck were the eighteen public hospitals which existed for that portion of the city population which could not afford private hospital service.

These hospitals were to get the management treatment in spades. The HSA choice for hospital administrator, Dr. Joseph Terenzio, was called a "McNamara type," to which Terenzio replied, "I wish I could be more like him." [158]

The Mayor's plans for the hospital (issued in a White Paper on New York's hospital crisis) called for the "decentralization" of responsibility "to reduce bureaucracy, red tape, inefficiency, and duplication," the "centralization of special activities," and the "modernization of methods and systems of administration." [159] The Mayor's office would spearhead these changes.

For many decades, the city had recognized an obligation to pay hospital bills for the "medically indigent." By the 1960s, nearly one half of the city's population relied on the city to pay at least part of its medical bills. To care for this population, the city supported a system of municipal hospitals. In 1965, Medicare and Medicaid were new, Federally sponsored programs that provided subsidy for aged and indigent patients. In New York City these Federal programs accompanied and accelerated continuing deterioration of the public half of a dual health care system.

The municipals coexisted alongside prestigious and rich "voluntary" or private hospitals. During the Fifties, it became clear that the privates were outdistancing the publics in attracting doctors and in providing quality care.

The municipals were buoyed in 1961, when the city contracted with the private hospitals to "affiliate" with municipals. Under affiliation plans, the privates agreed to supply medical personnel to the municipals, and in return, the city hospitals would be used for teaching and research. The affiliation contracts marked the first in a series of steps to place the management of city hospitals into private hands.

"Affiliation" was a stopgap measure, and by the time Mayor Lindsay was inaugurated the dikes had burst. A series of sensational public investigations showed that the privates were not providing the services promised. A 1966 State Senate investigation found gross waste. "Certainly," the investigatory committee reported, "the infusion of $200 million over a four-year period into the affiliation program must have had some effect, but the complexities of wastefulness, unnecessary expenditures, failures to perform services, duplicate charges, diversion of equipment, and mismanagement, etc., have deprived the hospital system of additional benefits that should have been realized." [160]

The committee attacked affiliation not only for mismanagement but also because private hospitals saw the municipals as experimental laboratories from which they turned away patients who were "just not interesting cases for experiments." [161] When Medicaid permitted patients to choose between public and private hospitals, the publics went begging for patients while the private hospitals quickly became overcrowded.

In sum, there was general agreement that something had to be done about the public hospitals and that whatever was done, it had to be more than just giving out money.

In December 1966, Mayor Lindsay called into being a Commission on Personal Health Services.

The Piel Commission

Gerard Piel, the publisher of *Scientific American*, headed the seven-man Commission on Personal Health Services. The other commissioners represented major voluntary hospitals, Blue Cross, the major health philanthropies, and the systems industry. (Although called into existence by a city official and functioning as a public body, the Commission was paid for by a host of private foundations.) One member was William Golden, Chairman of the Board of the Systems Development Corporation and a trustee of Mitre Corporation, and much staff work for the Commission was done by a spinoff of SDC. The Commission produced three major findings: health care in New York City was inadequate and costly; the dual hospital system was not only inequitable but uneconomical; and the villain of the piece was the city bureaucracy.[162] The Commission found that disarrayed medical records were months behind; beds were poorly distributed through the hospital system; delay and error plagued purchasing. Piel attributed such inefficiencies to bad administrative processes. Planning was fragmented; the municipals had to rely on other "overhead" agencies to hire personnel, construct buildings, buy supplies; civil service made a guild of the employment system; the archaic budgeting system contained outmoded categories; and authority was generally dispersed and confused.

The Commission's proposed remedy was a classic restatement of the management themes we have seen before. A system designed to enhance public accountability had become the enemy of the public. Since it was assumed that the responsible officials were distinguished and innovative people, the failings of the health system could not be blamed on them. Their efforts had been thwarted by the intricate and archaic system of "checks and balances . . . designed in another day to secure public accountability of elected and appointed officials." The Piel Commission was kind to the voluntary hospitals; its basic assumption was the same as that of the technology reformers: the private sector was where the solution to health problems lay.

The Commission called for the creation of a new corporation to run the public hospitals. It claimed that decentralized management reforms would not only revive the dying municipal system but would allow for greater freedom at the local hospital level. It proposed that HSA contract with the corporation for management of the hospitals.

How was the city to maintain control over the private operation? A board of directors of eminent citizens appointed by the Mayor would oversee the corporation. In addition, the corporation would operate under a "program budget" concurred in by the HSA. "The corporation will thus be held responsive to the public through the elected and appointed officials of the city by the power of appointment and of the purse, implemented by the techniques of program budgeting and benefit-cost analysis."

The Hospitals Corporation would run the system, while

the HSA would set performance standards and do analyses to guarantee the integrity of the corporation.

The gaping hole in the Piel report was a failure to explain how the corporation would integrate the dual system. The omission was deliberate because of the misinterpretations that might arise. The problem was considered in the Commission meetings where Technomics' Robert Parks and William Golden expressed the hope that the new corporation would "hold the carrot" to the private sector. The city intended to use the contract to lure private hospitals to accomplish public ends. Incentives would be offered to hospitals which processed patients and used facilities more efficiently.[163]

Piel's report gave legitimacy to the idea of a new hospital corporation, but it is difficult to trace its influence on future events. In part, the difficulty lies in the ambiguous management rhetoric of the report. There is, however, no doubt among its proponents that their ideas were not heeded. Gerald Piel was stung by the Mayor's refusal to endorse or comment publicly on the report. "The Mayor never came close to understanding what we were talking about.[164] His advisers confused the issue for the Mayor, and by the time the idea reached the Mayor's office, its meaning had been lost."

Indeed Werner Kramarsky, Lindsay's top health aide, recalled he had helped to "bury the report." [165]

Kramarsky differed with the Piel Commission's concept of health. The Commission's formal title, the Commission on Personal Health Services, implied that it would deal with nonhospital care as well. It did not, and Kramarsky felt that the most important element of health services was excluded from concern. Mayor Lindsay himself had objections to the Piel recommendations. He had expected a stronger public role for the Health Services Administration in operating, planning, and regulating the hospitals. Piel wanted an organization free from the traditional political process, whose accountability would be to the health and management experts on its board of directors.

The complex medical needs of the city did not look like the kind of system the management tradition could come to terms with. As Kramarsky noted, "When you deal with chaos, with nonsystems, you find it incredibly difficult to describe. . . . So instead the Piel Commission picked up management as the issue." [166] Kramarsky was accurate in his explanations of the basis for the Commission's failure—hospitals were easier for management analysts to deal with.

In rejecting the report, the Lindsay administration was not affirming a fondness for the status quo. Both Budget Director Hayes and Hospitals Commissioner Terenzio were anxious to get the city out of the hospital business. It was hard to be supportive of a hospitals department whose services declined as costs rose at an annual rate of 15 percent. Terenzio's McNamara-like qualities had been blunted by the "archaic system of checks and balances."

Hayes and Terenzio differed on the path to reform. Terenzio wanted a strong new organization which he would head and which would free the Department of Hospitals from city budgetary restrictions. "If there is one essential point you have to remember," Terenzio explained, "it was that I wanted to create a vehicle so that third-party monies (Blue Cross, Medicare, Medicaid, etc.) circumvented the City of New York and went into a separate treasury. All checks would be made payable to the Corporation and not to the City of New York." [167] Hayes was dead set against this idea. He was anxious to "get the city out of the health business, if possible," but was not as willing as Terenzio to create a new agency for this purpose. "The control of the Mayor ought not to be qualified," Hayes explained. "It is an integral part of democratic theory that things should not be given away to private interests." [168] While the Budget Director echoed the Mayor's position, it led him to revive the very corporation model discarded by the Mayor.

For Hayes, the ultimate solution lay in building the capabilities of the municipals so that they could be sold to the private sector.[169] He wanted to rid his budget of the deficit-ridden Department of Hospitals, but he saw a difference between maintaining executive control over executive functions and getting rid of the burden altogether.

In April 1968, a state investigatory committee told the city to clean up its hospitals mess or "get out and turn the municipals over to an authority or some other private body." [170] In January 1969, the State Legislature received from the city the first draft of a bill to create a "public benefit corporation" to run the municipal hospitals. Terenzio drafted the legislation, and Hayes oversaw the work with the assistance of budget officials, Carter Bales, and other McKinsey personnel.[171] Hayes recalls that the McKinsey staffers in the Budget Bureau played an influential role within the Budget Bureau in drafting the legislation. He recalls that they participated in discussions with union officials and served as liaison with the Department of Hospitals and City Hall.[172]

In drafting the legislation, the city inevitably consulted with the medical profession, the municipal hospitals workers' union, and ranking staff members from the Department of Hospitals, but it was not until the bill had been marked up by the State Legislature that citizens' groups heard about the plan at a public hearing required by city law. (The Corporation was created by state law, but the fact that only New York City was involved meant that the City Council had to pass the law first.) Civil rights organizations, independent health councils, and neighborhood associations appeared at the hearings to boo Commissioner Terenzio and protest the closed and secretive preparation of the plans for the Corporation.[173]

The opposition was especially intense because the city was going through an annual fiscal crisis which threatened to close hospital wards. The City Council responded to the public concern by adding to the HHC bill a requirement that each municipal hospital was to have a "community advisory board." The City Council's provision for community participation was vague, but sufficient to appease the citizens and lawmakers.

The final bill easily passed the State Legislature. Compared with the old Department of Hospitals, the Corporation was granted far more freedom from the city under the assumption that the problems of health required a system permitting "legal, financial, and managerial flexibility." The new Corporation would float its own construction bonds and establish its own personnel policies, independent of the civil service, though, through a deal with union leadership, it was agreed that the hospital workers would remain on the civil service pay scale for a six-month period with civil service privileges. The Corporation would then proceed to develop its own merit system. Most importantly, the Corporation could administer its own budget, although the relation of the HHC to the Bureau of the Budget remained to be worked out.

Hayes was to use his management consultants to ensure that, no matter how flexible the Corporation seemed to others, it would be controlled in fact by the Mayor and the Budget Bureau through their connection with McKinsey. In an interview Hayes explained that he "insisted" that consultants be used in planning the Corporation, if it was to come into existence at all.[174]

The legislation provided that the Corporation would operate hospitals under a contract with the Health Services Administration. There would still be two health care delivery systems, one private and one now quasi-public. Gerard Piel had hoped that at some point the municipal system would be phased out and that the Corporation would make this possible, but HHC plans did not indicate this. Terenzio thought that the Corporation would attract the poorer voluntary hospitals into the corporate fold, replacing the two-class system with a one-class corporate system.[175]

While they argued that a new corporation could create standards and goals to allow "measurement" of performance, Hayes and McKinsey staff neglected to incorporate these in the HHC legislation. Nor did the legislation clarify how the municipals were to be protected from the neglect and "rape" that had characterized their association with the private affiliates.

A month before the new state law was passed, the city government quietly put its consultants to work on the development of the Corporation. Carter Bales (who, of course, was also serving as Assistant Budget Director) signed, on behalf of McKinsey, a "letter of intent" to contract with the city to work on plans for the new Corporation. McKinsey, through Bales, agreed to provide $325,000 worth of "management assistance" to the Corporation.[176]

This was not the only occasion on which Bales's activities placed him on both sides of the contract table. He was also Assistant Budget Director when letters of intent were written for over $300,000 in Model Cities contracts which he later signed as a McKinsey partner.[177] In the eyes of both the City Council and the Mayor's office, fine legal distinctions preserved the integrity of Bales's position. Although he had the title of Assistant Budget Director, he was, as an embarrassed official explained, given a "formal" title rather than an "official" one.[178] He was a private citizen and not a civil servant, as is evident from the charge for his services— more than $200,000 a year.[179]

Controlling the Corporation

Once the legislation was passed, the formation of the Corporation proceeded in two stages. In June 1969, before a board of directors was appointed, the Mayor appointed an "Interim Organizational Task Force" to prepare the Corporation for its July 1970 birth. Four individuals manned the Task Force—Hospitals Commissioner Terenzio, Assistant Hospitals Commissioner Henry Manning, Lindsay health aide Werner Kramarsky, and McKinsey's Carter Bales.

As one of its first activities, the Task Force asked HEW to fund its planning work. Grants to the Corporation were solicited from HEW's Community Health Program and from the HEW-funded New York Metropolitan Regional

Medicine Program. Although the applications were turned down, the two proposals show the Interim Task Force's attempt to sell the new Corporation as an "experiment in research and development." Terenzio later granted that the R & D planning application was a "façade" to attract Federal largesse. Joseph English, who became President of the Corporation, acknowledged that the McKinsey proposal bore little resemblance to the reality of running the Corporation.[180] Long on rhetoric, the proposal glossed over major issues such as Corporation approaches to the city's dual health care system.

In asking for monies from the New York Regional Medical Program, McKinsey pushed for a "management consulting firm" to assist the "organizational task force in planning, negotiating, and scheduling the takeover of responsibilities and facilities from the city." The (unnamed) firm would also involve itself in the recruitment of managers and lower-level officials, would prepare the "detailed specifications" for contracts with other consultants, and would provide the "necessary clerical staff, office space, and office services to support the Task Force until the Corporation becomes operational." [181] McKinsey thus wrote into the genesis of the Corporation a solid role for itself and other consultants. Since the Corporation had no board of directors, HEW rejected the proposal. Undaunted, Hayes, under his own authority, agreed to commit the city to funding consultants.

Given its connections, McKinsey's participation in HHC was inevitable—but not very rational. Carter Bales could not recall any McKinsey experience in public health work. Task Force member Kramarsky was blunt; "McKinsey and every other consultant spent their time learning about health in the city," he complained. "They knew far less than we did, and this lack of knowledge was disastrous." Kramarsky, who has become a consultant himself, stated that "being a professional consultant now, I tell people when I can't do the job. This McKinsey never told us."

Nevertheless, McKinsey was turned to continually by the Task Force, says Kramarsky. "As all the people knowledgeable about the hospital situation were leaving and being displaced, we had to rely on McKinsey." [182]

The Task Force directed McKinsey to write proposals outlining consulting contracts through which the Corporation would be funded.[183] There were to be eight contracts, with a total value of over $3 million for the development of a fistful of information, accounting, and budgeting systems. Six of the proposals drew half a dozen competitors apiece. On two, competition was slack. One of these was not advertised at all, and the second drew only two competitors. These two contracts went to McKinsey, making good the letters of intent.

McKinsey received $240,000 to provide "overall management assistance," meaning that McKinsey was to oversee the other consultants. A second $105,000 contract went to McKinsey to produce the PPB system for the new Corporation. Henry Manning, an interim Task Force member, explained the reasoning behind the PPB award: "McKinsey was a storehouse of great information. I think you would have to say that McKinsey did have intimate knowledge of the workings of the Corporation and what was wanted. A. D. Little did make an effort, but they did not stand much of a chance." [184] (Arthur D. Little was the sole bidder against McKinsey, and HHC officials made up for Little's loss by recommending it for a study of health needs on Welfare Island.)

The HHC contracting was seen as an unethical departure from prevailing practices, and John Corson's reaction was typical. Bales's actions, he said, indicated that some of the "younger men" in McKinsey were not holding true to the firm's traditionally high ethical standards.[185]

With consultants safely on board, the selection of HHC officials was undertaken. The recruiting was done by a consortium of consultants—under the supervision of McKinsey. The pattern of selection was consistent with the character of the recruiters. The consortium chose men who had management experience but who lacked experience with hospitals or with New York City.

The recruiting work permitted McKinsey to help select its own supervisor. The firm reviewed the selection of Eli Francis, Senior Vice President for Finance.[186] Francis, a former Canada Dry executive, was to control payments to contractors.

HHC followed the promoters of the Postal Service, Amtrak, and, indeed, the entire Federal contract system, in arguing that public management will improve if it is made increasingly lucrative. A confidential McKinsey study for HHC recommended salaries that were considered, even by HHC supporters, to be out of the ballpark. Hayes called them outlandish. George Kalkines, special counsel to HHC, recalled that "McKinsey thought that the Corporation's salary scales should be equivalent to those of corporation presidents in the private sector. Their scales were outrageous." [187]

Though it rejected the McKinsey recommendations, the Corporation adopted pay schedules that clearly distinguished the HHC from the civil service. In its first year of operation, HHC recorded a 125 percent increase above the Department of Hospitals in the number of employees earning $20,000 or more. The President of the Corporation received $65,000 a year—more than the Mayor.

Management Systems

As the underpinnings of the HHC (see charts on following pages), the contractors had up to a year to design management systems for debt collections, payroll, purchasing, accounting and budget, cash management, data-processing, fixed assets, PPB, and information-gathering, before the Corporation went into operation on July 17, 1971. The systems were not merely important to the long-range improvement of the health system; they were crucial to HHC's immediate functioning.

It had been popular wisdom, promoted by commissions

The creation of the Health and Hospitals Corporation is one of the few instances where consultants have actually been located on the official government organization chart. Below is reprinted a condensed version of the HHC organization chart.

**Development and Implementation
of the New York City Health and Hospital Corporation
Implementation Organization Chart**

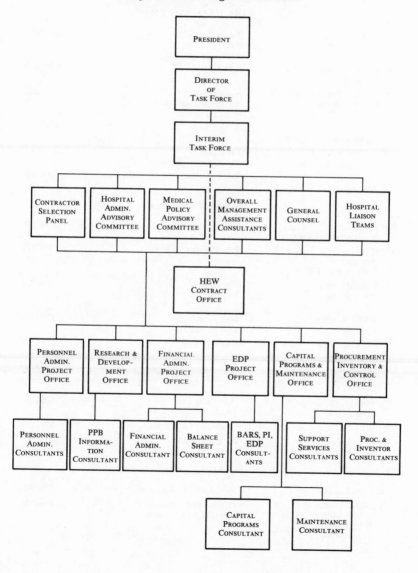

HHC Consultants

CONTRACTOR	PURPOSE OF CONTRACT	CONTRACT PRICE
1. McKinsey & Co.	Overall Management Assistance	$240,000
2. McKinsey & Co.	PPBS	$105,000
FINANCIAL SYSTEMS		
3. Peat, Marwick, Mitchell & Co.	Preparation of initial balance sheet	$46,800
4. Peat, Marwick, Mitchell & Co.	FIMARS	$445,049
5. Peat, Marwick, Mitchell & Co.	Assistance in implementation of financial system	$225,000
6. American Management Systems	Budget Support	$243,750
7. American Management Systems	Financial Management Systems	$240,000
8. American Management Systems	Review of Data-Base	$35,000
ADMINISTRATION		
9. American Management Systems	Payroll Systems	$284,550
10. Planning Research Corporation (PRC)	Procurement System	$266,815
11. H.B. Maynard & Co. (division of PRC)	Maintenance System	$296,028
12. MDC Systems Corporation	Like-Item Coding System	$279,850
13. MDC Systems Corporation	Capital Programs	$114,024
14. Burlington Management Services Co.	EDP and Payroll Systems	$153,324
15. Medical Data Systems	Admitting and Discharge System	$83,200
16. EPG Co.	Computer Programming	$50,000
17. Information Co. of America	Patient Census	$3,000
PERSONNEL		
18. C.W. Robinson	Personnel Management	$277,825
19. AERC (Association of Executive Recruitment Consultants)	Professional Consulting Services re: Recruitment	$48,500

CONTRACTOR	PURPOSE OF CONTRACT	CONTRACT PRICE
20. Battalia Lotz	Recruitment of Personnel	$15,382
21. PERT Services Corporation	Nurse Recruitment	$40,000
	OTHER	
22. Earl Graves Associates Inc.	Development of Pilot Plan—Community Involvement	$72,000
23. Arthur Andersen & Co.	External Audit	$150,000

and consultants, that the failings of the health bureaucracy were managerial and susceptible to the remedies of management experts. When at last the management consultants got free rein, they discovered that, somehow, things were far more complicated than suspected. Once again, things were obvious in retrospect that should have been apparent in prospect.

The New York health debate had given ample warning of the labor problems a new corporation would face. The requirement that the Corporation staff many areas that the old Department of Hospitals had not was one source of conflict with the local unions. New York City's dual health system had a dual union system, and, to fit the men into the management machine, the union had to be asked to agree to new job standards and performance measures.

Secondly, while HHC headquarters was to direct central administrative functions, the Corporation simultaneously claimed that decision-making would be decentralized. In the words of Terenzio and Manning,

> The Corporation's management systems must provide the maximum possible autonomy for each of the hospitals. Each hospital administrator ultimately will be free from overhead restrictions, and his hospital will be able to meet all of the medical needs of the community it serves. . . . The Corpo-

ration will then be free to coordinate the total system and monitor performance.[188]

The centralization-decentralization talk was based on the fact that the HHC had a massive information problem. As the Piel Commission, among others, had documented, the hospital system could not produce elementary patient and financial records. While the consultants were to improve information-gathering and processing, McKinsey was to introduce a PPB system that depended on sophisticated information development.

Peat, Marwick, Mitchell & Co. (PMM) was hired to produce a financial management, accounting, and reporting system (FIMARS), which would track collections, billings, and accounts receivable. In theory, FIMARS would give financial management autonomy both to the HHC and to local hospitals, making it possible for each hospital to balance its own budget and to allocate funds within the budget.

As July 1971 neared, it became obvious that things were not going well. Bales says he warned the new officials of the Corporation to ask the Legislature to extend the gestation period of HHC for another year, but the officials were apprehensive about returning to the Legislature and decided to "make a go of confusion." [189] At this juncture, Bales explains, McKinsey washed its hands of responsibility for the work of the consultants and for the health of the new Corporation.

HHC's officials recall no such warning from McKinsey.[190] The Health Services Administration itself warned McKinsey and the HHC that commencing operation of the new management systems would be enormously difficult.[191]

When the Corporation opened its doors, not a penny of collections was recorded in the first month; in the second it did little better.[192] From PMM's standpoint, the reporting system did what it was supposed to do.

The accounting and billing mess was compounded by labor problems. A high percentage (60 percent) of the experienced collections workers in the Department of Social Services (who had handled 65 percent of the collections) left when the activity was transferred to HHC. According to Director of the Health Services Administration Gordon Chase, most of the people objected to the civil service employment scales. Though HHC's executives received higher salaries than comparable Government officials, lower-echelon workers received lower wages than their peers in Government. Though PMM was paid to train new collection agents, when HHC opened, there was a dearth of trained personnel.

The accounting failure provoked a crisis. HHC was unable to present a budget to the city, as required by law. (The legislation stated that the Corporation could not exceed its budget.) Later, HHC President Joseph English wrote:

> The financial management and reporting system failed . . . to provide the information needed by the Corporation for monitoring and control of its basic encumbrances and expenditures. As a consequence of the system's various deficiencies, the Corporation spent the first eight months of its existence with no way of knowing whether it was spending within the budget appropriated by the City of New York or not.[193]

Thus management chose to blame others for budget embarrassments. PMM's contract was cut short after it had received close to $440,000 for its accounting system and $225,000 for training work. Corporation officials were displeased with the design of the financial system, and an independent review of the Corporation noted:

> The levels of employee productivity and effectiveness in almost all departments appear to be below those normally found. . . . Procedures for implementing new or existing systems are not adequately communicated to all levels. . . . Training of corporate and hospital personnel regarding the various aspects of their individual functions is inadequate.[194]

In a salvage effort, HHC junked FIMARS and switched back to the old accounting system.

Administrative Consultants

Other systems met a similar fate. Burlington Management Services, a division of Burlington Industries, received $153,324 to install an electronic data-processing and payroll system. Four weeks before it was to become operative, the system was called a failure.[195]

HHC paid Planning Research Corporation (PRC) $266,815 for an inoperable purchasing and inventory system. PRC's failure was analogous to PMM's. The PRC system decentralized the power to conduct purchasing operations, but central management refused to relinquish authority over these operations. (English's explanation for canceling the purchasing system was PRC's underestimation of purchasing volume.)

The Corporation paid Medical Data Systems $104,000 for a patient admission and discharge system. It failed to keep track of patients and was discarded. The McKinsey PPB system, for which $105,000 was paid, was never installed.

The failure of the most rudimentary systems both made planning an impossible luxury and put the HHC back to Square One in the management game. According to HHC directors, HHC abandoned efforts to replace the line-item budgeting with PPB and tried to make the old system work.

In February 1972, a report by the President of HHC termed the outcome of the consultants' work abysmal, a conclusion, English told us, which was "understated." The theme of the report was the irrelevance of the shiny "systems" to the real capabilities of the Corporation. The report concluded: "The Corporation was created by law in response to . . . desperate needs for better management. To accelerate the changeover from the Department of Hospitals to the Corporation, the Interim Task Force engaged consulting firms to design new systems, systems which later proved to be defective. . . ."

The Ongoing Consultant Game

English's disenchantment with consultants was not enduring. In 1971, to replace PMM, he hired American Management Systems, whose contracts as of 1973 cost the Corporation over $750,000. AMS was to provide budget support and design new financial and payroll information systems.

AMS was founded in 1970 by men who left the Systems Analysis Office of the Secretary for Defense. Operating under the illusion that he was still working for defense, the President of AMS, Ivan Sellin, refused to permit us to speak to any of his employees who work for the HHC. Along with McKinsey, PMM, and PRC, AMS was selected to be "on call" to the Federal Office of Management and the Budget. The notable overlap between firms used in the United States and New York City Budget Bureau levels was underlined in AMS's case, as in McKinsey's, by connections. When Kerz was with the Office of the President (of the United States), he had worked with AMS, and when he moved to the Bureau of the Budget of the State of Illinois, he awarded AMS several contracts.

English's vision for municipal hospitals was similar to that of Lindsay and Hayes—the reintroduction of centralized management. While English believes in management innovation, the Corporation has ceased to be sold as a "research and development" model.

How does the Corporation differ from the Department of Hospitals? Many think not at all. The critical difference is legal and financial, not managerial. (The city has created an organ to receive third-party monies.) Otherwise, as Gerard Piel notes, "The new Corporation is looking like the old Department of Hospitals more and more."

"Good centralized management" has not been without costs. Dr. English attempted to alleviate the Corporation's budgetary deficit by instituting an attrition policy in the hospitals. The policy was greeted with outrage from both hospital administrators and physicians, who argued that health care was relegated to second place in HHC management operations.

With the aid of AMS, English instituted new financial systems to bring about centralized management. A Case Management System would sort out collections received from third-party sources and enable the Corporation to distinguish receivables actually received from those outstanding. A second system was designed to keep track of purchases.

Although the Corporation has claimed great success with the collections system, an audit by the State Comptroller on third-party Medicare payments was not so optimistic. "To date," the Audit Report said late in 1972, "the Case Management System has not been an effective tool for monitoring and measuring the effectiveness of the billing process." [196] As for the purchasing system, an independent audit noted that it "is not yet operating effectively in order to provide for the timely processing of authorized corrections or changes to outstanding encumbrances." [197]

Despite these setbacks, Dr. English still claimed incredible progress toward financial stability. In 1972, he said the Corporation not only liquidated the $32.2 million deficit stemming from the first set of consultant failures but collected $42.2 million more than the adopted budget. (It is, of course, not to be forgotten that the Corporation abolished 1,500 positions in the hospitals, of which English estimated that one half were critical to the life of patients.)

These figures are, unfortunately, not actual receipts for the Corporation. Rather, they represent "receivables" which are anticipated by the Corporation's accounting system.

In 1971, the Corporation hired the firm of Arthur Andersen to conduct an "external 'audit.'" In its first effort, Andersen was unable to review the financial status of the Corporation because of the failures of systems. After a second audit—made as English was proclaiming the brilliancy of the management systems and the highest level of productivity of any agency in the city—Andersen issued a qualified statement. Its report said that "this statement . . . does not account for income earned but not received and expenses incurred but not not yet paid at June 30, 1971, and June 30, 1972; it does not purport to present the results of operations of the Corporation in conformity with generally accepted accounting principles." (In accounting, the failure to use accepted accounting principles simply means to corroborate the estimates a corporation puts out. In the accounting profession, Andersen's statement represents a disclaimer from being held responsible for the claims of Dr. English.)[198] The qualification was interpreted by some HHC directors to mean that the Corporation did not meet estimated goals. English downplayed the audit, insisting it was a management tool for the use of the Corporation.

The new Corporation had a legislative mandate to establish community advisory boards for each local hospital. In its writing, McKinsey never mentioned the function of the community boards. In no small part this was because the influence of consulting firms far exceeded that of citizens. While the central bureaucracy spent liberally to arm itself with consultant firepower, the low priority it put on citizen participation was indicated by the $20,000 consulting contract given to study community involvement. (It was not until 1972 that the HHC increased this contract amount by $50,000.) The first of the community boards was not appointed until 1972, when development of the Corporation had already been under way for two years. At the Corporation's first public meeting in June 1971, "not one member of the audience offered a favorable comment on the new system," in reaction to which, the Board of Directors voted to close meetings to the public.[199]

In 1971 six citizens' groups wrote to Dr. English to complain that, on the matter of accountability, they, as civic organizations, found that even less information was available on the performance of the Corporation than from its other predecessors, including the Department of Hospitals.[200]

In 1973, the Society of Urban Physicians, composed of municipal hospital physicians, issued a survey of the physicians' perceptions of HHC. The report concluded:

> The delivery of health services to the poor, in which the Municipal Hospitals play a central role, is plagued by many problems. The establishment of the Health and Hospitals Corporation has not, to date, been able to improve or resolve many of these problems according to the testimony of many of the chiefs of service at the MHs [municipal hospitals]. Rather, the HHC has aggravated certain problems and created new ones, leading to the low morale and sense of futility of those working in these hospitals.[201]

If the interests of citizens were ignored, so were the interests of physicians. The major "theme" extracted from the interviews was that physicians were not included in the decision-making process. Seventy percent of those interviewed complained of the separation between corporate goals and hospital needs. Majorities did not find any change in the quality (86 percent) and quantity (76 percent) of the staff of the municipal hospitals from the time of the HHC's inception.

Among other findings of the Society of Urban Physicians were: 77 percent of the medical directors indicated that the supportive staff (technical, clinical workers, messengers, and others) were not motivated in carrying out their tasks, and 60 percent stated that the reason for low productivity was lack of administrative control. (Dr. Alex Rosen, Director of Health Affairs at the New York University Medical Center notes that low productivity of support workers has forced physicians to perform managerial services.) Between 46 and 56 percent of the physicians indicated that they were having problems with the procurement of equipment and supplies because of stifling bureaucratic procedures; 77 percent of those interviewed stated that there was a general problem with all record-keeping systems, and 82 percent stated that the systems in their hospitals were poor; 50 percent stated that the municipal hospitals should have complete autonomy in all areas, and 75 percent stated that there should be substantial autonomy or local control over many decisions.

Finally, the report addressed the HHC's claim of productivity and said:

> Financing is one of the keystones of the system, and the one toward which the HHC has directed its most energetic efforts (with some success). As of yet, however, there is no basic incentive for personnel of the MH to aid in improving the rate of billing collection. The general attitude appears to be that the money gained will be siphoned off to other areas. Personnel believes that increased efforts on their part to collect payments will not bring about any resolution of their problems, nor benefit them in any way.[202]

NOTES

I. OFF THE ORGANIZATION CHART

1. According to Office of Management and Budget figures, Federal civilian employment was 2,794 million at the end of 1974, 2,469 million at the end of 1964, and 2,382 million at the end of 1954. The most current figure is an actual decline from the year-end 1969 peak of 2,980 million. These figures cover total end-of-year employment in full-time permanent, temporary, part-time, and intermittent positions, except for summer workers under the President's Youth Opportunity Programs and, for the 1974 figure, disadvantaged-worker trainee programs. Federal employees actually make up a smaller portion of the population today (13.0 per 1,000, estimated for 1976) than they did two decades ago (14.6 per 1,000 in 1954, and 14.0 per 1,000 in 1956). The comparative stability of the Federal work force is in sharp contrast to the substantial recent growth in the number of state and local employees. See *Budget of the United States Government, Fiscal Year 1976, Special Analyses,* pt. I H, "Civilian Employment in the Executive Branch," pp. 135–6. The budget figures compared in the opening paragraph are the 1956 actual expenditures and newspaper reports of the projected 1976 budget. (According to summary table 20 of the *Budget of the United States Government, Fiscal Year 1976,* the outlay for fiscal 1956 was $70.46 billion.)

2. The size of the procurement work force was estimated in *Summary Report of the Commission on Government Procurement,* December 1972, p. 1. On the overall dimensions of contracting, see, generally, Comptroller General of the United States, *Annual Report 1973,* chap. 6, "Procurement and Systems Acquisition." The figures appear to be rough estimates, for, as discussed in the text, the Government has little precise information on many characteristics of the contract bureaucracy.

3. Walter Lippmann, *Public Opinion* (1922; reprint ed., New York: Free Press, 1965), chap. 25. Quotation on pp. 233–34.

4. Report to the President and the Secretary of Defense by the Blue Ribbon Defense Panel (the Fitzhugh report), July 1970, pp. 158–59.

5. *A Report on the Manpower Policies and Practices of the Department of Health, Education, and Welfare,* Surveys and Investigation Staff, Committee on Appropriations U.S. House of Representatives, April 1971. Reprinted in *Department of Labor and Department of Health, Education, and Welfare Appropriations for Fiscal Year 1972,* Hearings Before a Subcommittee of the Committee on Appropriations, U.S. House of Representatives, 1971, pt. 4, pp. 1061–166. Quotation on p. 1107.

6. Telephone interview with Jack Donovan, Department of Health, Education, and Welfare procurement policy official, January 1973.

7. *Federal Funds for Research, Development and Other Scientific Activities, Fiscal Years 1973, 1974, 1975,* National Science Foundation, 1974. This volume is one of a series of periodic National Science Foundation reports on R & D spending and conduct.

8. *Improvement Needed in Training and Technical Assistance Services Provided to Antipoverty Agencies,* U.S. General Accounting Office, April, 26, 1972.

9. The Estimate appears in "Federal Grant Programs Assisting State and Local Governments in Functional and Comprehensive Planning," Executive Office of the President, Bureau of the Budget, Office of Executive Management, March 26, 1968, mimeographed. The Bureau study included funds for "functional and comprehensive planning," but did not include funds for planning specific projects—e.g., "river basin development as opposed to planning a small watershed project." The totals in both cases are larger today.

10. See, on evaluation spending, *Need for Improving the Administration of Study and Evaluation Contracts,* U.S. General Accounting Office, August 16, 1971; *Selected Contracting and Consulting Activities of the Office of Education,* U.S. General Accounting Office, June 30, 1970; *The Competitive Evaluation Research Industry,* Bureau of Social Science Research, May 1972; *Improvements Needed in the Administration of Contracts for Evaluations and Studies of Antipoverty Programs,* U.S. General Accounting Office, December 28, 1971.

11. Interviews with officials at the Springfield, Virginia, Federal document center, summer 1974. The clearinghouse issues a semimonthly *Government-wide Index to Federal Research and Development Reports.* The Army contracts were examined in *Administration of Contract Studies Should Be Improved,* U.S. General Accounting Office, December 11, 1972. The Army also spends a large portion of the total Federal expenditures for public relations contractors. Between 1970 and 1972 an estimated $80 million was placed by the Federal Government with private public-relations and advertising firms. See "Administration Tries Public Relations to Re-establish Image and Promote Its Efforts," *National Journal,* June 23, 1973.

12. The packet included brochures entitled "Westinghouse's Public Management Services Business Strategy," dated November 17, 1970, and "Business Strategy for 1970," by F. J. Carr.

13. The list of competitors appeared in Carr, "Business Strategy for 1970," pp. 25–26.

14. The contract is discussed in Chapter II.

15. The Arthur Andersen income statistics appear in *Arthur Andersen, March 31, 1974,* the firm's second annual report. (The annual reports are, in theory, designed for limited distribution to Andersen employees, clients, and others.) The Lyons quotation appears in John Lyons, "The Big Eight Accountants: How Far Should They Go?" *Corporate Financing,* December 1970. The accounting profession has rarely been subjected to accessible criticism. A highly readable exception is Abraham Briloff's *Unaccountable Accounting* (New York: Harper & Row, 1972).

16. The size of the Big Eight consulting services, as well as an upheaval in the structure of traditional consulting firms, is the subject of "Consultants Clash over Ownership," *Business Week,* November 27, 1971. *Business Week* found that accountants do not like the term "management consulting." The American Institute for Certified Public Accountants prefers "management advisory services," which is defined periodically in issuances by its Committee on Management Services.

17. "Statement Submitted by Peat, Marwick, Mitchell & Company," in *Legislative Oversight Review of the Civil Service Commission,* Hearings before the Subcommittee on Investigations, Committee on Post Office and Civil Service, U.S. House of Representatives, 1972, p. 236.

18. The Booz, Allen contracts are discussed in Chapter III. The large accounting firms, like elite law firms, traditionally have enjoyed an immunity from public scrutiny. *Fortune* magazine was prompted to title a July 1966 article on PMM "The Very Private World of Peat, Marwick, Mitchell." An article in the December 1970 *Staff Memo,* a PMM house organ, reveals that PMM's own employees may know little more about the firm than is told to the public. When PMM's senior partner gave candid talks to meetings of employees and even revealed the firm's "financial status in dollars," the *Staff Memo* recounted the reactions:

> As an indication of how unexpected Mr. Hanson's candor had been at the Northeast conference, house chairman Dick Ferguson noted that committee members had some difficulty getting participants to submit their questions at the coffee break preceding the presentation. However, by the time the Southeast conference met the following Thursday, the word had obviously filtered south because questions flooded in.
>
> Protected by the anonymity of 3 x 5 cards, the management group scribbled down exactly what was on their minds: Where are the black, female, and minority faces in the audience? Explain the mechanics of nomination and election of partners? Why are the firm's personnel changes made abruptly? What compensation can a newly admitted partner expect in his first year? Why are the partnership's activities cloaked in fraternity-like secrecy?

19. Interview with Felix Kauffman, Lybrand & Cooper, winter 1970–71. Accountants aver that their professional codes do not allow them to solicit business publicly. While they do not advertise, they employ other techniques to acquire and retain business. A "practice development primer" given to Lybrand's employees, for example, explains that the firm will be well served if accountants are seen at appropriate social clubs, accept speaking engagements, and employ their wives as corporate assets (James Mahon, *Practice Development Primer,* no date).

20. See *The Block Grant Programs of the Law Enforcement Assistance Administration,* Twelfth Report by the Committee on Government Operations, U.S. House of Representatives, October 1971, pp. 48–60. Quotation on p. 56.

21. Peter Drucker, *The Age of Discontinuity* (New York: Harper & Row, 1969). For an alternative view of the rise of efficiency expertise, see Loren Baritz, *The Servants of Power* (1960; reprint ed., Westport, Conn.: Greenwood Press, 1974).

22. *What ACME Is* (New York: Association of Consulting Management Engineers, n.d.).

23. Philip Shay, *Common Body of Knowledge for Management Consultants (in Summary Form)* (New York: Association of Consulting Management Engineers, 1970).

24. The estimates are those of ACME executive Philip Shay. Shay is quoted in the April 1973 issue of *Consultants' News,* an informative industry newsletter.

25. Booz, Allen, & Hamilton, *Annual Report 1973;* Booz, Allen, & Hamilton, *Fact Book,* 1970–71.

26. Interview with Harry Vincent, Booz, Allen, & Hamilton, winter 1971–72. Booz, Allen, & Hamilton staff directive, "Policy Statement on Security of Client Information."

27. On ADL's earlier successes see Arthur D. Little, *Industrial Bulletin,* October 1936; Herbert Solow, "Science for Sale at a Profit," *Fortune,* March 1955.

28. Arthur D. Little, *Annual Report 1969,* p. 13; telephone interviews with ADL employees, winter 1971–72; letters of Daniel Guttman to James M. Gavin, January 11 and March 1, 1972; letters of James M. Gavin to Daniel Guttman, January 20 and March 6, 1972.

29. ADL's development work has suffered a severe blow. The firm's promise to "bring modern industry to Manitoba's pine-covered northwest" resulted in what the *Wall Street Journal* termed "one of Canada's most celebrated scandals." See "How a Promising Plan Became a Scandal, Got Canadians Mad at Arthur D. Little, Inc.," *Wall Street Journal,* October 14, 1974.

30. Arthur D. Little, *Annual Reports.*

31. Abt Associates, *Annual Report 1974.* Abt was most successful in marketing to civilian agencies the brand of military analysis current in the early Sixties and embodied in his MIT thesis, "Termination of General War."

32. Planning Research Corporation, *Annual Reports.* Interview with Robert Krueger, winter 1970–71. Krueger made available a memo which defined the conception of the Council, "Representing the Interests of Profit-Making Professional Service Firms in Doing Business with the Federal Government on a Fair Basis," June 1971. The Council testifies periodically before Congressional committees considering procurement. See, e.g., Testimony of John F. Magnotti, Jr., in *Establishing Office of Federal Procurement Policy,* Hearings Before the Ad Hoc Subcommittee on Federal Procurement, Committee on Government Operations, U.S. Senate, 1973, pp. 167–76.

33. See, e.g., testimony of John F. Magnotti, Jr., National Council of Professional Service Firms, and William P. Sommers, Booz, Allen, & Hamilton, *Federal Grant and Cooperative Agreement Act of 1974,* Hearings Before the Ad Hoc Subcommittee on Federal Procurement and the Subcommittee on Intergovernmental Relations, Committee on Government Operations, U.S. Senate, 1974, pp. 162–67.

34. For descriptions and histories of nonprofit research institutions see, generally, Harold Orlans, *The Nonprofit Research Institute: Its Origins, Operations, Problems and Prospects* (New York: McGraw-Hill Book Co., 1972); *Contract Research and Development Adjuncts of Federal Agencies,* Denver Research Institute, 1969. Orlans has been the Brookings Institution's expert on research funding. The Denver report was prepared for the National Science Foundation. British and American scholars and officials discuss the growing role of "quasi-public" nonprofit institutions in Bruce L. R. Smith and D. C. Hague, eds., *The Dilemma of Accountability in Modern Government* (New York: St. Martin's Press, 1971). See also Paul Dickson, *Think Tanks* (New York: Ballantine Books, 1972).

35. We have excluded universities and trade associations from the primary focus of our study in order to make the work manageable. In general, however, money is not given to universities with the expectation that a product of immediate use to the Government will result. Money goes to support "basic research," or to provide, in effect, for supporting faculty and training graduate students.

Many nonprofit trade associations, such as the National League of Cities, support Washington activities with grant or contract funding. Trade associations, normally associated with interest groups, and "independent nonprofit research institutions" often perform similar political and technical functions.

36. R. R. Black and C. Foreman, *Technological Innovation in Civilian Public Areas,* Analytic Services Inc. (ANSER), September 1967. Quotation on p. 23. For descriptions of the nuclear laboratories, see "Atomic Energy Commission

Research and Development Laboratories (A National Resource), September 1973," reprinted in *AEC December 1, 1973 Report on Energy Research and Development,* Hearing Before the Joint Committee on Atomic Energy, U.S. Congress, 1973, app. 4.

37. See *Federal Funds for Research, Development, and Other Scientific Activities, Fiscal Years 1973, 1974, 1975,* National Science Foundation, 1974. The NSF also uses the terms "Federally Funded Research and Development Centers," or "FFRDC."

38. *Report of the Research Group on Federal Contract Research Centers,* Office of the Director of Defense Research and Engineering, August 1971, p. 9.

39. The corporate reorganization caused considerable controversy. Congressman Jack Brooks attacked the transition as a giveaway of public property, Krueger's group attacked it as the unfair subsidy of a competitor, and SDC's defenders argued that the deal was a fair arrangement necessary to sustain SDC. Interviews with Richard Goldstein (summer 1972), Edwin Huddleson, Jr., the San Francisco lawyer and RAND counsel who negotiated the deal with the Air Force (1973), and staff of the House Government Operations Committee. The terms of the deal are described in "An Air Force Baby Gets Set to Go Private," *Business Week,* December 9, 1972.

40. *Scientific Activities of Independent Nonprofit Institutions,* National Science Foundation, 1971.

41. In fiscal year 1972 the Federal Government obligated $40 million to SRI, close to three quarters of which came from the Defense Department (*Federal Support to Universities, Colleges, and Selected Nonprofit Institutions, Fiscal Year 1972,* National Science Foundation, 1974, p. 32). SRI's story of its growth is told in "20 Years: The Story of SRI," *SRI Journal,* December 1966.

42. See George A. W. Boehm and Alex Groner, *The Battelle Story: Science in the Service of Mankind,* Battelle Memorial Institute, 1972. This corporate history was commissioned by Battelle's "corporate communications" department.

43. "Battelle Institute Ordered to Donate Millions to Charity," *New York Times,* May 9, 1975.

44. Smith and Hague, eds., *Dilemma of Accountability in Modern Government,* p. 15. Just how small a step it can be is starkly illustrated by the use of "letter contracts." With the letter contract (literally, a brief letter), the Government has authorized work on projects as vast and complex as missiles on the assumption that a formal contract will be drawn up as the work proceeds.

45. Interview with Ralph Howard, fall 1972.

46. HEW contract evaluation, 1971.

47. It should be noted that half of the negotiated dollars represented renewals of prior contracts.

48. HEW contract evaluation, 1971.

49. Interview with Herbert Winokur, Inner City Fund, August 1971.

50. The quoted material appears in the contract file, HEW Contract OS-71-21.

51. The quoted material appears in the contract file, HEW Contract OS-71-187.

52. Interviews with Martin Duby, summer 1971.

53. The quoted material appears in the contract file, HEW Contract OS-71-110. The Health Maintenance program is another spinoff from the faith that social service crises can be remedied by mating Government dollars and private managerial techniques.

54. Contract files, HEW Contracts OS-71-134 and OS-71-180.

55. RAND received the large award to study the effectiveness of "performance contracting" in education. Performance contracting was a managerial bloodbrother of the Health Maintenance Organizations.

In the early Sixties, Defense Department management experts promised to control the costs of defense contracting by binding contractors to fixed prices and performance requirements and rewarding them for bettering the "targets." The concept, as discussed in Chapter IV, unraveled quickly and was largely discarded by the end of the decade. The myth of performance contracting spread far in advance of the reality, however, and by the late Sixties it was all the rage in the education research establishment. In line with the aerospace myth, local school districts contracted out to private corporations to "systems-manage" the classroom. In 1970 HEW and OEO undertook separate studies of school districts that employed performance contracts. The OEO "experiment in performance contracting" showed little positive benefit and effectively killed the fad.

56. Quotation from the contract file, HEW Contract OS-71-125.

57. Quotation from the contract file, HEW Contract OS-70-196. The report, *A Review of the Utilization of Research and Demonstration Results*, University Research Corporation, Washington, D.C., is dated May 13, 1971.

58. Depending upon the agency and the contract, the evaluators may be drawn from the program office alone, or from employees throughout the agency. On some occasions, outside experts will also be empaneled to judge proposals. On other occasions, a series of panels will weed out responses, and sometimes evaluations of the written responses will be followed by invitations to leading bidders to appear and discuss their proposals orally before the panel.

59. David Allison, ed., *The R & D Game: Technical Men, Technical Managers, and Research Productivity* (Cambridge, Mass.: MIT Press, 1969), p. 290.

60. *Small Business and Government: Research and Development*, Small Business Management Series No. 28 (Washington, D.C.: Small Business Administration, 1962), p. 33.

61. Interview with Karl Hereford, 1972. The quoted material, initially discovered in the Office of Education contract files, is cited in a letter of Daniel Guttman and Barry Willner to Anthony Natelli and Robert Sullivan, Peat, Marwick, Mitchell, January 22, 1973. PMM declined to comment on the incident; letter of Anthony Natelli for Robert Sullivan and Anthony Natelli to Guttman and Willner, February 14, 1973.

62. Response of Clark Abt to letter survey on contract industry, December 1970.

63. "Analysis of the Procurement Process for HEW Evaluation Studies, in FY 70," Office of the Deputy Assistant Secretary for Evaluation and Monitoring, HEW, May 1, 1971.

64. *The Competitive Evaluation Research Industry*, Bureau of Social Science Research, May 1972.

65. *A Report on the Investigation of the Contract Between Westinghouse Electric Corporation and the United States Postal Service*, Subcommittee on Investigations, Committee on Post Office and Civil Service, U.S. House of Representatives, October 19, 1971.

66. Ibid., p. 12.

67. Ibid., p. 16.

68. Hearings Before the Subcommittee on Investigations of the Committee on

Post Office and Civil Service, U.S. House of Representatives, July 30, 1971, pp. 318–19.

69. Ibid., p. 186.

II. PRIVATE MANAGERS OF THE PUBLIC DOMAIN

1. The quotation is from the draft of a report on a project on conflict of interest law, which was made available through Leonard Meeker of the Center.

2. Much of the information concerning PMM in this chapter was presented by the authors in testimony before the Special Investigations Subcommittee of the House of Representatives' Post Office and Civil Service Committee. The testimony appears in the print of that Committee's *Legislative Oversight Review of the Civil Service Commission*, 1972, pp. 159–83. The testimony was given under extraordinary conditions. The Subcommittee initially declined to permit the testimony to be read in public session, citing a House rule concerning testimony that may be potentially defaming, degrading, or incriminating. It was agreed that the testimony could be offered in public if, upon Committee staff investigation, it were determined to be accurate. The testimony was given in public session. PMM submitted a rebuttal, which appears at pages 236–49 of the hearing. The authors submitted a letter rejoinder to PMM, which invited further discussion. A brief PMM response acknowledged the letter, and stated: "Based on my recent telephone conversation with Mr. Willner, your continued predisposition concerning information provided to you by us in the past, and your policy of not permitting us to review your interpretation of such data prior to release of your opinions to the public, we see no useful purpose in our further response." Letter of Daniel Guttman and Barry Willner to Anthony Natelli and Robert Sullivan, PMM, January 22, 1972; letter to PMM (Anthony Natelli for Natelli and Robert Sullivan) to Guttman and Willner, February 14, 1973.

The *Fortune* article, "The Very Private World of Peat, Marwick, Mitchell," appeared in July 1966.

3. The evolution of defense cost-control consulting is described in Chapter IV.

4. Ernest Joss, J. Sterling Livingston, and John Wander, "How Much Will It Cost?" in *Cost Reduction Journal*, Department of Defense, winter 1966–67.

5. ORL's contracts with Management Systems Corporation (in October 1965, by novation agreement with Peat, Marwick, Mitchell & Co.) ran from November 1963 through January 1967. Contract numbers include B-231, R65-0645, and R66-339. The cost for these was $1,214,295.70. Letter of John Johnson, Director, ORL, to Daniel Guttman, March 28, 1972.

6. Transcript, "Sixty Minutes," as broadcast over the CBS television network, March 3, 1970.

7. "Torpedo Mk 48 Weapon System Project Manager Response to Center for Study of Responsive Law," May 31, 1973. PMM was hardly the only consulting firm at work on the Mark 48. Through the end of 1972 the Government had awarded Operations Research Inc. over $2 million; A. T. Kearney, over $1.3 million; Bolt, Beranek & Newman, over $2.2 million; Arthur D. Little, close to $.5 million; and the Vitro Corporation, nearly $4.5 million. Letter by Dolph M. Veach, Naval Ordnance Command, to Daniel Guttman, no date.

8. Interviews with Hassell Bell, winter 1971–72. Letter from Bell to Daniel Guttman, no date. The PMM-Wander track record was filed with GAO in an

October 15, 1969 letter from John Sieck of PMM to Bell. The GAO contract with PMM, first dated October 29, 1969, is GAO-715.

9. Interviews with Commander E. B. Coleman, Mark 48 Business Manager, and Mark 48 contract team, winter 1971–72. See also *The Acquisition of Weapons Systems*, Hearings Before the Subcommittee on Economy in Government, Joint Economic Committee, U.S. Congress, 1969, to 1, pp. 269–73.

10. *Legislative Oversight Review*, p. 241. While disavowing any obligation "to unilaterally disclose information about their clients to the public," PMM asserted that a "consultant, of course, does not have the right to knowingly support or hide irregularities, fraud, or illegal action. If he encounters such activity in the course of a consulting engagement, he should bring the matter to the attention of the proper authorities" (p. 241). The practical distinction between the two types of obligations is often not obvious. Anthony Natelli, a PMM partner who wrote the above response to the author's Mark 48 testimony, was convicted and sentenced to jail for participation in a stock fraud involving the National Student Marketing Corporation. Natelli was convicted after the judge asked for a determination whether he was "blinding himself to facts which he should have inquired about." The judge, in pronouncing sentence, noted that Natelli suffered from a myopia shared by many professionals, for there is no clear definition of the public responsibility of professionals. See "Two Auditors in National Student Case, Company's Founder Receive Jail Terms," *Wall Street Journal*, December 30, 1974.

11. Interviews with Ernest Fitzgerald, 1971–72.

12. Interview with John Macy, winter 1971–72.

13. Interview with Charles Bingman and Gene Tetterick, Office of Management and Budget, winter 1971–72.

14. Contract file, Office of Education Contract OEC-O-70-4750 (099).

15. Letter of W. Russell G. Beyers to Daniel Guttman, April 12, 1972.

16. HEW Procurement Regulations, subpart 3-22.5101.

17. *Ibid.*

18. Interviews with Robert Kane, summer 1971; interview with Steve Sklar, summer 1971.

19. Saunders' promise that managerial technique would restore the railroads is cited in Peter Binzen and Joseph Daughten, *The Wreck of the Penn Central* (Boston: Little, Brown, 1971), p. 61.

20. *Investigation into the Management of the Business of the Penn Central Transportation Company and Affiliated Companies*, Brief of the Bureau of Enforcement, Interstate Commerce Commission, Docket No. 35291, March 8, 1972. See also *The Financial Collapse of the Penn Central*, Staff Report of the Securities and Exchange Commission to Special Subcommittee on Investigations, U.S. House of Representatives, August 1972.

21. See "Amtrak Is About to Miss the Train," *Fortune*, May 1974. See also Richard Hebert, "Amtrak: Asleep at the Switch," *The Nation*, August 21, 1972. The information on Amtrak bidders was obtained from the files of the Amtrak "organization" contract, Department of Transportation Contract DOT-FR-10017.

22. Amtrak's commitments are enumerated in *The National Railroad Passenger Corporation*, Hearing Before the Subcommittee on Surface Transportation, Committee on Commerce, U.S. Senate, 1971, pp. 107–8. The Amtrak-McKinsey contract is Department of Transportation Contract DOT-FR-10017.

23. *Annual Report*, Form A submittals to the Interstate Commerce Commission, Schedule 563.

24. Letter to A. J. Greenough, President, Pennsylvania Railroad Company, and Wayne M. Hoffman, Executive Vice President, New York Central System, to John S. Crowley, McKinsey & Co., March 9, 1965.

25. The proposal appears in the contract file of DOT-FR-10017. The quotation is from *A Career with McKinsey & Company: Its Opportunities and Limitations*, McKinsey & Co., no date.

26. Interview with Bruce Rohrbacher, McKinsey & Co., July 1971.

27. *Report to the President and Congress, Amtrak—State of Rail Passenger Service—Effectiveness of the Act*, Interstate Commerce Commission, October 30, 1971.

28. On McKinsey's influence on Britain, see Derek Channon, "The Strategy and Structure of British Enterprise," Ph.D. thesis, Harvard Graduate School of Business Administration, 1971. On the influx of McKinsey, Booz, Allen, and other consultants, see "Europe's Lush Market for Advice," *Fortune*, July 1969.

Historian Alfred Chandler, Jr., whose graduate students at Harvard Business School set out to study the effects of American managerial thought on European corporation structure, found that McKinsey itself was a dominant purveyor of the corporate form developed by American corporations like DuPont and General Motors. The late Gilbert Clee, the prime mover in the development of McKinsey's international practice, linked managerial technique to cold-war ends. A *Harvard Business Review* article by Clee, for example, bore the subtitle "The system management concept has played a key role in weapons development. It can be equally indispensable in U.S. firms' efforts to develop the economies of nations in Africa, Asia, South America—before the Soviets do." McKinsey has adapted to, and perhaps led, the new corporate view of *détente*. In the late Sixties it began advising management in Yugoslavia. See Gilbert Clee and Frank Lindsay, "New Patterns for Overseas Operations," *Harvard Business Review*, January–February 1961.

29. The sums expended by railroads on professional services are reported in their *Annual Report*, Form A submittals to the Interstate Commerce Commission, Schedule 563.

30. Department of Transportation Contract DOT-FR-00025. The title of the contract is "Determine the Full Cost of Passenger Train Operation Between New York City and Washington, D.C."

31. Letter of Robert Monteverde, partner, PMM, to Clifford Gannett, Assistant Chief, Demonstration Division, Office of High Speed Ground Transportation, U.S. Department of Transportation, August 28, 1969.

32. *Legislative Oversight Review*, pp. 244–46.

33. Testimony of Willard Wirtz, et al., in *Failing Railroads*, Hearings Before the Committee on Commerce, U.S. Senate, 1970, p. 631.

34. Letter of Wright Patman to William J. Casey, January 3, 1972.

In July 1975 the Securities and Exchange Commission announced a settlement of controversies with PMM concerning the firm's role as auditor of the Penn Central and four other companies that had experienced financial collapse. The settlement barred PMM from seeking most new, publicly held audit clients for six months, and was said to be the strongest sanction the Commission has imposed on a major accounting firm. See "Peat, Marwick Sharply Curbed in Taking Clients for 6 Months Under SEC Accord," *Wall Street Journal*, July 3, 1975.

35. *Legislative Oversight Review*, pp. 244–46.

36. Letter of Frederick G. Bremer, Chief, Procurement Operations Division, Office of the Secretary of Transportation, to Barry Willner, April 23, 1971.

37. The Department even tried to withhold reports by "nongovernmental experts," arguing that "we regard them as intra-agency memoranda." It did so in response to a request for a study of departmental R & D management by Sperry Rand, an industrial corporation that is a substantial beneficiary of DOT R & D contracts. Letter of Oscar O. Griffin, Jr., Acting Director, Office of Public Affairs, Office of the Secretary of Transportation, to Daniel Guttman, January 14, 1972. Letter of John W. Barnum, General Counsel, Department of Transportation, to Daniel Guttman, March 31, 1972.

38. DOT listed the PMM highway studies in its contract files as "Studies to Fulfill Requirements of Section 138 (a) and (b) of the Federal Highway Act of 1973, Contract # DOT-OS-40064."

39. See, e.g., C. Corson and Harvard Business School citations in note 135, p. 314 below; *Business Week* citation in note 136, p. 314 below; and Malek's *Harvard Business Review* citation in note 124, p. 313 below.

40. On the evolution of American corporation structure, see Alfred D. Chandler, Jr., *Strategy and Structure: Chapters in the History of American Industrial Enterprise* (Cambridge, Mass.: MIT Press, 1969).

41. McKinsey & Co., *Supplementing Successful Management*, New York, 1940, p. 8; D. Ronald Daniel, "Reorganizing for Results," in Rolo Mann, ed., *The Art of Successful Management: A McKinsey Anthology* (New York: McGraw-Hill Book Co., 1971), pp. 66–78. Quotation on p. 66.

42. Stanley Ruttenberg, *Manpower Challenge of the 1970's: Institutions and Social Change* (Baltimore: Johns Hopkins Press, 1970), p. 79; interview with Stanley Ruttenberg, August 4, 1971.

43. In addition to intramural reorganizations, Federal organization charts may be changed by Congressional creation of new agencies (or alteration of existing agencies), and by Presidential orders issued pursuant to statutory authority. See, generally, *Executive Reorganization: A Summary Analysis*, Committee on Government Operations, U.S. House of Representatives, 1972.

44. Interview with Richard Cheney, February 1, 1972.

45. Interview with Bertrand Harding, January 25, 1972.

46. Ibid.

47. Interview with Ralph Howard, Procurement Division Chief, OEO, January 25, 1972.

48. Interview with Richard Cheney, February 1, 1972.

49. Interview with Richard Blumenthal, January 31, 1972.

50. Interview with Richard Cheney, February 1, 1972.

51. Ibid.

52. Interview with Paul Anderson, February 1972.

53. See OEO contract file, B99-4889.

54. Interview with Robert Cassidy, January 24, 1972.

55. Interview with Paul Anderson, February 1972; see also *Washington Star*, September 19, 1969.

56. Interviews with Russell LeFevre, January 1972.

57. Interviews with Gerson Green, January 12 and October 27, 1972.

58. Interview with Benjamin Zimmerman, January 1972.

59. Interview with Noel Klores, January 26, 1972.

60. See OEO contract file B99-4882.

61. Memorandum, "Background on OEO Reorganization," dated August 11, 1969, from the Executive Office of the President, p. 1.

62. Ibid., p. 4.

63. Because of the inactivity of the Compliance Division, it is impossible to tell how many of OEO's contractors were in compliance with equal employment regulations. Agency officials did know that many of the consulting firms they used employed few, if any, women or minority-group people in professional positions. The prime contractor for the major OEO study of minority-group training programs, Operations Research, Inc. (ORI), was a major offender. At the same time that OEO was paying ORI over $5 million for its study, a female employee was bringing ORI to court for its employment practices. The Federal Equal Employment Commission determined that ORI had, in fact, discriminated.

64. "Background on OEO Reorganization," p. 8.

65. Interview with Christopher Clancy, February 15, 1972.

66. Letter from Jacob Fuchsberg to Sargent Shriver, November 1967.

67. Interview with Jacob Fuchsberg, winter 1972.

68. Letter from Sargent Shriver to Jacob Fuchsberg, January 1968. For an excellent review of the regionalization of the Legal Services Program, see *Regionalization of Legal Services: An Examination of Problems and Issues*, Report by the Subcommittee on Regionalization, National Advisory Committee for OEO Legal Services, November 20, 1970.

69. Interview with Paul Anderson, February 1972.

70. Ibid.

71. Interview with Padraic Kennedy, winter 1972.

72. Interview with William Bozman, February 2, 1972.

73. Interview with Terry Lenzner, winter 1972.

74. Interview with Richard Blumenthal, January 31, 1972.

75. Interview with Thomas Bryant, winter 1972.

76. Interview with Paul Anderson, February 1972.

77. Ibid.

78. Interview with Bertrand Harding, January 25, 1972.

79. Interviews with Richard Ottman, January 14 and February 15, 1972.

80. Interview with Donald Wortman, February 16, 1972.

81. Interview with Robert Trachtenberg, February 1, 1972.

82. Interview with Donald Wortman, February 16, 1972.

83. Testimony of Frank Carlucci, Hearings Before the Committee on Education and Labor, U.S. House of Representatives, 1971, p. 219.

84. Interviews with Doc Drohat, February 14 and February 2, 1972.

85. Interviews with William Bozman, January 13 and February 2, 1972.

86. OEO contract file, B99-4889.

87. Interview with Richard Cheney, February 1, 1972.

88. On February 7, 1972, the authors of this study asked Senator Proxmire to instruct the General Accounting Office to review the relevant Booz, Allen contracts with OEO (B99-4889 and B99-5008). The results of this investigation, in part detailed in this chapter, are contained in "Charges of Improper Practices Regarding Two Contracts Between the Office of Economic Opportunity and Booz, Allen, and Hamilton, Inc.," General Accounting Office Report B-175394, dated August 25, 1972.

89. Letter from Floyd Hyde, Assistant Secretary, Department of Housing and Urban Development, to Clinton B. Anderson, September 4, 1970.

90. Interview with Bernard Russell, winter 1972.

91. The President's statement is reprinted in *Planning-Programming-Budgeting Inquiry of the Subcommittee on National Security and International Operations*, Committee on Government Operations, U.S. Senate, 1970, pp. 503–4. PPB has been the subject of countless speeches, articles, courses, and memoranda. The more notable statements by PPB experts and critics were collected by the Joint Economic Committee of Congress in *The Analysis and Evaluation of Public Expenditures*, the three volumes of which were issued in June 1969. The Committee itself deemed PPB to be of little use to the Executive and less use to Congress in *Economic Analysis and the Efficiency of Government*, Report of the Subcommittee on Economy in Government, Joint Economic Committee, U.S. Congress, February 9, 1970. The spirit of PPB is expounded in Charles Schultze, *The Politics and Economics of Public Spending*, (Washington, D.C.: Brookings Institution, 1968). Schultze, now a senior Brookings economist, directed the Budget Bureau during PPB's heyday. PPB was a boon to public administration scholars, justifying numerous exercises in scholasticism. See, e.g., "Symposium on PPBS Reexamined," *Public Administration Review*, March–April 1969. The assembled scholars, the editor of the *Review* explained, could not agree on the very name to be applied to the subject of their study. Some preferred PPB, but others insisted on PPBS. "Obviously," the editor concluded, "in most cases the usage does not represent mere whim, but rather an important point of logic or matter of emphasis." The dilemma was dire. "To the extent that PPBS presents us with new tools, we need to sharpen them and use them; to the extent that it represents makework and delusion, we need to know it. Both urgently."

92. The Office of Management and Budget's characterization of "controllables" and "uncontrollables" appears in *Budget of the United States Government, Fiscal Year 1975*, summary table 14.

93. This distinction is suggested by Harvey Sapolsky in *The Polaris System Development: Bureaucratic and Programmatic Success in Government* (Cambridge, Mass.: Harvard University Press, 1972), p. 78, n. 32. On the evolution of systems management, see, generally, Fremont E. Kast and James E. Rosenzweig, *Management in the Space Age: An Analysis of the Concept of Weapons Systems Management and its Nonmilitary Applications* (New York: Exposition Press, 1962); *Organization and Management of Missile Programs*, Hearings Before a Subcommittee of the Committee on Government Operations, U.S. House of Representatives, 1959; *Systems Development and Management*, Hearings Before a Subcommittee of the Committee on Government Operations, U.S. House of Representatives, 1962.

94. On early governmental work see, e.g., Otto Eckstein, *Water Resources Development: The Economics of Project Evaluation* (Cambridge, Mass.: Harvard University Press 1958).

95. David Novick, "Origin and History of Program Budgeting," RAND Paper P-3427, October 1966. The paper was presented at training sessions in which RAND experts helped introduce civil servants to PPB. Nonclassified RAND documents are available at depository libraries throughout the country.

96. Ibid.

97. Ibid.

98. Alain C. Enthoven and K. Wayne Smith, *How Much Is Enough? Shaping the Defense Program 1961–1969* (New York: Harper & Row, 1971), p. 33.

99. Charles Hitch himself tried to import PPB to the University of California, of which he became President.

100. The OEO Research Office awarded RAND contracts which gave RAND a beachhead in civilian agencies. The awards were the source of conflict between the "action-oriented" Community Action Program R & D division of OEO and the study-oriented Research, Planning, and Revaluation Office. The latter was initially headed by Robert Levine, formerly a RAND arms control analyst, who was succeeded by RAND's Tom Glennan. In 1969 RAND was hired to recommend a reorganization of the Office of Education's struggling R & D spending. The RAND study resulted in the National Institute of Education, a body that was to stimulate educational R & D through liberal use of grants and contracts. Glennan was tapped to direct the Institute, and struggled, with little success, to get it off the ground.

101. The OEO Institute for Research on Poverty was evaluated by a National Academy of Sciences team headed by Yale economist and former RAND analyst Richard Nelson. See *Policy and Program Research in a University Setting*, National Academy of Sciences, 1971.

102. The Secretary is quoted in John Burby, *The Great American Motion Sickness* (Boston: Little, Brown, 1971), p. 45.

103. Interviews with: Leo Werts, former Assistant Secretary for Administration; Frank Zarb, Assistant Secretary for Administration; Ed Salner and Thomas O'Brien, Office of the Assistant Secretary for Administration, Department of Labor, 1971–72. Booz, Allen, & Hamilton, "Department-Wide Data Systems Study," February 1967.

104. Memorandum, Ed Salner to Leo Werts, January 30, 1967.

105. David K. Carlisle, "Results of a Department-Wide Survey on Evaluating Program Effectiveness," March 22, 1968.

106. "The Work of the Steering Group in Evaluation of the Bureau of the Budget: A Staff Summary," Bureau of the Budget, July 1967.

107. Bureau of the Budget Contract EB-108.

108. McKinsey & Co., "Strengthening Program Planning, Budgeting and Management in the Federal Government," Office of Management and Budget, December 1970.

109. Interviews with Velma Baldwin, Charles Bingman, Jack Carlson, Walter Haase, Joseph Laitin, William Niskanen, John Pinckney, and William Taft, Office of Management and Budget, 1971–72. Interviews with Robert Fri, Bruce Rohrbacher, McKinsey & Co., 1971. Fri returned to McKinsey in 1974. In 1975 Fri left McKinsey again for a high administrative post in the newly created Energy Research and Development Administration.

110. See, e.g., "Defense Reverses PPB Process," *Armed Forces Management*, February 1970; "Military Planners Muscle in on Role of Defense Department's Whiz Kids," *National Journal*, December 5, 1970.

111. Interview with Allen Schick, June 1971. See also Allen Schick, "PPB: The View from the States," *State Government*, winter 1972.

112. Only a small portion of the Ash council's work was published. See, e.g., *A New Regulatory Framework: Report on Selected Independent Regulatory Agencies*, President's Advisory Council on Executive Organization, January 1971. The council's theme, that regulatory ills could be cured by a dose of reorganization, was critiqued by a conference of economists and lawyers convened by Brookings.

See Roger G. Noll, *Reforming Regulation: An Evaluation of the Ash Council Proposals* (Washington, D.C.: Brookings Institution, 1971). Details of the evolution and operation of MBO appear in "OMB's Management Team to Review Agencies' Programs," *National Journal*, June 2, 1973; "OMB's Management by Objectives Produce Goals of Uneven Quality," *National Journal*, August 18, 1973.

113. Marvin Bower, *The Will to Manage: Corporate Success Through Programmed Management* (New York: McGraw-Hill Book Co., 1966).

114. Corson left McKinsey in the early Sixties, and later returned to consulting as the director of the Washington office of Fry Consultants.

115. The Carnegie Foundation sponsors reports which often serve as the basis for subsequent public and private education planning. Social critic Paul Goodman commented on the attempt of one such study, John Corson's *The Governance of Colleges and Universities* (New York: McGraw-Hill Book Co., 1960) to relegate learning to the priorities of educational management (Paul Goodman, *Compulsory Mis-education and the Community of Scholars* [New York: Vintage Books, 1964], chap. 4, "The Community of Scholars.") The Institute for Educational Development's (IED) government-education-industry promotions are chronicled in items such as *Industry and Education: A New Partnership*, Report on a Conference Held at the Harvard Club, New York, December 4, 1968; Institute for Educational Development, U.S. Office of Education, and American Telephone and Telegraph Company, *Conference on Dissemination of Educational Products Developed Under USOE Sponsorship*, Report of a Conference, April 23–24, 1970; the Carnegie Corporation–inspired study, *Research and Development in the Educational Materials Industry*, 1969; and the Mitre-IED seminar, "On the Creation of an Institute for the Application of Technology to the Problems of National and World Illiteracy," December 1969. As the titles indicate, IED hoped to turn education into a profit-making business, and thereby lead to its reform. The "Conference on Dissemination" was the most successful venture. It led directly to a revision of the Office of Education's copyright rules, which were modified to permit the profit-making textbook business to acquire marketing rights to educational "products" developed by the Office of Education's FCRCs. The FCRCs were floundering, and the Office of Education hoped to save them by gaining industrial support.

116. Interview with Warren Cannon, McKinsey & Co., spring 1971; interview with John Macy, February 1972.

117. John J. Corson, *Business in the Humane Society* (New York: McGraw-Hill Book Co., 1971).

118. Ibid., pp. 12–18.

119. *Supplementing Successful Management*, McKinsey & Co., 1940, p. 27. Interview with John Corson, July 1971.

120. "Restaffing the Executive Branch of the Federal Government at the Policy Level," McKinsey & Co., 1952, sec. i. Quotation on p. i-1.

121. "Restaffing the Temporary Mobilization and Stabilization Agencies," sec. xiv, p. v.

122. "Restaffing the Executive Branch of the Federal Government at the Policy Level," sec. i, pp. i-17 to i-18.

123. Interview with John Corson, July 1971; interview with George Graham (Director of Brookings' Government Studies in 1960), August 1971.

124. Malek's rough tactics were the talk of Washington. See, e.g., Robert

Sherrill, "The Hatchetman and the Hatchetmyth," *Washington Post, Potomac Magazine*, February 6, 1972. See also "Nixon's Talent Hunter Also Wields Executive Hatchet," *New York Times*, July 12, 1972. For Malek's view, which borrows from Corson, see "Mr. Executive Goes to Washington," *Harvard Business Review*, November 10, 1972.

125. John J. Corson and R. Shale Paul, *Men Near the Top: Filling Key Posts in the Federal Service*, prepared for the Committee for Economic Development (Baltimore: Johns Hopkins Press, 1966). Quotation on p. 1.

126. John Corson, *Executives for the Federal Service: A Program for Action in Time of Crisis* (New York: Columbia University Press, 1952).

127. Ibid., pp. 51, 55.

128. Ibid., pp. 52, 54.

129. Testimony by John Corson, in *Organizing for National Security*, Hearings Before the Subcommittee on National Policy Machinery, Committee on Government Operations, U.S. Senate, 1960, pp. 518–44. Quotations on pp. 529, 541.

McKinsey encourages its professionals to contribute to conferences and scholarly journals, and the firm is a major source of contributors to the prestigious *Harvard Business Review* (which offers an annual "McKinsey award" for an outstanding article). Corson's themes were taken up by other firm members.

In a 1962 article, for example, Gilbert Clee told the story of the "Appointment Book of J. Edward Ellis." Corporate executive Ellis, feeling uneasy, keeps a diary to pinpoint the source of his anxiety. He discovers that the Government's activities continually affect his business. This upsets him; then he reflects on all the defense contracts the company has received:

> In his own lifetime, the United States had moved rapidly away from a high degree of free enterprise. But what had it moved to? It was not true, he knew, that (as some of his friends seemed to believe, judging by the way they extolled the past and lamented about the future) the United States had moved from Adam Smith to socialism or any other known "ism." What existed now seemed to Ellis economically and politically to be an undefined and indefinite agglomerate. . . . the race run by the United States against the communist world for military superiority, economic strength, and the support of the uncommitted nations would require more than a structure that just "works." . . . It was neither practical nor praiseworthy, Ellis felt, to sit back and let someone else generate the ideas and establish the rules as to the relative position of Government and private enterprise. If he and others like him in business simply allowed a vacuum to exist, economic power would move further toward the Government—by default.

With the source of sickness revealed, Ellis is liberated. The article concludes with his memo to the "operating committee," re steps to be taken to make the corporation's will felt in Washington. See Gilbert Clee, "The Appointment Book of J. Edward Ellis," *Harvard Business Review*, November–December 1962.

130. Corson testimony, *Organizing for National Security*, p. 529.

131. The 1958 Brookings-McKinsey seminar inspired "The Company Representative in Washington," *Harvard Business Review*, May–June 1961. The membership and topics of the Government-industry seminars were communicated in a letter of Frederic N. Cleveland, National Institute of Public Administration, to Daniel Guttman, December 27, 1971; a letter of Richard B. Simons, Senior Staff member, Brookings Institution, to Daniel Guttman, January 4, 1972.

132. According to the "Orientation Program for the Presidential Interchange Program September 10–15, 1972," conducted by Brookings' Advanced Study Program, participants heard speakers that ranged from Congressman Gerald Ford (on "effective legislative action") to McKinsey *éminence grise* Marvin Bower ("improving Federal program performance").

133. Interview with George Graham, August 1971.

134. Clinton Rossiter, *The American Presidency* (New York: New American Library, 1960), pp. 164–65.

135. Corson testimony, *Organizing for National Security*, pp. 518–44; Harvard Business School Club of Washington, D.C., "Businessmen in Government," 1958. We could find only two scholarly references to McKinsey's role in the 1952 transition, for example. One appears in a Brookings study of Presidential transition. In *The Power Elite* sociologist C. Wright Mills cited a *Time* magazine story of the use of business consultants by Eisenhower as further evidence of America's inability to sustain an independent civil service.

136. Interview with Charles Edwards, Commissioner, U.S. Food and Drug Administration, November 1972.

The career of John Sheehan is an almost archetypal illustration of the forces and motives that power the Government-industry conveyor belt. Sheehan told *Business Week*, "I began thinking relatively long-term about my life plan very early in life, around high school." Sheehan attended the Naval Academy, but "began to study the Navy system for promotion, and I was very dissatisfied." He left the Navy for Harvard Business School, and, as a top-ranking scholar, again departed from career plans (to become an industrial salesman) to take a job with McKinsey. When McKinsey reorganized Martin Marietta Corporation, Sheehan went to work for the firm on the assumption that he would ride the reorganization to an important position. Martin Marietta, however, failed to reorganize as McKinsey recommended, and Sheehan joined Corning Glass. He grew restless again, and the McKinsey grapevine recommended him to McKinsey alumnus Malek and the White House. Malek helped the forty-one-year-old Sheehan secure appointment to the powerful Board of Governors of the Federal Reserve Board. Placed in a position of responsibility for the entire American economy, Sheehan was not overawed. "It doesn't take a deep knowledge of the techniques; it takes a knowledge of the fundamentals . . . you don't have to understand the details of how the bond markets work to understand what the level of interest rates means to the economy." The task of national economic management, however, was just a stepping-stone in Sheehan's career. "The average tenure of a Government official at this level," he told *Business Week*, "is about twenty-two months. I had already been here 50 percent longer than average." In spring 1975, therefore, Sheehan announced that he would leave the Federal Reserve Board to become the number two man at White Motors Corporation. See "I'm Ready to Run My Own Show Now," *Business Week*, May 26, 1975; see also "He's Not an Economist or Banker, but Sheehan Helps to Guide the Fed," *Wall Street Journal*, May 7, 1973.

137. For Patton's views on the Government salary morass, see Arch Patton, "Government Pay Disincentive," *Business Week*, January 19, 1974, and "Fallacies in Federal Pay Standards," *Business Week*, January 26, 1974.

138. The "Federal Political Personnel Manual" is reprinted in *Presidential Campaign Activities of 1972: Senate Resolution 60*, Executive Session Hearings Before the Select Committee on Presidential Campaign Activities, U.S. Senate, 1974, pt. 19, pp. 8903–9017. Quotation on p. 8976.

The "rape" of the merit system was illustrated by an amusing example from the manual (ibid., pp. 8976–78):

> Let us assume that you have a career opening in your Department's personnel office for a Staff Recruitment Officer. Sitting in front of you is your college roommate from Stanford University in California who was born and raised in San Francisco. He received his law degree from Boalt Hall at the University of California. While studying for the bar he worked at an advertising agency handling newspaper accounts. He also worked as a reporter on the college newspaper. Your personnel experts judge that he could receive an eligibility rating for a GS-11.
>
> The first thing you do is tear up the old job description that goes with that job. You then have a new one written, to be classified at GS-11, describing the duties of that specific Staff Recruitment Officer as directed toward the recruitment of recent law graduates for entry level attorney positions, entry level public information officers for the creative arts and college new liaison sections of your public information shop, and to be responsible for general recruiting for entry level candidates on the West Coast. You follow that by listing your selective criteria as follows: Education: BA and LLB, stating that the candidate should have extensive experience and knowledge by reason of employment or residence on the West Coast. Candidate should have attended or be familiar with law schools, and institutions of higher education, preferably on the West Coast. The candidate should also possess some knowledge by reasons of education or experience of the fields of college journalism, advertising, and law.
>
> You then trot this candidate's Application for Federal Employment over to the Civil Service Commission, and shortly thereafter he receives an eligibility rating for a GS-11. Your personnel office then sends over the job description (GS-11) along with the selective criteria which was based on the duties of the job description. When the moment arrives for the panel to "spin the register" you insure that your personnel office sends over two "friendly" bureaucrats. The register is then spun and your candidate will certainly be among the only three who even meet the selective criteria, much less be rated by your two "friendly" panel members as among the "highest qualified" that meet the selection criteria. In short, you write the job description and selective criteria around your candidate's Form 171.
>
> There is no merit in the merit system!

139. Ibid., pp. 8907–8.

140. Ibid., p. 8937.

141. Ibid., pp. 8996–97.

142. Corson testimony, *Organizing for National Security*, p. 525.

143. Robert L. Rosholt, *An Administrative History of NASA 1958–1963* (Washington, D.C.: NASA, 1963), pp. 50–56.

144. Interview with John Young, Office of Management and Budget, summer 1972.

145. Rosholt, *Administrative History of NASA*, pp. 161–69; John J. Corson, "Partners in the Space Age," *Management Review*, September 1959.

146. *The Production of Documents by NASA*, Hearing Before the Committee on Science and Astronautics, U.S. House of Representatives, 1960, pp. 2–78. Years later Congress and the GAO questioned the legality of NASA's excessive use of contractors. See, e.g., *Support Service Contracts*, Hearings Before a Subcommittee of the Committee on Government Operations, U.S. House of Representatives, 1967.

147. Rosholt, *Administrative History of NASA*, p. 164.

148. Rosholt, *Administrative History of NASA*, pp. 168–69.

149. Corson, *Business in the Humane Society*, p. 18.

III. THE PROLIFERATION OF THINK TANKS

1. David Eakins, *The Development of Corporate Liberal Research in the United States*, is an exhaustive intellectual history of Brookings, the National Bureau of Economic Research, the National Planning Association, and other "corporate liberal" nonprofits. The work, completed in 1966, was the author's Ph.D. thesis at the University of Wisconsin and is available from University Micofilms.

2. Congress traditionally examined the budget through the actions of its committees. As the budget grew, the fragmented committee jurisdictions frustrated Congressional attempts to provide a coherent view of the budget, thus permitting the Executive budget to serve as the ultimate standard against which discrete decisions are measured. Aficionados of budgeting note that there are several versions of the Executive budget which are prepared for different purposes.

3. Charles B. Saunders, Jr., *The Brookings Institution—A 50 Year History* (Washington, D.C.: Brookings Institution, 1966), p. 24.

4. Eakins, *Development of Corporate Liberal Research.* Business historian Alfred Chandler suggested the early usefulness of national economic information to the first giant corporations (interview, Boston, February 1972).

5. NBER's works are described in *Economics—A Half Century of Research 1920–1970: 50th Annual Report 1970*, National Bureau of Economic Research, New York, 1970.

6. See, generally, Eakins, *Development of Corporate Liberal Research.*

7. NBER Vice President Geoffrey Moore, who served as Commissioner of Labor Statistics in the Nixon Administration, details the development of income measurements in "The Analysis of Economic Indicators," *Scientific American*, January 1975. See also, "From the People Who Brought You the GNP . . . New Concern for Social Issues," *New York Times*, December 24, 1972.

8. *Brookings Biennial Report 1968–69*, pp. 2–3.

9. Quoted in Eakins, *Development of Corporate Liberal Research*, p. 213.

10. Cited in ibid., pp. 129–30.

11. See Robert Brookings, *Industrial Ownership: Its Economic and Social Significance* (New York: Macmillan Co., 1925); *Economic Democracy: America's Answer to Socialism and Communism* (New York: Macmillan Co., 1929); *The Way Forward* (New York: Macmillan Co., 1932). Quotations are from *Economic Democracy*, p. 22; *The Way Forward*, p. 73.

12. Grant McConnell's *Private Power and American Democracy* (New York: Alfred A. Knopf, 1967), is an excellent study of, *inter alia*, the influence of private trade associations.

13. The numerous energy-related nonprofit research-lobby groups include those related to special components of the industry (National Petroleum Refiners' Association, National Oil Jobbers Council); to industry-related services (National Tank Truck Carriers, National Association of Truck Stop Operators); energy-dependent industries (Gas Appliance Manufacturers' Association, Rubber Manufacturers' Association); public producers of energy (American Public Power Association, American Public Gas Association); energy byproducts (National Slag Association, National Solid Waste Management Association); and energy expertise (Petroleum Industry Research Foundation, American Association of Petroleum Geologists).

14. Robert Engler, *The Politics of Oil: Private Power and Democratic Directions* (Chicago: University of Chicago Press, 1961), provides an early (pre-energy crisis) description of the oil lobby (see pp. 59–63).

15. The Federal Reports Act of 1942 provides a particularly interesting example of the delegation of authority to industry advisers. The law requires special clearance for all surveys or questionnaires to be administered by Government. This clearance has been administered by an office of the Budget Bureau (now the Office of Management and Budget), which has worked closely with industry groups. The law was designed to minimize paperwork, but gave industry groups effective veto power over all Federal attempts to gather information about industry. The advisory groups were purely private, but acquired official status, and their meetings with Government were closed to the public. It was only in the early Seventies that Congressional action opened such meetings to the public.

In March 1975, attorneys in the Federal Trade Commission's Bureau of Competition recommended that the Commission issue a complaint against the American Gas Association and leading oil and gas companies. The attorneys, following over four years of investigation, had concluded that the organizations violated the Federal Trade Commission Act by maintaining a deficient natural-gas reserve reporting program, and thereby influencing the price of natural gas. See "FTC Suit on Gas Data Urged," *Washington Post*, June 10, 1975.

16. Arthur D. Little's role in setting asbestos standards is considered in Paul Brodeur, *Expendable Americans* (New York: Viking Press, 1973), pt. 3, "Some Conflicts of Interest."

17. See, generally, Eakins, *Development of Corporate Liberal Research.*

18. For a history of CED, see Karl Schriftgiesser, *Business and Public Policy: The Role of the Committee for Economic Development 1942–1967* (Englewood Cliffs, N.J.: Prentice-Hall, 1967).

19. See "CED's Impact on Federal Policies Enhanced by Close Ties to Executive Branch," *National Journal*, June 17, 1972. The Committee staffer is quoted on p. 1022.

20. Herbert Stein, *The Fiscal Revolution in America* (Chicago: University of Chicago Press, 1969), p. 197.

21. See, generally, Eakins, *Development of Corporate Liberal Research*, chaps. 6 and 7. The nonprofits worked closely with the Government in foreign policy planning. In 1942, for example, the CED appointed a "committee on inter-American affairs" while the State Department was simultaneously naming a "committee on inter-American development." (Nelson Rockefeller, then a State Department official, commissioned the latter.) The two groups had identical memberships. They paid separate bills, however.

22. The Agency for International Development, the Economic Cooperation Administration's current incarnation, is one of the few agencies that possesses a readily accessible list of contractors. The contracts listed, of course, may or may not reveal intelligence-related projects.

Popular ignorance of the extensiveness of foreign aid contracting was illustrated in early 1975 when the press revealed that the military had employed a Los Angeles contractor to train Saudi Arabian troops. The contractor was to receive close to $80 million to send Vietnam veterans to the Middle East, and critics suggested that America had hired a mercenary army for the Saudis. The press then discovered that the contractor had done much prior business with the Government and that the terms of the contract were not all that uncommon.

23. The memo appears as Appendix A in Seymour Melman, *Pentagon Capitalism: The Political Economy of War* (New York: McGraw-Hill Book Co., 1970).

24. Bruce L. R. Smith, a Columbia University political scientist who worked at RAND, authored the corporation's biography, *The RAND Corporation: Case Study of a Nonprofit Advisory Corporation* (Cambridge, Mass.: Harvard University Press, 1966). RAND has also been the subject of numerous articles in periodicals. For a view of RAND as the "model" for the proliferation of nonprofits, see Roger Levien, "Independent Public Policy Analysis Organizations—A Major Social Innovation," RAND Paper P-4231, November 1969.

25. The genesis of RAND is described in Smith, *The RAND Corporation.* There is disagreement over the original meaning of the name. Some insist that "RAND" stands for "Research and Development," while others say that "Research and No Development" was intended. The latter was to signify that RAND was a producer of ideas, not hardware.

26. Smith, ibid., pp. 46–47.

27. Speech by J. R. Goldstein, reprinted as RAND Paper P-2236-1. RAND's nonclassified works are generally available in major public and university libraries.

28. Testimony of F. R. Collbohm, President, RAND Corporation, in *Systems Development and Management*, Hearings Before a Subcommittee of the Committee on Government Operations, U.S. House of Representatives, 1962, pt. 3, p. 940. The selection of "industrial," "academic and scientific," and "public interest" trustees was provided for by Section 14 of the RAND Bylaws.

In 1951 the Ford Foundation added $900,000 to its original $100,000 loan, and in 1952 turned the loans into an outright grant. The RAND charter provides that, should RAND ever dissolve, the Ford Foundation will direct the distribution of its assets. Ford also helped the Institute for Defense Analyses convert itself from an office in the Defense Department into a private nonprofit corporation. The Rockefeller Foundation provided seed money for RAND's social science department.

29. Rivers is cited in Richard J. Barnet, *The Economy of Death* (New York: Atheneum Publishers, 1969), p. 53.

30. The basing study is described at length in Smith, *The RAND Corporation*, pp. 195–240.

31. Arnold is quoted in Barnet, *Economy of Death*, p. 116.

32. Letter of Edwin E. Huddleson, Jr., to Daniel Guttman, June 6, 1973.

33. Interview with J. R. Goldstein, summer 1972. Smith, *The RAND Corporation.* When Daniel Ellsberg, a former RAND employee, released the Pentagon Papers to the press, he violated the RAND code. The incident, and RAND's association with the McNamara administration, were grist for Congressional attempts to impose a ceiling on the budgets of the Defense Department's "policy research" FCRCs. The FCRCs were compelled to justify themselves in *Fiscal Year*

1973 Authorization for Military Procurement, Research and Development, Construction, Authorization for the Safeguard ABM, and Active Duty and Selected Reserve Strengths, Hearings Before the Armed Services Committee, U.S. Senate, pt. 5. See pp. 3283–84 for Congressional inquiry concerning allegations that RAND's service to the Office of the Secretary of Defense conflicted with its service to the Air Force.

34. The literature of deterrence is vast. For a critique of the theory see Phillip Green, *Deadly Logic* (New York: Schocken Books, 1968). On the deterrence theorists themselves, see Bernard Brodie, "The American Scientific Strategists," RAND Paper P-2979; Colin Gray, "What RAND Hath Wrought," *Foreign Policy*, fall 1971.

35. See Gene H. Fisher, "Aspects of Corporate Planning in the Defense Industry," and Harold Linstone, "An Approach to Long-Range Planning," in J. Stockfisch, ed., *Planning and Forecasting in the Defense Industry* (Belmont, Calif.: Wadsworth Publishing Co., 1962), pp. 67–81, 89–113. Quotation on p. 80. Linstone later moved on to the Defense Department, RAND, and Lockheed—where he worked on Mirages 80 and 85.

36. Henry Rowen, an early RAND employee who served as its president during the latter part of the Vietnam war, argues that it is a mistake to assume that RAND's systems analysts should have been prepared to advise in wartime decisions. The successes of systems analysis, Rowen explained, are largely technical, e.g., the suggestion that missile sites should be hardened or fail-safe systems installed. The social scientists who developed systems analysis, Rowen claimed, had no claim to knowledge of the "political systems" at issue in Vietnam. (Interview with Rowen, fall 1973. The *Congressional Record*, however, shows that from 1955 on, RAND had "from fifty to one hundred people working on limited war." *Planning Programming Budgeting*, Inquiry of the Subcommittee on National Security and International Operations, Government Operations Committee, U.S. Senate, 1970, p. 293.

37. Herbert York, *Race to Oblivion: A Participant's View of the Arms Race* (New York: Simon & Schuster, 1970), pp. 157–58.

38. Morton Halperin, "The Gaither Committee and the Policy Process," *World Politics*, April 1961, pp. 360–84. Quoted material on p. 360. McKinsey's work for the Gaither Commission led to a prestigious contract to consolidate Federal civil defense agencies. The fallout shelter studies provided to the Commission were the springboard for the career of RAND's Herman Kahn. Kahn's work for the Commission was incorporated in his famous tracts on "thinking the unthinkable."

39. The President's reaction is cited in *Office of Science and Technology*, A Report Prepared by the Science Policy Research Division for the Military Operations Subcommittee, Committee on Government Operations, U.S. House of Representatives, March 1967, p. 98.

40. Albert Wohlstetter, "The Delicate Balance of Terror," *Foreign Affairs*, January 1959.

41. Theodore C. Sorenson, *Kennedy* (New York: Harper & Row, 1965), chap. 22. Quotations on pp. 680, 686.

42. Speech by J. R. Goldstein (RAND Paper P-2236-1); William W. Kaufmann, *The McNamara Strategy* (New York: Harper & Row, 1964).

43. Alain C. Enthoven and K. Wayne Smith, *How Much Is Enough? Shaping the Defense Program 1961–69* (New York: Harper & Row, 1971). Enthoven and Smith explain (pp. 172–84) how the systems analysts, having little information on actual Russian intentions, planned for overkill by assuming a "greater than expected threat."

44. Bernard Brodie, *Strategy in the Missile Age* (Princeton, N.J.: Princeton University Press, 1959), chap. 10, "Strategy Wears a Dollar Sign." Quotation on p. 373. In the mid-Seventies the Brookings Institution appears to be assuming RAND's mantle as the source of independent justification for an increased defense budget. In 1975 the promise that Congress would cut the postwar defense budget disappeared, and Congress accepted the country's first $100 billion defense budget. Previously critical Congressmen cited new Brookings studies to justify their action. "Many of those interviewed," reported the *New York Times*, "said their thinking had been affected by as-yet unpublished studies by the Brookings Institution." The *Washington Post* took Brookings' word as "a final bit of evidence that the defense debate is over. . . . The study is of a series, and out of an institution, identified with liberal alternatives to official policy. Yet in this instance, they [the study's authors] . . . do not offer any fundamental critique of the administration-congressional budget." See "Move for Big Cut in Defense Wanes," *New York Times*, May 6, 1975; Stephen S. Rosenfeld, "The Defense Debate Is Over," *Washington Post*, July 4, 1975.

45. The study group was one of many summer retreats sponsored by the military. Held in attractive settings in California or on Cape Cod, these retreats have given rise to many costly defense programs. They complement the work of year-round research centers and attract expertise that otherwise might not serve the military.

46. The TRW story is recounted in H. L. Nieburg, *In the Name of Science* (Chicago: Quadrangle Books, 1966), chap. 11. Nieburg's work describes and critiques the rise of DOD-NASA systems management contracting.

47. The National Science Foundation hired the Denver Research Institute to survey nonprofits, and in 1969 it produced *Contract Research and Development Adjuncts of Federal Agencies*. Harvey Sapolsky, *Polaris System Development* (Cambridge, Mass.: Harvard University Press, 1972), describes the delegation implicit in systems management; see chap. 3, "Structure of Organizational Relationships."

48. Harold Seidman, *Politics, Position and Power: The Dynamics of Federal Organization* (New York: Oxford University Press, 1970), chap. 8. Quotations on pp. 259–60.

49. Clarence Danhof, in his Brookings study, *Government Contracting and Technological Change* (Washington, D.C.: Brookings Institution, 1968), notes that the Comptroller General actually issued a statement that found systems management contracting to be beyond the law because of the excessive delegation of authority it implied. Senators drafted a bill to declare its legality, but the proposal died.

As the classic work on weapons contracting explains, "the preference for private enterprise conduct of U.S. weapons development and production work . . . is essentially an unwritten law, and, indeed, statutory references seem to contradict it, for the Secretary of the Army is directed to have supplies needed for the Department of the Army made in factories or arsenals owned by the United States, so far as those factories or arsenals can make those supplies on an economical basis. However, in practice, private enterprise has been favored to meet the expanded military needs of the past two decades, and the role of

Government arsenals and shipyards has declined both relatively and absolutely."
(Merton Peck and Frederick Scherer, *Weapons Acquisition Process* [Cambridge,
Mass.: Harvard University Press, 1962], p. 97.)

The Presidential panel was headed by Budget Director David Bell and
culminated in a "Report to the President on Government Contracting for
Research and Development," April 30, 1962. The report was the subject of 1962
hearings on *Systems Development and Management* before a subcommittee of the
House Committee on Government Operations. The Bell panel and the House
begged the big questions, as the following excerpt from the Bell report explains:

> Finally, the developments of recent years have inevitably blurred the
> traditional dividing lines between the public and private sectors of our
> Nation. A number of profound questions affecting the structure of our
> society are raised by our inability to apply the classical distinctions
> between what is public and what is private. For example, should a
> corporation created to provide services to Government and receiving
> 100 percent of its financial support from Government be considered a
> "public" or a "private" agency? In what sense is a business corporation
> doing nearly 100 percent of its business with the Government engaged
> in "free enterprise"?
>
> In light of these criticisms and concerns, an appraisal of the
> experience in using contracts to accomplish the Government's research
> and development purposes is evidently timely. We have not, however,
> in the course of the present review attempted to treat the fundamental
> philosophical issues indicated in the preceding paragraph. We accept as
> desirable the present high degree of interdependence and collaboration
> between Government and private institutions. We believe the present
> intermingling of the public and private sectors is in the national interest
> because it affords the largest opportunity for initiative and the
> competition of ideas from all elements of the technical community.
> Consequently, it is our judgment that the present complex partnership
> between Government and private institutions should continue.

The report appears as Appendix 1 of *Systems Development and Management*, pt. 1.
Quotation on pp. 209–10.

The Price quotation is from *The Scientific Estate* (Cambridge, Mass.: Harvard
University Press, 1965), p. 51.

50. Interview with William Golden, October 1972; letter from Edwin Huddleson
to Daniel Guttman, June 6, 1973.

51. *Fiscal Year 1973 Authorization for Military Procurement*, pt. 5, p. 3239.

52. The Air Force FCRC's trustees police themselves. The Aerospace Corporation's rules, for example, were drawn up by Roswell Gilpatric, a Wall Street
lawyer, Aerospace incorporator, and counsel for the aerospace industry. When
Aerospace was created, the proposed conflict rules for trustees prohibited them
from "acting" for companies with Aerospace related interests. Gilpatric told the
Air Force's general counsel that he construed the term "act" in the narrow
sense—to participate in negotiations with Aerospace, or to sign a contract with it.
"The fact that the trustee is an officer or a director of such a company but does not
'act' for it in the manner just described should not, I believe, disqualify him as an
Aerospace trustee. . . . if the word 'act' were to be interpreted more broadly or
loosely, it would not be possible for some trustees to remain on the Aerospace
Board." Gilpatric argued that the public interest would be protected if trustees

were placed on their honor to disclose their interests to the Board. The Senate Committee on Government Operations found that Gilpatric himself could not be trusted in this respect, as note 55 below describes. Yet such trust is the substance of the FCRC's conflict "rules."

"Nothing," according to Ed Huddleson "has ever come before the Mitre Board which influenced whether the Government did or did not buy a system." The Board is never informed in detail about Mitre's role in selecting a contractor. "I wouldn't," says Huddleson, "want to know a damn thing" about whether IBM or RCA has a better proposal "and would be unhappy if any of the nonmanagement board members did."

The creation of the conflict rules, and the Gilpatric letter, are described in *Systems Development and Management*, pt. 3. The Gilpatric letter is on p. 1225. The Huddleson quotations, in the text and above, are from the letter of Edwin Huddleson to Daniel Guttman, June 6, 1973.

53. Interview with William Golden, October 1972.

54. Letter from Edwin Huddleson to Daniel Guttman, June 6, 1973.

55. We are concerned with indirect conflicts in the contract bureaucracy, for they appear to be essential to the concentration of power and are accepted as "the way the world works." By contrast, the practice of direct self-dealing is undoubtedly restrained. Even so, painstaking investigation has given the lie to the "honorable man" position. Wall Street lawyer Roswell Gilpatric, for example, served in the Eisenhower Defense Department, and returned to Wall Street to work for aerospace industry clients. Gilpatric incorporated the Aerospace Corporation, wrote its rules on conflict of interest, which govern employees and not trustees, and then became McNamara's Deputy Secretary of Defense. As McNamara's adviser he was involved in the most controversial procurement of its time, the decision to award a multibillion-dollar contract to General Dynamics. Through the better part of the Sixties, a Senate investigations subcommittee tried to uncover the basis for the choice. By the end of the decade, the contract had turned into a disaster. The investigation was concluded only when the Republicans permitted access to defense records. The Senate concluded that Gilpatric had misled Congress, that he had urged the selection of General Dynamics, that General Dynamics was a major source of his legal income, and that he had not severed his ties with Wall Street while serving as a defense official. Gilpatric, in short, was guilty of a "flagrant conflict of interest in the TFX award." Congress could not touch the elite lawyer. Gilpatric not only received a Wall Street promotion after his defense experience but was named as a "public trustee" of the Institute for Defense Analyses. Honorable men, in this sense, do no wrong. While Gilpatric served on the IDA board, its chairman was William Braden, a financier who also was a director of Lockheed. Braden too was listed as a "public interest" trustee. The Senate's brief against Gilpatric appears in *TFX Investigation*, Final Report, Permanent Subcommittee on Investigations, Committee on Government Operations, U.S. Senate, 1970.

56. United States v. Mississippi Valley Generating Co. (Dixon-Yates), 364 U.S. 520, 1961, pp. 549–50.

57. Ibid., pp. 554–55.

58. Ibid., p. 561.

59. Letter of Norman Waks, Chief Management Scientist, The Mitre Corporation, to Daniel Guttman, January 26, 1972. Interview with Waks, winter 1972. Interview with Edward Roberts, January 1972.

60. The Mitre *Matrix*, a publicly available periodical, offers lengthy descriptions of Mitre's work. The magazine is carefully tailored to reflect none of the controversy and gore that is inherent in much of it. Mitre, for example, has been a primary planner for the "electronic battlefield." As conceived for Vietnam, this highly costly weapon system, developed in great secrecy, was to employ sensors to locate enemy troops, who would then be destroyed by American firepower. This epitomized American hopes that technology could produce a costly but painless solution to the problem of guerrilla warfare. The public announcement of plans for "electronic battlefields," caused great controversy. Mitre viewed the sensors neither from the perspective of world politics nor from that of military strategy. The *Matrix* article was a paean to the challenging technical life of Mitre employees. There were no dead or wounded bodies in the ten pages of illustrations, and sketches portrayed forested combat fields that looked more like Vermont than Vietnam. The absence of bloodshed reflected conscious editorial policy. As a *Matrix* staff member explained, "the way I understand that system, it's a sensor system . . . any killing of the enemy is done with other weapons. We don't have any connection with that." Congress tried to cut off funding of the defense agency created to plan the sensor program, but the Department kept the innocuously titled "Defense Special Projects Group" (DSPG) rolling, putting it to work on the application of sensors to European battlefields. The Senate Armed Services Committee discovered that the Air Force wanted $2.1 million for Mitre's DSPG work in fiscal year 1972, even though the DSPG itself was not officially funded. *Matrix*'s account of the closedown of DSPG omitted any references to the confusion. "DSPG's last day was June 30, 1972. Nostalgic memories remain for the team that participated in this high-priority project which may be only the beginning of the electronic battlefields of the future."

61. Interview with William Golden, October 1972. The Aerospace presentation was part of a general review of defense FCRCs, and appears in *Fiscal Year 1973 for Military Procurement Authorization*, pt. 5.

62. The panel, headed by Metropolitan Life executive Gilbert Fitzhugh, was studded with members who had interests in matters of defense. Its staff was headed by a nonprofit alumnus, and staff work was done by staple defense contractors such as Stanford Research Institute and Harbridge House. The conflicts of interest embodied in the panel are discussed by Ernest Fitzgerald in "Gilbert Fitzhugh's Golden Fleece," *Washington Monthly*, November 1970.

63. The report passed blithely over well-publicized scandals, such as the Mark 48 Torpedo, a major procurement disaster whose cost increased from a planned $680 million to close to $4 billion. The Navy's technical director for the project, the Penn State Ordnance Research Laboratory, received high marks for its expertise. *Report of the Research Group on Federal Contract Research Centers*, Office of the Director of Defense Research and Engineering, August 1971.

64. Letter of R. W. Gutmann, Director, Procurement and Systems Acquisition Division, General Accounting Office, to Daniel Guttman, March 29, 1972. Cf. the statement from the 1971 defense study that, "unlike Mitre, there is very little flavor of an arm's-length relationship" between the Air Force Systems Command and Aerospace.

65. Hearings Before the Subcommittee on Investigations of the Committee on Post Office and Civil Service, U.S. House of Representatives, July 30, 1971.

66. "DOD's Computer Critics Nearly Unplug Ailing Worldwide Military

Command and Control System," *Armed Forces Journal*, December 21, 1970. See also *Armed Forces Management*, July 1969, special issue on command and control.

67. J. C. R. Licklider, "Underestimates and Overexpectation," in Abram Chayes and Jerome Weisner, eds., *ABM: An Evaluation of the Decision to Deploy an Antiballistic Missile* (New York: New American Library, 1969). Interviews with Leonard Rodberg, Institute for Policy Studies, 1971; Licklider, February 1972; Charles Zraket and Charles Grandy, Vice Presidents, Mitre Corporation, November 1972.

68. Interview with Charles Zraket, November 1972. Mitre's annual reports list the L systems on which it has worked. These range from the seemingly esoteric, such as an air defense system for the Ryukyu Islands, to the grandiose, such as the military's automated voice communications network (Autovon).

69. See *The Military Budget and National Economic Priorities*, Hearings Before the Subcommittee on Economy in Government, Joint Economic Committee, U.S. Congress, 1969, pt. 1. The Schultze quotation appears at p. 72, and the Hoag quotation at p. 239. See also Richard English and Dan Bolef, "Defense Against Bomber Attack," *Scientific American*, August 1973. The AWACS battle continues. See, e.g., "GAO Challenges 111 Million Dollar Plane," *New York Times*, February 23, 1975.

70. Interview with Charles Grandy, November 1972. The "simple engineer" pronouncements must be understood in the context of the grand claims for systems engineering. The systems engineer does not think of developing discrete products but of creating new markets and industries. "Why," asks Mitre Vice President Charles Zraket, are we "propping up" the medical schools, when we should be planning a "reorganization" of the medical "system"? The grand scheme "is the part of the problem I want to work on." Engineers with ambitions of such magnitude lose sight of traditional concerns for efficiency. Zraket does not understand defense critics who "arm-wave about cutting defense budgets by thirty billion dollars." It is idle to debate such a relatively small sum, he contends, when the attack on major social problems requires "something like a few hundred billions a year" (interview, November 1972).

71. The Wyer, Dick study is debated in exchanges that appear in *Passenger Train Service*, Hearings Before the Subcommittee on Transportation and Aeronautics, Committee on Interstate and Foreign Commerce, U.S. House of Representatives, 1970, pp. 77–84, 90–94.

72. Contract FDA-66-186.

73. See *Product and Process Development*, Foster D. Snell Co., 1970.

74. The quotations appear in Booz reports located in the files for Contracts FDA-66-186 and FDA-67-59.

75. Telephone interviews with Association staff and with Harry Vincent of Booz, Allen, winter 1971–72. Letter from John T. Walden, Acting Assistant Commissioner for Public Affairs, FDA, to Daniel Guttman, February 10, 1972.

In 1969, Dr. Charles Edwards, head of Booz's health division, was named Commissioner of FDA. Edwards stated that he did not work on Booz's contracts for the drug lobby or the FDA. He also volunteered that the consultants had never gotten very far with their system and that the Booz studies were gathering dust when he entered the agency. Edwards saw nothing improper about Booz's dual service. In 1975, he left HEW for an executive position with Becton-Dickinson, a major drug company.

Edwards was interviewed in November 1972.

76. The contract was with SRS's predecessor agency, Vocational Rehabilitation.

77. Contract file, SAV-105-61. See also contract file, SRS-69-37.

78. Letter from Herbert M. Temple III, Vice President of Harbridge House, to Miss Mary Switzer, Director, Social and Rehabilitation Services Administration, dated March 14, 1963.

79. Harbridge House actually presented the report four months late.

80. Memorandum from Aubrey Villenes to the Assistant Administrator for Administration Re: Questionable Procurement Practices, January 31, 1969.

81. Contract file, SRS-69-37.

82. Interview with Lowell Genebach, March 1972. The Federal Council for Science and Technology, now defunct, hired Harbridge House to perform a major study of patent rights attending grants and contracts. The study recommended the liberalization of grants of rights to contractors. See Harbridge House, *Government Patent Policy*, for the Federal Council on Science and Technology, 1968. (The Nixon Administration subsequently did liberalize grants. See "U.S. to Revise Policy on Patents It Owns to Let Developers Buy Exclusive Licenses," *Wall Street Journal*, August 25, 1971.) Harbridge House simultaneously offered its services to contractors and grantees. It taught a course in proprietary rights for the National Defense Education Institute, a co-venture of Harbridge House and the National Security Industrial Association. It also helped the University of California plan its approach to Federal funding. See Harbridge House, "A Report on the Economic Potential of Patent Exploitation at the University of California," October 1967.

83. Contract file, SRS-70-87.

84. Interview with Miss Mary Switzer, August 1971.

IV. EFFICIENCY IN GOVERNMENT:
Private Control of Public Spending

1. Charles Schultze, "The Reviewers Reviewed," *American Economic Review*, May 1971. The remarks were part of a symposium on the "state of economics" attending the completion of a National Academy of Sciences survey of the behavioral and social sciences. This quotation and those in the following paragraph are from pp. 47–49.

2. See the Commissioner's *Annual Report*, March 31, 1971. (The report was largely ghostwritten by a contractor.) The Office of Education hired the American Institutes for Research to study "Models" of "educational product development." See reports pursuant to Contract OEC-0-70-4892.

3. Followthrough serves the disadvantaged in the years following their graduation from the better-known Head Start program. Head Start, the showpiece War on Poverty program, provides prekindergarteners not only with a foretaste of academe but with critical extra-academic needs, such as health care, food, and affection. Followthrough would offer similar fare through third grade.

As evaluators sought further control over data, the practice of "evaluation" merged into the practice of "social experimentation." Both terms were applied to the Head Start–Followthrough studies discussed. While evaluations are generally incidental to ongoing programs, the experimenter creates a program to suit the needs of science. Employees of organizations such as Battelle, RAND, Brookings, and the Urban Institute became leading exponents of the "theory and practice" of evaluation and experimentation. See, e.g., Thomas Glennan, "Using Experiments for Social Research Planning," *Monthly Labor Review*, February 1972; Alice Rivlin, *Systematic Thinking for Social Action* (Washington, D.C.: Brookings Institution, 1971); Walter Williams, *Social Policy Research and Analysis* (New York: Elsevier, 1971). In spring 1973 Brookings held a conference on social experimentation which featured papers on the "planned variation" techniques applied in the Head Start–Followthrough evaluation-experiment that is discussed in this chapter. For details of other major experiments see *Income Maintenance Experiment*, Material Submitted by the Department of Health, Education, and Welfare to the Committee on Finance, U.S. Senate, February 1972; *An Experiment in Performance Contracting*, Office of Economic Opportunity, June 1972.

4. Gorham and Rivlin, recruited by HEW in response to the planning-programming-budgeting pressure, had traveled impeccable routes to the Department. Gorham came from RAND and the Defense Department; Rivlin came from Brookings. Gorham left HEW for the Urban Institute; Rivlin returned to Brookings.

5. Quotations concerning Head Start and Followthrough, unless otherwise indicated, were obtained from the HEW contract files. The Stanford Research Institute Followthrough contract is OEO-0-8-522480, and the Head Start contract is HEW-OS-70-134. In addition, the Followthrough files of the Bureau of Elementary and Secondary Education were made available.

6. The decision to turn Followthrough into an R & D program was abetted by a Gorham-headed task force on childhood education. On the Johnson era education task forces, see Address of Wilbur J. Cohen at the Lyndon Baines Johnson Library Education Symposium, reprinted in *Congressional Record*, February 2, 1972.

7. Memorandum from J. Graham Sullivan, Deputy Commissioner of Education, to Nolan Estes, Associate Commissioner, Bureau of Elementary and Secondary Education, July 10, 1967. Memorandum, Estes to Sullivan, July 14, 1967.

8. The SRI "educational policy research center" was supposed to support SRI's Followthrough–Head Start team. In 1972, however, members of HEW's Followthrough staff hardly knew that the Policy Research Center even existed. The Center, in fact, provided little or no useful "input" to the Office of Education. Its numerous papers on the world "macroproblem" may have been well received at conferences of futurists and humanistic psychologists, but they had little to do with ghetto education. Nonetheless, the Center, and a parallel "policy" center at the Syracuse University Research Corporation, continued to obtain funding renewals.

9. Interview with Richard Snyder, summer 1971.

10. Contract OEC-0-71-1341, "Legislative-Administrative History of Followthrough Program Under the Economic Opportunity Act."

11. The SSRC grant is OEC-0-8-5 22495-4635.

12. Ibid., files.

13. Letter of Daniel Guttman and Barry Willner to Elliot Richardson, May 24, 1974.

14. Letters of Richardson to Guttman and Willner, June 28, 1972, and October 23, 1972.

15. *Defense Industry Profit Study of the General Accounting Office*, Hearing Before a Subcommittee of the Committee on Government Operations, U.S. House of Representatives, 1971.

16. *Review of Head Start and Followthrough Evaluation Contracts with Stanford Research Institute*, Audit Agency, Office of the Assistant Secretary, Comptroller, U.S. Department of Health, Education, and Welfare, March 30, 1973. Quotations on pp. 2, 28.

17. The Head Start–Followthrough disaster was not unique. During the same period the Department of Labor and OEO cosponsored a major "evaluation" of four manpower programs. Operations Research Inc., a firm with little social expertise, was the prime contractor. The initial estimated cost of ORI's work was under $1 million, but by 1972 the estimate had increased to close to $5.8 million. (The contract was modified no fewer than fourteen times, and five of the modifications, totaling $830,000, were labeled "cost overruns.") The manpower evaluation sustained setbacks analgous to those suffered by Head Start–Followthrough. ORI mistakenly assumed that the Government possessed a substantial amount of data, the contractors found it difficult to locate mobile job trainees for follow-up interviews, and contractor and Government project managers often changed.

18. Stephen K. Bailey and Edith K. Mosher, *ESEA: The Office of Education Administers a Law* (Syracuse, N.Y.: Syracuse University Press, 1968), p. 163.

19. Interview with John Evans, 1973. *Title I in the Great City Schools*, Research Council of the Great City Schools, no date.

While the Followthrough–Head Start "experiment" fit spending to the needs of research, the evaluators of the largest compensatory education program—Title I of the Elementary and Secondary Education Act (ESEA)—had far less control over their subjects. In 1968 a Federal-State Task Force on Evaluation was created to administer the evaluation requirements for ESEA. The Task Force developed two massive questionnaires for administration, on a sample basis, to school districts throughout the country. The computerized results were the source material for "evaluation," Congress was told. Insiders knew that the system was a paper tiger. The questionnaires measured the "input" to schools—the amounts spent—but not the effect of spending. Further, the Office of Education deferred to local districts that chose to produce incomplete or erroneous information. Contractors were the primary beneficiaries of the evaluation. Between mid-1969 and mid-1971 no fewer than 120 contracts were awarded, with price tags ranging from hundreds to hundreds of thousands of dollars. Contractors were paid to plan the evaluation, to design tests, to write public relations material, to train evaluators, to criticize one another's work, and to write RFPs. For $87,000 Clark Abt & Associates wrote the official guide to the evaluation. Many contracts were curious. OE gave the State of Texas $200,000 to develop an information system, and Texas shuffled the money off to Abt. The exercise was useless, for Karl Hereford, the evaluation director, found the "contract was finally adjudged not worthy of continuing." When Director Hereford left OE he received a $2,500 "purchase order" for some work, and a White House Fellow who had worked at OE received the same amount to prepare some material for a conference on the evaluation. The Research Council for the Great Cities Schools, an association of urban school systems, wrote its own sole-source justification. Cynics in OE suggested that the $194,000 award (to develop a model local information system) was essentially a subsidy for the Council's Washington operations. Finally, OE relied on outsiders to write the official evaluation report received by Congress. The 1968–69 version was passed to Congress with scarcely an official alteration, and a contractor was paid $5,000 to abstract it. By 1973 the OE discarded the pretense of evaluation. The operation was moved into OE's Bureau of Educational Statistics. The system, Bert Mogin of the OE evaluation staff admitted, never was an evaluation: "That was part of the rhetoric."

Interviews with Sue Smith and Larry LaMoure, Bureau of Elementary and Secondary Education, 1971–72; interview with Bert Mogin, spring 1972; interview with Frank Reilly, Macro Systems, spring 1971; interview with Karl Hereford, former director of the evaluation, 1972. The Bureau permitted review of its contract files.

20. *ESEA Title I: A Reanalysis and Synthesis of Evaluation Data from Fiscal Year 1965 Through 1970*, American Institutes for Research in the Behavioral Sciences, Palo Alto, Calif., March 1972.

21. *Title I of ESEA: Is It Helping Children?* Washington Research Project, Washington, D.C., 1969. Quotations on pp. V and 57.

22. Interviews, Bureau of Elementary and Secondary Education, 1971–72; interviews, HEW Office of Special Concern, 1971–72; interview with Michael Trister, summer 1971.

23. "An Evaluation System to Support Planning, Allocation and Control in a Decentralized, Comprehensive Manpower Program," Urban Institute, March 1971; "An Evaluation System to Support a Decentralized, Comprehensive Manpower Program," paper presented at the Conference on the Evaluation of the Impact of Manpower Programs," Columbus, Ohio, June 16, 1971. As John Scanlon, a young Urban Institute employee who cut his teeth on the evaluation studies, lamented, "My steelworker friends are amazed to learn how little information government decisions are based on."

24. Interview with Sterling Livingston, 1972.

25. Harbridge House brochure, no date; *PMM & Co., Directory of Services*, 1970. Harbridge House emphasizes the usefulness of its Government experience to industry quite explicitly. "For sixteen years," one of its brochures explains, "Harbridge House has maintained a close relationship with the Federal agencies and their major contractors. In the theory and practice of defense procurement systems and source selection practices, our experience exceeds that of any other civilian organization. . . . This capability is made available to the defense aerospace industry through the services of the Harbridge House Government Marketing Division (*Government Marketing Services for Industry*, no date).

26. *NSIA's 26th Year, Annual Report 1970*, p. 5. The Defense Department provided the information about procurement training in *Government Procurement and Contracting*, Hearings Before a Subcommittee of the Committee on Government Operations, U.S. House of Representatives, 1969, pt. 1, pp. 59–60.

Consultant-produced textbooks—generally thick looseleaf binders filled with excerpts from Federal regulations, exhortatory speeches by bigwigs, magazine articles from management journals, and a surfeit of charts—have become standard items on the Government contract office bookshelf. The consultants have long sold contract education to civilian agencies as well as to the Defense Department. The mention of Harbridge House in HEW, for example, may bring a chuckle from contract officials who know that a Harbridge House–type course is the standard bromide for endemic contracting problems. "The teachers," remarked a former Livingston employee, "are the blandest."

According to Harbridge House's Richard Miller, about $20,000 is invested in the average Harbridge House training course, and the "quality of teaching is much higher than in any school I've ever attended." Miller is a Yale Law School graduate. See, e.g., Harbridge House, *Defense Procurement Executive Refresher Course*, developed under the direction of headquarters, Naval Material Command, January 1970.

27. The origins of LMI are discussed in *Systems Development and Management*, Hearings Before a Subcommittee of the Committee on Government Operations, U.S. House of Representatives, 1962, pt. 2, pp. 590–604. Also, interview with Tom Morris, currently Assistant Comptroller General of the United States, July 1971.

The Logistics Management Institute (LMI) studies such logistics matters as food service management, overhaul scheduling, and manpower practices, as well as being a continual source of expertise on contracting. The Institute has a small budget of approximately $1 million a year.

The creation of the Institute is a further example of the primary role of profit forces in the shaping of "public interest" nonprofit research organizations. The Institute did not take business away from firms like those run by Livingston, but stimulated the acceptance and production of management techniques. LMI even subcontracted out the production of manuals to Livingston consultants.

28. That the consultant bureaucracy is only one of several buffers between the Defense Department and its contractors is illustrated by the Department's statement that proposed revisions in procurement regulations are submitted to sixteen trade associations. *Government Procurement and Contracting*, p. 52. Secretary McNamara, for his part, formed the Defense Industry Advisory Committee to promote continuing discussion with the complex.

29. Merton J. Peck and Frederic M. Scherer, *The Weapons Acquisition Process: An Economic Analysis* (Boston: Harvard Business School, 1962). See also Frederic M. Scherer, *The Weapons Acquisition Process: Economic Incentives* (Boston: Harvard Business School, 1964).

30. The reforms of the Sixties, and the consultants who produced them, were central to the Mark 48 Torpedo disaster, discussed in Chapter II. The rise of the McNamara reforms, and their fall, produced numerous volumes of testimony. On their rise, see, generally, *Systems Development and Management*. On their fall, see *The Military Budget and National Economic Priorities*, Hearings Before the Subcommittee on Economy in Government, Joint Economic Committee, U.S. Congress, 1969; *Capability of GAO to Analyze and Audit F Defense Expenditures*, Hearings Before the Subcommittee on Executive Reorganization, Committee on Government Operations, U.S. Senate, 1969; *TFX Contract Investigation* (Second Series), Hearings Before the Permanent Subcommittee on Investigations, Committee on Government Operations, U.S. Senate, 1970; *Policy Changes in Weapons System Procurement*, Hearings Before a Subcommittee of the Committee on Government Operations, U.S. House of Representatives, 1970; *The Acquisition of Weapon Systems*, Hearings Before the Subcommittee on Economy in Government, Joint Economic Committee, U.S. Congress, 1970; *Weapon System Acquisition Process*, Hearings Before the Committee on Armed Services, U.S. Senate, 1972.

31. The 1970 reflections of Congress are located in *Policy Changes in Weapons System Procurement*. Forty-second Report of the Committee on Government Operations, U.S. House of Representatives, 1970. Quotation on p. 9. Morris explained the McNamara reforms to Congress in *Systems Development and Management*, pt. 2. Quotation on p. 550.

32. See Scherer, *Economic Incentives*, chaps. 7 and 8.

33. The incentive contract responded to industry demands for both increased profit opportunity and lessened governmental intervention in industry management. As Frederic Scherer later suggested, the industry was really suffering from overcapacity created by the aerospace boom of the late Fifties. The Department should have pruned the industry in the early Sixties, but, via the incentive contract, it permitted it to grow—under the umbrella of profit-motivated self-discipline.

The McNamara reforms were buoyed by industry-sponsored contractor studies that documented the threatened health of the aerospace industry. In one major study for the Aerospace Industries Association, the Stanford Research Institute, itself increasingly reliant on defense dollars, called for more "communication" and less regulation. See George Hayes, Director of Planning, SRI, "The Industry-Government-Aerospace Relationship," Presentation to Aerospace Industries Association, September 1963. When President Kennedy commissioned his Budget Director to head a panel on R & D contracting, the industry prepared a parallel report, which was also presented at the Systems Development hearings before Congress in 1962. See testimony of Arthur D. Little's Helge Holst, *Systems Development*, pt. 1, pp. 80–121. (Both the official and the private reports advocated continued extensive use of R & D contracts.) When, in 1969, President Nixon commissioned his Blue Ribbon Panel to study the legacy of the McNamara era, Stanford Research Institute was hired as the primary panel contractor.

34. The Air Force hired McKinsey to design a management system to control modifications. See James Reece, "The Effects of Contract Changes on Control of a Major Weapons System," Ph.D. thesis, Harvard Graduate School of Business Administration, undated.

35. Interviews with Ivan Fisher and J. R. Goldstein, Acting President, RAND, 1972. The Fisher incident is discussed in A. Ernest Fitzgerald, *The High Priests of Waste* (New York: W. W. Norton, 1972), pp. 94–98, 221–22.

36. See Logistics Management Institute, "An Examination of the Foundations of Incentive Contracting," May 1968. See also Albert J. Gravallese, "An Evaluation of the Total Package Procurement Concept as Exemplified by Three Air Force Weapon System Contracts," M.S. thesis, Massachusetts Institute of Technology, June 1968.

37. *Policy Changes in Weapons System Procurement*, p. 11.

38. Interview with Sterling Livingston, 1972.

39. The origins of PERT are testified to in *Systems Development and Management*, pt. 2, pp. 575–90. Quotation appears in the testimony of Vice Admiral W. F. Raborn, Jr., pt. 4, p. 1461.

40. PERT/Cost illustrated the triumph of salesmanship over science. The PERT network was not very useful for the collection of cost information, so the PERT/Cost system was not really a PERT system at all, but a system created to capitalize on the PERT name. Interviews with A. Ernest Fitzgerald, Dave Moran, and Mert Tyrell, former Livingston employees, 1971–72.

41. The Booz quotation appears in an undated Booz brochure entitled "The Management Implications of PERT." On the proliferation of PERT see, e.g., Sterling Livingston, "The New Management Elite," *Journal of the Armed Forces Management Association*, 1961; Sterling Livingston and Ronald Fox, "PERT Gains New Dimensions," *Aerospace Management*, January 1962; Management

Systems Corporation, *A Survey of Planning and Control Systems for Development Projects*, August 1963.

42. Telephone interview with Frederic Scherer, 1972. See Harvey Sapolsky, *The Polaris System Development: Bureaucratic and Programmatic Success in Government* (Cambridge, Mass.: Harvard University Press, 1972), chap. 4, "PERT and Managerial Effectiveness." Quotation on p. 106.

43. Sapolsky, *Polaris System Development;* interview with Mert Tyrell. Tyrell worked on Lockheed's Polaris contract prior to employment with Livingston's Management Systems Corporation.

44. Dr. J. Ronald Fox, "The Development of the Department of Defense Cost and Schedule Specifications (C/SPCS)," 1967, mimeographed material for Harvard Business School curriculum. See also Fox's testimony in *Policy Changes in Weapons System Procurement*, p. 128.

45. Sapolsky, *Polaris System Development*, p. 124.

46. Antony Oettinger, "A Bull's-Eye View of Information Systems," in Alan F. Westin, ed., *Information Technology in a Democracy* (Cambridge, Mass.: Harvard University Press, 1971). Quotation on p. 259.

47. Interview with Sterling Livingston, 1972.

48. Interviews with J. Ronald Fox, A. Ernest Fitzgerald, Robert Anthony, and Joseph Warren, 1971-72. The McKinsey episode is described in Fitzgerald's *High Priests*, pp. 26–28, 79–85, 106–8. McKinsey did not respond to a request for an interview concerning its cost control work and the relation between such work and its work for major aerospace contractors.

49. See testimony of A. Ernest Fitzgerald in *The Military Budget and National Economic Priorities*, vol. 2, pp. 595–617 (quotation on p. 605). Estimates placed the cost of complying with management systems requirements at 10 to 14 percent of the defense contract budget, possibly $6 billion or more. See Harbridge House, "A Study of Requirements for Data and Management Control Systems in Three Engineering Programs," A Report to the Office of the Director of Defense Research and Engineering, February 1970; Aerospace Industries Association, "Management Systems in Future Government Procurement," July 1971.

50. Report to the President and the Secretary of Defense by the Blue Ribbon Defense Panel (the Fitzhugh report), July 1970, p. 82.

51. Interview with J. Ronald Fox; Fox, *Arming America: How the United States Buys Arms* (Cambridge, Mass.: Harvard University Press, 1974).

52. P. Suver, "A Comparison of the Management Control Systems Being Utilized in Commercial and Governmental Programs in the Aerospace and Defense Industries," Ph.D. thesis, Harvard Graduate School of Business Administration, 1971.

53. David Packard, "David Packard for the Defense," *Business Week*, October 28, 1972. Packard condemned the "whole host of 'experts' like Fitzgerald [who] invented all kinds of schemes like the ones Fitzgerald describes in his book— Should Cost, CWAS, CIMR, PERT—and many others. The program managers manipulated these schemes, produced tons of paper reports, but never really managed what they were supposed to be managing."

54. The Packard era's procurement reforms are extolled in an anthology of articles on "The Weapons System Acquisition Process," in the fall 1971 *Defense Management Journal.*

55. The dollar figures appear in a letter by Peter A. Erickson, Staff Assistant,

Public Affairs, Office of the Assistant Secretary of Defense, to Daniel Guttman, January 19, 1973. They appear to be incomplete, for PMM must have received substantial sums in 1969 for its Mark 48 work, discussed in Chapter II above.

56. Brigadier General Winfield Scott III, USA, "Educating the DOD Program Manager," *Defense Management Journal*, April 1972; letter of Lieutenant Colonel William O. Thurston, USA, to Daniel Guttman, December 29, 1972.

57. *Background Papers on Washington State*, the Final Report of the Commission on Intergovernmental Relations, Washington, D.C., 1955, p. 88.

58. Title 42, United States Code, section 3301.

59. Judson James, *Evaluation Report on the Model Cities Program*, in Papers Submitted to the Subcommittee on Housing Panels on Housing Production, Housing Demand, and Developing a Suitable Living Environment, Committee on Banking and Currency, U.S. House of Representatives, June 1971, pt. 2, p. 839.

60. Ernest Erber, ed., *Urban Planning in Transition* (New York: Grossman Publishers, 1970), p. xxi.

61. Hammer, Greene, Siler Associates, *Comprehensive Planning Assistance in the Small Community*, A Report Prepared for the Department of Housing and Urban Development, March 1, 1969.

62. Ibid., p. 55.

63. Marshall Kaplan, Gans & Kahn, *The Effectiveness of the Section 701 Urban Planning Assistance Program*, A Report Prepared for the Department of Housing and Urban Development, September 28, 1967, p. 37.

64. Letters from George M. Raymond to Robert Siler, Jr., Hammer, Greene, Siler Associates, September 6 and November 11, 1968.

65. Ibid.

66. "Urban Report/Model Cities Program Faces Uncertain Future Despite Romney Overhaul," *National Journal*, July 11, 1970, p. 1474.

67. *Model Cities: A Step Towards the New Federalism*, Report of the President's Task Force on Model Cities, August 1970, p. 7.

68. Management Assistance Program, Westinghouse Public Management Services, Model Cities Observation Report No. 1, December 1971, pp. 2-1, 2-2.

69. Ibid., p. 2-6.

70. McKinsey interoffice memorandum from Robin Foote to Bob Haas, June 17, 1970, re NYC Model Cities work.

71. Interview with Thomas Ubois, August 1971.

72. District of Columbia City Council Report from Vice Chairman Sterling Tucker, July 30, 1971.

73. *The Block Grant Programs of the Law Enforcement Assistance Administration*, Twelfth Report by the Committee on Government Operations, U.S. House of Representatives, October 1971. Quotations on pp. 8, 10, 56, 57.

74. Marshall Kaplan, "The Irrelevancy of the Planner in the Sixties," unpublished paper, no date.

75. Letter from Marshall Kaplan to Donald Dodge, Office of Community Development, October 4, 1972.

76. Kaplan's self-definition melds the jargons of social science, management, and political reform. He regards his firm as the best available vehicle for effective change, a means for improving the life of the disadvantaged without being sidetracked by concerns for profit and growth or by irrelevant academic and bureaucratic considerations. Letter of Marshall Kaplan to Barry Willner, October 30, 1970.

77. *Simplification and Consolidation of Community Development Programs*, HUD Task Force Report, July 2, 1972.

78. Hyde first retained Kaplan for seventeen and one-half days between August 29, 1969, and September 30, 1970. In this period Kaplan's firm received two contracts from HUD. The largest increment in the firm's income came from amendments to the Model Cities evaluation contract. The contract was initially priced at approximately $40,000, and during Kaplan's consultancy Amendment Number 4 (for $201,000) and Amendment Number 5 (for $399,997) were added to the contract. Letter from David O. Maxwell, General Counsel, Department of Housing and Urban Development, to Barry Willner, February 25, 1972.

79. "City Will Get Its Second Model Cities Grant of $65 Million," *New York Times*, August 6, 1971.

80. Letter from David O. Maxwell, General Counsel, Department of Housing and Urban Development, to Barry Willner, February 25, 1972.

81. *Simplification and Consolidation of Community Development Programs*, p. 1.

82. Letter from David O. Maxwell, General Counsel, Department of Housing and Urban Development, to Barry Willner, February 25, 1972.

83. Interview with Joseph Crane, October 30, 1972.

84. Arnold Schuchter, "Model Cities Relevancy and Results—Prospects for the Model Cities Program," paper presented at the 1970 National Planning Conference of Planning Officials, New York, April 8, 1970.

85. See Urban Institute memorandum from John Scanlon to Evaluation Staff, March 12, 1969.

86. To ascertain CDA reactions to the consultant work, we conducted interviews by phone and sent out questionnaires to 144 CDAs. Both the telephone interviews and nearly thirty responses to the questionnaires expressed almost universal disappointment with CDAIS. In Reading, Pennsylvania, for example, the CDA director explained that he had just finished firing the incompetent who claimed responsibility for the CDAIS work. Interviews with Government officials include Howard Ball, Director, State and Local Information Systems, and Charles Orlebeck, HUD Deputy Under Secretary, fall 1972. Contractor reports include Management Assistance Program, Westinghouse Public Management Services, Final Report, June 1972.

87. Management Assistance Program, Westinghouse Public Management Services, Final Report, June 1972, p. 6-4.

88. Ibid.

V. EFFICIENCY IN INDUSTRY:
Public Funding of Corporate Growth

1. The housing component of the Civilian Industrial Technology Program is the subject of Dorothy Nelkin, *The Politics of Housing Innovation; the Fate of the Civilian Technology Program* (Ithaca, N.Y.: Cornell University Press, 1971). The material quoted is on p. 19.

2. See Burnham Kelley, *The Lustron House: The Prefabrication of Housing* (Cambridge, Mass.: MIT Press, 1951).

3. Ibid., p. 116.

4. Interview with Milton Semer, August 1972.

5. *Better Housing for the Future*, White House Panel on Civilian Technology, Executive Office of the President, U.S. Office of Science and Technology, April 1963. For a fuller analysis of this report see Nelkin, *Politics of Housing Innovation.*

6. *A Decent Home,* President's Commission on Urban Housing, December 11, 1967, p. 5.

7. See, for instance, Arthur D. Little, Inc., *Patterns and Problems of Technical Innovation in American Industry: Report to the National Science Foundation,* U.S. Department of Commerce, September 1963, pp. 136ff.

8. *Better Housing for the Future,* pp. 15, 6.

9. Ibid., p. 13.

10. *A Decent Home,* p. 10.

11. Address by Congressman Frank Bow to the House of Representatives, February 21, 1963, *Congressional Record,* 1963, vol. 109, pt. 2, p. 2754.

12. Donald Schon, *Beyond the Stable State* (New York: Random House, 1971), p. 41.

13. Ibid., p. 42.

14. See Little, *Patterns and Problems of Technical Innovation in American Industry.*

15. *Proceedings of a Conference on Technology Transfer* (NSF 67-5) held under the auspices of the National Planning Association and National Science Foundation, May 15–17, 1966.

16. Ibid., pp. 32, 46.

17. *Industrialized Housing: An Inquiry into Factors Influencing Entry Decisions by Major Manufacturing Corporations,* A Report Prepared by the Committee on Industrialized Housing of the National Academy of Engineering, Washington, D.C., 1972, p. 14.

18. Transcript of Conference on Science and Urban Affairs, held by the Housing and Home Finance Agency at Washington, D.C., p. 17.

19. Several of those represented (e.g., SRI and SDC) were later to alter their status and become profit-making ventures.

Many of the organizations represented at Woods Hole were to receive major HUD R & D contracts. Among other conferees from private organizations were representatives from the Defense Research Corporation, Rutgers University, MIT-Harvard Joint Center for Urban Studies, Oak Ridge National Laboratory, Institute of Public Administration, Thomas Watson Research Center, Matson Research Corporation, National Planning Association, Brookings Institution, Resources for the Future, T. Y. Lin Associates, Institute for Defense Analyses, and Basic Systems, Inc.

20. *Science and the City* (HUD-MP-39), Department of Housing and Urban Development, Washington, D.C., 1967.

21. Interview with Hortense Gabel, January 14, 1972.

22. *Science and the City* (HUD-MP-39).

23. Summer Study on Science and Urban Development, Woods Hole, Mass., June 5–25, 1966, mimeographed. See A Report of the Rehabilitation Panel, July 1966. Among the panel members were Anthony Downs (Real Estate Research Corporation), Ezra Ehrenkrantz (BSDI), James Simpson (HUD), and Thomas O. Paine (GE Tempo). Quotations on pp. 7, 12.

24. Ibid., p. 13.

25. Tempo was established on the RAND model to perform studies for the Government as well as for General Electric itself, which had great ambitions in housing and was one of several corporations planning to build entire "new towns."

26. Correspondence from Hortense Gabel and Thomas O. Paine to Secretary Robert Weaver and Under Secretary Robert Wood of the Department of Housing and Urban Development, June 28, 1966.

27. Interview with Donald Schon, fall 1972.

28. Schon, *Beyond the Stable State*, p. 136.

29. "The Proposal" (from Gabel and Paine to Weaver), November 7, 1966, mimeographed, pp. 5–7.

30. Ibid.

31. See Abt Associates Inc., Urban Development Applications Project, Quarterly Report No. 4 K (NASA-2022), December 31, 1970, app. E-2.

32. Memorandum from Secretary Robert C. Weaver, of the Department of Housing and Urban Development for the President, The White House, November 8, 1966 (6 pages).

33. Interview with Milton Semer, August 1972.

34. For the Demonstration Cities and Metropolitan Development Act of 1966, see Title 42, United States Code Annotated, section 3301.

35. *A Decent Home*, p. 10.

36. For an excellent review of this dispute see Harold Wolman, *The Politics of Federal Housing* (New York: Dodd, Mead & Co., 1971).

37. *A Decent Home*, p. 10.

38. For a review of the founding of the National Housing Partnership, see Carter L. Burgess and Sidney Friedberg, "NHP—a New Opportunity for Housing," *George Washington Law Review* 39 (May 1971).

39. Part 5 of the Douglas Commission Report, "Reducing Housing Costs," was substantially written by Ezra Ehrenkrantz, President of Building Systems Development, Inc. It represents a classic statement of Ehrenkrantz's position on industrialized housing, and as such, a misleading statement on the reality. (See above.) The report recommended Federally subsidized R & D and concluded: "There can be little doubt that prefabrication techniques and large-scale production (on- and off-site) have produced cost savings in the past and should continue to do so in the future. Such savings are not merely theoretical; they have been proved. At the same time, no dramatic industrial breakthrough has occurred in this country." *Building the American City*, Report of the National Commission on Urban Problems to the Congress and the President, December 12, 1968, pp. 476, 445.

40. *A Decent Home*, p. 39.

41. Henry Aaron, *Shelter and Subsidies: Who Benefits from Federal Housing Policies?* (Washington, D.C.: Brookings Institution, 1972), p. 43.

42. Miles Colean article in *New York Times* Sunday edition, June 24, 1973.

43. Interviews with Thomas Rogers, August 17, 1970, and October 14, 1971.

44. HUD Contract H-978 (1968) to the Massachusetts Institute of Technology, "Summer Study on Urban Information Systems and Matching Advanced Technology to Urban Needs."

45. Robert C. Wood, "The Rediscovery of the American City," address to the MIT Alumni Seminar, Cambridge, Mass., September 8, 1967, p. 8.

46. The awards resulted in two studies: *A Strategic Approach to Urban Research and Development: Social and Behavorial Considerations,* National Academy of Sciences, Washington, D.C., 1969; *Long-Range Planning for Urban Research and Development: Technological Considerations,* National Academy of Sciences, Washington, D.C., 1969.

47. The RAND Corporation, *Recommendations for Research in Support of Federal Urban Programs* (Memorandum RM-5503 HUD), Santa Monica, Calif., April 1968, p. 22.

48. James D. Carroll, "Science and the City: The Question of Authority," *Science,* February 28, 1969, p. 906. Interviews with Thomas Rogers, August 17, 1970, and Joseph Stockfisch, Vice President, Institute for Defense Analyses, November 1971.

49. In a January 8, 1972 letter to HUD's Research and Technology Assistant Secretary Harold Finger, we requested a statement on final costs of Rehab. In a February 10, 1972 reply, Mr. Finger referred us to Mr. Robert Philpott, Assistant Commissioner for Rehabilitation, HUD-FHA, stating that no figures were available from R. & T. Philpott's assistant Paul Lydens informed us that no figures were available.

50. Interview with David Moore, HUD Research and Technology, August 1970.

51. Robert C. Wood, untitled speech to the Southeastern Region National Association of Housing and Redevelopment Officials (NAHRRO), New Orleans, La. June 12, 1967, p. 8.

52. *Rapid Rehabilitation of Old Law Tenements: An Evaluation,* Institute of Public Administration, New York, September 1968, pp. 35, 3.

53. Ibid., p. 4.

54. John R. Boice, "A History and Evaluation of the School Construction Systems Development Project 1961–1967," Building Systems Information Clearinghouse, Educational Facilities Laboratories, Menlo Park, Calif., undated.

55. Interview with Howard Moskof, assistant to Senator Proximire, winter, 1972. Moskof was executive director of the President's Committee report known as *A Decent Home.*

56. J. Karl Justin, "Can We Rebuild an Industry?" *Technology Review,* May 1970, pp. 23–29. Also interview with Justin, summer 1972.

57. Summary Report of the Ad Hoc Housing Committee to the Executive Committeee of the Metropolitan Detroit Citizens Development Authority and the Housing Committee of New Detroit Inc. (hereinafter New Detroit Report), mimeographed, August 1971, p. ix-4.

58. Confidential interviews.

59. Interview with William Hawkins, December 14, 1971.

60. New Detroit Report, p. ix-12.

61. New Detroit Report, p. ix-6.

62. In-Cities Experimental Housing and Research and Development Project—Phase I: Composite Report (hereinafter called In-Cities Report), March 1969, vol. 1, p. ii.

63. Interview with Hortense Gabel, January 14, 1972. Although neither Edgar nor Henry Kaiser attended the Wood's Hole conference, Walter Rosenblith is a member of the Board of Directors of Kaiser Industries.

64. Testimony of Robert C. Weaver, Hearings Before Subcommittee of the Committee on Appropriations, U.S. House of Representatives, May 22, 1968, pt. 2, p. 92.

65. In-Cities Report, p. ii.

66. Ibid., pp. iii, iv.

67. Ibid., p. iv.

68. Ibid., p. iii-5.

69. Ibid., p. iv-9.

70. Ibid., pp. ii-1, 2.

71. Testimony of Harold Finger, Hearings Before a Subcommittee of the Committee on Appropriations, U.S. House of Representatives, April 30, 1969, pt. 4, pp. 467–68.

72. In-Cities Report, pp. vi-1–31.

73. Correspondence from Harold Finger to authors, January 19, 1972.

74. Interview with William Meyers, January 15, 1972.

75. Interview with Clark Abt, November 18, 1971.

76. Interview with Milton Semer, August 1972.

77. Correspondence from Harold Finger to authors, January 19, 1972.

78. Interview with William Meyers, January 15, 1972.

79. The Mitre Corporation, "The In-Cities Project, Some Initial Results" (MTP-334), June 30, 1969, mimeographed, pp. 4, 64.

80. Interview with David Moore, August 1970.

81. Hearings Before a Subcommittee of the Committee on Appropriations, U.S. House of Representatives, March 16, 1970, pt. 3, p. 503.

82. Testimony of George Romney, Hearings Before a Subcommittee of the Committee on Appropriations, U.S. House of Representatives, April 28, 1969, pt. 4, p. 457.

83. HUD was careful in all its releases not to say that it would be the market aggregator.

84. Michael Stegman, ed., *Housing and Economics: The American Dilemma* (Cambridge, Mass.: MIT Press, 1971), p. 114.

85. Speech of George Romney to the NAACP, July 3, 1969, mimeographed.

86. Editorial, *House and Home*, August 1971, p. 1.

87. Testimony of Charles Biederman, Hearings Before the Subcommittee on Urban Affairs, Joint Economic Committee, U.S. Congress, July 9, 1969, pt. 1, p. 12.

88. Ibid., pt. 2, p. 246.

89. Stegman, *Housing and Economics*, p. 114.

90. Interview with Donald Loomis, summer 1972.

91. *Housing Systems Proposals for Operation Breakthrough,* Department of Housing and Urban Development, December 1970.

92. Interview with Arthur Newburgh, July 1972.

93. Robertson Ward, Jr., "Breakthrough?" *AIA Journal*, March 1971, pp. 21–22.

94. For a breakdown of costing, see HUD's statement reprinted in *House and Home*, October 1971, p. 20.

95. Interview with Richard O'Neill, fall 1972.

96. Interview with Arthur Newburgh, April 27, 1972.

97. Interview with Ezra Ehrenkrantz, January 15, 1972.

98. Interview with Bert Greenglass, September 18, 1972.

99. Interview with Ezra Ehrenkrantz, January 15, 1972.

100. Interview with Professor Niles Thompson, University of Texas and head of NAE review panel, October 1, 1972.

101. "Big Battles over Rules for Builders," *Business Week*, January 1, 1972, p. 48.

102. Interview with Ezra Ehrenkrantz, January 15, 1972.

103. Computer Sciences Corporation, "Quality Programs of Existing Manufactured Housing Producers," Summary Report, Contract H-1449, October 1970, p. 2-1.

104. See symposium brochure, "NAS-NAE Symposium on Industrialized Housing," April 27, 1972.

105. Speech by Clarence Broley to the NAS-NAE Symposium on Industrialized Housing, April 27, 1972.

106. Speech by Arthur Newburgh to the NAS-NAE Symposium on Industrialized Housing, April 27, 1972.

107. Interview with Arthur Newburgh, April 27, 1972.

108. According to the 1969 *Summary*, HRB awarded 161 contracts between 1963 and 1969, of which 41 percent went to universities, 24 percent to "research institutions," 23 percent to "consulting firms," 7 percent to "commercial research firms," and 1 percent to "industrial firms."

109. John Burby, *The Great American Motion Sickness* (Boston: Little, Brown, 1971), p. 311; see also Ben Kelley, "The Highway Lobby in Ambush," *The Nation*, November 15, 1971.

110. The Wilbur Smith story is told in the firm's thick, midnight-blue, felt-covered brochure, which provides capsule descriptions of work in Africa, Australasia, Latin America, Europe, and seemingly every corner of the United States.

111. An early explication of the "gravity model" appears in Alan Voorhees, Gordon Sharpe, and T. Stegmaer, "Shopping Habits and Travel Patterns," supplement to Special Report II, "Parking as a Factor in Business," presented at the 34th Annual Meeting, Highway Research Board, 1955.

112. In late 1975 the District of Columbia freeway battle was still being fought. Its earlier years are recounted in Helen Leavitt, *Superhighway—Superhoax* (New York: Ballantine Books, 1970).

113. The Little study appeared as Arthur D. Little, *Transportation Planning in the District of Columbia, 1955 to 1965: A Review and Critique.* Independent critiques of District of Columbia highway planning were presented by a citizens' group, and authored by transportation lawyer Peter Craig: *The 1965 "Gravity Model" Traffic Forecast of the Mass Transportation Survey: Forecast vs. Actual Traffic Growth,* A Report Submitted to the National Capital Regional Planning Council, September 9, 1965, revised February 15, 1966; *Forecasting 1985 Transportation Requirements,* a report submitted to the National Capital Planning Council, February 26, 1966, p. 495.

114. Testimony of Peter Craig, in *Economic Analysis and Efficiency in Government*, Hearings Before the Subcommittee on Economy in Government, Joint Economic Committee, U.S. Congress, 1970, pt. 5, pp. 1120–83.

115. Interview with George All, Wilbur Smith & Associates, summer 1971.

116. "An Evaluation of Urban Transportation Planning," Office of the Assistant

Secretary for Environment and Urban Systems, Department of Transportation, February 12, 1971. The study is summarized by Michael Cafferty, then Acting Assistant Secretary for Environment and Urban Systems, in "Urban Goals and Priorities: The Increasing Role of Transportation Planning," *Traffic Quarterly*, July 1971.

117. Wilbur Smith & Associates, "Evaluation of the Transit Planning Process," a proposal to the Department of Transportation in response to RFP DOT-OS-10063, December 21, 1970.

118. The Northeast Corridor and Civil Aviation studies produced numerous volumes of contractor reports. The work is summarized in *Joint DOT-NASA Civil Aviation Research and Development Report*, Summary Volume, DOT Report TST-10-4, NASA Report SP-265, 1971; *Recommendations for Northeast Corridor Transportation Project, Final Report*, Department of Transportation, May 1971.

119. "New Systems" was the subject of a paper by David Lawrence for the Urban Transportation Center Consortium of Universities, "The Politics of Innovation in Urban Mass Transportation: The New Systems Example," Washington, D.C., 1970.

120. Interviews with Paul Sitton, Thomas Floyd, Franz Gimmler, 1971.

121. According to NHSB staff, corporate consultants were relied on because, in 1966, the only "expertise" on automobiles was expertise that had been bankrolled by the automobile companies.

122. Interviews with Paul Sitton, 1971. Sitton recalled, in particular, his experience with one fabled systems study. As a Bureau of the Budget examiner he followed the progress of Booz, Allen's "Analyses of the Functions of Transportation," a multimillion-dollar work that rests heavily on a DOT library shelf.

123. Information on UMTA contracts, unless otherwise noted, was located in the UMTA administrative files. The initial Mitre contract is TRD-52 and the IDA contract is TRD-51. The means by which access to the files was gained is worth noting. UMTA and the Department offered to make contracts available on generally unacceptable terms: high fees and only minimal access. The authors could not afford the fees and abandoned hope. They assumed, however, that they were at least entitled to see final reports, which were not always available in the agency's ample library. In search for reports produced by the "Center Cities" project one author was finally referred to the "administrative file room." When he found the room and asked clerks for the report, they told him that it was somewhere in the files and that he should find it for himself. The room apparently contained duplicates of the UMTA contract files, which the co-author spent several weeks examining. The documents were often quite revealing, and allusion to them facilitated interviews with contractors who had previously refused to discuss their work.

124. The memo of agreement underlying Mitre's relationship with UMTA stated that "his contract establishes a special relationship between the Mitre Corporation and UMTA founded on the relationship between Mitre and the Air Force. It is the desire of the UMTA to employ the special capabilities which the Mitre Corporation has developed in serving the needs of the Air Force to furthering the mission and objectives of UMTA." Mitre was to perform a vast range of tasks, as UMTA would from time to time specify: "These studies shall include systems analyses of transportation systems in our urban environment, analyses of performance and performance requirements for transportation, evaluation of proposed transportation systems with respect to their capability to satisfy performance requirements, cost analyses of transportation systems, including development, investment, and operating costs, technological forecasting, and feasibility studies of urban transportation systems" (contract file, TRD-52).

The tragicomic development of civilian air-traffic control, which Mitre was supposed to help oversee, was testified to in *Problems Confronting FAA in the Development of Air Traffic Control System for the 1970s.* Hearing Before a Subcommittee of the Committee on Government Operations, U.S. House of Representatives, 1970.

125. Hassler's departure from Mitre may have further enhanced Mitre's clout at UMTA. He left Mitre to take a position with the Transportation Systems Center, an electronics laboratory in Cambridge, Massachusetts, that had been funded by NASA. Northeastern Congressmen successfully protested NASA's termination of the laboratory's funding, and the Department of Transportation awarded it a $20 million budget. The Center quickly went to work with Mitre in the promotion of high-technology transportation, including the "personal rapid transit" technology discussed above.

126. Proposal 70-6, which appeared in the file of Mitre Contract TRD-52, promised that Mitre would help develop UMTA's yearly plans. "Mitre will assist UMTA in the development of concepts and procedures to systematically and rationally respond to program planning and budgeting submission requirements. Assistance will also be provided in preparing the necessary documentation to accompany such submission and the detailed work plans derived from them."

127. Unless otherwise noted, quotations concerning Center Cities appear in the Center Cities contracts. The primary Center Cities contracts were with Arthur D. Little (TRD-44), the National League of Cities (TRD-62), and Urban America (DC-MOT-6).

128. Interview with Michael Michaelis and Harry Broley, Arthur D. Little, August 1971.

129. Interviews with Paul Sitton, 1971. Interview with Gordon Murray, Department of Transportation, July 1971.

130. Villarreal appeared before the Senate Banking and Currency Committee on March 3, 1969.

131. Keynote address by John A. Volpe, Secretary of Transportation, at the fourth annual International Conference on Urban Transportation, at the Pittsburgh Hilton, March 10, 1969.

132. Sitton and ADL consortium employees, for their part, felt that the Villarreal administration did not understand CCTP. Villarreal was an aerospace technician who, as Sitton assistant Tom Floyd put it, "had never ridden a bus in his previous life . . . was abysmally ignorant about mass transportation." Clearly Villarreal was not excited by the "concept" of Center Cities. In one touching memo, an UMTA staffer pleaded with him not to change the CCTP acronym. "Unlike MIRV, or TOPICS, or PPBS," wrote Franz Gimmler, "it [CCTP] does mean something."

133. Interviews with Larry Stinchombe, 1970, 1971. Contract files.

134. The Anderson contract was TRD-80.

135. Interview with Franz Gimmler, 1971.

136. Interview with Robert Hemmes, summer 1971.

137. Sperry Systems Management Corporation, Critique of Current DOT R & D Management Practice, August 1971. The Department grudgingly revealed a scissored copy of the Sperry report, after arguing that it contained no information, was an "internal" document, and therefore was not subject to required disclosure. The report followed on the heels of similar studies by Operations Research Inc. and the Jet Propulsion Laboratory. In 1973 McKinsey was hired to review departmental R & D management. It produced a compendium of typical recommendations in *Strengthening Grant and Research Management in the DOT*, July 1974.

138. Interview with Robert Hemmes, summer 1971. Federal funding had a dramatic effect on the "people-mover" industry. Many of the early people-mover designs were produced by entrepreneurs who formed small companies to promote their work. They found that Federal support was forthcoming only if they could provide the government with reputable corporate backing. Howard Ross, for example, had worked at Stanford Research Institute on the New Systems study, then left to join General Motors employees in the creation of Transportation Technology Incorporated. TTI soon found that "it is necessary to create corporate stability with long-term muscle that will permit you to market to government agencies. You can get a preliminary hearing for your ideas, but most agencies will not seriously entertain building an advanced system without knowing that some large corporate entity stands behind it to guarantee it in some way." TTI was acquired by Otis Elevator. See Howard Ross, "Bringing Advanced Technology to the Public Sector," *Innovation,* no. 27, 1971.

139. See, e.g., "Morgantown Boondoggle," *Engineering News Record,* April 25, 1974. UMTA may spend over $60 million to make Morgantown operational. See " 'People-Mover' May Get Reprieve," *New York Times,* April 17, 1975.

140. See "Congress Roasts Transit R & D," *Business Week,* June 2, 1975.

141. See "High Speed Trains Hit a Red Signal," *Business Week,* January 13, 1975.

142. Interview with Thomas Floyd, 1971.

143. Interview with Franz Gimmler, 1971.

144. See, e.g., "Congress Roasts Transit R & D."

145. New York Metropolitan Regional Medicine Program Application, mimeographed, July 9, 1969. (Adapted from "Proposal for Demonstration and Study Through Extensive Reorganization of Personal Health Services in a Large Urban Environment.") Although McKinsey's name does not appear on the application, according to the "author of the report, Dr. J. Jay Brightman, McKinsey wrote the application and simply placed Brightman's name on it with his permission. Interview with Dr. J. Jay Brightman, January 5, 1973.

146. Joseph V. Terenzio and Henry E. Manning, "Case Study: New York City Hospitals," *Journal of American Hospital Associations,* July 1, 1970, Vol. 44, pp. 66–75.

147. New York Metropolitan Regional Medicine Program Application.

148. Interview with Carter Bales, March 16, 1972.

149. IPA boasts of being the oldest center for policy research in the country. Lyle Fitch, IPA president, had offered the Institute's services to the candidates running for Mayor, and Lindsay had accepted. IPA's predecessor, the New York Bureau of Municipal Research, was instrumental in establishing the Brookings Institution. IPA's work on the organization of New York's government has paralleled, in continuity and influence, that of Brookings at the national level.

IPA was an old hand at the game of administration and reorganization. Its efforts at home and abroad are naturally marked by varying degrees of success. IPA, for instance, established a National Institute for Administration in Vietnam. "This," according to IPA staffer Howard Mantel, who worked with the Craco Commission, "was one of our less successful jobs" (interview, April 20, 1972).

150. Lyle C. Fitch and Annmarie H. Walsh, *Agenda for a City: Issues Confronting New York* (Beverly Hills, Calif.: Sage Publications, 1970), introduction.

151. Interview with Henry Cohen, executive director of the Craco Commission, April 1972.

152. The early returns on the superagencies mark them as failures. In early 1972, the City Council termed the housing superagency a "large and clumsy bureaucracy which serves to frustrate rather than further housing goals." (*New York Times*, March 1, 1972). The Human Resources Administration, which IPA served as a fiscal agent, was the subject of a Department of Labor study by David Rogers, a professor at New York University who was sympathetic to the work of IPA ("Inter-Organizational Relations and Inner City Manpower Programs," U.S. Department of Labor Contract 81-34-69-16, 1971). Ironically, Rogers concluded that HRA's failure stemmed from its poor management. The most serious defect of HRA was its failure to coordinate its operating agencies into a coherent program. He found that the agency failed to pay sufficient attention to developing its political base, to dealing with other agencies, and to administrative detail. It bungled the job of managing performance contracts with local labor suppliers. Comparing the promise of long-range management planning with the reality, "It was," Rogers states, "a noble design that moved from a promising blueprint to a delicatessen store, crisis management operation from its inception."

153. It is difficult to discern any grand scheme which knits together the work of all the groups. The late Wallace Syre, who, as chairman of Columbia University's political science program, was one of the most respected authorities on New York government, suggested in an interview (January 1972) that, in fact, there was no coordination.

154. "Creative Budgeting in New York City: An Interview With Former Budget Director Frederick O'R. Hayes," An Urban Institute Paper, Washington, D.C., June 1971, p. 10.

155. John V. Lindsay, *The City* (New York: W. W. Norton & Co., 1970).

156. "Creative Budgeting in New York City," p. 30.

157. McKinsey employees billed at a rate of $75,000 per man year. The sum was far more than that paid for New York's civil servants, although McKinsey had free use of city office space and facilities. (It was $25,000 more than the comparable billing rate for RAND's analysts.)

158. Interview with Joseph Terenzio, January 4, 1973.

159. John V. Lindsay, *White Paper on New York City's Crisis in Hospital Facilities and Care*, October 15, 1965. Available in Municipal Reference Library, New York City.

160. Seymour Thaler, Interim Report, The New York City Municipal Hospitals, 1966, unpublished.

161. Ibid.

162. Gerard Piel, et al., *Comprehensive Community Health Services for New York City*, Report of the Commission on the Delivery of Personal Health Services, 1967.

163. Interview with Robert Parks, March 8, 1972.

164. Interview with Gerard Piel, March 2, 1972.

165. Interview with Werner Kramarsky, March 14, 1972.

166. Ibid.

167. Interview with Joseph Terenzio, January 4, 1973. See also Barbara Ehrenreich, "New York Tries a New Model," *Social Policy*, January–February 1971, pp. 25–31.

168. Interview with Frederick Hayes, March 15, 1972.

169. Ibid.

170. Ehrenreich, "New York Tries a New Model."

171. Interview with Joseph Terenzio, January 4, 1973.

172. Interview with Frederick Hayes, March 15, 1972.

173. Ehrenreich, "New York Tries a New Model."

174. Interview with Frederick Hayes, March 15, 1972.

175. Interviews with Gerard Piel, March 2, 1972, and Joseph Terenzio, January 4, 1973.

176. New York City Board of Ethics Opinion 153.

177. Ibid. Also, confidential interviews with McKinsey employees.

178. The "letter of intent" is a common device employed by the city with consultants. It permits consultants to begin work without requiring the city to account for expenditures which, legally speaking, have not yet been requested. In the McKinsey case, the firm received its position in the HHC on Carter Bales's signed letters of intent committing the Corporation to contracts even before the Corporation came legally into existence.

The law relevant to this case reads (in part):

> No councilman or other official, employee, or person whose salary is payable in whole or part from the City treasury shall be or become interested directly or indirectly in any manner whatsoever except by operation of law in any business dealings with the City; shall act as any person, firm, or corporation interested directly or indirectly in any matter whatsoever in business dealings with the City shall represent private interests before the City.

At a Code of Ethics Board inquiry into Bales's role, Budget Director Hayes said that Bales was not involved in a conflict of interest: "I regard the designation of Bales as operationally useful but legally without meaning. However unorthodox the application of the nomenclature, Carter Bales remained a consultant to the BOB, not an officer or employee."

The Code of Ethics Board accepted this explanation.

179. New York City Board of Ethics Opinion 153.

180. Interview with Joseph English, January 4, 1972.

181. New York Metropolitan Regional Medicine Program Application.

182. Interviews with Carter Bales, March 16, 1972, and Werner Kramarsky, March 14, 1972.

183. The Code of Ethics Board was never able to prove that McKinsey did in fact write the proposals for the contracts they were to bid on and later receive. However, a memorandum entitled "New York City Health and Hospitals Corporation to Do List," dated September 3, 1969, states that the task of writing the proposals for which McKinsey received contracts would be assigned to Carter Bales and his associate Ms. R. Foote. Carter Bales denies that he wrote the proposals, and HHC's General Counsel George Kalkines (March 7, 1972) explains, "We wrote lots of memorandums during this period." Henry Manning, one of the four Interim Task Force members, and Robert Derson, an individual designated by the Task Force to help coordinate the creation of HHC, recall that McKinsey in fact wrote the proposals (interviews with Henry Manning, February 21, 1972, and Robert Derson, March 6, 1972).

184. Interview with Henry Manning, February 21, 1972.

185. Interview with John Corson, July 1971.

186. Confidential interview.

187. Interview with George Kalkines, March 7, 1972.

188. Terenzio and Manning, "Case Study: New York City Hospitals."

189. Interview with Carter Bales, March 16, 1972.

190. Interviews with Joseph English and HHC's Vice President for Finances, August 15, 1972.

191. Interview with Jeff Weiss, March 1972.

192. Interview with John Brady, HHC Junior Vice President for Finance, March 2, 1972.

193. A Report by the President of the Health and Hospitals Corporation to the People of the City of New York: Financial Condition, February 10, 1972.

194. Arthur Andersen & Co., Confidential Audit Report, February 1, 1972.

195. Interview with George Kalkines, March 7, 1972.

196. Audit Report on a Review of Medicare Payments Due to the New York City Health and Hospitals Corporation, (Report NYC 7-73), Office of the State Comptroller, Division of Audits and Accounts, June 29, 1972. A 1973 report sponsored by the Society of Urban Physicians noted that although the HHC "has developed a Case Management System which is supposed to track the patient from the point of his admission to the hospital through the final collection of the bill, the HHC admits that the quality of the information set down on the forms is poor, and that some type of training has to be provided so that intake personnel can obtain the information necessary to keep track of the patient." The report also noted that "the physicians interviewed in this study have noted that record-keeping is poor. Although the area of improved medical services to the patient is their major concern, they find that poor or unavailable records hinder them in their attempt to serve the patient." (Howard D. Young, Ph.D., "New York City's Municipal Hospital System: Physicians' Perceptions," Report Sponsored by the Society of Urban Physicians, mimeographed and undated.)

197. Arthur Andersen & Co., Statements of Recorded Cash Receipts and Cash Disbursements of Unrestricted Funds, Personal Services and Other Personal Services for the Year Ended June 30, 1972, Together with Auditor's Report, October 31, 1972.

198. Ibid.

199. A Report by the President of the Health and Hospitals Corporation to the People of New York City, November 1972. The HHC has been totally inaccessible to citizens, and the Board of Directors never took up our request to see minutes.

200. Letter from the New York Urban Coalition to Dr. Joseph English, August 10, 1971.

201. Young, "New York City's Municipal Hospital System."

202. Ibid.

INDEX